SWEET
INVENTION

SWEET INVENTION

A HISTORY

OF

DESSERT

michael krondl

CHICAGO
REVIEW
PRESS

Library of Congress Cataloging-in-Publication Data
Krondl, Michael.
Sweet invention : a history of dessert / Michael Krondl. — 1st ed.
  p. cm.
Includes bibliographical references and index.
ISBN 978-1-55652-954-2 (hardback)
1. Desserts—History. 2. Confectionery—History. 3. Pastry—History.
4. Food habits—History. I. Title.

TX773.K7154 2011
641.8'6—dc23

                                    2011016804

Interior design: Jonathan Hahn

Published by Chicago Review Press, Incorporated
814 North Franklin Street
Chicago, Illinois 60610
ISBN 978-1-55652-954-2
Printed in the United States of America
5 4 3 2 1

CONTENTS

INTRODUCTION

———— ∞∞∞ ————

BRUGES

I suppose you could call it an epiphany—if crumbling sweet pleasure can be given that name.

We were traveling in Belgium, Lucia and I. We told ourselves that it was a research expedition of sorts. A little like ornithologists delving into the swamps of the Orinoco delta, we were here to explore Flanders' astonishing diversity. I am, naturally, not referring to Brussels' pigeons but rather to another field of inquiry, mainly chocolates and beer. In the mornings we took on the assignment of spotting chocolate shops so we could rate and classify their bonbons and pralines. In the afternoons we found respite from the interminable rain behind the steamy windows of pastry shops and cafés, ever vigilant for a break in the clouds so that we might continue our reconnaissance. The evenings were, of necessity, devoted to beer—patisseries close early in Belgium.

The revelation came on a predictably drizzly day in Bruges, or rather a short distance from that delightfully medieval tourist trap. We'd decided to get a little exercise and bicycle out into the countryside—as you can imagine, all those cream-filled tortes and abbey ales take their toll. And we'd heard of an especially fine

1

pastry shop in the nearby hamlet of Damme. So we pedaled into the mist, emerging thirty minutes later onto Damme's picturesque square, the church on one side, the patisserie on the other. Once inside, there was nothing especially quaint or ye olde about Patisserie Tante Marie: just a few plain tables, a freezer full of homemade ice cream, and a long display case of cakes and tarts. But what cakes and tarts! Lumpy golden fruit tarts oozing sweet nectar were lined up beside fudge-brown disks floating above clouds of mousse. Sheets of almond sponge barely contained a lava flow of coffee cream. Lemon tarts, the color of butter, almost shivered with fragility.

This is perhaps the place where I should point out the difference between French and Belgian desserts. The distinction is subtle but essential. In France, the pastry cook's art is a kind of ornament to the fabulous physique of French cuisine. The vitrines of Parisian patisseries resemble jewelry displays, all sparkling and precious but somehow insubstantial, all mousse and no body. In Belgium, desserts are no mere baubles. They can seem a little less polished at first, but there is depth to their sparkle. Here, dessert is not some embellishment to a meal; it is the meal, served with due ceremony, with both knife and fork.

Which brings me back to Tante Marie and to two ladies of a certain age who were the only ones in the pastry shop when we sat down. They were perfectly coiffed and fashionably trim, fully absorbed in muted conversation—at least until their dessert arrived. Each had ordered one of the café's tasting plates of three desserts, a tart and two tortes, as best as I could determine without staring too rudely. But don't think for a minute that these were the sorts of effete portions served in multistarred restaurants. These were great plates luxuriant with sweetness. The tête-à-tête now ended and both ladies assumed a purposeful air of concentration, the kind of look you see in the eyes of a Beethoven devotee listening to a particularly profound rendition of the master's final quartets. Much like the music aficionado, the women were washed over by a wave of complete pleasure, an ode to joy that makes you sigh rather than smile.

And this was the epiphany. That dessert could be a great deal more than merely a pleasant ending to a meal, a frilly encore played after the weighty symphony was done. That the dessert itself was the purpose, the goal, the raison d'être—perhaps not for a whole lifetime, but quite possibly for a day spent in its anticipation and most certainly for an afternoon washed in its delights. Too often, our puritanical culture dismisses pleasure as, at best, a means to an end and, at worst, a sign of moral turpitude, an indicator of weakness. We are repeatedly told that immortality—or at least a long life—comes from self-denial. And yet, is a life of abstemiousness worth living? Is pleasure so inessential? I looked to the women's lips, still pursed in rapt attention even as they finished the final bite, and had my answer.

THE NEED FOR DESSERT

There is a great deal to say in favor of the joy elicited by the chilly smoothness of ice cream or the buttery tang of a lemon tart; nonetheless, pleasure provides only part of the explanation for the pastry cook's art. It may seem churlish to look for a reason for dessert beyond the sweet delight that it gives, but that is, in large part, what this book is about.

While the liking for sweetness is undoubtedly evolutionary in origin, dessert is a purely cultural phenomenon. From a biological standpoint, dessert is frivolous, unnecessary, and even harmful in excess, yet that's precisely why it's interesting. When you talk about dessert you step away from analyzing basic human needs to a conversation about culture. A discussion about dessert is more like a dialogue about painting and sculpture than it is about such staples of our diet as bread or rice or even salt. It fulfills the sort of needs that make our species unique, it feeds the same desires that led us to build Notre Dame and the Taj Mahal, that brought us Chanel and Tiffany's, and, yes, Mickey Mouse and plastic pink flamingos. It resembles both fine and decorative arts in another way as well, in that it has historically been the preserve of the elite. That said, an éclair or a slice of baklava was always a much more affordable luxury than a ruby pendant.

Food history is, at times, a ragged discipline, drawing in elements of social history, economics, and even considerations of artistry and fashion. It would be neater, for example, to follow the example of art historians, or scholars of the applied arts, who usually limit themselves to the rise and fall of aesthetic movements, to the influence of one artist upon another. This would result in a clean, linear narrative narrowly focused on the subject at hand. And yet, even though I appreciate the scholarly virtues of such an approach, it doesn't quite satisfy my curiosity about the subject. I am fascinated by the way the culinary arts interact with society at large: with religion, gender, class consciousness, and national identity, to name a few topics broached in the following chapters. I just can't ignore the reality that the European taste for sweet foods and beverages caused ripple effects that were felt around the world. Sugar was the prime mover of the transatlantic traffic in human beings. In Europe, the sweetener was a rare and expensive spice before the slave plantations of the New World made the raw stuff of the confectioner's art widely available, if not necessarily cheap. The biscotti of the Italian Renaissance as much as the cream tarts of Marie Antoinette's France were made possible by the sweat of enslaved Africans. Does that make dessert immoral? I don't think so, but it does lend a bitter undercurrent to the sweet tale.

Unlike cooking, which for most of its history was less an art than a daily chore carried out by women with little time or money, the creation of sweetmeats has long been reserved for special occasions where cost was no object. As a result, it was often a narrowly defined craft practiced by male specialists. Imperial Rome and Abbasid Baghdad both had professional sweet makers and their pastry shops. In Renaissance Venice, confectioners not only had to know how to concoct a batch of marzipan but were also expected to be skilled sculptors, sometimes working hand in hand with noted artists to create ornate sugary monuments. In France, pastry chefs constructed edible edifices that would make even the most elaborate of today's wedding cakes look like a fourth-grade craft project. It was no hyperbole when the famed French pastry chef Antonin Carême declared patisserie a branch of architecture. Because the work of a pastry chef is highly technical, it takes years of practice to get right. This is one reason why many people who are perfectly happy roasting a chicken or cooking up a batch of stew turn to a professional when it comes to an ornate dessert. The explanation for this is simple. Even dedicated amateurs are unlikely to frost a cake more than a few times a year. Compare that to the dozens of pastries iced and decorated in any modest pastry shop day in, day out. Enthusiasm and even talent only go so far as a substitute for years of training. With all respect to Carême, rather than architecture, I think better analogies to confectionary are decorative arts like jewelry making or fine cabinetry. A gorgeous dessert also has something of a virtuoso musical performance, perfectly crafted but also impermanent and fleeting.

Confectionary, like other applied arts, has long been tossed about by the whims of fashion. Perhaps because it is so superfluous (at least nutritionally speaking), the trends in pastry tend to come and go faster than in cooking as a whole. Certainly sweet makers have been under pressure from their patrons to keep up with the competition but also to innovate. Not that every generation is as inventive as the next. It seems that pastry often goes through a golden age when there is aesthetic ferment in other cultural disciplines too. Italy certainly went through such a phase in the Renaissance, when painting, sculpture, architecture, and confectionary were all reexamined and reinvented. So did Vienna at the turn of the twentieth century, a time when every aesthetic seemed up for grabs. In comparison to these two revolutionary moments, the court of Versailles was perhaps less artistically innovative. Decorative painting, porcelain manufacture, tapestry making, and cuisine nonetheless flourished, encouraged by the pressures of social competition and royal largesse. Similar cases could be made for other laboratories of sweet invention such as medieval Baghdad or nineteenth-century Calcutta.

Throughout history, cultures have found many uses for dessert. Sweets were fed to the gods in ancient Mesopotamia and continue to be the preferred sacred offering among Hindus. Meanwhile, in Europe, numerous pastries take the form of anthropomorphic fetishes consumed with more or less pious devotion. Southern Italy has its Saint Agatha's breasts, Portugal its angel bellies, and throughout northern Europe, gingerbread saints are gobbled up throughout the winter season. Almost everywhere, religious holidays are marked by eating cookies and other sweetmeats. Jews celebrate the New Year (Rosh Hashanah) with honey-sweetened treats, Christians bake Christmas cookies, and Hindus shower friends and family alike with sweetmeats during Diwali.

Around the globe, life's passages are marked with confections both simple and complex. In Muslim countries, newborns are traditionally given a taste of a date or of honey in a ceremony called *tahneek*. In India, a child's first taste of solid food is sweet rice pudding. In the West, birthday cakes mark the passing of each year. And once it's all over, in many parts of the Catholic world, the living munch on bone-shaped treats to remember their dear departed.

In our age of cheap sugar, it is hard to imagine desserts being used to score points in the competition for power, but there was a time when Renaissance princes weighed down their banquet tables with gilded sugar sculptures just to show off their opulence. Patronage of the sugary arts was just one more way to keep up with the Joneses. A rare reminder of that long-gone era are our multistoried wedding cakes, which still recall a time when ornate sugar work decorated the tables of royalty. But cakes and tarts are also put to more subtle uses, as the ladies in Damme inadvertently made clear. In Europe, women of a certain class have long used the afternoon pause between lunch and dinner to socialize over coffee, tea, and patisserie. In the West, dessert is an accessory to femininity. After all, aren't girls made of sugar and spice and everything nice?

SWEET GENES

As a matter of fact, the liking for sweetness is hardwired in our species, irrespective of gender. All infants will naturally gravitate to foods that are sweet while avoiding those that are bitter and sour. From a physiological standpoint this is perfectly logical. At the simplest level, the body is no more than a chemical processing unit that runs on water, oxygen, and sugar. The food you put into your body is eventually reduced into glucose, a simple sugar. This takes a great deal less effort when the input is itself a sugar— whether in the form of lactose from mother's milk, fructose in apple juice, or sucrose in lollipops. (Not that I'm recommending this as a diet.) The predilection for foods high in sugar makes sense from an evolutionary standpoint too; in the wild, bitterness often signals toxins while sweetness tells us that a food is good to eat. As parents will avow and scientists confirm, children can't get enough of the flavor. They are different from grown-ups in this respect. Researchers have found that when you give a sucrose solution to an adult and gradually increase the sweetener, he or she will eventually find it unpalatable. Not kids—with them, the sweeter, the better. This gluttony for sweetness only seems to drop off after adolescence.[1] Sweet food also has a demonstrable effect on mood. It has been shown that sugar comforts crying infants. Newborns given a sucrose solution seem to feel less pain.[2] But it isn't children alone who are susceptible to sugar's sweet charm. Scientists have noted a higher intake of sweets during women's menstrual periods and among those prone to psychiatric symptoms. They may be self-medicating. Studies of rats have shown that the taste of sweetness releases opiates into the blood.[3]

Age is hardly the only factor that affects any given person's fondness for sugary snacks. Not everyone is equally sensitive to sweetness. When fed sucrose solutions, some people can detect the flavor in lower concentrations than others can. Interestingly, this doesn't seem to have much bearing on how sweet they actually like their food. Here, culture may be the stronger influence. For example, Americans of African descent have been shown to like sweeter concentrations of laboratory solutions than their countrymen of European ancestry. This may partly explain why Southerners like their baked goods sweeter than Yankees do. But a taste for sweet food doesn't necessarily translate into a fondness for dessert. In at least one American study that surveyed the snacking preferences of men and women, the guys, when given a range of sweet foods, liked the sweetest ones the best. Yet, given the choice, they'd rather opt out of dessert altogether and go for the nachos and wings. The women, on the other hand, migrated toward the sugary snacks even though in other respects they didn't like their food as sweet as the men did. Numerous other studies point to the gender divide, at least in the West. In another one of these surveys, a sample group of obese Americans was asked to list their top ten favorite foods. The female respondents overwhelmingly preferred doughnuts, cake, cookies, chocolate, pies, and other desserts while the males preferred steaks, roasts, hamburgers, french fries, and pizza. The only item that showed up on both lists was ice cream.* But is this a matter of genetics? Does the Y chromosome direct one-half of humanity toward bacon cheeseburgers while the X makes the other half crave triple chocolate mousse cakes? History points to a cultural rather than genetic explanation for this, as do some international surveys. In Egypt, for example, there seems to be no difference between men's and women's dessert cravings, while in India, sweets are associated more with men than with women.

Even if all children are born with an innate sweet tooth, not all cultures nurture it in the same way. In food-obsessed France, children are quickly socialized into the national eating patterns. For school lunch, children are served a three-course meal that finishes with dessert, to be eaten with the appropriate tableware. In India, boys tend to be fed sweets more than girls are, which undoubtedly influences their tastes as adults. Austrian children, following adult example, often make meals of mostly sweet foods (pancakes, dumplings, and such) for lunch or supper. In England, food writers have theorized that that nation's penchant for certain kinds of very sweet, mushy puddings stems from the Victorian era, when it was precisely these sorts of desserts that were recommended for the nursery. In the United States, in the meantime, the distinction between food for adults and food for children is increasingly becoming blurred, with the grown-ups following the kids' lead. In this respect it is almost exactly the opposite of what occurs in France. American adults retain a liking for the direct, uncomplicated flavors of childhood, for des-

---

* For what it's worth, there seems to be no correlation between eating sweet foods and obesity. In fact, studies have shown that lean people eat more of their calories as sugar than obese people do. Fat is another matter altogether, and, given how much butter and cream many desserts contain, the cheesecake diet has yet to prove its efficacy.

serts that can be picked up by the hand, for cookies and cupcakes. Since children here grow up eating highly sweetened products like breakfast cereal, ketchup, and soda, it makes sense that our desserts would tend to use more sugar than those in many parts of Europe.*

DEFINING DESSERT

Yet if there is incontrovertibly a biologically based craving for sweetness in our species, it hardly explains the existence of a Sacher torte or a Snickers bar. For that we need to look to a cultural but more especially a historical approach. For reasons both personal (I am not much of a candy fan) and professional (since the subject has been dealt with in other recent works), I have chosen to focus on the history of dessert rather than candy. When I say dessert, I am more or less following Merriam-Webster's definition of the term: "a usually sweet course or dish usually served at the end of a meal"; in other words, creamy dishes like pudding and ice cream, baked goods including cakes and pies, but also cookies and doughnuts. Clearly, many of these foods are not eaten just at the end of a meal, but we consider them dessert nevertheless. Yet in spite of this tidy definition, it can be tricky to draw a neat line in the sand between dessert and candy. The distinction between the two isn't always so obvious. Why is fudge candy and a brownie isn't? What makes a Kit Kat a candy bar and an *Oblatentorte* (a cake made of layers of wafers and chocolate cream) dessert? For that matter, why is a carrot muffin, made from an identical batter as carrot cake, breakfast

---

* At almost a cup of sweetener (190 grams, to be precise) per person per day, the United States gets the gold in world sweetener (sugar, corn syrup, etc.) consumption. The French eat about half that amount.[4]

while the latter belongs to a different category? And what should we call General Mills Reese's Puffs® cereal? Candy? Dessert? Anything but breakfast, I hope. Needless to say, the distinctions are culturally specific. I am comfortable calling waffles dessert in Brussels but not in Baltimore, and crêpes suzette are clearly dessert even if blueberry pancakes aren't. In the end I've just had to trust my own sweet tooth, or, to quote Justice Potter Stewart, who admittedly was speaking of a somewhat different temptation (he was addressing the subject of pornography): "I shall not today attempt further to define the kinds of material I understand to be embraced . . . [b]ut I know it when I see it."

The way each culture parses its repertoire of sweet foods is reflected in language. Even American and British English have totally different nomenclatures that don't entirely translate. In Britain "sweets" are what Americans call "candy." (I have chosen to use the word "sweets" in a more generic way that encompasses both cakes and candy.) They buy chocolate bars, we eat candy bars; they serve pudding, we have dessert. But their idea of "pudding" has a narrower sense than "dessert" does in America. In the context of a meal, pudding refers to the sweet course that follows lunch or dinner. At other times of day, cookies ("biscuits" in the queen's English), doughnuts, or even an ice cream cone would not be called pudding.

In many countries, the rules about how sweet foods are defined as well as how and when they are served are quite different from our own. In Austria, some sweet dishes such as fruit-filled dumplings can be served either as a main dish or as a dessert course but never as a mid-afternoon snack. *Gugelhupf* (bundt cake) is normally served for breakfast, or as an accompaniment to afternoon coffee, but hardly ever at the end of a meal. Nonetheless they both fall under the rather broad category of *Mehlspeise*, literally "flour foods." Meanwhile, in France, they have their own way of dividing up the pastry repertoire. A *pain au chocolat* would never be categorized as dessert, yet virtually the identical ingredients formed into a *tarte au chocolat* would. The first belongs to a category of dishes called *viennoiserie*, which are eaten for breakfast or as a snack, while the latter is classified as *pâtisserie* and generally consumed at the end of a meal. The main distinction between the two seems to be that one may be eaten out of the hand, while for the other you need a plate and flatware. Only barbarians (and Americans) would eat *le dessert* any other way.

DESSERT SUPERPOWERS

For historical and cultural reasons, some nations are just more into dessert than others. I've chosen to focus on a mere six, in part because I think they have wielded the greatest influence on other societies' sweet-eating customs but also because any more would be utterly overwhelming. As it is, I will doubtless be accused of biting off more than I can chew.

I begin in India because of its national obsession with dessert, something that even curry-loving foreigners are often unaware of. Then I move on to the Middle East, which, from a historical standpoint, is critical to understanding not only the sweets found in the region today but also the backstory of later developments in Europe and even India. Then comes Italy. Today's Italians are nowhere near as dessert-obsessed as some of their neighbors, but without their contributions it is hard to imagine desserts in contemporary France or Austria. Those two remain the world's pastry superpowers. Finally, America is fascinating, not only because I live here but also due to its immense influence on every aspect of world culture, sweet eating included. But what of Spain and Portugal, Mexico and Brazil, or China and Japan? To those, and other nations with fascinating dessert repertoires, I can only humbly apologize. Even my appetite is not without limits.

My story emphasizes breadth over depth with all the pluses and minuses that brings. It allows me to make connections between Venice and Vienna and to trace trends from Baghdad to Delhi, but there is inevitably less detail than a book devoted to a single tradition can offer. I have focused on desserts that I thought were culturally significant rather than attempting to discuss every single sweet. As a result, my grand tour has had to skip over many delightful local specialties.

Because the spread of sugarcane around the world is so essential to the subject, the order of the chapters roughly follows the crop's path: from India, where sugar was first refined, to the Middle East, where it was enthusiastically adopted in the later years of the first millennium, then to Europe and finally America.

Of course sugar is hardly the only sweetener that has historically been used to make dessert. Dried dates, figs, and other fruits were commonly used for this purpose in the ancient Middle East, and they continue to be used in such things as fruitcakes and Fig Newtons. Grape juice used to be boiled down to a thick, sweet syrup, or must, for sweetening pastries. Trees have been tapped for their sweet juices too, whether by Native Americans for maple syrup or south Asians for palm sugar. The most widespread ancient sweetener is honey, which humans have been gathering in the wild since time immemorial. In Egypt, apiculture goes back at least forty-five hundred years, and you can bet that honey began to be used to sweeten breads and other dishes soon after. Certainly the ancient Greeks and Romans served all sorts of honey-sweetened cakes at their banquets.

But sugar is special. The vast majority of our favorite sweets could never have been invented without pure, refined sucrose. There are just so many things you can do with sugar that can't be done with liquid sweeteners like honey and fruit juices. You can turn it into spun sugar, caramel, meringues, crispy cookies, moist madeleines, and towering angel food cakes. Sugar lowers the melting/freezing point of ice cream so that it remains smooth even when frozen solid. Melted sugar can be transformed into candy textures that vary from chewy to rock hard. But perhaps the most appealing thing about this particular sweetener is a quality that it lacks: flavor. Refined sucrose is simply, plainly, sweet. Chocolate sweetened with sugar tastes only of chocolate. A spoonful of sugar won't get in the way of vanilla's aroma. A thriving dessert culture has almost always depended on abundant sugar.

In the past, dessert was available only to the wealthy elite, and even to that minority it was undeniably tangential to their existence, at least if you consider the needs of the body. But then so are so many of the other frills that add up to what we call civilization. We don't require cream puffs and cupcakes in the same way we do bread and salt. But we do need them, much as we need "The Blue Danube" and "Hey Jude." By studying dessert, maybe we can learn just a little more about what makes humans human. And let's face it, for some people happiness *is* a hot fudge sundae. Or perhaps an ample tasting plate of tarts and tortes on a drizzly Belgian afternoon. Isn't it worth finding out how that came to be?

I

SACRED FUDGE

❋ *India* ❋

KALI PUJA

In Kolkata, the air is always thick with poison and perfume but never more so than on the eve of Kali Puja, the holiday dedicated to Kali, the goddess of destruction and rebirth. That night, the atmosphere fills with the sulfurous plumes of rockets and exploding fireworks. The traffic that gives the city its insistent backbeat of honks and beeps crawls even more slowly than usual so that the noxious exhaust pools at the intersections instead of dissolving into the yellow air. Yet in the narrow alleys, the diesel fumes periodically give way to an altogether different smell, a sweet and sweaty scent that brings to mind breasts and mother's milk. But it is a very Indian mother's milk: musky, and perfumed with cardamom and rosewater. The odor oozes from thousands of sweetshops across the metropolis, where cauldrons of sweet cow's milk and fat buffalo milk are boiled, simmered, curdled, and formed into sweetmeats for this holiday—and for the next.

For Kali Puja, block associations, sports clubs, and everyone else with the time and money put up pandals (temporary

15

shrines). There are perhaps two thousand of these miniature temples set up around the city's neighborhoods. Kali is everywhere. In a working-class enclave, where every street is bedecked with streamers of colored lights, the warrior mother towers above her temporary shrine, her blue, four-armed body surrounded by an electric violet halo of flowers and mandalas. A collection of fruit and sweetmeat offerings is arranged at her feet. Across town, on a busy commercial strip, the pandal almost blocks the sidewalk, while the black-skinned, naked goddess peruses the passersby, her blood-red tongue protruding as if in surprise. Next to a ferry pontoon dock tugged at by the mud-brown Hooghly River, the shrine is no bigger than a broom closet, yet this diminutive Kali looks pleased, perhaps because one of her acolytes has smeared her mouth with milky sweets.

At the Kalighat temple in south Kolkata, her devotees wait for hours to see her awesome countenance on her holiday. Kali's most revered shrine is a relatively modest affair, a two-story-high ziggurat that sits at the end of a broad pedestrian street lined with stands selling devotional postcards and tourist gimcracks. As you get closer to the holy structure, there is that sweet, milky smell again, emanating from the shops that crowd around the temple's two entrances. Here the stands sell just two things, garlands of Kali's favorite flower, the blood-red hibiscus, and her beloved sweet, a concentrate of milk and sugar called *pedha*. The shopkeepers spend their day unhurriedly forming great mounds of sweet paste into disks about the size of a silver dollar, pressing a few grains of cardamom into each. The pilgrims, in their festive best, buy these by twos and threes to present to the deity. The vendors wrap each in a cone of leaves and garnish it with a hibiscus blossom. There is something primeval, even elemental, about the sweets—the dense, fudgy concentrate of almost pure fat, protein, and carbohydrate, almost like an emergency military ration or space food more than a sweetmeat. Ancient Hindu texts over two thousand years ago mention much the same sweet offering. The Indian gods are renowned for their sweet tooth. So are their people.

In West Bengal, Kali Puja comes fast on the heels of Durga Puja, a ten-day celebration held in honor of Durga, a sunnier mother goddess. Here too, the deity is regaled with sweetmeats. Her worshippers follow suit, sending boxes of sugary snacks to everyone on their list. Immediately after Kali's festival comes Bhai Phota, or brother's day. This, several confectioners tell me, is their busiest day of the year, for it isn't merely brothers who are blessed with a present of sweets but any male in the vicinity.

Kali Puja also happens to coincide with Diwali, a five-day holiday celebrated throughout India. Diwali has many of the elements of Christmas. Presents are exchanged, and oil lamps (or more commonly these days streamers of electric "Christmas" lights) illuminate homes, businesses, and streets. But mostly people gorge on sweets. According to one study, Indians gain two to three kilograms around the time of Diwali.[1] Children get little toys molded out of pure sugar while the adults go in for more elaborate preparations. These vary somewhat according to the region. There are puddings of various kinds. In north India, favorite items include *kheer* (elsewhere called *pāyesh* or *pāyasam*), a thick rice pudding with raisins and nuts, as well as other custardlike desserts thickened with wheat germ or almonds. Fritters are popular too. The most widely dispersed are *jalebis*, those violent yellow strands of tangled dough soaked in syrup. And everywhere there are *laddus*. To make this ubiquitous dessert, confectioners begin with a thinnish batter (typically based on chickpea flour, though there are variations that use sesame or semolina), which they dribble into hot butter to form little drops. These deep-fried drops, now looking a little like corn kernels, are then soaked in saffron-tinted sugar syrup. This is referred to as *bonde*. When formed into two-bite-sized balls it is called a *laddu*.

Even cattle aren't left out of Diwali. In rural areas, farmers will feed their cows sweetmeats to mark the holiday.[2] Needless to say, cows are holy to Hindus and so by extension are butter and milk. The holy texts of India's most ancient religion are full of references to these sacred fluids. Ghee, or clarified butter, is considered especially precious.

DINING WITH GODS

Ghee is mentioned over and over in the sacred Hindu texts. In the *Mahābhārata* you read how the gods extracted the nectar of immortality from the deep ocean. This divine greasy fluid, called *amrita*, takes the form of ghee. The gods, led by Narayana (an avatar of the great god Vishnu), devise a way to get their hands on this ambrosia. They grab hold of a towering mountain, uproot it, and set it down on the immense shell of the tortoise king. Holding this mammoth contraption, they whirl it round and round, a little like a fantastical immersion blender that liquefies everything in its path: the beasts and fishes of the sea as well as the lions, elephants, and other unfortunate creatures are flung off the whirling mountain. Along the way, the trees and herbs and all their sap are churned into the milky sea. This gradually transforms the liquid into ghee, out of which emerges the divine Dhanvantari (yet another avatar of Vishnu) holding up a beaker filled with the liquid of life. The story doesn't end there, for as the gods continue to churn the sea, poison emerges as well. But this is luckily taken care of by the god Shiva and all's well that ends well. The gods are assured of their immortality.

Early holy texts are an invaluable source on the culinary tastes of ancient Indian gods and mortals alike. Some of the earliest references to food in India come from the religious poems and songs called the Vedas, which date back as far as 1000 BCE, if not earlier. Many more come from epic works like the *Ramayana* and *Mahābhārata* that detail the exploits of the Hindu pantheon. Like any good epic, these stories are full of sex, gore, betrayal, and redemption. There are also plenty of feasts and edible sacrifices.*

Hinduism isn't a religion in quite the same way as Christianity or Islam. There is no Bible or Koran, or the equivalent of a Catholic mass or Friday prayers. There is no religious hierarchy. A priest, a Brahman, is any male who has been born into the priestly caste. India's dominant faith is often called a path (*dharma* in Sanskrit), a way of life, and the details of that life are what really matter. In this context, food, with its rituals and taboos, is central, even if culinary customs do not strictly follow any universally accepted orthodoxy. Unlike in Jewish dietary law, say, where the taboos are highly codified, in India, rules about acceptable foods seem to float in a nebulous cloud of common consensus. Many of the restrictions are determined by class and caste, though age and marital status can come into it as well; Hindu widows, for example, traditionally followed an excruciatingly limited diet, devoid of seasoning or any other potentially "stimulating" flavor. Generally, an orthodox Hindu may only eat with his own caste; however, a lower caste member may always receive food from an upper caste member. It's one reason why cooking has been the second most popular profession for a Brahman, since he was the only one whose food was acceptable to everyone.[3]

Contrary to common belief, upper-caste Hindus were not historically vegetarians, and even today the taboo against eating animal flesh is observed to varying degrees. Similarly with the gods. Some, like Kali, are regularly appeased by the sacrifice of a

---

* Scholars generally think that both texts were first composed around 400 BCE, with the *Mahābhārata* probably a little older. The trouble is that they were so heavily edited and expanded over the succeeding centuries that it's almost impossible to reliably date any particular food occurrence.

live goat, which is then ritually eaten by the participants.[4] Many ceremonies involve food. One of the most basic forms of worship or *puja* is to present offerings of fruits, sweets, and other delicacies to the idols of the gods. (*Puja* can refer to both the ritual and the holiday.)

A family portrait of India's gods can be bewildering to non-Hindus. At the center of the snapshot is four-headed Brahma, the creator. To one side is Shiva the destroyer outfitted in a tiger skin with a necklace of snakes. On the other side is blue-complexioned Vishnu, the preserver, with his wife, variously known as Uma, Parvati, Durga, Lakshmi, and Kali. Then there are their children Ayyappan, Subramanya, Ganesha, and others. But that's just the nuclear family that fits in the camera frame. The extended clan of Hindu deities numbers in the thousands (or even millions), and, just to make it more confusing, some take on other incarnations or "avatars." Still, most Hindus have an attachment to one, or at most a few, of their favorite deities.

Vishnu's most notable avatar (there are ten in all), and certainly the best known in the west, is Krishna. There's no end of stories told about this transcendent celebrity. In one oft-told tale, the baby Krishna was in mortal danger due to the machinations of his murderous uncle, who had usurped Krishna's father's rightful throne. To keep the infant safe, he was secreted away and deposited with a band of cowherds. There he soon grew fat and happy on all the milk and its by-products. He was known to sneak into the houses of milkmaids to steal butter for himself and his companions. In the south of India, you often see the chubby-cheeked baby Krishna with a pot of butter tucked under his left arm even while he nibbles on a ball of butter in his right hand. This taste for butter apparently never left him because there are countless sculptures, paintings, and cheap reproductions that show the now-svelte adolescent god dancing with the never-melting butter ball still in his grasp. According to popular belief, he also has a thing for *laddu*s, presumably because they are fried in his favorite fat.

Each year in the northern Indian province of Uttar Pradesh, his followers celebrate Krishna's birthday by abstaining all day from food. At midnight they break their fast with a feast of sweetmeats, predictably all based on dairy. Instead of birthday cake, there is *bhog kheer*, an ancient pudding made by simmering parboiled rice in fresh milk.* Another traditional dessert is *shrikand*, which is made by straining yogurt and flavoring it with sugar and cardamom, as it was twenty-five hundred years ago when it was called *shikarini*. Fudgy *pedha* is served too, much as it is in Kali's temple.

But Krishna is a veritable ascetic compared with the rotund Ganesha, the affable god prayed to all over India for good fortune and success. He is instantly recognizable for his elephant head and fat belly. Ganesha is notorious for his sweet tooth. Inevitably you'll see him holding at least one *modaka* or even a towering plateful of them in one of his palms. The *modaka* is a steamed (or fried) rice-flour dumpling stuffed with a mixture of unrefined sugar and coconut. One of the many anecdotes told about baby Krishna is how the elephant god introduced the tubby toddler to this, his beloved snack. Evidently Krishna's mother had put an offering of *modaka* in front of a Ganesha idol, but, well aware of her young rascal's thieving ways, she tied her son's hands behind his back to keep the sweets safe. The good-hearted Ganesha would have none of this. The idol came to life and lifted the sweets with his trunk right into the happy infant's mouth. Or, according to some versions, maybe what he gave him was actually a *laddu*. The confusion arises because in early Sanskrit, the term *modaka* refers to what is now called a *laddu*.[5] In either case,

---

* Literally, *bhog* means offering, but also pleasure and delight, while *kheer* refers to thickened milk.

I can't see baby Krishna objecting. What's more, Ganesha is not known for turning up his trunk at *laddus* either. At opposite ends of India, in both Rajasthan and Andhra Pradesh, *laddus* are regularly offered to the elephant god. In southern India, in the meantime, he supposedly prefers *unni-āppam*, a spongy fritter made of rice flour, plantain, jackfruit, and jaggery (raw palm sugar).

Ganesha's gluttony is legendary. Hindu children are told the story of the elephant god who was returning one moonlit night from a banquet where he had stuffed himself with *modakas*. He had eaten so many sweets that he was fit to burst, quite literally. When he stumbled, his belly exploded, scattering the sweet dumplings across the forest. Miffed, the deity gathered them up and tied up his stomach with a snake. Seeing this, the moon, who had been watching the scene, couldn't restrain himself and burst into peals of laughter. For once, the amiable Ganesha lost his temper, cursing the moon into eternal darkness. He was later convinced to relent, but even so he forced the moon to wax and wane as a reminder that it isn't nice to laugh at a god, even a fat and jolly one.

It should be said that not every food presented to supernatural beings takes the form of a sweetmeat. There are gods who are happy with fruit. Others like a nicely spiced vegetable curry, while the more ferocious ones (like Kali) will need to be appeased with blood sacrifice. Some of the more unsavory gods even have a taste for alcohol, tobacco, and hashish.[6] That said, most would rather go straight to dessert.

Accordingly, Hindu temples across India specialize in sweets. The Vishnu temple at Srīmushnam in the southern state of Tamil Nadu makes a sort of *laddu* from ground-up *korai*, a tuber that Varāha (the boar incarnation of Vishnu) apparently likes to root around for. On the opposite coast, in Kerala, the monks at the Krishna temple of Ambalappuhza are renowned for their *pāyasam*, a creamy rice and milk pudding scented with cardamom.[8] For certain festivals, temples are turned into great catering halls providing confections to hundreds, if not thousands, of pilgrims. The devotees present the sweets to the deity, who blesses them; subsequently, when they nibble the sugary morsels, they are blessed in turn. Conveniently, this edible blessing is highly portable so pilgrims can take it home.

Back in 1708, the British captain Alexander Hamilton was duly impressed when he visited the famous pilgrimage site of Jagannatha. "There are, in all, about 500 [priests] that belong to the Pagod [temple], who daily boyl Rice and Pulse for the Use of the God," he wrote. But that was nothing compared to the sweets:

> They report, that there are five Candies [sweets] daily drest, each Candy containing 1600 lb. Weight. When some Part has been carried before the Idol, and the Smoke had saluted his Mouth and Nose then the Remainder is sold out, in small Parcels, to those who will buy it, at very reasonable Rates, and the Surplus is served out to the Poor, who are ever attending the Pagod out of a pretended Devotion.

His final comment is telling too, for it explains why sweets hold such a privileged role in Hindu culture: "And this Food, that is drest for the Pagod, has a particular Privilege above other Eatables, that the purified *Heathen* [i.e., Brahman] is not contaminated by eating out of the [s]ame Dish with polluted Christians or Mahometans, tho' in another Place, it would be reckoned a mortal Sin."[9]

At some temples today, the crowds (and sweetmeats) can number in the tens of thousands. In the southern temple at Tirupati, dedicated to Venkateshwara (Vishnu, yet again), *laddu*s are handed out to pilgrims after they have been duly blessed by the deity. In the 1990s, it was reported that as many as seventy thousand were cooked up by a staff of thirty cooks each day. In the process they went through three metric tons of *urad dhāl* (black bean flour), six tons of sugar, and two and a half tons of ghee as well as small mountains of raisins, cashews, and cardamom pods.[10]

What all these temple sweets have in common is that they contain milk or are fried in ghee. That we, as mammals, should consider milk sacred is hardly comment-worthy, but that cow's milk should attain a similar status in India requires a little explanation.

A LAND OF MILK AND CANDY

For the purpose of understanding the evolution of dessert in India, it is useful to divide its history into three epochs. The first, between about 1000 BCE and 1000 CE, saw the rise and consolidation of Hinduism, along with many of its food rules and rituals. This was the era of milky sweets, when sugar cultivation spread and methods of preserving and processing milk were developed. The second period endured for the next eight hundred years or so. This was when desserts of Middle Eastern origin arrived with Muslim invaders from central Asia. These typically flour-based desserts did not have the same religious overtones as the earlier milk-based sweets and were eventually adopted by the indigenous culture. The third era came with the British, who imposed an ostensibly secular regime on a society where religion had previously ordered everything from politics to home life. Though the colonial government transformed South Asia in profound ways, its influence on dessert was indirect. Mainly, what the new cities of the British raj did was to provide a space for a new class of Indian. It was this new indigenous elite that encouraged sweet makers to innovate, especially in the bourgeoning colonial capital of Calcutta, though here, too, religion played its part.

The idea that cows and consequently their milk are sacred seems to date back to the early part of our first epoch, to the so-called Vedic Aryans (the ones who composed the Vedas). These nomadic Indo-Europeans migrated to the great fertile plains of the upper Indus and Ganges sometime in the middle of the second millennium BCE.* They were a semipastoral people who measured their wealth in cattle. Their reluctance to kill cows may have originated from the fact that they were more valuable as plough animals and providers of cooking fuel and milk than as sources for beefsteaks. Nonetheless, eating beef doesn't seem to have been altogether forbidden as yet. In part this was because bulls and cows continued to be sacrificed, if only on special occasions. And what were you to do with the meat? Most likely, the sacred aspect of milk products came from their association with the sacrificed animal. Certainly the gods profiled in the Vedas had no issues with consuming cattle (or other animals) as well as the milk, yogurt, and butter they produced. The worshipers simply followed suit.[11] Just why beef eating became taboo is unclear. It seems to have occurred sometime in the middle of our first millennium (Hindus of all castes continued to eat other meats for another thousand years or so). Once the actual meat became taboo, dairy products were the next best thing.

In this early period, Hinduism, even in its many heterogeneous forms, didn't have a monopoly on Indians' souls. Buddhism traces its origins to the teachings of the Siddhārtha Gautama, called the Buddha, who may have lived in the fifth century BCE. Buddhists tended to be vegetarian, and their influence (at

---

* The tradition of the holy cow may go back even further. Archeologists have found numerous images of what seems to be a sacred bull that date back to the sophisticated civilization that flourished in the Indus Valley around 2000 BCE.

least one powerful emperor converted to Buddhism around 200 BCE) likely had an effect on weaning Hindus from animal sacrifice. More restrictive yet are the dietary rules of Jainism. Jainism is even more ancient than Buddhism, but it never had the popular following of India's other two main indigenous faiths.* Even so, the Jains have had an outsize influence, particularly in matters of diet. Jains not only avoid any form of meat, they also restrict numerous fruits and vegetables on the theory that they might harbor potential life. Any fermented food is taboo, and even honey is out of bounds on the assumption that bees are harmed in the process. With so little allowed, where could a Jain find pleasure in life? Well, in dessert, for one. Their literature is fertile ground for early mentions of certain sweets. The first reference to *payasam*, rice pudding, can be traced to a Jain-Buddhist text from around 400 BCE.[12] Indians' beloved *jalebis* are likely of Persian origin (the word derives from the Persian *zalibīya*), but they are first mentioned in India by a Jain writer around 1450. And much of what is known of the ancient food traditions of the western state of Gujarat and the southern state of Karnataka comes from Jain sources. Not all Jain desserts are milk-based, but many are.

It hardly bears pointing out that most of India does not have a climate conducive to long storage of fresh milk, and indeed most milk is processed before it is consumed. Yogurt, what Indians call "curds," has been common at least since the Vedic era. So has a kind of fresh cheese called *paneer* made by curdling milk (typically with lactic acid from sour milk but also with citric acid or even vinegar), then draining off the whey.[13]

Several other techniques were developed to preserve milk. Milk could be boiled down to make very thick evaporated milk

---

* According to the 2001 Indian census, there are only about four million Jains and eight million Buddhists in India compared to more than eight hundred million Hindus!

or even to the point where it turned into powder. Alternatively it was churned to make butter and then cooked to produce ghee.* What is somewhat mysterious is that salt was not widely used as a preservative as it was just about everywhere else, including in next-door Afghanistan. Was salt too difficult to come by in the upper Indus? Or was sugar just too commonly available?

The idea of sweetening yogurt probably came early, first with honey and then with sugar itself. *Madhuparka*, a preparation of honey and yogurt that is still used today in ritual offerings, seems to date back to Vedic times.[14] The creamy yogurt-based dessert called *shikarini* mentioned in Krishna's birthday celebrations was first noted around 500 BCE. Early Sanskrit literature makes mention of honey but not sugar. According to the *Mahāvastu*, a compilation of stories about the Buddha, the seer is supposed to have broken the seven-week fast when he attained enlightenment with a bowl of honey and ghee.[15] At the same time, it is apparent from numerous references to sugar dealers and confectioners in the text that sugar was hardly rare. Nonetheless it wasn't considered quite holy enough for this blessed moment. Yet even while honey retained a somewhat more sacred image, sugar became much more commonplace in the early Indus valley.

Milk (or its derivatives) is indisputably the most revered element in Hindu desserts, but it's self-evident that without sugar (and to a lesser degree other sweeteners) there would be no holy sweets. And in fact honey and sugar are recognized as kinds of junior partners to the holy trinity of milk, yogurt, and ghee. Together, these five elements or hallowed liquids (since sugar

---

* Before refrigeration, butter was commonly cooked to pasteurize it and boil off the whey that might cause spoilage. This occurred even in temperate climates. In Germany, old cookbooks often call for "schmaltz," which, confusingly, sometimes refers to lard and at other times ghee. (The Yiddish term *shmalts*, referring to rendered poultry fat, derives from the decidedly unkosher German original.) Incidentally, the difference between clarified butter and ghee is that the former is gently heated to separate the butterfat from the milk solids and whey, while for the latter, the whey is boiled off, resulting in a slightly nutty caramelized taste.

also begins as a fluid) make up a mixture called *panchamrita*.*
This sacred slurry may be presented as an offering, but it is also
used to wash down idols (presumably in a diluted form) and, in
parts of India, ritually consumed by women in pregnancy.[16]

By the time the Buddhist *Mahāvastu* was finally edited into
its current form (around the fourth century CE), sugar in its
crystalline form had been around at least eight hundred years.
Most likely, the early and broad adoption of sugarcane cultivation across the subcontinent goes far in explaining Indians' sweet
tooth. Compare this to the other dessert-obsessed cultures featured in the coming chapters: in India, sugar was widely available
more than a millennium before the foodies of medieval Baghdad
started writing odes to their favorite desserts and easily fifteen
hundred years before Italians began showering their pies and
tortes with the white crystals.

Today, Indian nutritionists bemoan the dietary habits of
their more affluent countrymen almost as much as they worry
about malnutrition among the poor, and perhaps rightfully so.
India has an enormous rate of diabetes, which is growing by
leaps and bounds. But sweets didn't used to be an everyday treat,
something to nibble on at breakfast, lunch, and dinner as they
are today. They were special, even holy, used not only to honor
the gods but also to mark holidays and life's rituals from birth to
death, and just about every event that comes in between.

SWEET CIRCLE OF LIFE

Seated in her cluttered but prim living room on the sixth floor
of a sprawling Kolkata apartment building, Rajashi Gupta feeds

* In the south, fruit is often added to the mix. In the southern state of Tamil Nadu, the Muruga
temple stirs in cardamom, plantains, dates, and raisins.

me *laddu*s and expounds on the sweet circle of life. Rajashi is an immensely hospitable Kolkatan. In her youth she earned a degree in comparative literature and competed as a state table tennis champion. These days she gives classes to curious foreigners in the fine art of Bengali cooking. Though hardly conservative by Indian standards, she is a pious Hindu. And like every other Hindu, her first taste of food was of dessert.

"When there's a newborn in the family," she explains, "there is a rice feeding ceremony. For the son it is after three months or six months, for the girl it is an odd month, it could be seven or nine." A maternal uncle or comparable relative feeds the infant a little sweet rice pudding or *pāyesh*. "That's very, very auspicious," she continues, "and it has to be sweet because we believe in Bengal that the first thing served to a child should be sweet."

This last idea is widespread in India. A hundred years ago, anthropologists in Punjab noted that infants' lips used be smeared with jaggery (raw sugar) before they were allowed to suckle for the first time.[17] A similar ritual is described in the eleventh-century text called *Mānasôllāsa*, though there it is honey mixed with ghee that is applied to the infant's lips.[18] The tradition stems from the Manu Smirti (the closest thing Hinduism has to a uniform code of law), which prescribes that a newborn should be fed with a mixture of honey and ghee from a golden spoon before its umbilical cord has been cut.

At one time, this ceremony could draw the whole clan into a celebration as elaborate and costly as a wedding. It used to be that the rite was limited to males, something that drew the ire of at least one reformer in the late 1800s. Nand Lal Ghose was a barrister who authored a curious protofeminist work, *A Guide for Indian Females from Infancy to Old Age*, with the intent of improving the second-class status of women in colonial India. As part of his crusade to expose the gender inequalities in every aspect of daily life, he documented in great detail the boy-centric ceremony. The "Anna Prasadam" (first feeding) he described is a far cry from Rajashi's modest domestic event. Among status-conscious Punjabi Brahmans, he wrote, it was common to spend thousands of rupees on the occasion—if it involved a son. (A skilled laborer earned little more than a quarter-rupee a day.)[19] The cost even led some to bankruptcy.

In the days leading up to the first feeding there were banquets and parties, Ghose tells us. Fish, oil, vegetables, spices, and sweetmeats were handed out to villagers. At a vegetarian feast given for sometimes hundreds of fellow Brahmans, a meal of vegetable "curry" and buttery dal-filled *puri* (puffy bread) was followed by "sweetmeats of different kinds," then a sort of palate cleanser of yogurt and cream, and then yet another course of sweets. The author goes on to explain how, on the assigned day, the infant boy took part in a complex ceremony of venerating the ancestors during which the dearly departed were symbolically fed with a blessed mélange of rice mixed with yogurt, clarified butter, sugar, sesame seed, and banana. (He notes that a similar rite is performed before marriage.) Before the first feeding, the child was ritually bathed, dressed, anointed, and decorated, then placed on a stone normally used for grinding spices. There was a naming ceremony, and then the first feeding occurred. This was another point at which males were shown preference, for the little boy's first taste was of sweet rice pudding, while the unfortunate girl got fish. (She would get some of the sweet gruel before all was said and done.) The sweet *pāyesh*, here called *payasa*, was apparently meant to increase life for the boy, while the fish was supposed to promote conjugal life, deemed more essential for the girl. Society has progressed over the last hundred years, though Mr. Ghose might be perturbed that in many respects a double standard still applies to all too many Indian women, and not just when it comes to dessert.

It's worth underlining that in India sweets are decidedly not associated with femininity, as they are in most of Europe. It is boys who are traditionally the recipients of sweets, not girls. Bhai Phota, or brother's day, the holiday right after Kali Puja, when sisters regale their male siblings with sweet snacks, has no female equivalent. Rajashi, for one, tells me that she doesn't care for sweets—even as she offers me yet another *laddu*.

In South Asia it isn't just Hindus who turn to sweets to mark life's passages. Sugary snacks are omnipresent in Indian Muslim rituals and ceremonies as well. Some of these were exhaustively documented by an English contemporary of Nand Lal Ghose. Horace Arthur Rose arrived in Punjab in the late nineteenth century tasked with organizing the government census of the province, though it's a wonder he got the job done because he evidently became obsessed with every minute detail of the lives of the people he had been sent to count. In later years this compulsive amateur would send detailed accounts of his findings to the Royal Anthropological Institute back in London. At the time the British province of Punjab included not only the current west Indian state but much of the densely populated Indus Valley in what is now Pakistan. The population was fairly evenly split between Hindus and Muslims.

Rose detailed, for example, the elaborate choreography of offer and counteroffer involved in Muslim engagement rituals and weddings. These necessitated sweetmeats during every move. The process often began even as the betrothed couple were still only children. One of the first steps required the women of both families to come together at the fiancée's house to seal the deal. This was referred to as "sweetening the mouth." The bride's family might then send rings to the groom, the golden bands nestled in a container filled with sugar. The groom's father would respond with a present of sweetmeats and fancy fabric. In one district, the sweets were always a mixture of *patasha* and *nuqul* (both candies) along with cardamom. The bride's father was then expected to reciprocate with fruit and more sweets. The details of the ceremonies and the specific sweetmeats varied from region to region, but they were always there. They might be *khajârs*, fritters shaped like dates made of wheat flour and coarse sugar, or *chobba*, a dish of sweet rice. In one district 101 *laddus* were presented to the bride's family once the engagement was confirmed.

Once a child was born, more sweets ensued. The compulsive Englishman described a delightful celebration when the grandmother sends ball-shaped sweets to her daughter's family when the child is approximately six months old. These might be a *marunda* or *murunda* (a ball of parched sugar mixed with raw sugar), or *laddus,* the point being that at this age the toddler begins to open and close its fists and this is how both sweetmeats are made. As you might expect, the first birthday is celebrated with sweets, as is the first day of school. When girls' noses and ears are pierced, they are bribed with sugary snacks. When boys are circumcised (generally between the ages of seven and twelve), the members of their Muslim fraternity are regaled with sugar or dates. The boy undergoing the operation, on the other hand, often gets a sweetmeat called *majun*, made of sugar, ghee, and milk, mercifully spiked with marijuana.[20]

Is it any wonder that both Muslim and Hindu Indians (the men especially) have such a developed sweet tooth?

SUGAR

In Kolkata, the intersection of Park Street and Jawaharlal Nehru Road is even busier than most. There is a metro stop here, so at clockwork intervals torrents of humanity gush from beneath the ground. Some wait at the curb edge, taking heed of the automated announcement that chants, "Do not cross the road now, please wait for the light to turn red, someone (or your near one) is waiting for you at home." Others plunge heedless into the fitful flow of yellow taxis, oblivious to the wailing horns and the belching exhaust. On one corner, altogether indifferent to the barely contained chaos around him, a skinny, bare-chested man tends to a small shrine. It's not much of a shrine, really, just a platform of marble and concrete about the size of a washing machine. There is a scattering of idols on top: a strapping sculpture of Hanuman, the monkey god, garlanded with a splendid necklace of orange and yellow marigolds, and little figurines of Ganesha and Durga wrapped in their own radiant blooms. There are also a handful of coins, a little brass cup of holy water, and a paper plate of sugar crystals. For a small contribution you can step away from the surging masses, sip a little of the sacred water, and nibble on a sugar crystal. Rajashi explains to me that when you drink the holy water you are taking in a part of the god and when you eat the sugar you'll be sweet like the god. You will not speak ill of others. Since whatever has been given to the god becomes pure, in eating it you purify yourself. In consuming the sugar, you are blessed. The analogy to the Christian sacrament of bread and wine is inescapable.

In India, sugar is hardly some esoteric ambrosia. It is, like bread in the Christian West, ordinary and essential. Around the corner from the sugar shrine, two men have commandeered prime sidewalk real estate to set up their sugarcane press under an improvised lemon-yellow awning. As one peels the sugarcane, the other feeds the denuded stalks between two rollers, spinning a large blue hand wheel that keeps the mechanism whirring. The clunky machine, which looks like it was designed by some ingenious Victorian, exudes the clear sweet liquid into a galvanized bucket set amid the cane peelings and a heap of broken crockery. It costs only a few pennies for a serving of cane juice served in little unglazed pottery beakers, the local answer to Dixie cups. When done, you are expected to dispose of the container in the gutter. You see these cane juice stands everywhere in India. The machine may be of relatively recent vintage but the process of extracting cane juice has been going on here for millennia.

It is generally accepted that Indians first perfected the art of extracting and refining sugar from cane. As far as the origin of sugarcane itself goes, there is a lack of consensus. Some varieties of cane appear to be indigenous to India, others to southeast Asia, and still others to Polynesia, especially to Papua New Guinea and the nearby islands. Among botanists, the majority view is that people started to cultivate cane independently in all these places as a kind of fruit, to be chewed for its juice. Some cane varieties are grown solely for this purpose. There is still a market for the sugary nectar, as Kolkata's cane juice vendors will attest.[21]

Historians of agriculture surmise that at some point the New Guinea varieties reached India, where they hybridized with the local varieties. By the sixth century BCE, Indians had figured out how to turn the sweet juice into something we might recognize as sugar. In its simplest, most unrefined form—what Indians call *gur* (Hindi, Bengali), *vellam* (Tamil), or jaggery (English)—it is made by simply boiling away the liquid from the cane extract. The result is lumpy, moist, and brown with a pronounced molasses taste. Indian cooks still use it extensively in both sweet and savory dishes. This first step in sugar refining must have taken place before 500 BCE, because by that date references to a more refined, sweeter *sarkara*, the Sanskrit term for granular sugar, begin to appear. Originally *sarkara* referred to granular particles or gravel, a meaning that eventually migrated to crystalline sugar. By around 300 BCE, a government bureaucrat was already mentioning five kinds of sugar including something called *khanda*, which would later come to mean the kind of pure sugar crystals offered at the Kolkata sidewalk shrine.* In the coming centuries, fields of sugarcane spread all across northern India so that, by the

* The English word "jaggery" is descended indirectly from *sarkara*, the Sanskrit word for sugar, by way of the Portuguese *xagara* or *jagara*. "Sugar" derives from the same word, this time through the Persian *shakar* and the Arabic *sukkar*. Candy comes from *khanda*, the meaning of which was originally "a piece," from *khand*, to break.[22]

Gupta era (300–550 CE), the commercial cultivation of sugar-cane was widespread throughout the fertile plain of the Ganges.[23]

⌒ Gur ⌒

Sugar and honey aren't the only sweeteners historically used by Indian sweet makers. Another popular form of sugar comes from date palm sap. *Gur* is boiled down over wood fires, much like maple syrup, absorbing a lightly smoky taste. (Like the native American sweetener, it is also occasionally used like pancake syrup, poured over breads for an instant dessert.) In Bengal, jaggery derived from palms is called *gur* while unrefined cane sugar is called *akhi gur*, which suggests that it predates cane sugar in the region. Many consider palm jaggery superior in taste, and, in winter when the palms are tapped, numerous sweets use *gur*, as liquid molasses or as a dry paste. During its short season you'll find nuggets of the palm sugar embedded in *rossogolla* and *kalojam*.

When Ibn Battuta, a famed Moroccan traveler and chronicler, visited northern India in the mid-1300s, he was most impressed by the quantity and the cheapness of sugar. In Delhi, the sultan maintained a sugar market and controlled the prices. The sweetener was still expensive but nowhere near as dear as in Ibn Battuta's North African home. At the sultan's market, a pound of sugar cost about as much as twelve pounds of rice and about the same as a pound of ghee.* Sugar and candy (presumably crystal sugar) were also dispensed to the sultan's employees as part of their wages.

---

* As a gauge of comparison, the price of sugar in England at the time was more than forty times the price of wheat, the local staple.

Two hundred years later, sugar was ubiquitous in the subcontinent. Vasco da Gama commented on it when he made landfall in Calicut in 1498. Ludovico di Varthema (an Italian traveler) and Duarte Barbosa (one of Magellan's sailing partners) were both impressed by the quantities of sugar they found in the first decades of the sixteenth century. By that century's end, Abul Fazl, the vizier (high minister) to the great Mughal emperor Akbar, documented that fine white sugar now cost merely three times the better grades of rice; brown sugar was almost equivalent in price. Sugar was now sufficiently cheap to be a staple food. Even horses and elephants got a daily allowance of either sugar or molasses (as well as ghee), depending on the season. The best imperial horses could count on as much as three pounds of sugar a day. The Mughal emperor's hundred elephants typically received some ten pounds of sugar as well as three hundred sugarcanes per day during the two-month harvest season.[24] Today, India is easily the world's leading producer, growing enough cane to produce over twenty million metric tons of raw sugar a year. What is more, that doesn't even count all the sugarcane juice consumed on street corners or the undocumented jaggery boiled down in rural backyards.

Needless to say, without the early and widespread availability of sugar, India's confectioners couldn't have come up with the thousand and one incarnations of sweet ambrosia that feed gods and mortals alike.

MAKING SENSE OF THE SWEETS

A Westerner wandering into a large Indian sweetshop can feel like a birdwatcher venturing for the first time into the Amazon. The profusion of color, shape, and size is bewildering. It's hard to make sense of it all. Much as ornithologists must learn to distinguish among fifty species of parrot, sweetshop clients must learn a whole new taxonomy of sweets. First they must study the different species, the *burfi*s, *halvah*s, *jalebi*s, *laddu*s, and others, and then learn to distinguish among the myriad subspecies that often look quite different but are really no more than a variation on a single genotype. Take the popular northern India sweet called *burfi*. This is made by cooking down milk along with sugar to a fudgelike consistency. But then the mixture can be colored, flavored with nuts, legumes, fresh or dried fruit, spices, and even carrots. It may be cut into squares like American fudge, formed into balls, layered, or rolled into multicolored slices and decorated with ground nuts, dried milk, coconut, or silver foil.

Another difficulty for a student of Indian confectionary is that the American distinction between candy and cake, between sweet snack and dessert, is not applicable here. The twisted ropes of *jalebi* manage to split the difference between candy and doughnuts. What do you call a *moong dal burfi*, a sweet mung bean–based nugget with the consistency of marzipan? European languages simply don't have the vocabulary to describe the many sugary foods Indians categorize as *mithai* in Hindi and *mishti* in Bengali (the two most widely spoken of India's thousand-plus languages).

Cakes and pastry are virtually unknown in India except as foreign—and thus often highly desirable—imports. As a rule, Indians don't bake anything, though in a nation often rightly described as more continent than country there will be exceptions. The only ovens traditionally used in South Asia are the cylindrical clay ovens called tandoors introduced from the Middle East by medieval invaders. These are, however, utterly unsuitable for most kinds of Western-style pastry. The only Indian oasis of cakes is Goa, the former Portuguese colony on the west coast, which has a five-hundred-year-old tradition of baking. Given that length of time, it's all the more surprising that their techniques did not leak out of the European enclave. But perhaps it was the Portuguese penchant for sweets laced with eggs that made it all but impossible for the Hindu majority to consider adopting the foreigners' ways. Observant upper-caste Hindus don't eat eggs, which naturally eliminates a whole range of techniques commonplace in European desserts. Thus no cakes or meringues, no mousses or custards. In India, creamy desserts are made by condensing milk or thickening it with starch. These days, in Mumbai and Bangalore, pastry shops advertise their egg-free cakes to their religious customers. But this is a new phenomenon.

Traditionally, all Indian desserts are made on top of a stove, whether steamed, simmered, boiled in syrup, toasted, panfried, or deep-fried, or sometimes a combination of all these techniques. The popular *gulab jamun*, for example, is a syrup-soaked fritter about the size of a Ping-Pong ball.* Like so many Indian sweets, its ingredients are simple, essentially sugar and milk, but the recipe requires a great deal of precision, technique, and labor—again, like so many of the subcontinent's confections. The process begins by making *mawa* (also known as *khoa* or *khaya*), produced by cooking milk over a slow fire for hours to evaporate almost all of its moisture. Ideally the result should be fairly dry with a delicate golden color and a taste hinting of caramel. *Mawa* is used in numerous Indian desserts. (Some cookbook authors suggest substituting milk powder for the *mawa*, but then all the complexity is lost.) Once the *mawa* is ready, the cook mixes it with flour and more milk or cream, forms the batter into balls, then deep-fries them. Finally, they get a soak in syrup. The resulting *gulab jamun* is part doughnut, part baba rum with a pleas-

---

* A fritter of very similar appearance is made in the Middle East under the name *luqmat al qadi* (see page 102). It is conceivable that they both developed from an earlier Persian antecedent. *Gulab* comes from the Persian word for rosewater, while *jamun* refers to a local fruit of roughly this size. The two batters are made entirely differently, though, so the only Persian connection may be the common use of rosewater syrup.

antly bitter edge from the twice-caramelized milk sugars. Most Americans find it too sweet. Indians adore it.

Other fritters are based on *chhana* (fresh curd cheese), yogurt, rice, or wheat, bean, or chickpea flour. They vary in color from pale gold to Day-Glo yellow to jet black. Some, like the *bonde*, are no more than little droplets. Others, like the knotted *jalebis* (made with wheat flour) and the similar *amriti* (made with a chickpea dough), are poured into the hot fat carefully so that they end up resembling a rose.

While certain confections are found across India, others remain local specialties. Visitors to the Taj Mahal shouldn't leave without tasting *Agra ka petha*, the local candied pumpkin. *Pithe*, a rice pancake typically stuffed with some sort of sweet mixture, is typical of the northeast. In Karnataka, to the south of Mumbai, they make a crêpe-thin wheat bread called *hōlīge* stuffed with dal, coconut, and jaggery that goes back at least to the tenth century. Chances are you will not find *murmura* in a confectionary store. These are typically made at home with puffed rice (you make it by spreading a special kind of rice on hot sand) mixed with dense molasses. The result is surprisingly like rice crispy squares except for the fact that they are the size and shape of a tennis ball. This was another recipe that was around in the Middle Ages.[25] How old some of these preparations are is often difficult to nail down. Many, however, show up in documents that go back hundreds if not thousands of years.

MĀNASÔLLĀSA

Unfortunately, most documentary evidence of the early history of food in India comes in such tattered scraps that it's hard to assemble it all into a meaningful whole. There does exist, however, a large, richly embroidered tapestry that details the feasts

and other entertainments of at least one medieval Hindu potentate. Sometime around 1131, King Sômêśvara III sat down to pen
a handbook on how to run a kingdom that came to be known
as the *Mānasôllāsa*. Sômêśvara's realm, the western Chalukya
empire, was enormous, covering a large swath of southern India.
In his how-to manual, the king went into enormous detail, covering everything from alchemy to military strategy to issues of
taxation. He gave advice on religious topics, interior design, and
child rearing. He listed varieties of umbrellas and the best kinds
of beds. (This last item was clearly of great concern to the author
given his affection for the fairer sex.) Not only are there rules for
work, there are instructions for play. Sômêśvara dwelt at length
on what the monarch should do on his days off. According to the
Mānasôllāsa the ideal ruler should spend most days frolicking
in fragrant gardens and playing hide and go seek with beautiful
women. Perhaps so he can work up an appetite for lunch?

With his hedonistic temperament, it is to be expected that
Sômêśvara would have plenty of opinions about food and dining.
It seems, for example, that the monarch was much taken with eating en plein air. A royal picnic demanded a sensual setting, amid
beautiful farms or pasture grounds, aromatic with flowering trees
and plants, "the air full of the fragrance of ketaki flowers," which
the author found especially suggestive. In this idyllic location the
thump of elephants brings on erotic thoughts and the peacocks
mimic the sound made by the flying arrows of the Cupid-like
Manmadha. The royal servants prepare the spot with carpets and
tents to greet the monarch as he arrives on an elephant decorated
with flowers, golden bells, and vermillion powder, surrounded by
his women, "who shine with jewels." There are singers and dancers—and more women. When the ruler and his lovers dismount
they are feasted with "a variety of tasty items." He then gives away
jewels, flowers, and clothes to his concubines. Song and dance fill
the rest of the afternoon until the party finally departs for home.

In this particular case, the author leaves the details of the romantic afternoon somewhat to the imagination. Elsewhere he is more graphic. In medieval India, sugar wasn't merely used in confectionary. It was also fermented into an alcoholic toddy. Apparently Sômêśvara enjoyed getting his lovers drunk "for relaxation and satisfying his sensual feelings" so that he could "enjoy the different moods of the intoxicated women."

He was also cryptic about the "tasty items" served at the picnic, but his meals must have been a delight. In another passage, his model king is directed to sit on a cushioned seat, his lap covered by a large white napkin. The food arrives on a great platter of gold. First there is rice with a kind of dal made of green lentils, then tender meat with more legumes and side dishes of vegetable curries. There is a pause in the middle of the meal for *pāyasam* (sweet rice pudding) before proceeding to other savory preparations. The *pāyasam* is the only dessert he mentions in the context of a meal, though elsewhere he describes the preparation of many others. Perhaps among these were the tasty items served at his outdoor fête.

The king was not above sharing his favorite recipes. He gives instructions for cooking rice (seven kinds are mentioned), pulses, meat, vegetables, and numerous sweets. The Indian penchant for frying is evident here. There are many recipes for savory legume flour–based fritters, but he also gives instructions for *gôlamu*, a sugar-sweetened doughnut made with wheat flour and scented with cardamom and pepper. He describes *ghārikās* ("the best of all eatables"), fried cakes made of black gram flour that are subsequently soaked in sugar syrup. In another recipe he gives directions for a syrup-soaked fritter many modern Indians would recognize. To make it, the cook is told to curdle warm milk by adding buttermilk, then strain it to remove the liquid. (Nowadays this fresh cheese would be called *chhana*.) The resulting curds are then mixed with a little rice flour, formed into balls, and fried in ghee. Finally, they are soaked in syrup. Visitors can taste just about the same dessert in any Bengali sweetshop today. It is called *pantua* or *ledikeni*. The only noteworthy difference is that the Bengali sweet uses wheat rather than rice flour. The *Mānasôllāsa* mentions many other milk-based sweets as well, in addition to spelling out several ways to condense and sour milk, all methods that would be familiar to contemporary confectioners.[26]

The *Mānasôllāsa* was composed at a time of great political upheaval. Up until this time the subcontinent had been divided into numerous kingdoms that fluctuated in size and dominance. They were, however, indigenous and predominantly Hindu, although there were sizable Buddhist and Jain minorities. Yet even before the sensual prince had begun his encyclopedic opus, northern Indians had no choice but to confront a religion and a people with a very different food tradition than their own. A new, Muslim-dominated era swept down from the mountains of Central Asia.

THE MUGHALS

The relatively insular nature of Indian society was rent asunder when, in 997, Mahmud of Ghazni and his Turkish, Afghan, and Persian warriors spilled out of the Afghanistan passes to pillage and plunder the rich Indus valley. Others followed, until by 1200 much of the north Indian plain was under Muslim rule. The invaders set up their capital in Delhi; accordingly, their empire is referred to as the Delhi Sultanate. Dominated by Turkic and Afghan dynasties, the Muslim overlords looked to Persia for many of their cultural cues, whether in language, religion, architecture, painting, or dining habits.

Despite their best efforts, the foreigners were only partly successful in imposing their culture. There just weren't enough of them. In the end they had to accommodate themselves to the mostly Hindu population. Many local Hindu chiefs were left in place, and petty rajas were allowed to keep ruling their domains as long as they paid their taxes.[27]

In the early sixteenth century, the sultans of Delhi were replaced by yet another invasion of Turks from Central Asia, the so-called Mughals, who would rule for the next three hundred years. Under the new dynasty, there was once again a great deal of political accommodation and seemingly very little forcible conversion of the Hindu population. Apparently one could rise quite high in the Mughal administration and remain Hindu.

Yet Persia remained the model to be emulated. In Delhi, Persian became the official language of court despite the fact that it wasn't even the invaders' mother tongue. But India—as every visitor will attest—is hard to resist. Mughal culture, whether in dress, decor, manners, or morals, began to acquire something of a national patina, leading to a subtle marriage of Persian design with Indian style.

The one cultural sphere where mutual influence occurred only at arm's remove was in the matter of food. Hindu dietary rules, which grew even more restrictive during the years of Muslim rule (perhaps precisely to keep the new elite at a distance?), would not allow an upper-caste Brahman to break bread with a Muslim. As a result, two parallel cuisines developed in the parts of India with a substantial Muslim population: a meat-based Mughal cuisine and a mostly vegetarian Hindu style of cooking. The sweets were different too. Hindus had their milk-based sweets, while Muslims typically preferred the *halvah*s and other desserts that originated in the Middle East.

Robert Montgomery Martin, a British census official, reporting on conditions in northern Bengal, noted how separate the two groups of sweet makers were even as late as the 1830s. "The people, who prepare sweetmeats from curds," he wrote, "are called Moyra among the Bengalese, and Haluyikors [a word derived from *halvah*] in western India. The artists of the two countries, however, keep totally distinct; and those of Bengal use most milk, while those originally from western India use more flour in their sweetmeats." It's amusing to note how his Victorian taste buds were aghast at the local delicacies. "These sweetmeats," he noted with palpable distaste, "please neither the eye nor palate of Europeans . . . [though] the rich natives use large quantities."[28]

Historians know a great deal more about the food of the Mughal era than about earlier periods, in part due to the swarm of Western visitors who descended upon India to make their fortune after 1498. Most were not as closed-minded as Mr. Martin, even if they were equally amazed by the amount of sweet snacks consumed by the locals.

One awestruck European was Edward Terry, a young chaplain assigned to the English ambassador at the Mughal court between 1616 and 1619. Terry was barely out of divinity school at Oxford when he reached India, and he hadn't expected such a prominent post. But the ambassador's chaplain had recently died, so the English country boy was thrust into hobnobbing with India's nabobs. Keep in mind that at this time the Mughal sovereign ruled an empire of a hundred million, while all of Great Britain could claim fewer than five million souls. What's more, the emperor claimed between a third and one-half of all crops in taxes. And money flowed even more freely than these statistics suggest. Much of the imperial revenue was ceded to courtiers and officials, though only for their lifetime. This gave Mughal grandees every incentive to spend as much as possible, since they could not pass on their wealth to the next generation. Whatever was left over would revert to the emperor upon their death. As a result, the Mughal elite burned through their cash in a great conflagration of conspicuous consumption. Courtiers of relatively modest rank packed their stables with Arabian horses, populated their harems with Indian and African dancing girls, and filled their servants' quarters with slaves. To the English, this level of spending beggared belief. When it came to food, week-day suppers in Delhi grew to resemble imperial banquets. Terry had the chance to witness one of these quotidian meals when he and the ambassador were invited to supper by Asaf Khan, the monarch's brother-in-law.[29] Today, Asaf Khan is best known as the father to Mumtaz Mahal, whose tomb, the Taj Mahal, would become one of Mughal India's greatest ornaments, but in his day he was in the emperor's inner circle and one of the most powerful men in India.

The dinner Terry described is served in a large, ornate tent, the air filled with perfume, the floor piled with expensive carpets on which the host, the ambassador, and the chaplain recline. There are no other guests. Servants arrive bearing silver dishes trimmed with gold. They are not enormous ("not larger than our largest trencher plates," Terry noted), but they descend upon the diners in a seemingly endless cascade. The chaplain counts fifty for himself, sixty for the host, and seventy for the ambassador. Even if our impressionable informant exaggerated a little, there must have been a huge amount of food for just the three of them. Terry made a conscientious effort to taste just about everything within reach and reported that he was most pleased with the result.

What is noteworthy about Asaf Khan's menu is that it is fundamentally Persian, not Indian. There are numerous pilafs, or rice dishes, made both with meat and without, some tinted yellow with saffron, others purple ("by what ingredient I know not; but this I am sure, that it all tasted very well"). There are stews of various kinds of meat and poultry. But the Englishman seemed especially impressed by the sweetmeats:

> To [accompany these meat dishes] we had many jellies
> and culices [aspics]; rice ground to flour, then boiled,

and after sweeten'd with sugar-candy and rose-water, to be eaten cold. The flour of rice, mingled with sweet almonds, made as small as they could, and with some of the most fleshy parts of hens, stewed with it, and after, the flesh so beaten into pieces, that it could not be discerned, all made sweet with rose-water and sugar-candy, and scented with Ambergrease; this was another of our dishes, and a most luscious one, which the Portuguese call *mangee real* [*manjar real*], food for a King. Many other dishes we had, made up in cakes, of several forms, of the finest of the wheat flour, mingled with almonds and sugar-candy, whereof some were scented, and some not. To these potatoes [sweet potatoes?] excellently well dressed; and to them divers sallads of the curious fruits of that country, some preserved in sugar, and others raw; and to these many roots candied, almonds blanched, raisons of the sun, prunellas, and I know not what, of all enough to make up the [fifty and more] number of dishes before named . . .

The almonds, the rosewater, the ambergris, the candied fruit—these were all Middle Eastern imports. Some of the combinations Terry described would certainly have been too alien for the Hindu palate; others were too pricey. The blancmange, the sweet pudding of rice, almond, and chicken scented with ambergris, was both.* This *mangee real*, as he calls it, was a common enough dish in Europe and the Muslim world at the time, but to observant Hindus the presence of chicken would have made it taboo. And the ambergris was fantastically expensive. Yet even while many dishes never made it out of the Sultan's kitchen, others were adapted and absorbed into the dessert repertoire of the country's Hindu majority.

---

* For more on chicken puddings and ambergris, see the following chapter, pages 97 and 99.

The cakes Terry described must have been *halvah*, and Indians of all creeds took to them with glee. The origin of Indian *halvah* is unmistakably Middle Eastern; the name itself is originally Arabic (*ḥalwā*, meaning sweetmeat). In the Middle East there are two types of *halvah*, an older type, made with flour, and a more recent variant that substitutes a nut or, more commonly, sesame seed paste. It is the former version that Terry would have tasted. In today's India this is called *sooji* (semolina) *halvah*. It has the consistency of a dense brownie or a slightly crumbly cake and is made by frying semolina in ghee, then adding syrup. This is cooked briefly until the water is absorbed. A Mughal era recipe calls for equal parts flour, ghee, and refined sugar. Today *halvah* is often enriched with dried fruit, nuts, and spices. Generally it is cut into diamonds and is often decorated with a little silver foil. As with *burfi*, there are dozens of variants. *Moong dal halvah* substitutes crushed mung beans for the semolina and stirs in milk and sugar instead of plain syrup. The fudgelike *gajar* (carrot) *halvah* is made by cooking down carrots with milk and sugar, then stirring in ghee and dry milk. There are bottle gourd *halvah*s, fig *halvah*s, pumpkin *halvah*s, and rice *halvah*s, to name just a few. Not surprisingly, most are associated with north India, but the southern state of Kerala has its own "banana" *halvah* made with ripe plantains, ghee, and sugar.* The dessert became so popular that in many parts of India *halwai* is the generic name for a sweet maker.

Another fashion imported from the Middle East was a taste for sorbets, which is what the Mughals called a flavored syrup (rather than a frozen dessert). The ever-informative Moroccan travel writer Ibn Battuta mentioned an event in Delhi where great basins were filled with a kind of sugar-sweetened soft drink flavored with rosewater. In yet another passage he noted: "They

---

* Somewhat confusingly, Indians typically refer to eating bananas as plantains and to the larger cooking variety (known as plantains in the United States) as bananas.

offer cups of gold, silver and glass, filled with sugar-water. They call it sherbert [sic] and drink it before eating."[30] This was still in the mid-1300s, in the days of the Delhi sultanate.

By the Mughal period, these soft drinks were often chilled, and a great deal of money and effort were devoted to procuring ice and snow to this end. Abul Fazl devoted several pages to the matter in the *Ain-i-Akbari,* his meticulous dissertation on the administration of emperor Akbar's empire. Ice and snow were transported five hundred miles from the Himalayas by carriage, by boat, and on foot. Even more intriguing, the Mughals had figured out how to chill water by the use of saltpeter.[31] If enough of the chemical is stirred into water it will actually cause the water to freeze.

It is this technology, initially developed to chill drinks, that likely led to *kulfi,* the Indian answer to ice cream, certainly one of the more delightful outcomes of the encounter of Mughal and indigenous sweet makers. According to the Indian food historian K. T. Achaya, these desserts were first made in the sixteenth century. A mixture of the dense evaporated milk so common in Hindu sweetmeats was flavored with pistachios and saffron, then packed in metal cones before being immersed in an ice slurry, a procedure that is still followed today.[32] The word *kulfi* comes from the Persian term *qulfi,* meaning a covered cup.

Even if there may have been many sweets at Terry's meal, they were certainly not served as a final dessert course. This seems to have been the case among the Muslim elite earlier as well. Ibn Battuta described a meal in Delhi that began with glasses of sweet sherbet scented with rosewater. After this came a roast accompanied by bread served with different sorts of *halvah* placed in the middle of it. Presumably one ate this as a kind of wrap, or sweetmeat sandwich, to accompany the meat. (Persians still eat *halvah* in this way.)[33] The next course consisted of more meat dishes, meat-stuffed samosas, and a pilaf with a whole roast chicken on top. Then came another sweet and a kind of pudding. Though the meal Ibn Battuta outlined is more modest than Terry's feast (a mere forty dishes instead of about sixty), the pattern is similar—platters of meat, rice, and bread interspersed with what we would call dessert.[34]

Yet despite their well-developed sweet tooth, the Muslim elite could never quite catch up to their Hindu neighbors. During his sojourn, Terry noted with some amazement that the more observant Hindus lived on no more than "herbs and roots, and bread, milk, butter, cheese, and sweetmeats." Not that anyone should conclude from this that the vegetarian Brahmans were necessarily abstemious. The long-lived poet Surdas (1478–1583) devoted several verses to the breakfasting habits of the North Indian upper classes. He related that the day's first meal consisted of bread, ghee, milk, and yogurt but also some ten confections and a half-dozen kinds of fruit and nuts. The dinners he described were equally blessed with sweets.[35]

Other European visitors who arrived in India at the height of Mughal rule were as impressed as Terry by the mountains of sweetmeats everywhere. The Spanish friar Sebastian Manrique, who traveled from Bengal to Punjab in the 1630s, reported on how the Bengalis had "many kinds of lecteus [lacteous or milk-based] food and of sweetmeats prepared in their own way, for they have a great abundance of sugar in those parts." He was impressed to find "huge amounts of foodstuffs and dainties of all sorts" in the "numerous Bazars or markets." He wrote, "Entire streets could be seen wholly occupied by skilled sweetmeat makers who proved their skill by offering wonderful sweet scented daunties of all kinds which would stimulate the most jaded appetite to gluttony."[36] In later years the British would reward their native troops with sweets instead of the liquor rations provided for their own soldiers.[37]

Europeans Come to India

By Terry's day, India had been crisscrossed by Westerners. Goa had been seized as a Portuguese colony, and smaller groups of Portuguese, Dutch, French, and English had settled along both east and west coasts.

The European—particularly the Portuguese—influence on the Indian diet was huge. Unlike the earlier Muslim invaders, however, it was mostly restricted to introducing new foods, not new dishes. New World chilies slipped effortlessly into the regional spice mixtures. South American cashews became a cheaper substitute for almonds and cashews in *burfis* and *halvahs*. At the markets, American squash sat side by side with local gourds; tomatoes nestled next to indigenous eggplant. The one spot where cuisine really was fundamentally transformed was in Goa. There the miscegenated residents invented a hybrid cuisine by using vinegar and pork to make distinct "curries" like pork vindaloo, but also by commingling eggs with local ingredients to beget desserts like *bibinça* (a multilayered egg custard made with coconut milk). However, the tiny colony existed as little more than a Portuguese–Indian culinary ghetto on the vast subcontinent utterly dominated by the Mughals in Delhi. Somewhat surprisingly, Lisbon would hang on to its little pied-à-terre until 1961, well over a decade after the British had been ejected from India.

Led by the English East India Company, British encroachment into the subcontinent was initially incremental and slow. The first English settlement was at Surat in 1612, eventually followed by Madras in 1639, Bombay in 1668, and Calcutta in 1690. The company's subsequent rapid infiltration into the interior was made possible by the gangrenous decay of the Mughal elite in the eighteenth century. Thomas Babington Macaulay, an East India Company functionary, later captured this decline with cruel precision: "A succession of nominal sovereigns, sunk in indolence and debauchery, sauntered away life in secluded places, chewing bhang, fondling concubines and listening to buffoons [even as] a succession of ferocious invaders descended through the western passes to prey on the defenceless wealth of Hindostan."[38] In the eighteenth century, the Mughal empire cracked apart into a jigsaw puzzle of more or less independent statelets run by more or less despotic *nawabs* (governors) who soon styled themselves *maharajas* (literally "great rulers"). In and of itself this might not have been so bad if the British hadn't been there to scavenge the pieces.

The Company picked off one *nawab* after another until by 1800 it was running most of coastal India and large parts of the Ganges valley. The result wasn't pretty. In 1769, the English trader Richard Becher wrote home from Bengal that since the takeover by the Company four years previously "the condition of the people of this Country has been worse than it was before . . . verging towards its Ruin." The following year famine wiped out an estimated one-third of Bengal's peasantry even as the Company hoarded grain and merchant speculators made a killing on the disaster.[39]

The nineteenth century saw the Europeans' single-minded predation gradually replaced by a more schizophrenic attitude toward the Indians. On the one hand, enlightened Englishmen sought to "civilize" the "natives." (Without a trace of irony, Rudyard Kipling would later call this "the white man's burden.") On the other hand, they brutally suppressed any demands for self-rule. Eventually, when a massive uprising threatened to liberate India in 1857, the British government took the reins of power away from the East India Company.

Though Britain ruled or dominated the subcontinent for over two hundred years, it's noteworthy how little direct impact they had on Indian cuisine (though, given the state of English cooking in the Victorian era, perhaps it isn't as remarkable as all that). But in other ways—in economics, culture, and even religion—the influence of far-off England was transformational. In Bengal, the colonial government's policy disrupted centuries-old patterns of agriculture and settlement. In the countryside, displaced peasants were pushed into growing cash crops such as cotton and indigo, while absentee landlords resident in the colonial capital raked in the profits. In the meantime, the old provincial capitals of Mughal rule hemorrhaged their populations of skilled laborers. Many of the artisans couldn't compete with the new industrially produced cloth and metal goods imported from Manchester and Birmingham and cast their lot with the landless peasants. Others joined the stream of the desperate and the ambitious to settle in the new centers of British power, in Bombay and Madras but most especially in Calcutta.

Calcutta wasn't much more than a collection of villages on the banks of the Hooghly River (a branch of the Ganges) when, in 1690, Job Chamok set up the East India trading post in what is now the city's central business district. The city grew rapidly and by 1821 numbered approximately two hundred thousand people. Fifty years later that had doubled. With English patronage, Calcutta became a magnet for entrepreneurs and day laborers, for government hacks and revolutionaries, for holy men and confectioners.

⌒ Portuguese in Asia ⌒

To the great Mughals, the arrival of the Portuguese in India in 1498 was as noteworthy as a gnat landing on an elephant. Even the little outposts the Europeans seized on the empire's periphery were barely noted in Delhi. Yet the tiny Iberian nation would have an outsize effect on eating habits throughout South Asia, admittedly mostly because of the chilies, tomatoes, and other American imports they introduced to the region.

When it came to dessert, their influence was more modest. During the Mughal era, there were two notable Portuguese communities in India, one on the west coast around Goa and the other in Bengal. Goa developed its own particular fusion cuisine, at times using indigenous ingredients and imported techniques, or in some cases re-creating Indian sweets with the cashews they'd brought from South America. There is a sort of Goan *barfi* made with cashews called *doce de castanhas*—which contains no chestnuts (*castanhas*) whatsoever. In other sweets, cashews and coconut would occasionally replace the almonds more common in Portugal proper.

Though they were perhaps as numerous as in Goa, the Bengali Portuguese never formed a cohesive community. Nonetheless their confectioners were apparently well known. François Bernier, a French doctor who spent 1659–1666 in India, wrote, "Bengal likewise is celebrated for its sweetmeats [*confitures*] especially in places inhabited by the Portuguese, who are skillful in the art of preparing them and with whom they are an article of considerable trade."[40] In his day *confitures* referred to sugar-preserved fruit, which in this case apparently included citrons, mangoes, pineapples, and other tropical produce. It's plausible to conclude that the technique used today to candy pumpkins in Agra was picked up from the foreign confectioners; after all, pumpkin preserves are a staple of Portuguese dessert makers.

Curiously, the greatest Portuguese influence on local dessert culture may not have been in India but elsewhere in Asia. Portugal has numberless desserts based on a mixture of eggs and sugar, some the consistency of creamy custards, others as dense as fudge. Many use just egg yolks, probably a by-product of the fact that Portuguese confectioners used egg whites to clarify sugar, leaving them with a surfeit of yolks. One such decidedly peculiar dessert is called *fios de ovos*, made by drizzling a batter of egg yolks into boiling syrup. The result looks like a tangle of yellow vermicelli and has a chewy, even rubbery, texture. The only other places this seems to exist are in Thailand, where it is called *foy thong*, and in Japan, where it goes under the name of *keiran somen*.

The evidence that these are both of Portuguese origin may be circumstantial but is pretty convincing. The Portuguese were the first Europeans to have prolonged contact with the Japanese in the second half of the sixteenth century, trading with the insular nation as well as sending missionaries. The Japanese language retains more than a score of Portuguese words from these contacts, including *pan* (from *paõ*, bread), tempura (from *tempero*, seasoning), and *kasutera*, or "castela cake" (from *paõ de Castela*, literally bread of Castile but in this case referring to sponge cake, what the Italians, in a similar vein, would later call *pan di Spagna*). Thailand seems to have forgone the sponge cake, perhaps because of the lack of ovens. But there are at least four egg-based sweets whose appearance makes the Portuguese parentage hard to disguise. *Thong yawd* is cooked in syrup much like *foy thong*, though in this case it results in tear-shaped drops of the yolk mixture instead of threads. *Thong yib* uses much the same process as a Portuguese dessert called *trouxas das caldas*. To make it, the cook floats a layer of egg yolks on gently simmering syrup. The texture that results is vaguely reminiscent of sheets of tempeh. In the Portuguese case these are typically rolled, while the Thai sweet is pinched into a flower shape. For *med khanoon*, the technique is taken one step further. Here a sweet bean and coconut paste is dipped in yolks before a final dip in hot syrup. The most plausible explanation for how these arrived in Southeast Asia is that Thais picked up the technique from Portuguese confectioners living in the European enclave in the Thai capital of Ayutthaya sometime after their arrival in 1516. The egg desserts are now considered thoroughly indigenous and no marriage ceremony would be complete without them.[41]

THE COLUMBUS OF *ROSSOGOLLA*

In present-day Kolkata (the spelling was changed from Calcutta in 2001 to reflect the Bengali pronunciation), it is mostly the holy men and revolutionaries who are commemorated in the names of squares and boulevards, but the confectioners aren't entirely forgotten. In the north Kolkata neighborhood of Bagbazar there is a small plaque set into a newish building on Rabindra Sarani (street). The sign, put up in 1968, memorializes the invention on this very spot of *rossogolla* by Nobin Chandra Das a hundred years earlier.* *Rossogolla*, a syrup-poached dumpling of fresh curd, is arguably India's favorite dessert. Today the family business Das founded (now called K. C. Das after his son) is one of

---

* Ironically, the plaque went up one year after the Bengali government almost put all of Kolkata's sweet makers out of business. In 1967, the ruling Communist party banned the use of milk in confectionary in an attempt to control the price of milk. The outcry from sweet-obsessed Bengalis was such that the regime quickly backpedaled. Hedging his bets, Das opened up shop in Bangalore, where the company still produces sweets and has its research lab.

India's largest producers of traditional sweets, with production facilities in Kolkata and Bangalore, with, at latest count, seventeen shops in both cities.

I had the opportunity to contemplate the photograph of Nobin Chandra Das at length as I sat waiting for his great-great-grandson in the family's ancestral house just a few blocks from the commemorative plaque. A servant took me up through the inner courtyard into a dim, old-fashioned parlor hung with family portraits, religious icons, and early modern art (the founder's grandson was an art patron). A white-haired Nobin Chandra gazed down from the wall, looking impatient to have the photographer finish so he could get back to business.

Today the company's day-to-day operations are under the direction of Dhiman Das. When he finally arrives, this latest Das gives the impression of a software engineer more than a pastry chef, which is not entirely surprising given how detailed the business can be. He is meticulously polite but only modestly forthcoming. The family has its stories, he tells me, but there's little documentation to speak of.

The Das clan traces its roots to Burdwan (or Barddhaman), seventy-five miles north of Kolkata. The city, once a district capital of the Mughal empire, had come under British rule in the 1770s and, like so many similar towns, it lost both its importance and its population in the coming years. The Das joined the stream of migrants to Calcutta, where the family apparently worked as sugar merchants. Nobin Chandra Das was born in 1846, by which point the family had fallen on hard times. As a consequence, the young Nobin Chandra slipped down the social ladder and opened up a sweetshop. In the early days, it is likely that he specialized in *sandesh*, the fresh curd cheese confection that is Bengal's most characteristic sweet.[42] It was here, Dhiman Das tells me, that his ancestor invented *rossogolla* through a long process of trial and error. The ingredients of *rossogolla* are simple, though the technique can be tricky to get just right. To make it, confectioners combine *chhana* (fresh curd cheese) with a little wheat flour. This dough is then formed into balls about an inch in diameter that are boiled in syrup, drained, and then placed in cool syrup. In the process, they blow up to more than twice their diameter and become light and almost bouncy, with a slightly squeaky texture that Indians adore.

As we sit, Dhiman sets a feast of sweets before me. Today the company produces numerous variations of *rossogolla*, some flavored with fruit like mango, others sandwiched with creamier *sandesh*. My favorite is *rossomalai* (*rosso* refers to syrup and *malai* to milk), created by the founder's son, Krishna Chandra Das, in the early years of the twentieth century according to company lore. This is made exactly the same way as *rossogolla* except that in this case it is finished off in a milk-based and saffron-tinted syrup. The result is creamy, delicate, and a little like a French *île flottante*, but less insipid. Dhiman Das tells me all the Westerners like it the best.

Given the passion Indians feel for *rossogolla*, it follows that it would occasionally be the subject of fierce controversy. Not everyone credits Nobin Chandra Das with the invention, but few can argue with the fact that it was he who made it popular. Kolkatans have called him (only a little facetiously) the "Columbus of *Rossogolla*," and even if he did not discover *rossogolla* any more than Columbus discovered the Indians, he is most definitely worthy of a plaque.

⌒ *Rossogolla* ⌒

That a dessert should elicit war, even if only a war of words, is hardly surprising in a country as obsessed with sweets as India. The matter of *rossogolla*'s origin is not without dispute. Despite the Bagbazar plaque, which identifies the time, the place, and the inventor of the dessert, there are earlier claimants to this moist and bouncy ball of *chhana*. Many natives of Orissa make the claim that *rossogolla* has been around for hundreds of years and that those arrogant, big-city Kolkatans have usurped their Oriya birthright. That Orissa is the much smaller southern neighbor to Bengal makes the battle even more vicious. On the Internet the subject is discussed with the tact and subtlety of soccer hooligans.

Yet a cursory glance through the history books suggests it is perfectly reasonable that foods and the artisans who make them would have migrated from Orissa to the population centers of the north. Under both the Mughals and the British, Orissa was part and parcel of Bengal. According to J. B. Padhi, who has published several books on the great Hindu temple at Puri, *rossogolla*—or something much like it—has been produced here for hundreds of years. The priests serve it to pilgrims at the end of the great annual chariot procession in honor of the temple's gods. Even if local sweet makers didn't make it to Kolkata, there were surely many Bengalis among the pilgrims to this, one of India's most important temples. In Bengal, sweets made with *chhana* have traditionally not been permitted in Hindu temples, yet it is entirely possible that this restriction didn't exist in Orissa; Hindu dietary rules vary greatly from region to region.

Just to muddle the picture further, at least one Bengali writer made the point that "*rasagollá*" was the specialty of the French colony of Chandannagar. He wrote this in 1874, that is, only six years after the purported invention by Das.[43]

Many Kolkata *moira* (confectioners) originally hail from Hooghly district, where Chandannagar is located, so could that be the connection? Certainly the French were partial to fresh curd cheese, but then so were the English; they too occasionally used an acid to coagulate milk as was the common practice in India.[44]

Yet no matter its origin, *rossogolla* likely predates Nobin Chandra Das. But then, even the company's sales brochure hedges its bets, noting, "it is hard to tell whether or not cruder versions of similar sweets existed anywhere at that time. Even if they did, they did not match the quality of Nobin Chandra and having failed to excite the Bengali palate they slipped into oblivion." And there is something to this, for it was Nobin Chandra Das's marketing savvy, or at any rate his access to the tastemakers of India's most powerful city, that made *rossogolla* the favorite of Indians the world over.

For you see, in Bengal, all this matters. No one is as fond of sweets as Indians and no Indian is as obsessed with confectionary as the Bengali. In 2003, the *Times of India* estimated that West Bengal, with about 8 percent of India's population, spent half the sixteen billion rupees that the country paid for sweetmeats that year.[45] Nobody in Kolkata would be surprised. Here there are blocks with three, four *moira*. Some are large operations with many branches like K. C. Das, while others are no bigger than a newsstand. In certain cases they are known for a certain specialty, but many make simply what will sell.

There are shops renowned for their *mishti doi,* a custard-like dessert made by introducing yogurt cultures into sweetened evaporated milk. (*Mishti* is the Bengali word for both "sweet" and "a sweet," while *doi* means "thick yogurt.") This is then allowed to set in unglazed earthenware cups that have the double advantage of cooling the mixture through evaporation and absorbing any excess whey. The result has the creaminess of crème caramel but the refreshing quality of yogurt. It is much appreciated in the summer.

What Bengal is most renowned for, however, are desserts based on *chhana* (also spelled *chhena*). *Chhana*, like *paneer*, is made by curdling milk and extracting the whey. *Paneer* is typically pressed into bricks and used in savory dishes like the ubiquitous curry joint staple, *saag paneer*, a creamy dish of spinach with chunks of *paneer*. The name clearly comes from the Persian, *panir*, though the actual cheese is quite different from its Middle Eastern cousin. *Chhana* is moister, more like ricotta, and almost invariably goes into sweets.

The process used to make it hasn't changed much over the last two hundred years. The East India Company functionary Robert Montgomery Martin may not have been enthusiastic about the result, but he dutifully described the technique in 1833. "The *chhana* or curd is prepared by boiling the milk, and by adding to it, while hot, some acid milk, which coagulates the whole into one mass. This is put into a cloth, and the whey is expressed, so that it is a kind of cheese."[46] Today both buffalo and cow milk are trucked into town each day from small producers. Small batches of *chhana* are made daily and hung in muslin to extract the moisture. Finally, the most traditional *moira* knead the resulting *chhana* by hand to achieve a creamy consistency. *Mishti* mavens swear that they can tell the difference between machine- and hand-kneaded *chhana*.

The purest of the cheese-based desserts is *sandesh*. A sweet known by this name has been around at least since the Middle Ages, though it is uncertain how it was made. Most likely it was what is currently called *kheer sandesh*, similar to the milky fudge based on desiccated milk sold at Kali's temple, rather than today's more common *chhana sandesh*. In Bengali, the word *sandesh* also means "good news." The story goes that the sweet got its name because people would bring it along when they came bringing good news. As the British captain Alexander Hamilton pointed out as early as 1708, these sorts of milk-based sweetmeats are especially incorruptible even when they come in contact with persons deemed to be unclean, which makes them a safe present. A British nineteenth-century guide to the intricacies of the Indian caste system noted: "The social standing of the Halwai is respectable, and Brahmans will take water from his hands. There is no caste in India which is too pure to eat what a confectioner has made."[47] In a similar vein, it's been postulated that Bengali Brahmans, loathe to accept an edible present that might have come in contact with other castes, were willing to accept gifts of *sandesh* but not more easily polluted sweets cooked with rice or legume flour.[48]

To make today's beloved *chhana sandesh*, the curd cheese is cooked with sugar until the desired consistency is reached. The mixture can simply be scented with rosewater—that favorite flavor of the Mughals—and formed into two-bite-sized pillows with a texture reminiscent of Italian cheesecake. This will last at most a day in a *moira*'s unrefrigerated display case. With a drier base, the sweet maker has more options: the *sandesh* can be pressed into forms, molded, and stuffed with any number of fillings. Palm sugar jaggery is one favorite during the winter season, when the palms are tapped for their sweet juices. Fruit can be used as well. Nobin Chandra Das, according to his descendants, pioneered the use of fresh jackfruit and custard apple in two of his *sandesh* creations.[*]

Chhana can also be used as a base for numerous fritters, much as it was in Sômêśvara's medieval kingdom. In contempo-

---

[*] Jackfruit, which grows like a giant, extraterrestrial tumor out of the thick trunk of the tree, tastes a little of bananas and chewing gum. Custard apples are a New World import that resemble large fat pinecones and have a vanilla and pineapple flavor with a texture resembling a ripe pear.

rary recipes, the fresh cheese is typically mixed with a little wheat flour, formed into balls, fried, and then soaked in sugar syrup. Names vary depending on the shape, size, degree of cooking, and whether the fritter is stuffed or not. (Americans make similar distinctions among doughnuts, jelly doughnuts, and crullers; it's just that our repertoire is much more limited.) *Pantua*, for example, is a doughnut-brown ball about the size of a lime, a little like a very moist baba rum but with a more intriguing texture. About the same size are the slightly sinister *kalojam*, black spheres that contradictorily are both rich and airy, penetratingly sweet yet with an undercurrent of bitter caramel. When you bite into *kalojam*, a concealed nugget of melted brown sugar spills its sweet juices. The nearly jet black color comes from the caramelization of the lactose in the cheese.

Nobin Chandra Das was just one of many *moira* who trace their roots to nineteenth-century Kolkata. It was a revolutionary time that had an impact on every facet of society, not least the sweet makers. According to local lore, the *chhana*-based sweets for which Kolkata is renowned only came into their own in the mid-nineteenth century as a consequence of shifting attitudes to Hinduism and a general loosening up of society. Yet it turns out that even under the ostensibly secular rule of the British, religion and sweets were once again intertwined.

CALCUTTA

Today's Kolkata sprawls across the Ganges delta in shantytowns and glitzy shopping malls, in crumbling Raj-era apartment blocks and shiny new towers, often all intermingling in a single block. Yet look beyond the grime, behind the invading bushes and vines, and you will spot elegant columns and delicate detail, even whole mansions reminding you of the long-lived British

Raj. In many ways, Calcutta was a British invention, a city with almost no history, a place where you could come and reinvent yourself. It wasn't just confectioners who came to the city to seek their fortune.

In the years previous to British rule, there were numerous Bengali Hindus serving the Mughal rulers. In the eighteenth century, almost all the tax collection was in Hindu hands. This didn't change much as the reins of power shifted from Delhi to London. Now, however, there were more opportunities to get rich quick. In some cases, already-prosperous Hindus became moneylenders to the East India Company, but others got jobs as pencil pushers, messengers, or servants. The melting pot of nineteenth-century Calcutta seemed to dissolve away many social distinctions. Opportunities in business and government meant that arrivistes could aspire to power. In one case, a laundry man reincarnated himself as an interpreter, learning English on the job and making a mint in the process.[49]

But there was a curious side effect that resulted from Indians rubbing up against the pink-skinned pudding eaters. In part due to the new educational opportunities offered by English schools, and in part as a reaction to the foreigners' patronizing attitude, Bengal's young intelligentsia began reawakening to India's rich cultural past. This Bengali Renaissance (as the movement came to be called) influenced every aspect of culture including food and religion. While some of the new generation hitched their fortunes to the corrupt colonial system, others sought reform in society by turning to their Hindu roots, though admittedly in a way that often conformed to contemporary Western ideas. Part of their agenda was to bring religion, along with its dietary rules, into the modern age.

The most influential of the new gurus of this movement, at least as far as Kolkata's *moira* are concerned, was Gadadhar Chattopadhyay, better known as Ramakrishna. You'll see his picture in just about every one of the most revered Kolkata sweetshops. In the most widely circulated photograph he sits cross-legged with an expression that seems more incredulous than beatific. Tellingly, he appears to have particularly bad teeth.

It was surely no coincidence that Ramakrishna hailed from the area around Barddhaman, the same city the Das family claims as its ancestral home. He was a simple priest who was entrusted to carry out ceremonies at the flashy new Dakshineswar Kali Temple funded (around 1855) by Rani Rashmoni, a rich, low-caste businesswoman. From all accounts the young priest was largely uneducated but given to visions and cryptic epigrams. He was also a revolutionary of sorts, rejecting the rules of caste and embracing the unity of all religions, something that seemed to mesh perfectly with the progressive and ecumenical thinking of the Bengali Renaissance. In capturing the zeitgeist, Ramakrishna soon developed a following not only among Calcutta's intelligentsia but also the city's progressive business owners. Yet, as the photographs hint, the holy man didn't have his thoughts merely on the divine. Apparently, he also had a sweet tooth.

According to Haradhan Nag, an aged scion of Kolkata's oldest sweetshop, Bhim Chandra Nag, the temple's founder, is said to have bought over a ton of *sandesh* from the confectioner for the celebration of its inauguration. Haradhan adds that whenever Rani Rashmoni went to Dakshineswar, she invariably carried two big packets of Bhim Chandra Nag sweets—one for the goddess Kali and the other for Ramakrishna, who would then apparently share it with his disciples.[50]

The reason this was a big deal to the confectioners is that in Bengal, *chhana* had previously been considered unacceptable for observant Brahmans and certainly not anything one would take to the temple as an offering. Dhiman Das tells me that some ultratraditional priests will still turn away *chhana*-based *sandesh*. The prohibition seems to be specific to Bengal. Just to the south, in Orissa, *chhana*-based sweets appear to have been common even within the temple at Puri for hundreds of years. In Gujarat, where observant upper-caste Hindus are typically much more strictly vegetarian than Bengalis, *paneer*, *chhana*'s denser cousin, is eaten without any qualms. How far back this regional taboo goes is unclear. Certainly the first published Bengali cookbooks, *Pakrajeswar* (1831) and *Byanjan Ratnakar* (1858), contain plenty of desserts but none using *chhana*, yet by 1874 a writer for the influential women's magazine *Bamabodhini patrika* (Journal for the Enlightenment of Women) enumerated a list of dishes every educated woman should know, which specifically included sweetmeats made from *chhana* as well as coconut, semolina, lentils, pumpkin, and thickened milk. Incidentally, she was also to learn to prepare meat in the Mughal style as well as English-style desserts like cakes, biscuits, and puddings.[51] The implication is that *chhana* was part and parcel of educated, cosmopolitan Bengali society.

One way the new Hindu *babu*s (as they were dubbed) showed off their worldly bona fides was by stuffing their houses with fake Claudes and Raphaels, Chippendale sofas, and gilded clocks. Bankim Chandra Chattopadhyay (Chatterjee), an influential writer of the Bengali Renaissance, couldn't help but skewer their pretensions:

> [W]e have exchanged . . . the tight-fitting jackets and loose-flowing chapkans of our grandfathers for shirts a l'anglaise and chapkans that are everyday steadily approaching towards the shape and size of English coats. . . .
>
> In the houses built by English-educated Bengalis, the poojah dalan [hall of worship] is conspicuous only by its absence. . . . Chairs, tables, punkahs [a type of ceiling fan] seldom meant to be pulled, American clocks, glassware

of variegated hues, pictures for which the Illustrated London News is liberally laid under contribution, kerosene lamps, bookshelves filled with Reynolds' *Mysteries*, Tom Paine's *Age of Reason* and the *Complete Poetical Works* of Lord Byron, English musical-boxes, compose the fashionable furniture of the Young Bengal.[52]

Another way they showed off was through ostentatious spending on food. Here the *babus* tended to stick closer to their Bengali roots. What that meant was that every engagement, every wedding, every *puja* would be celebrated with sweets and more sweets.

Nineteenth-century Bengalis were as obsessed with dessert as they are today. Writing in 1874, Lal Behari Day noted:

> I do not know that any other nation in the world consumes so many sweetmeats as the higher and middle classes of the people of Bengal. In other countries sweets and comfits are for the most part eaten by children; in Bengal they are eaten as much by grown men and women as by children. In some feasts all the courses consist of sweetmeats from beginning to end. . . . Hence confectioners are as plentiful in the land as crows.[53]

In Calcutta, people could discern the fine distinctions among sweets in much the way Angelinos can parse the meaning of a passing automobile.

Ever since Thorstein Veblen coined the phrase "conspicuous consumption" in 1899, it has been widely understood that one way people move up the social ladder and then broadcast their new position is through targeted spending to buy goods and services conspicuous to their peers. Every society has the equivalent of box seats at Yankee Stadium. In earlier eras, with fewer ways of keeping up with the Joneses, the public meal was one of the primary tools of one-upmanship. Quantity was important, of course, as the meals served by the Mughals make clear, but so was preciousness and expense. For most of history, foods containing sugar, preferably a lot of it, fit just those criteria. It is the reason early modern European banquets were cluttered with hundreds of pounds' worth of sugar sculptures.

In Bengal, where the love of sugar seems hardwired into the DNA, quantity in and of itself was not enough. The sweets had to be luxurious, naturally, made of the best ingredients, and covered with silver or preferably gold foil. But they also had to be innovative and comment-worthy in a society that cultivated connoisseurship, or at least pretended to. There was, accordingly, not only competition among the many sweet makers who had come to the colonial capital to make their fortune but also a rivalry among their customers to seek out the greatest and the latest. It is no wonder that in this hothouse atmosphere, innovation flourished.

If a single food could represent the Bengali Renaissance it would certainly be *chhana*-based *sandesh*, that urbane, artisanal sweet made by craftsmen in neighborhood shops rather than a caste of priests a breath away from the goddess. Unlike the almost primordial sweets you find in Kali's temple, *sandesh*, with its myriad forms, textures, and flavors, obeys the rules of human invention, of the marketplace of ideas. It is secular, even profane in its use of the mildly prohibited *chhana*. But it was its profanity, its modernity, that made it so attractive to Calcutta's *babus*. Consequently, like Bengali poems, novels, and broadsheets, its forms multiplied, and it became inextricably linked to the city's vernacular.

The deeply ambivalent script played out between the *babus* and the English rulers is neatly condensed in another *chhana*-based sweetmeat called the Lady Kenny or *ledikeni*. The lady in

question was Lady Charlotte Canning, the wife of the last governor general of the East India Company and subsequently the
viceroy when Parliament took control of the Raj in 1857. From
her published correspondence, Lady Canning emerges as no
wallflower. Her stay in India coincided with a precarious time for
the imperialists as Indian nationalists attacked British representatives across the subcontinent. Despite the considerable danger
and discomfort, the Victorian aristocrat traveled all over India,
folding her voluminous Victorian crinolines into carriages and
palanquins in order to spend time with her husband instead of
hosting tea parties at her Calcutta palace. Her letters show much
more interest in matters of war and politics than in the frequent
entertaining she had to do as the viceroy's wife. That she had a taste
for Indian food is doubtful, though she must have encountered
it in her visits to the palaces of local potentates. When it came
to Indian sweets, the English mostly seemed horrified by them.
So what of the *ledikeni*? There are multiple versions of the story,
but one of the earliest is told by Sivachandra Vasu in 1883. It is
telling that the writer, an Indian writing for an English-speaking
audience, sees the sweet as a sign of Bengali assimilation:

> The Bengalis have become so much anglicised of late that
> they have not hesitated to give an English name to their
> sweetmeats. When the late Lord Canning was the Gov-
> ernor-General of India, it was said, his Babu made a pre-
> sent of some native sweetmeats to Lady Canning, who
> was kindly pleased to accept them. Hence that sweetmeat
> is called the "Lady Canning," and to this day no grand
> feast among the Bengalis is considered complete unless
> the "Lady Canning" sort is offered to the guests. The man
> that first made it is said to have gained much money by
> its sale. It is not the savoury taste of the thing that makes
> it so popular, but the name of the illustrious Lady.[54]

Later stories embroidered the tale, claiming that it became her favorite dessert and she would demand it on every occasion. Whether she ever even tasted the confection named in her honor is, of course, unknowable. More plausibly she had her secretary send a thank-you letter to the sender with some prim Victorian phrase that deemed the sweets "delightful" without having so much as put them to her lips. Incidentally, the *moira* credited with inventing the confection was Ramakrishna's favorite, Bhim Chandra Nag.

Bhim Chandra Nag is still in business on a narrow shop-lined street in the old northern end of the city. It is still renowned for its *ledikeni*, which are to all intents and purposes a larger version of *pantua*. To make it, a nugget of *gur* is enclosed in a dough of *chhana* and a little flour. This is then fried until golden and finally soaked in syrup. As it cooks, the sugar in the center liquefies so that when you bite into it, a sweet, earthy syrup oozes out. Apparently these used to be made quite large and sliced into portions, though nowadays the average *ledikeni* is a little smaller than a tennis ball.

Today it is not as easy to find a *ledikeni* in Kolkata as it used to be. India's flourishing middle class has other ways of showing status than with fancy sweets. A 2008 article on Diwali, north India's traditional sweetmeat blowout, listed linens, toasters, and iPods as the preferred gifts of that season.[55] Today, *mishti* are still expected, but they come with a lot less symbolic baggage. In part the confectioners have become victims of prosperity, as the epidemic of obesity and diabetes threatens to engulf the affluent. Indian sweetshops now regularly sell artificially sweetened desserts to their diabetic or dieting clients. In Kolkata, Hindustan Sweets has even developed a line of sweets with purported nutraceutical properties to counter *mishti*'s unhealthy reputation. But Bengalis, at least, don't seem to be taking the nutritionists' warnings too much to heart. As best as I can tell, the sweet makers are thriving and, in certain cases at least, their creativity is unabated.

PRINCE OF *SANDESH*

When in December of 2007 Ravi Shankar, the Bengali-born sitar virtuoso, returned to Kolkata after an absence of seven years, he was given a hero's welcome. Cameramen milled at the foot of the ramp, reporters primped, readying for their cues, and VIPs elbowed their way to front and center. But when the aging maestro descended the stairs, he did not immediately address the media huddle. Rather he turned to a group of friends with a question that made it clear why he had really made the trip. "Tell me," he whispered, "is it that Nakur still makes that *sandesh*?" Of course they all knew what he meant. In Kolkata, Nakur is a prince among *moira*, renowned for its *sandesh*. And yes, it still does make that *sandesh*.

I visited the shop on the day after Bhai Phota, the festival devoted to brothers, which ends the cycle of holidays when the confectioners labor without respite to satisfy the sweet cravings of deities and mortals alike. At Girish Chandra Dey & Nakur Chandra Nandy (to give Nakur its full name), the workers were understandably lethargic after this explosion of sweets giving. Nevertheless they had to satisfy the customers who were already crowding at the window. Nakur is on a busy commercial lane in the tangle of densely trafficked streets that make up the old Shyambazar district. The shop itself is little more than a grated hole in the wall, but the locals who line up at the window and the connoisseurs who have braved the traffic across town know that this is where you can find some of the finest *sandesh* in Kolkata.

When I arrive, Prasanta Nandy, the shop's guiding light, sits fitfully on a worn, embroidered dining room chair, gesturing at the apprentices of his atelier. He is young and earnest, one moment shouting with indignation and the next chuckling with irony. In short, he is an artist. It's just that his raw material happens to be *chhana* rather than clay. He has come up with dozens of new flavors, stretching the idea of *sandesh* in much the same way that chocolatiers in the West have expanded their repertoire. Where they often add Indian spices to their trendy confections, Prasanta returns the compliment, making his own *sandesh* with dark chocolate. He fills his confections with lemon, black currants, and even vodka and scotch.

He can't stop himself. As I watch the next day's batch of *chhana* transmute into *sandesh*, he sends one of his workers scuttling into the back to bring out his new invention, which he presents with a sly but slightly hesitant grin. He admits it is a work in progress: a nugget of *sandesh* rolled in sesame with a few morsels of pistachio secreted inside. It's good but could use a little work, I tell him, playing the critic. He looks thoughtful and smiles. As I say my good-byes to venture out into Kolkata's purple night, he hands me one last morsel, a simple white *sandesh* filled with a mix of soft *chhana* and evaporated milk. It's perfect, like an edible haiku on the many forms of creaminess.

Rossomalai

This is *rossogolla*'s less famous and less controversial cousin. As with *rossogolla*, the Das family of the famous K. C. Das confectionary empire claims *rossomalai* as a family invention, this time attributing its creation to Krishna Chandra Das, the second-generation owner after whom the company is named. Like so many origin stories, this one is impossible to verify, but the fact remains that the K. C. Das version of this sweetmeat is very tasty indeed. Unlike *rossogolla*, which has a texture that isn't immediately appealing to Westerners, *rossomalai* has a melt-in-the-mouth creaminess that any fan of crème caramel will immediately recognize. What's more, it is much less sweet than many South Asian desserts. To make it you will need the traditional Bengali fresh cheese called *chhana*. It's not difficult to make but does take some preliminary planning.

Makes 6 servings

Chhana

1 cup cultured buttermilk
2 quarts whole milk
2 tablespoons all-purpose flour

Milk sauce

8 cups whole milk
6 green cardamom pods
4–6 tablespoons sugar
2 tablespoons rosewater (or to taste)
Pinch saffron, lightly bruised

Poaching syrup

6 cups water
3 cups sugar
½ cup whole milk

About ½ cup coarsely chopped pistachios and almonds for garnish

1. Make the *chhana*: Leave the buttermilk out overnight at room temperature. This increases its acidity.

2. Heat the whole milk in a large heavy nonreactive saucepan, stirring every so often so that the bottom doesn't scorch. When the milk is almost ready to boil, remove from heat, stir in the buttermilk, and continue to stir very gently until curds form. Cool to room temperature. Strain in a colander lined with two or three layers of cheesecloth. Allow to drip about 1 hour. Gather up the cheesecloth and squeeze out the liquid. You're looking for a texture a little firmer than ricotta. Knead this mixture with your hands until it is somewhat smoother than ricotta. Measure 2 cups. Stir in the flour. Using slightly damp hands, form the mixture into about two dozen balls. Flatten each lightly to make disks about 1½ inches in diameter and 1 inch high. Make sure they are very smooth.

2. While the *chhana* is draining, make the milk sauce: In a wide, heavy, and ideally nonstick pan, simmer the 8 cups whole milk with the cardamom pods until it is reduced to about 3 cups, stirring regularly so it doesn't scorch. Strain. Stir in the sugar, rosewater, and saffron. Remove from heat and let cool to room temperature.

4. Make the poaching syrup: Combine the 6 cups water and 3 cups sugar. Bring to a rolling boil until sugar is dissolved. Ladle out 2 cups of this into a shallow bowl and let cool to room temperature. Stir ½ cup milk back into the pot with the hot syrup. Bring back to a boil, skimming the top of any impurities.

5. Slip the disks of *chhana* into the boiling syrup and cook at a gentle but continuous rolling boil about 15 minutes, until firm. Lower heat to a gentle simmer and continue cooking another 10 minutes. Very gently remove disks from the syrup and place in the cool sugar syrup. Let stand at least four hours to allow them to absorb the syrup.

6. Transfer disks to the cooled milk syrup and let stand at least 1 hour and as long as overnight before serving. If you refrigerate the dessert overnight, return it to room temperature before serving. Serve the *rossomalai* in shallow bowls along with the milk sauce. Garnish with the chopped nuts.

2

❀❀❀

A THOUSAND AND ONE
SWEET LAYERS

※ *Middle East* ※

BAKLAVA UNIVERSITY

"You should have come earlier!" Fatih Güllü tells me as I step in the door of the family baklava factory at nine in the morning. By earlier, he means about six hours ago, when the place was abuzz with activity. Now, the vast, spotless building is virtually silent. Though, in Turkey, baklava may be an ancient, treasured heirloom, there is nothing picturesque, quaint, or old about the Güllüoğlu production facilities in suburban Istanbul. The seventy-thousand-square-foot bakery is housed in an anonymous white sugar cube of a building that could just as easily be in a suburban American industrial park.

Fatih looks younger than his thirty-one years, his cheeks still retaining the imprint of a cherubic mold. Despite the fact that he has been up all night supervising production, he is fresh and animated—and intensely enthusiastic about his family's métier. "I knew that—Bismillah [God willing]—I would be a baklava

maker by the age of three," he recalls in a moment of rare grav-
ity. Fatih runs the day-to-day operation while his father, Faruk
Güllü, looks after the big picture from a high tech office outfitted with banks of computer screens. The younger Güllü is the
sixth generation in the family business, having worked his way
up from cleaning floors and waiting tables, finally graduating to
making baklava. "Baklava is like an art," he tells me. "In one piece
of baklava are thirty-five layers of dough. The learning process is
like a university, it takes years to learn."

The first step to making baklava begins even as normal people have just gone to bed. Workers start by taking two-pound
lumps of prepared wheat dough out of mechanical kneaders and
feeding them through the rollers of what looks like an oversized
pasta machine. The result is a thin sheet of dough, but thin is a
relative term. To make *yufka* (or phyllo—from the Greek *phyl-
lon*), layers must be as thin as onionskin. At Güllüoğlu the next
step is done entirely by hand. The pastry cooks cut the sheets into
ten pieces, dust a little cornstarch between them, and then begin
to roll all ten together, adding more starch as needed and where
needed. That is where the human eye still beats the machine.*
After a certain point, the dough is measured by microns, not mil-
limeters, and a machine just wouldn't be able to tell where the
dusting of starch needs to go. It takes a year or more to learn to
do this properly, and some people never get the hang of it. Fatih
assures me that his father has no sentimental attachment to the
hand process; he just hasn't been able to find a machine that can
do the work. When *yufka* is rolled entirely by machine—as is

---

* Wheat starch (not to be confused with flour) has long been used in Middle Eastern (and to
some degree in early European) pastries. To make it, medieval manuals instruct the reader to
knead a stiff dough in water and then to evaporate away the starchy liquid. In rural Turkey,
wheat starch was traditionally made by soaking wheat grains for several weeks in water and
then drying them out to capture the resulting starch. When commercial cornstarch was introduced in the early twentieth century, most *yufka* producers switched to the new product.[1]

more typically done at large commercial operations—the dough needs to be made with a harder flour so that it won't tear during the rolling process. The side effect, however, is that the resulting pastry is necessarily more brittle.

"When you eat our baklava, it is melting in the mouth," is Fatih's not entirely unbiased explanation. "You don't have to bite too much. When you make it with the hard flour it is like a needle in the mouth." I'm not sure I'd go quite that far, but Güllüoğlu's baklava does manage a sort of ephemeral crispiness that entirely transcends the chewy, and often soggy, baklava found in the United States.

At the Güllü factory, the pastry is finished by brushing some seventeen sheets of *yufka* with clarified butter. Then comes a layer of pistachio or other filling, and another seventeen sheets go on top. This is scored and baked, and then finally bathed in sugar syrup.

"If you cook baklava three minutes too long it is too dry, if three minutes less it is too soft," the baklava professor goes on to explain. "The degree of the syrup is critical—half a degree more and it will be very hard to eat, half a degree less and it is too soft." But even that factor is apparently not so simple, because the syrup has to be adjusted according to the weather since ambient humidity will affect the final texture.* Cake baking is a cinch by comparison, Fatih quips.

But of course texture isn't (quite) everything with baklava; the ingredients matter too. Due to its reputation, Güllüoğlu can get away with charging premium prices and accordingly can afford good ingredients. Connoisseurs can immediately identify their baklava by the rich and slightly funky flavor that comes from the

---

* Sugar syrup is made by mixing refined sugar with water and boiling it until it reaches a specific temperature. This measurement tells you the proportion of water and sugar in it. Recipes for homemade baklava typically omit this level of detail—but then they're not producing baklava by the ton.

sheep and goat butter spread between the layers of dough. The pistachios are fat and aromatic. Both the butter and the nuts hail from the ancient city of Gaziantep near the Syrian border. The region is renowned for its pistachios and, not coincidentally, its baklava.

This is where the company got its start. According to Güllü family lore, it was their ancestor, Güllü Çelebi, who brought baklava to these parts in 1871. "Here in Turkey we love our history," Fatih tells me when I ask if there's any documentation of this, "but we are not used to taking notes."

The tale begins with Güllü Çelebi on his way to make the Hajj, the ritual pilgrimage to Mecca required of every Muslim. The trip unavoidably took him through next-door Syria (an Ottoman province at the time), where he apparently lingered and picked up the local technique for making the pastry. Returning to Gaziantep, Çelebi tweaked the recipe so that it worked with the local ingredients—the superb local pistachios, the sheep and goat butter—and next thing you know the family dynasty was on its way to fame and fortune. Or maybe not. More plausibly, he was simply another provincial confectioner producing a local specialty. It was only when his grandson brought the Gaziantep version of baklava to Istanbul in 1949 that Güllüoğlu was on its way to becoming a household word in the metropolis.

Nowadays baklava is integral to Turkish culture, whether it is the kind sold at Güllüoğlu—dear, delicate, and filled with expensive nuts—or the kind you find in Anatolia's small villages—where the dough is rough and homemade with no filling to speak of. When you visit a Turkish home you are likely to be served baklava. A wedding or circumcision ceremony would be incomplete without the dessert. During Ramadan the daylong fast is that much more tolerable because you get to look forward to baklava at *iftar*, the evening meal.

Of course baklava isn't limited to Turkey. It exists, in many permutations and variations, from Belgrade to Kabul. Some of the differences are quite subtle. Syrians make a slightly drier baklava that is baked longer and uses a stronger syrup, according to Fatih. Turks don't think much of the Syrian version, a sentiment that is returned by their southern neighbors. In Damascus, they also like the scent of orange flower or rosewater, a taste shared by Persians, who, additionally, tend to add cardamom to the mix. Greeks often use honey in combination with the sugar syrup and like to stir cinnamon into the nuts. Across the baklava diaspora, the layers can be filled with ground nuts (pistachios, walnuts, almonds, pine nuts, cashews) or with cheese and cream. In Istanbul, Güllüoğlu sells varieties filled with sour cherries and candied chestnuts (both Turkish obsessions). At Dubai airport, the gift shops sell chocolate baklava next to the miniature Persian rugs. Other than baklava, what all these places share is that they were once part of the Ottoman Empire. Some foods have a half-life that long outlasts empires. Witness the *Krapfen* (jelly doughnuts) sold in Venice, Vienna, and Kraków even today, a hundred years after the disintegration of the Hapsburg realm that once contained all three cities. In the case of baklava, pry apart the layers and you continue to find a common culinary tradition that knits together groups of disparate language, ethnicity, and religion even though the political bond that once forced them to live together is long gone. Baklava is now part and parcel of *their* identity as much as it is for the Turks.

Yet even if the dessert doesn't belong to any one narrow ethnic group, there is some evidence that baklava developed into its current form in the Ottoman capital. The first mention of baklava comes from Kaygusuz Abdal, a Turkish mystic and poet who lived in the first half of the fifteenth century. He mentions "Two hundred trays of baklava," adding the curious fact that some were made with almonds and others with lentils. The pastry is mentioned once again in 1473 in the imperial kitchen register during the reign of Sultan Mehmet II, a mere twenty years after the Turks captured Constantinople. A decade on, an account of the dishes served at a circumcision feast for the sultan's son mentions "trays of many-layered baklava made of thin pastry."

With baklava, as with other recipes, it can be hard to nail down a precise sequence of cause and effect. The brittle, multilayered masterpiece was surely the culmination of a long evolutionary process. Cooks no doubt picked up and adapted ideas from others. Pastry isn't rocket science, and it is always plausible that similar techniques may have been "invented" by cooks widely separated by both time and place.

The food historian Charles Perry theorizes that the dish was developed from layered flatbreads made by Turkish nomads in Central Asia before they settled down in Anatolia. He points, for example, to a contemporary Azerbaijani sweet called *Baki pakhlavast*, or Baku-style baklava, as a kind of ur-baklava. Here, rather than thirty or forty paper-thin sheets, there are eight, rolled no thinner than lasagne noodles, with nuts alternating with the dough. These early flatbreads were referred to as *yufka* (from the word for thin or fragile) as early as the eleventh century. An eleventh-century Turkish–Arabic dictionary describes a *yufka* folded and fried in butter, and another variety (*yalaci yuga*) so thin it crumbled at a touch. In Turkey *yufka* is still used to refer to both a thin flatbread and phyllo.

Yet the whole baklava idea, if not the contemporary recipe, may well be much more ancient. Even a cursory scan of the Old Testament yields plenty of unleavened bread (i.e., *yufka*), milk, and honey. Pistachios were cultivated in the gardens of Babylon around 700 BCE.[2] Ancient Greeks certainly used crushed nuts and honey for filling their confections. In Athenaeus's third-century treatise on eating, *The Deipnosophists*, the author describes a contemporary Cretan sweetmeat called *gastris* made with a filling of walnuts, filberts, almonds, and poppy seeds sweetened with honey and heavily spiced with pepper, which is then wrapped in a paste of honey-sweetened sesame. The Romans made something called *placenta*, a sort of cheese and honey pie enclosed in a thin pastry exterior.[3]

A more immediate ancestor can probably be found among medieval Arabs, who seemed to have been as obsessed with sweets as any modern-day Kolkatan or Viennese. The early medieval pastry that most resembles today's baklava was called *lauzīnaj*. In one of several variations it was made from "the thinnest of the thin bread," flavored with mastic and rosewater, stuffed with almonds and sugar. It was, however, fried in almond oil rather than baked. When you ate it, it was supposed to melt in your mouth even as it encountered your tongue. The pastry wrappers were so ephemeral that the Baghdadi poet Ibn al-Rumi described them as more delicate than the morning breeze and as thin as the inner skin of the eggshell and locusts' wings.[4] In other variations, the sheets of dough were more like very thin, crisp crêpes, rolled around the filling to create multiple layers. Something similar is done today when *yufka* is rolled around a filling rather than layered in sheets. In Iraq, this rolled version of baklava has the delightfully evocative name of "bride's fingers."[5]

Even closer in resemblance to today's layered dessert is a medieval Arab dish that comes across as decidedly peculiar to modern tastes in its mixture of sweet and savory. This is the so-called *jūdhāba*, a sort of pastry, or sometimes pudding, placed under spit-roasting meat so that it can absorb the savory juices. One version of the dish was made by layering superthin bread or crisp crêpes with sweetened nuts and rosewater and then finally pouring syrup on top. The result was probably more like a sweet-savory lasagna than a crispy baklava, but the layering technique is suggestively similar. The word *jūdhāba* is Persian, hinting once again at a Central Asian origin for this penchant for layering.[6]

There is also a curious reference to a baklavalike preparation from a fourteenth-century Venetian cookbook that describes a

"*Torta ungaresca*" (Hungarian pie) made by sandwiching a cooked meat filling between a top and bottom layer, each made of nine sheets of thin dough brushed with fat in between.* This dough is stretched rather than rolled, making it the first description of the classic Hungarian technique for making *rétes* (strudel).[7] Later, Italian Renaissance–era *torte* recipes also commonly call for several layers of thin dough for baklavalike piecrusts, but the dough is invariably rolled rather than stretched.[8] Most writers assume that the central European dough was an adaptation of Turkish *yufka* since the Turks ruled Hungary for over 150 years following the battle of Mohács in 1526. But in the fourteenth century, Hungary was nowhere near the Ottoman frontier, and though the results are not dissimilar, the technique for making the two kinds of dough are entirely different. It would be rash to infer too much from a single recipe, especially since it comes from an Italian source, but I wouldn't be too surprised if strudel dough wasn't invented independently somewhere in central Europe.**

As the Hungarian pie recipe shows, flaky pastry wasn't limited to the Middle East, nor was it only used for baklava. Medieval Arab cookbooks also contain recipes for making a kind of puff pastry. An anonymous cookbook from thirteenth-century Andalusia, then under Muslim rule, describes a pastry called *musammana* made by spreading a thin layer of dough with clarified butter, then rolling it up "like a cloth until it becomes a reed." The dough is then flattened. In a preparation called Toledan cheese pie, it is stuffed with cheese much like a Neapolitan *sfogliatelle*.*** (The Neapolitan dough uses the same technique.)

---

* What this dish mostly resembles is the savory meat- or vegetable-filled *börek* commonplace in Turkey and throughout the Balkans. In Hungary, *rétes* is typically sweet, though savory versions such as cabbage or spinach *rétes* are not uncommon.
** It so happens that a transparent, stretched dough is also made in Turkey, for example in the traditional Gaziantep *katmer* (a sort of sweet pie filled with cheese and sometimes pistachios). Is there some connection to strudel? I doubt it. My guess is that the two cultures developed the similar technique quite autonomously.
*** Bartolomeo Scappi, in his sixteenth-century cookbook, outlines a similar technique for making a *pizza sfogliata*, a sort of sugar-dusted puff pastry pie.[9]

Yet all of this still doesn't add up to baklava, a dish of ephemeral sheets of dough filled with nuts (or lentils?) and soaked in syrup. The most likely explanation is that this was created by the cosmopolitan confectioners of the Ottoman capital, who put the pieces together for the pastry we know today.

In sixteenth-century Istanbul, the baklava could be as thick as a hundred layers, yet had to be so insubstantial that a coin dropped from a two-foot height would supposedly pierce every layer right down to the tray. Evliyâ Çelebi, a seventeenth-century Turkish travel writer, described the legendary cream-filled baklava made a hundred years earlier by the cooks of Ferhad Pasha. It was "without equal in the world, so delicate and crisp that a coin dropped onto it penetrates right through." When visiting Belgrade, Çelebi (who had a habit of embellishing the facts) reported on baklava made up of a thousand layers that could pass the money-dropping test. These pastries were apparently the size of cart wheels and baked, somewhat improbably, in a tandoor-type oven. In later years, aspiring master cooks had to pass guild examinations where they had to roll out the *yufka* not only superthin but also so round that it would perfectly fit the circular baklava-baking tray. Once the pastry was baked, the examiners naturally subjected it to the coin toss.

The high standing of baklava in Turkish culinary culture is nicely captured in an anecdote told by Sir Harry Luke, a British colonial functionary who traveled in Turkey in the early decades of the twentieth century:

A Turkish grand vizier once gave a dinner in Constantinople to a certain Ambassador. The dinner was ample and, by the time that the plat doux (it was baqlawa) had arrived, the ambassador could eat no more. "Supposing," asked the grand vizier, who noticed that his guest had passed the dish, "that you were in a very crowded apartment and that your king wanted to enter, what would you do?"

"I would press against the others," said the ambassador, "and make room for him somehow."

"That is exactly what you must do," retorted the grand vizier, "for the baqlawa, who is the king of sweets."

ANCIENT SWEETS

In the Middle East, desserts have played an important role in society since time immemorial. The region's sweet tooth is undoubtedly as old as civilization—if not older. By local standards, the Turks were the new kids on the block, having only arrived in Anatolia around the turn of the first millennium. Eleven thousand years before that, hunter-gatherers had planted their roots between the Tigris and Euphrates Rivers (Mesopotamia is Greek for "between the rivers"). There they began to cultivate wheat and raise livestock; they also undoubtedly collected honey and dates. Eventually these agricultural revolutionaries would build cities and write cookbooks.

The Sumerians, who thrived in ancient Mesopotamia until about the year 2000 BCE, had no doubt about the superiority of their cuisine compared with that of the nearby nomads. The surrounding desert dwellers were so primitive, claimed Sumer's food snobs, that they ate their food raw. If you presented these uncouth barbarians with flour, eggs, and honey for a cake, they would not know what to do with them.[10] So what exactly would a civilized cook do with these ingredients? The closest thing to specific instruction that exists is a contemporary record that describes cakes (or possibly breads) that "have gone to the palace." They are made with three parts butter, one part white cheese, nine parts dates, and one part raisins. Presumably there was flour in there as well, though there's no mention of it. One of the oldest cake recipes in the world (more of a recipe fragment, really) is for something called *mersu* that dates back to about 1400 BCE. As best as archeologists can make out, given the damage to the tablet, the cake was a kind of enriched bread that was made by a professional pastry cook specializing in such things. The baker apparently mixed the dough in a large pot, adding dates, pistachios, dried figs, raisins, and possibly apples. Spices were part of the recipe too. The cuneiforms seem to indicate nigella, cumin, coriander, and, somewhat incongruously, garlic. Since there are no quantities given, it's impossible to determine what the texture of the resulting confection was. Did it resemble an Italian panettone or was it more like a dense fruitcake? We'll probably never know.

There must have been many of these enriched breads or cakes. A sort of Sumerian–Akkadian dictionary preserved on ancient tablets records approximately three hundred varieties of breads, some of which were enriched with oil and fruit, or flavored with date syrup and honey. They ranged in size from "very large" to "tiny." (Were these the original cookies?) Anticipating a tradition that still endures, the bakers sometimes shaped them in the form of body parts: a heart, a head, a hand, an ear, and even a woman's breast. The most exquisite ones were reserved for kings and gods. One frequently mentioned sweetmeat worthy of the gods was called *giri.lam*, made of dates and sometimes figs, bound with honey and a little flour.

As in India, the gods of ancient Mesopotamia seem to have liked their sweets, though they apparently preferred them as part of a balanced diet instead of gorging on dessert alone. Their spreads included savories as well. To feed their appetites, confectioners were attached to temples. They specialized in making sacred cakes, which were consumed in large numbers during religious rituals. Mere mortals got a taste too, but not always. For the love goddess Ishtar, the cooks made cakes with an especially sensual mixture of flour, date syrup, honey, butter, sesame seeds, sesame oil, and fragrant rosewater. These, however, were not intended for the likes of you and me. They were crumbled and fed to the goddess's sacred doves.[11]

This and other Mesopotamian recipes had to depend on honey or fruit-based sweeteners since sugar was, as yet, unknown. Honey, perhaps due to the difficulty of collecting it, was expensive, however, so in many cases raisins but especially dates were used. The latter were boiled down to produce "date-honey" as a cheap substitute for the real thing.

There is evidence of dates in the region going back fifty thousand years, and the ubiquitous palms may have supported Sumerian civilization as much as the wheat and barley granaries. Dates were so abundant that they could be cheaper than grain. Pound for pound they certainly provided way more calories than any staple cereal.* At the time, what is now southern Iraq was crisscrossed with irrigation canals, and palms flourished on their banks. This was equally true in later years, when the classical Greek historian Herodotus would write of the Assyrians (who inhabited the land between the Tigris and the Euphrates): "They have palm trees growing throughout the entire plain; the majority of these bear fruit from which food, wine and honey are made."[12]

The tree of life is an ancient Mesopotamia idea, and it often took the form of a date palm. The Assyrians considered it a symbol of fertility. A variation on this theme was later picked up by Islam. In the Muslim version of the birth of Jesus, the tree provides nourishment for Mary as she is ready to give birth. In the Koran, the virgin mother finds herself in labor beside the trunk of a date palm. "Oh, would that I had died before this, and had

---

* A pound of pitted dates has about 1,280 calories whereas a pound of whole wheat bread is somewhere in the range of 500 calories.

been a thing quite forgotten!" she cries out in pain, only to have the as yet unborn Isa (Jesus) pipe up, "Grieve not, surely your Lord has made a stream to flow beneath you; And shake towards you the trunk of the palm tree, it will drop on you fresh ripe dates: So eat and drink and refresh the eye."

Dates also have a place in a Muslim ritual called *tahneek* in which a piece of well-chewed date (or a suitable sweet substitute) is placed in the mouth of a newborn before he or she suckles for the first time. According to the Sunnah, a compilation of the acts of Muhammad, dates were the first food to break the prophet's fast at the conclusion of Ramadan, a habit that is now practiced by his followers.

The Middle Eastern taste for dates may well explain the impassioned taste for tooth-numbingly sweet desserts in the region. Yet with strongly flavored liquid sweeteners like honey and date syrup, the sweetmeat repertoire was necessarily limited. The creative outburst that would make medieval Baghdad a magnet for dessert mavens everywhere had to await the arrival of the candy crystals from the East.

THE CANE AND THE CRESCENT

Given how active trade was with India since at least classical times, it's surprising how long it took sugarcane to reach the Mediterranean. Pliny the Elder described sugar as a rare and exotic medicament in the first century, at a time when Indian pepper was more than abundant in the Roman marketplace. Estimates vary, but sugar cultivation didn't begin in the Middle East until well after the fall of Rome. The first plantations probably took root in Persia around 600 CE and in modern-day Iraq about a hundred years later. The new crop arrived at a particularly pivotal moment. Its appearance more or less coincided with the downfall of the four-hundred-year-old Persian Sassanid Empire and the rise of Arab Islam, which would sweep like a desert wind across Central Asia, North Africa, and the Iberian peninsula. Sugarcane, which had taken more than a millennium to travel the distance between today's Pakistan and neighboring Iran, now spread across the Middle East and the Mediterranean with the rapidity of the advancing Muslim armies. The local climate was hardly ideal for a tropical plant like sugarcane, but Arab improvements in irrigation and agriculture made sugar production viable from the Palestinian littoral to the coast of Andalusia, from the Nile basin to the narrow valleys of Sicily. Sugar remained expensive but it was no longer rare and exotic.

You can't just pick sugar off a tree like you can a date. Processing it is an arduous and time-consuming task. A thousand years ago, the stalks were typically first chopped into pieces and then ground up using millstones powered by animals (or later by wind or water). This released only some of the juice. The remaining crushed, soggy reeds were packed into sacks and squashed further by a mechanical press. All the resulting liquid was then boiled, and continually skimmed of scum, until the gooey brown syrup in the bottom of the pot was thick enough to crystallize. Somewhere along the way, the Arabs had the bright idea of packing the damp raw sugar into inverted earthenware cones with a small hole in the bottom, which allowed the molasses to drain out. This technique would remain more or less the standard way of doing things until the nineteenth century, resulting in the traditional sugar loaf shape. Turned upside down, this was shaded from molasses brown at the very tip to a milky white base where the sucrose became almost pure. The best-quality sugar was produced by dissolving the crystals once more, then reboiling and recrystallizing them two or three more times, the cones becoming paler and paler each time. But even this wasn't enough for the purpose of some confectionary. Cookbooks as early as the tenth century recommend refining the sugar further by reboiling it once again and adding egg whites to absorb the impurities.

By the early Middle Ages, Arab sugar was traded across the Mediterranean—mostly in the holds of Italian ships. A how-to guide for merchants from the early 1300s written by the Florentine merchant Francesco Pegolotti identifies over a dozen sources of sugar, including Alexandria, Cairo, Cyprus (the only Christian source mentioned), Muscat (on the Arabian Sea), Kerak (Jordan), and Damascus (or more generically Syria). Sugar came in the form of powder, lozenges, lumps, large loaves, and basket sugar (perhaps drained in baskets rather than earthenware?) as well as rock sugar candy and refined sugar. It might also be scented with violets and roses.[13] Yet it seems that the Arabs kept the best for themselves. Pegolotti wrote that the highest quality sugar—"for it is more thoroughly boiled, and its paste is whiter, and more solid that any other sugar"—hardly ever made it to the West "because nearly the whole is kept for the mouth and the use of the [Egyptian Mamluk] Sultan himself."[14]

∽ Sugar Versus Honey ∾

There is a tale in the *One Thousand and One Nights* that tells the story of Ma'aruf, a poor Cairo cobbler, and Fatimah, his shrewish wife. One day Fatimah wakes up with a yen for *kunāfah*, but not just any old *kunāfah*; she wants hers drenched with expensive honey, something that is far beyond the underemployed cobbler's means. Distraught, the fearful husband stands in front of the *kunāfah* seller's shop, his eyes filling with tears. "O Master Ma'aruf, why do you weep?" the confectioner inquires. "Tell me what has befallen you." So our henpecked hero recounts his woes, at which the pastry cook laughs and, taking pity on him, agrees to give him five pounds of the pastry on credit. First he fries it in clarified butter, but having no honey he drenches it in molasses.[15] He also gives Ma'aruf some bread and, with a few parting words about how to deal with his wife, sends him home.

True to form, the wife is furious because the *kunāfah* was sweetened with cheap molasses. "Begone, you pimp, and bring me other than this!" she spits out, as she throws it in his face and whacks him with such force that she knocks out one of his teeth. At this point Ma'aruf loses it and actually hits back. His self-assertiveness doesn't last long though, and soon enough he is groveling at her feet promising to bring the honey-sweetened *kunāfah*. This sort of torment goes on for several days until Ma'aruf flees the city. This being the *One Thousand and One Nights*, he encounters a benevolent jinn who flies him to a distant kingdom.

The tale continues through many twists and turns involving more jinns but also kings and princesses (but neither Fatima nor *kunāfah*). In the end Fatima does show up. By this point the cobbler is the sultan of a great realm, and, being the kind-hearted soul that he is, he sets up his wife in his harem. But the scorpion can't change her ways. One night, as Ma'aruf is sleeping, Fatima creeps up on him with the intention of killing him and taking over the kingdom. But as luck would have it, she is spotted and beheaded as she is about to strike. You know there had to be a happy ending.

So what does the reader learn, other than that human nature doesn't change? First, that there was some sort of fried dessert called *kunāfah* made in the ninth century (when the *One Thousand and One Nights* are presumed to have been collected). (Note that the *kunāfah* in question was most likely a pancake at the time rather than the vermicelli-type dessert we're familiar with today.)[16] But the other thing the story reveals is that in Egypt, molasses was a common, cheap sweetener, much less desirable than honey.

The penchant for dousing sweets with syrup clearly comes from the early availability of not only honey in the Middle East but also the so-called date honey. When sugar came along, it gradually replaced the earlier sweeteners. But that took several centuries. *Kitāb al-tabikh*, a cookbook (roughly contemporary to *One Thousand and One Nights*), contains many more recipes for honey syrup than later sources do. Fruit, for example, had been preserved in honey even in ancient Mesopotamia, but gradually sugar replaced honey for those who could afford it, for the very obvious reason that it did not mask the fruit's flavor. This transition took place in Europe as well. In Paris, the fourteenth-century author of *Ménagier de Paris* used honey to candy orange rind. A hundred years later, Nostradamus (who also wrote a popular guide to confectionary) offered the choice between sugar and honey. By the mid-sixteenth century, sugar had won the day. Though still expensive, it was now widely available.

It's clear from the cobbler's tale that molasses was cheap, certainly more affordable than honey, but it doesn't say anything about the price of sugar itself. Records from a few centuries later do. In the early 1400s in Egypt, refined sugar cost six to eight times as much as honey, though there is some indication that the ratio may not have been as wide in earlier years.[17] (Unrefined sugar was roughly half the price of refined.)[18] In France around this time, sugar was about ten times the price of honey. But the pattern is much the same in Istanbul a hundred years later, where sugar was about six times the price of honey.[19] As a result, honey remained the sweetener of choice for those who couldn't afford sugar up until the nineteenth century. Fatima had plenty of company.

In Europe, the imported sweetener was undeniably a luxury, comparable in cost to Indian spices. Even in the Arab world, however, it was relatively dear. Scholars estimate that sugar cost about six to ten times the price of wheat in Egypt and Syria during the early Middle Ages; in other words pricey but comparable to contemporary India and vastly cheaper than in northern Europe.[20] Yet whatever the cost, for the foodies of Muslim Mesopotamia, sugar was a necessity.

Baghdad

Medieval Baghdadis would do just about anything to satisfy their craving for sweets. If they had to cheat and steal to achieve their goal, so be it. Or at least that's the implication of a tale told by the late tenth-century writer Badā' al-Zamān al-Hamadhānī. The author's alter ego and protagonist 'Īsā ibn Hishām is a wily young scholar who is as bereft of scruples as he is of money. Arriving at the crowded Baghdad market, his nostrils fill with the smell of roasting meat blending with the perfume of caramelized sugar. Ravenous, 'Īsā looks around for a way to fill his growling stomach. He quickly spots a likely victim in the shape of a country bumpkin weighed down with a purse of money.

"Greetings, Abū Zaid!" he addresses the complete stranger. "Where have you come from, where are you staying, and when did you get here?"

"I am not Abū Zaid, but Abū ʿUbaid," the increasingly muddled rube stumbles to explain. But he is out of his league.

He is soon convinced that ʿĪsā was once best of friends with his father. Next thing you know, the two are celebrating their reunion at the roasted meat seller's, devouring platters of meat accompanied by *jūdhāba*s soaked with the meat's fatty pan juices. (You will recall that a *jūdhāba* was a sort of sweetened multi-layered pastry or bread pudding cooked beneath roasting meat.) They make quick work of this, but ʿĪsā isn't quite done yet. Did not their long-lost acquaintance need to be celebrated with a little dessert?

So now the young con artist conducts his companion to the confectioner. "Weigh out for Abū Zaid two pounds of throat-easing *lauzīnaj*, for it slips into the veins," ʿĪsā commands. "And let it be but one night old, on sale just this morning, the crust paper-thin, generously filled, pearled with almond oil, starry in color, melting before it meets the teeth, that Abū Zaid may relish it." The narrator adds that once it was served, both hunter and prey "kneeled and fell to like locusts."

Having played his mark, ʿĪsā now extricates himself by offering to fetch some ice water to slake their thirst. Needless to say, that's the last "Abū Zaid" sees of him. He has little choice but to pay an extravagant bill of twenty dirhams.[21]

By the tenth century, with over a million inhabitants, Baghdad was the world's largest city. It was no longer the capital of a huge empire as it had been two hundred years earlier, but it had continued to grow and flourish. The Abbasid rulers had moved their capital from Damascus to Baghdad in 762, at a time when their empire extended from the Spanish Pyrenees to the mountains of Afghanistan. The next hundred or so years has justifiably been described as an Islamic golden age, a time when the city became the unrivaled world's capital for science, mathematics, philosophy, and medicine. Its boosters called Baghdad the "mother of the world" and "navel of the nations." It became a vortex that gathered up scholars, poets, musicians—and cooks—from Byzantium, Persia, North Africa, and even as far as India. Certainly Indian medicine was hugely influential and the expansion in the use of Indian spices (sugar included) may well be traced to prescriptions of Indian physicians or their local acolytes living in the Abbasid capital.[22] Luxury goods both edible and inedible arrived from the four corners of the world for the delectation of the leisure classes. Even the spartan desert Bedouin who had been the founders of Islam were soon seduced by the charms of a cosmopolitan lifestyle.

Before the rise of Islam, the Middle East had been roughly split between the Christian Byzantine (or Eastern Roman) Empire in the west and the Zoroastrian Sassanid Empire in the east. In both cultures there was a deeply ingrained tradition of luxury living that the Abbasids happily acquired and improved.

Perhaps the most famous Abbasid foodie was a prince and, even briefly, a caliph. Ibrāhīm ibn al-Mahdī was born in 779 in the Rusafa palace on the left bank of the Tigris, the son of an African wife of an Abbasid monarch. The young Ibrāhīm cultivated an eclectic collection of talents. (Politics wasn't one of them—he ruled less than two years before he was forced to abdicate.) He was a renowned poet and musician but was equally famous for his culinary skills. When he wasn't sitting down to pen an ode to his favorite sweetmeat, he seemed to spend much of his time in the kitchen in the company of his Byzantine slave girl Bid'a, who also happened to be his favorite cook. He wasn't entirely exceptional in this; a tenth-century bibliography of Arab cookbooks lists at least three other Abbasid caliphs so interested in cooking that they spent time in the kitchen supervising their cooks.[23] However, none of them could compare with our prince. Ibrāhīm even wrote a cookbook to set down his favorite dishes for posterity. Sadly, the book is lost to history, though some of his recipes and poetry do remain.

A record exists, for example, of Ibrāhim's ecstatic response to a gift of round sesame cookies called *aqrāṣ fatīt* from his nephew al-Amīn. Ibrāhim was so thrilled with the treat that he dashed off a versed description in lieu of a thank-you note:

> *So kind and generous was it of al-Amīn to send me a gift of*
>   khubz al-fatīt, *and his affection proved.*
> *Shaped like perfect discs of equal size, each of which the full*
>   *moon resembles.*
> *As luscious as honey they taste and like the breeze sweetly*
>   *perfumed.*
> *Like silver and gold, white and yellow juxtaposed.*[24]

The foodie poet is even thoughtful enough to include the ingredients, which included saffron, mastic, and almond oil. Finally the cookies were coated with sesame seeds, almonds, and pine nuts. The culinary obsession of Abbasid poets and politicians brings to mind nineteenth-century Paris with its dissertations on the fine points of cuisine. It's hard to point to another time in history when the nation's upper classes devoted quite so much ink to writing about food and comparing recipes. In medieval Baghdad, pleasure wasn't something people merely experienced, they needed to discuss and analyze it too. Writing around the year 1200, a Baghdadi author divided the pleasures of the world into six classes in the introduction to his cookbook:

> They are food, drink, clothing, sex, scent and sound. The most eminent and perfect of these is food; for food is the foundation of the body and the material of life. There is no way to enjoy anything else but with health, which it supports. It is not forbidden to be meticulous about food,

and to take an interest in it and specialize in it. . . . I am one who prefers the pleasure of food over all the other pleasures, so I composed this book for myself, and for whoever may want to use it in the making of dishes.[25]

The Abbasid passion for fine cooking as well as the recipes themselves were often derived from Sassanid sources, something that was recognized at the time. (It's worth noting that earlier Persian traditions were as syncretic as the Arab culture, having absorbed Central Asian, Indian, and even far-off Chinese influences.) Given that sugar spread from India through Iran, it isn't entirely surprising that the medieval Arabic dessert repertoire is full of Persian loan words. The endings on the word *fālūdhaj* or *fālūdhaq* (a sweet resembling Turkish delight) betray a Persian origin, as do numerous other sweetmeats.* The Sassanids were especially fond of these transparent confections, at least if we are to believe a story told about one sixth-century Persian ruler. The tale recounts a meeting between an orphaned page and King Chosroes. Despite the loss of his father, the young man boasts of his education in every sphere of learning—in religion, literature, horse riding, music, and sport—and challenges the monarch to probe his knowledge. The king, though, has a different sort of test in mind. He queries the young man on which are the best dishes, the most beautiful birds, the most attractive meats, the freshest *fālūdhaj*, the best broths, the most delicious fruits, the most wholesome seeds, the most excellent wines, the most attractive tunes, the seven best ingredients for soup, the flowers with the sweetest perfume, the most beautiful women, and the best war-

---

* Medieval Arab cookbooks contain numerous recipes for something called *fālūdhaj*, which vary considerably in texture and consistency. Some resemble Turkish delight (*lokum* in Turkish) in that a sugar or honey syrup is cooked with starch until it reaches the proper chewy consistency, somewhere between a fruit jelly and toffee. In some cases it was thickened with egg yolks, yielding an almost chewy custard. Other recipes include almonds, resulting in a sort of candy that was molded into shapes, a little like marzipan.

horses.[26] The youth is quickly corrected as to what it really means to be cultured. It was a story the Abbasids knew well since it was translated into Arabic, just like so much other Persian literature.

Falūdhaj (confusingly rendered as a "jelly" in some translations) was just one of a vast repertoire of starch-thickened desserts in medieval Baghdad. A number of these also seem to trace their origin to Persian cuisine.

Rice pudding, for example, certainly traveled to the Middle East via Iran even if that was only a stopover from the Indus valley. Nonetheless, by the time it reached Baghdad, the original pudding was transformed into dishes no Hindu would recognize. The *Kitāb al-tabikh*, the oldest surviving Arab cookbook, compiled by Abū Muhammad al-Muzaffar ibn Sayyār al-Warrāq in the second half of the tenth century, contains at least a half-dozen rice-thickened desserts. In some cases they are as thick as *halvah*, while others have the consistency of Turkish delight. *Muhallabiyya* (named after an early Arab governor of Iraq who was especially fond of the dish) was the sort of rice pudding we might find familiar, made by simmering finely ground rice in milk until thickened. Powdered sugar was sprinkled on top. The dessert, more commonly transcribed as *mahalabiya* in modern Arabic, is still common in the region. There was, however, a variation on this same dish that will strike the modern Western palate as bizarre. It was made with whole rice and cooked chicken, all heavily sweetened with honey. Other sources call the dish *maʾmūniyya* (this time supposedly named after Ibrāhim al-Mahdī's great rival, Caliph al-Maʾmūn). In Europe this kind of sweet chicken and rice pudding would remain long in vogue under the name blancmange (see the following chapter). To the best of my knowledge nothing similar exists in the Arab world today, but a very similar dessert is still popular in Turkey. *Tavuk göğsü* is about the closest thing to medieval *maʾmūniyya* or blancmange. It is a milk-based pudding, thickened with rice starch and chicken. It has a consistency that is oddly both smooth and chewy, which comes from the little shreds of chicken breast in it. These days, when the pudding is made, the bottom is sometimes caramelized to give it a contrasting bitter-sweet dimension.

Even more commonly than rice, wheat flour was used to thicken sweetmeats. This resulted in textures ranging from creamy to chewy to dense and crumbly. There are many medieval desserts that resemble *halvah*, which are made by frying flour in fat (butter, sesame oil, or some other vegetable oil) and then adding honey or sugar syrup. Several recipes from al-Warrāq's tenth-century cookbook basically follow the same procedure. He also gives instruction for making date, apple, and carrot *halvah*. Many of these were the sorts of sweetmeats that arrived in India with the Mughals, and today *halvah*, *halva*, or *halwa* are all widespread from Albania to Bangladesh.

Though it shares the name, this starch-thickened sweetmeat shouldn't be confused with that other *halvah* in which syrup is incorporated into crushed sesame seeds. This seems to be of more recent origin. While the medieval sources have plenty of recipes using crushed nuts along with the flour, and sesame oil is ubiquitous, there are no recipes using tahini (ground sesame seed). This sort of *halvah* may well be a later Ottoman invention. It was commonplace by the 1700s and likely dates to at least the previous century.[27]

Medieval Arab sources don't just emphasize taste and texture. Dessert wasn't merely meant to be delicious, it was supposed to be pretty too. One recipe from al-Warrāq's opus is for a thick pudding made with honey, milk, starch, and walnut oil. This is allowed to set in four bowls, one large and three small. The cook then unmolds them, setting the large pudding at the center, clustering the little ones around like the domes of a mosque, and finally dotting the outside with drops of saffron-colored water. Other dishes are dyed green, red, or even black. In one case, *halvah* is even decorated with a dome made with a sort of honey taffy, decked with colored almonds, and topped off by a candy minaret. Confectioners molded marzipan into fish shapes, anticipating an Italian industry of modeling almond paste into every sort of shape imaginable. Al-Warrāq's almond fishes are scented with camphor and, somewhat gruesomely, set atop a little pond of blood-red honey and sugar syrup.

Even as the texture and appearance of many medieval desserts might be familiar to Westerners today, we would have a hard time dealing with the smell. A visit to a Baghdad confectioner had the olfactory impact of the perfume department at Macy's. Aroma was hugely important to medieval Arabs, and not just a dab behind the ears either. Perfumes were seen as necessary for both health and hygiene. Rooms were scented with cooling aromatics or perfumes to counter the "foulness of the air." The use of perfumes even extended to the cleaning of pots and pans. Lemon Joy would not have cut it. The Baghdadi author of a thirteenth-century cookbook gave explicit instructions for doing the dishes: "Likewise he will wash the vessels and pots that have been used in cooking and beat them with brick dust, then with potash and pounded dry rose (petals). [He will perfume bowls with mastic and galangal . . .] And he will wipe the pot, after washing it, with fresh citron [and orange] leaves."

Desserts got the perfume treatment as well. There is still some residue of this in Middle Eastern desserts scented with mastic or rosewater, but the use of other intense aromas like musk, camphor, and ambergris is more or less extinct. Musk, valued for its sexy undertones as well as its ability to fix other scents, was extracted from the glands of the musk deer of Tibet and Nepal. Ambergris is a peculiar substance produced by the digestive system of sperm whales that is collected at sea. In its fresh state the smell of ambergris is sometimes compared to cow dung or a damp forest floor, though when it dries the odor is sweeter and muskier. Both mastic and camphor are kinds of resin. To get a sense of the aromatic impact of certain dishes, you need to imagine sweet sweat mixed with turpentine and perhaps a hint of ripe fruit or flowers. *Nāṭif,* for example, was a nougatlike confection made with honey, egg whites, and nuts, scented with the pungent smell of musk and ambergris as well as the resinous mastic. At least one writer was moved to poetry on tasting an especially fine *nāṭif,* this one made with almonds, walnuts, pistachios, and dried fruit: "How lovely in hue, taste, and sight, sweeter still than the stealthy touch of a gazelle. . . . Break it, and the inside even surpasses how it looks when on a platter displayed./What the honey, what the musk and ambergris, what the mastic, crushed and mixed!"

No doubt, part of the appeal of these funky perfumes was their very expense and reputation as aphrodisiacs. Gradually, though, the fashion turned to lighter, more floral aromas. In the case of dessert, I suspect the gradual substitution of sugar for honey may have had something to do with it. Those powerful aromas make a lot more sense with a strong-flavored substance like honey than they do with a neutral sweetener like sugar.

While the flavorings may have changed, many of the medieval desserts still exist. Not only is *halvah* ubiquitous but so are various kinds of cookies. Al-Warrāq gives instructions for a cookie called *khushkanānaj* filled with ground almonds scented as usual with camphor and musk. Subtract the medieval scents and much the same pastry can be found in today's *klecha.* In Iraq, it is traditional to hand out these date- or nut-filled cookies during the Eid al-Adha holiday (celebrating Abraham's willingness to sacrifice his son).*

Another dessert that has not lost any of its popularity in the intervening centuries is the yeast-leavened eggless pancake called *qatayif.* Like so many other Muslim sweets, it is tradition-

---

* At the height of the second Gulf war, *klechas* became a casualty of the conflict. Since the cookies are baked in bulk for the holiday, people often rent out ovens in commercial bakeries. But in 2007, people didn't dare to venture out. One baker complained that he was down from thirty families to two. What's more, the pastries typically had been distributed to family and neighbors, but now, *USA Today* reported, people were stuck at home exchanging congratulations by mobile phones or via text messages.[28]

ally eaten during Ramadan. In the version popular in Palestine, the pancake is folded into a half-moon shape around a filling of fresh cheese or nuts.[29] This is fried, then drizzled or dipped in sugar syrup. Rosewater or orange flower water are the typical flavorings, though mastic is not unheard of. Much the same recipe exists in thirteenth- and fourteenth-century sources.[30]

Other syrup-soaked fritters are also ubiquitous now, as in the past. Today, the fried tangle of dough called *zalabia* is common across the Arab world and even finds an echo in Indian *jalebis*. Once again the origin may lie in Persia, where *zulbia* (*zulabiya*) is still made almost exactly the same way as described by al-Warrāq. The medieval guide explains how to make a thin batter, which is then drizzled into hot fat through a hole drilled in half a coconut, resulting in a loose knot of crispy strands. These are then dipped in honey. Apparently the author adored these crispy doughnuts. Certainly they were worthy of a few lines of verse:

[They are} soft to the touch, smooth,
dipped in white honey,
lined up one after the other like nuggets,
like incised bars of gold.[31]

Today sugar syrup is more common and the fritter varies widely in form, but then al-Warrāq also provides several options in terms of shape. In Morocco as elsewhere in the greater Middle East, the fritter is, once again, associated with Ramadan. Men generally go to buy *shebbakia* (as they are known here) in the evening, while they are still warm, just after the meal that breaks the day's fast. Some confectioners devote themselves to this sweetmeat and nothing else for the duration of the month of fasting.* Middle Eastern Jews may not have shared in the celebration

---

* There is an economic dimension to the Ramadan fritter fest. Across the Arab world, the price of cooking oil spikes during the holiday, as do the costs of sugar and honey. Importers of dates and other dried fruit make out like bandits.[32]

of Ramadan, but they were just as fond of *zalabia*; in their case it was traditional for Hanukah.[33]

A dessert that is closely related to *zalabia* is *luqmat al qadi*. In this case the fritter is closer in shape and size to a Ping-Pong ball. It makes its first appearance in a thirteenth-century Baghdadi recipe collection, there called *luqam al-qāḍī* or "judge's morsel." More evocative yet was the name "virgin's breasts," referring to cookies with a nut center, or "Zainab's fingers" (named after a famous queen), which resemble nut-filled cannoli.[34] These still exist, as do such other delightfully named desserts as *asabi' al-'arous*, the above-mentioned bride's fingers, made by rolling *yufka* around a nut filling. *Znoud el set* are larger and stuffed with a cream filling. Ideally they are fat and sweet just like a lady's upper arms—which is what the name means.

Many of the medieval desserts have not survived merely in the Arab lands; they left their imprint across the Mediterranean world. The Greeks have their own version of *luqmat al qadi* called *loukoumades*. We've already seen how the recipe for pastry used in Neapolitan *sfogliatelle* follows a Middle Eastern antecedent. But southern Italians also make a traditional Christmas confection called *struffoli* by frying tiny balls of dough and then immersing them in a honey-sugar syrup. They are flavored with candied fruit, obviously a later addition, but in other respects the recipe could be pure medieval Arab, or even Persian if you will. Cannoli have a similar lineage. Given the fact that Sicily was under Muslim rule for over a hundred years, it isn't entirely surprising to find that these Italian café fixtures are Arab in origin. The old texts describe a process of rolling dough around a length of cane or reed before frying it and filling it with a sweetened nut paste. (*Cannolo* means "little tube," derived from *canna* or cane.) The same process is used in Italy today. All that was needed was to substitute a ricotta filling for the nuts.

What strikes the modern reader perusing the thousand-year-old Arab recipe collections is the incredible variety in flavor, texture, and seasoning—in a word, the sophistication of this cuisine, especially when compared to the modern Middle East, which favors a much simpler approach to cooking. In the case of desserts, only a small fraction of the old recipes survive. The transformation underlines the need for a cosmopolitan society with plenty of spare cash for an evolved dessert repertoire to blossom and flourish. With the near annihilation of Baghdad in 1259 by the grandson of Genghis Khan and his Mongol army, and a second punishing sacking in 1401 by Tamerlane, the city could maintain none of this. The center of power and consequently of fine confectionary moved north and west to Ottoman Turkey.

ISTANBUL

Like many a young man, Friedrich Unger was anxious to see the world, so when the German-speaking sweet maker was offered a job as chief confectioner to the king of Greece, he jumped at the chance. "When opportunity arose," he would write in his treatise on Turkish confectionery in 1837, "I was overjoyed to have the opportunity to enrich my knowledge of Eastern confectionery . . . and from the very start I missed no opportunity wherever it arose that would advance me in this object." That a German should have been offered the top pastry cook position isn't as weird as it sounds; the king of newly independent Greece happened to be a Bavarian. What was more unusual in this age of European chauvinism was that he was deeply curious about the local techniques.

Starting sometime around 1832, Unger wasted no time poking around pastry shops and confectioners, not only in Greece but in the next-door Ottoman Empire.[35] Admittedly, with his sense of Western superiority, what he found wasn't always to his taste. "The general opinion about the high level of Oriental confectionery is exaggerated," he sniffed. "The ordinary French or German confectioner supplies articles out of his laboratory which not only in variety far outdo the Oriental products but also are more suited to our European palate . . ." Yet despite his prejudices he painted a vivid picture of the Turkish capital that would make any sweet lover salivate.

Vendors wandered through the narrow streets like ancient caryatids come to life, balancing trays stacked with plates of cookies and candy on their heads. Scruffy Albanian boys shoved their way through the city's crowds shouting to attract attention to their lumps of sesame *halvah*, which they would hack off with a little knife and weigh out on a flimsy scale. Then there were the languorous pastry sellers who set up their stands in the squares, where they quietly sold their doughnuts, pies, and the like.

Unger went out of his way to learn as much as he could, given his language and cultural limitations. He came across a then-recent German translation of the writings of the seventeenth-century Turkish travel writer Evliyâ Çelebi, who remains a valuable source on his countrymen's sweet fixation. In one passage, Çelebi describes the procession of artisans (lasting three days!) that circled the Sultan's palace in his day. Among them, he lists twenty-one kinds of confectioners who specialized in myriad types of candy and pastry, many still sold in twenty-first-century sweetshops. Leaving aside the candy assortment, the parade featured pastries of every kind. The *güllaç* makers layered gauzelike sheets of starch wafer with nuts and milk into a puddinglike dessert.* Entirely different yet also vaguely puddinglike was saffron-colored *zerde*. This was a dairy-free dessert made by thickening long-simmered rice with starch. These days, *zerde* is traditional for weddings, births, and other special occasions. Another spe-

---

* In Ottoman days, *güllaç* used to be made from egg whites and wheat starch in almost the same way as medieval Arab/Persian *lauzīnaj*. Today, the sheets are often made with cornstarch and people buy them already cooked, though they will typically finish the dessert at home by soaking these with hot milk and nuts. It's yet another sweet typical of Ramadan.

cialty still common today was a dessert made with *kadayıf*, the infinitesimally thin strips of dough (Unger describes the people who make it as "noodle bakers") that most Americans mistakenly call shredded wheat. In fact *kadayıf* is cooked more like a crêpe. In Unger's day, Istanbul pastry cooks had a series of specialized implements to help them achieve the right texture. The most critical gadget was a sort of copper udder with a dozen little pipes or nipples on the bottom. They filled this with a thin flour and water batter and drizzled it in a circle onto a heated four-foot-wide copper plate. The resulting strands were then layered with fat or butter and baked. Much like baklava, the *kadayıf* was finished with a drizzle of honey syrup. Today, it is typically filled with nuts or fresh cheese. In Turkey the recipe seems to be as old as baklava itself, dating back to at least the fifteenth century.* Beyond the *kadayıf* makers, Çelebi goes on to list rosewater distillers, pastry cooks, doughnut makers, cake bakers, and *halvah* producers. According to our seventeenth-century tour guide, the sweet makers' parade concluded with the sugar bakers of Galata, who sold fruit preserves and candied fruit that, for the procession, they mounted and carried on cypresses and fruit trees made entirely of sugar.

As interesting as Unger found these old reports, he was ultimately no antiquarian; rather he was a working confectioner who wanted his information firsthand. Accordingly, he talked or bribed his way into sweet makers' workshops. He even managed—after a judicious application of baksheesh—to get into the old imperial Topkapı palace, now no longer occupied by the Sultan but nevertheless sporting an impressive array of kitchens. The German confectioner counted nine different kitchens,

---

* The word, if not the dessert, *kadayıf* clearly comes from the Arab *qatayif*, and there is indeed a sort of pancake in Turkey, now called *yassı kadayıf*, that resembles it. The vermicelli variety is called *tel kadayıf* or literally string *kadayıf*. In Arabic this is now called *knafa* or *kunafah*.

all but two or three abandoned by this point. Unsurprisingly, he was especially eager to see the separate confectionary facilities. These, like the regular kitchens, consisted of large domed rooms, their ceilings black from soot. Ovens were ranged against the wall while cooking was done in tinned copper pans set over charcoal fires set into a long sort of gutter. There were specially designed pans for sesame *halvah* and equipment purpose-built for making *kadayıf*. Seed mills, pans, tins, spatulas, sieves, and mortars signaled the specialized nature of the cooking that had once gone on here, though by the time Unger visited, all this was lying helter-skelter on the filthy floor.

Worse yet for our inquisitive pastry cook was the fact that he could get no one to talk to him. Confectioners everywhere are notoriously secretive, and these palace artisans were no exception. Moreover, they were constantly under the eye of the supervising imperial sugar baker, who towered over them in his white pointed felt hat. There wasn't a chance that they would divulge anything to the nosy foreigner. "My questions . . . were answered in monosyllables," the frustrated Unger fumed. "I saw that here I could see and hear little that was useful and left the court with a feeling of disappointment." Happily, in the end he was able to find a Greek confectioner who had once worked for the sultan to show him the state of the art in Ottoman sweet making.

When Unger visited Istanbul, in the 1830s, the once mighty Ottoman Empire was in precipitous decline. Greece had escaped Turkish rule in 1829, to be followed by the rest of the Balkans over the coming decades. Austria nabbed its share in the north while the British and French poached North Africa. European visitors like Unger had some justification for their superiority complex. It hadn't used to be like this. In earlier centuries, when Turkish troops had surrounded Vienna and seemed on the verge of adding central Europe to their already vast domains in the Middle East and Africa, Europeans had been nowhere near as smug.

Sugar Feast

The Turks first swept into the Middle East a thousand years ago during Abbasid times, and, soon enough, many of the Muslim emirate's soldiers were of Turkish origin. By the eleventh century they were running the place. Persia was ruled for a time by a Turkish dynasty, as was much of Mesopotamia and Anatolia during the time of the Crusades. As a result, Turkish culture was heavily inflected by both Persian and medieval Arab influence. This once nomadic people now turned to Mecca to pray and acquired a taste for syrup-soaked pastry. The desserts listed at early Turkish banquets—"*me'muniye* and *halvah*s with musk and fragrances"—were just the sort of thing you might have bought at the marketplace in Baghdad.*

The first mention of the Ottoman dynasty comes relatively late, in a Byzantine account of a battle against a hitherto obscure chieftain by the name of Osman in 1301. But Osman made an impression. His successors rapidly expanded his domain into the Balkans, Anatolia, Eastern Europe, the Middle East, and Africa. At its height, in the sixteenth and seventeenth centuries, the food-stuffs of three continents (four if you count the new arrivals from the New World) filled Istanbul's thriving bazaars, while Italians, Slavs, Arabs, Greeks, Egyptians, and Persians milled through its congested streets. Like Baghdad before it, the city became a melting pot of culinary influences.

In Çelebi's day, Istanbul, with perhaps seven hundred thousand residents, may have been the world's largest city. The palace alone was home to forty thousand residents in the 1640s.[37] (The whole of Vienna had a population of only about seventy thousand at this time.) There were numerous kitchens and hundreds of

---

* "*Me'muniye*" (more commonly rendered as *ma'mūniyya*), the rice pudding made with chicken, would latter be known as the *tavuk göğsü* described above.[36]

cooks, some specifically catering to the sultan, to his harem (the term in Turkish is *darüssaade*, meaning "house of happiness"), or to other members of the household. The French traveler Jean-Baptiste Tavernier, who described his visit to the Topkapı palace in 1675, wrote that there were six or seven kitchens dedicated to confectionary alone where perhaps four hundred "Halvagis" practiced their craft. He added, "They work incessantly in those seven pantries [he used the French term "offices"] making all sorts of confections both dry and wet."

The confectioners' job included making sorbet (*şerbet* in Turkish) and conserves but also pickles.[38] Here sorbet should be understood as the sort of dense, flavored syrup that we've met among the Mughals rather than the frozen dessert we think of today. It was typically stirred into water—often chilled with snow or ice—to make a kind of soft drink. Given the name, the recipe is probably of Arab origin and may have developed out of the same sort of rosewater and sugar syrups used to soak pastries in the Middle Ages. Tavernier noted that the favorite sorbet of the reigning Sultan Mehmet IV was made with violets. Those medieval flavorings, amber and musk, were also much esteemed, a fashion that had waned by the time Unger visited the Turkish capital. By the nineteenth century, fruit flavors were more typical.* Wealthy Ottomans used to serve these scented sweet soft drinks throughout dinner.

By Renaissance European, or, for that matter, contemporaneous Mughal norms, the Turkish meal took a highly unusual form. It was served sequentially, one dish following another, each platter cleared before the next was offered. This is, of course, how

---

* This Turkish-style sorbet had a huge fad in seventeenth-century Europe, where it was launched by the same emigrants from the Ottoman Empire who had introduced the idea of the coffeehouse from Istanbul. You still find these fruit-based syrups today in Central Europe but also in Italy, where they are more commonly flavored with almond, hazelnut, or vanilla, though pomegranate, orange, and watermelon are also not unheard of.

we eat today, but before the nineteenth century, Europeans typically ate buffet style, picking from numerous dishes both salty and sweet that were served more or less simultaneously. Yet even if, at the Topkapı palace, desserts did not have to share center stage with roasts and ragouts, as they did at the Louvre and the Vatican, there was, as in the West, no sense that sweet should follow savory.

The writings of the English chaplain John Covel, who visited the court of Mehmet IV at more or less the same time as Tavernier, offer a glimpse of Ottoman dining habits. Covel was in the employ of the ambassador, which allowed him an intimate view of the Ottoman ruling class. It also gave him an overweening sense of self-importance, all too evident in his writings. The nosy vicar never penned a sentence where a paragraph would do. But it is precisely this "wearisome in the extreme" quality (as his nineteenth-century editors termed it) that led him to put down details that others thought too unimportant—such as what he had to eat when invited to dine with the vizier (the sultan's chief minister) on July 27, 1674. Covel recalled the menu as best as he could, given how little sleep he must have had the night before. The English entourage had to arrive at the palace gates at five-thirty in the morning to get through all the formalities to be on time for the eight-thirty A.M. banquet. In Turkey, it was typical to finish the day's main meal before the muezzin's call to the noon-day prayer. Covel counted some twenty dishes served in quick succession: kebabs and roast poultry, rice pilaf with chicken, stuffed gourds and vine leaves, sweet and savory puddings, a *börek* (baklava's savory cousin), and honey-drenched baklava itself. All this was a prelude to the ambassador's interview with the bejeweled sultan, to which the inquisitive chaplain, much to his chagrin, was not invited.[39]

Although the catalogue of dishes is incomplete, there is enough detail here to explain the order, or lack thereof, of the

Ottoman meal. This remained much the same two hundred years later, when Unger described a model Turkish feast. Unsurprisingly, the professional cook paints a more complete picture. Here too, dessert is not served for dessert. In a twenty-two-course meal, baklava arrives as course number nine, preceded by stuffed vine leaves and followed by (savory) cheese *börek*. Course number fourteen, *asure* (a sweet wheat berry pudding made with dried fruits and still popular today), is followed by meat dishes. Admittedly, the very last course is sweet. At the end of the meal the Ottomans traditionally served fruit (some dried, some fresh), nuts, and what we might call candy. Two centuries earlier, the French used to finish their meals in much the same way, calling this "dessert." At one time in Turkey, there were also some festive meals that consisted almost entirely of dessert as people today would call it. In the sixteenth century, Ogier Ghiselin de Busbecq, the Flemish Hapsburg ambassador to Suleiman the Magnificent, complained: "Even their formal banquets generally consist only of cakes and buns and sweets of other kinds, with numerous courses of rice, to which are added mutton and chicken."[40] Mary Işin, a Turkish food historian, points to a contemporary palace document that lists a banquet consisting solely of about fifty different sweets, puddings, and fruit preserves. The occasion for this cavalcade of sweetmeats was the circumcision of Suleiman's sons. And this was just one meal among many. Most of the others included a mere dozen dishes, some sweet, some savory.

It's all too clear from these menus that conspicuous consumption was as much a part of the Ottoman lifestyle as it was for any Renaissance prince or Mughal potentate. When the occasion demanded it (circumcisions were a big favorite), the Turkish monarchs mounted celebrations that were, well, worthy of a sultan. The ever-informative John Covel reported that the preparations for the festivities that marked Mehmet IV's son's circumcision in 1675 began six months before the actual event. The two-week-long jamboree included dancers, acrobats, and fireworks. High society attended feasts day after day even as the common people were showered with candy. Wax was fashioned into gardens and fountains for the occasion. The most spectacular display, however, was a parade made up of a menagerie of 120 sugar sculptures, each born aloft by two slaves. According to Covel, who wasn't much impressed by their workmanship ("they were done brutishly and bunglingly"), the pieces were between a yard and a yard and a half in height, the sugar paste formed into ostriches, peacocks, swans, pelicans, lions, bears, greyhounds, deer, horses, elephants, rams, buffaloes, and so on. These sorts of sugar sculptures were all the rage in Renaissance Italy, and it is perfectly plausible that this was an Ottoman import, or even that foreigners (presumably not especially skilled ones) created the sugar beasts. Çelebi did point out that the Galata confectioners were Greeks from the former Genoese colony of Chios and were Frankish (i.e., Western) "infidels."

Confectionary was also integral to more mundane court rituals. The imperial Janissary Corps and other military classes were paid their salaries every three months. During the ceremony that accompanied the payout, the Janissary general would show his good intent and allegiance by distributing candy to the sultan's ministers. These sweets were called *akide şekeri*, meaning literally "good faith or allegiance candy." People still use this name for the traditional hard candy, even though the Janissaries have been gone close to two hundred years.

Candy and dessert continue to be important in the lives of ordinary Turks. Marriages, births, and religious festivals all have their symbolic sweets. However, no holiday is as associated with sweet eating as Ramadan. Some writers suggest that the tradition of gorging on sweets during the holiday—something that happens throughout the Muslim world—has its origin in Muhammad's prescription to break the fast with dates, Mesopotamia's original sweetmeat. That may well be. But there is clearly also an element of compensation here, the feast that follows the famine, and nothing signals indulgence more than dessert. You find something similar in the tradition of doughnut-eating that precedes Lent in parts of Catholic Europe, to say nothing of the cascade of chocolate bunnies and eggs that comes on the heels of the Christian fast. Arabs also have their share of Ramadan sweets, but in Turkey the holiday's sweet orgy is exponentially more intense. Hans Dernschwam, a Hungarian who accompanied Busbecq and the rest of the Austrian delegation to Turkey in the 1550s, was mortified at the Ottoman sweet tooth, especially during Ramadan. "In Constantinople there are lots of different cooks who bake and fry in fat all kinds of cakes and doughnuts in many forms," he wrote, "[and] electuaries filled with herbs and eggs. In particular during the four weeks of fasting, they stuff themselves with such foods in the evenings. It is all made from honey and sometimes sugar, that one feels quite sick afterwards." Today, the three-day celebration following Ramadan is known as the "sugar feast," and every family stocks up with a supply of hard candy, Turkish delight, candied almonds, and other sweet snacks to offer guests.[41]

And then there is baklava. In the fading years of the Ottoman Empire it used to be traditional for upper-class families to give trays of the pastry to friends, neighbors, absent college students, even their children's schoolteachers during the holiday. The flaky pastry's association with Ramadan goes back at least to the sixteenth century, when, on the fifteenth day of the month-long fast, trays of baklava from the imperial kitchens were presented to the Janissaries of the imperial Ottoman army in what came to be known as the baklava procession. The tradition lasted until 1826, when the Janissary Corps was abolished as a result of their mutinies and general insurrection. Toward the end they didn't even return the baklava trays as had always been the custom, insolently claiming that they had eaten the copper trays along with the pastry!

In an earlier, more obedient era, two members of each squad of ten would pick up the circular tray, tied in cloth to protect it from the dust, and march with great pomp and din from the sultan's palace down the main road known as Divanyolu to their barracks. All of Istanbul paused while the city's dusty air filled with the sweet buttery aroma of baklava. At one time there may have been as many as ten thousand of these elite imperial troops, so it is conceivable that close to a thousand trays of baklava left the palace kitchens that day.[42] Today, during Ramadan, according to Fatih Güllü, his family's factory in Istanbul produces four metric tons of baklava a day. Lucky thing they don't have to depend on rowdy soldiers to deliver it.

THE BAKLAVA WARS

"Baklava Tension Increases; Protests Planned for Istanbul" was the headline in the English-language edition of one Turkey's largest newspapers, *Hürriyet*, on May 12, 2006. Turkish baklava makers were up in arms, and two hundred or so of them planned to march through central Istanbul bearing banners proclaiming BAKLAVA IS TURKISH. At a press conference, the president of the Baklava and Dessert Producers Foundation, Mehmet Yildirim, declared, "It is time for Turkey to stand up and claim its national treasures; Turkey brought baklava with them all the way from Central Asia. There are official documents proving that baklava rightfully belongs to Turkey."[43] At the EU General Secretariat, the top Turkish representative was launching a protest. Needless to say, baklava is still taken very seriously by the people of the eastern Mediterranean.

The impetus for the row was a thousand years of history and an indelicate poster put out by the European Union presidency featuring the "national" desserts of the current twenty-five members. One little corner representing Cyprus depicted baklava. Cyprus is a small island nation with fewer than a million people, but it is divided between a Greek (majority) and Turkish (minority) population. For years, both Greece and Turkey have used the island to poke the other in the eye; sad to say, Cyprus's accession to the EU has yet to make matters any better. Dessert is just another weapon in the conflict. Cyprus does have a long tradition of dessert making that goes back at least to the days when it was one of the region's major sugar producers. But that was in the fourteenth century, when Cyprus was under the foreign control of Venice. When the Ottomans conquered the island from the Venetians in 1570, Turks replaced Italians as the ruling class even as the majority remained Greek. It is perfectly logical that Cypriots would consider baklava their national dessert. But much the same could be said for every nation once ruled by the Ottomans, Turkey included. If you look at the communities that eat baklava today, you can make out the outline of an Ottoman Empire that disappeared a century ago.

Nations define themselves in different ways. Some do it by language or religion. Others have built states based on ideas of race or bloodlines. In each polity there is an inevitable feedback loop that reinforces a people's ideas of itself, of its history, of its culture. Cooking has an ambivalent role to play in this because, like religion and language, it ties us intimately to our own particular community, yet even a superficial analysis of the food we eat makes it clear how it also connects us to a wider world. There is something comical, but also slightly painful, when a dish like baklava is used in a political food fight. It is especially absurd in the case of baklava, which is the sum of all the nations that once ruled this corner of the world. There is a bit of ancient Greece in the nuts and medieval Mesopotamia in the syrup, and in the thin sheets there is certainly more than a little of the nomadic peoples of Central Asia.

But I'm not the only one who has the Pollyannaish idea that sticky sweet layers of nuts and dough can and should bring us together. Among the anti-Cypriot protesters in the streets of Istanbul there were some who held up banners that read BAKLAVA SHOULD UNIFY US, NOT DIVIDE US. Bismillah. And amen.

Qatayif
Crêpes Stuffed with Nuts and Cheese
. . . .

Like many fried sweets, *qatayif* is very traditional for Ramadan in many parts of the Arab world. Variations for it exist throughout the Middle East. Some call it *kataif* and others *ataif*. The name and the recipe for the pancakes go back to at least the tenth century. This particular version is adapted from a recipe described by Palestinian journalist Laila El-Haddad on her blog gazamom. com. Laila writes that, in Palestine, most people buy the pancakes premade but stuff them at home. I suspect that this dates from a time when the batter was made through a laborious process in which a dense dough was first kneaded to develop the gluten in the flour before working in water until a liquid batter resulted. Depending on the region, these little turnovers are filled with various fillings. In Palestine, a fresh cheese called Nabusli is often used. To all intents and purposes this is the same thing as unsalted mozzarella, though drier than the typical fresh-made Italian product. If you can't get the traditional cheese, use fresh mozzarella instead. Just shred it and let drain on several layers of paper towel before using to dry it out a little. Use one or both stuffings; each recipe is enough for one batch.

Makes about 3 dozen

Qatayif

6 ounces (about 1¾ cups) all-purpose flour
1½ cups lukewarm water
1 ounce (about ¼ cup) powdered milk
1½ teaspoons active dry yeast
1 tablespoon sugar
¼ teaspoon salt
¼ teaspoon turmeric
¼ teaspoon mastic* (optional)
½ teaspoon ground *mahlab*** (optional)
½ teaspoon baking soda

Stuffing

(see recipes below)

Syrup

1½ cups sugar
1 cup water
1 teaspoon lemon juice
2 teaspoons rosewater or orange blossom water

White sesame oil or grapeseed oil for frying

---

* Mastic is a type of resin used widely in Greece and to some degree the Middle East. To use it, crush it with some of the sugar with a mortar and pestle.

***Mahlab* is an aromatic spice made from the seeds of the St. Lucie Cherry (*Prunus mahaleb*), the flavor being similar to a combination of bitter almond and cherry. You may be able to find it in a store with Middle Eastern specialties. Crush with the sugar in a mortar before using.

1. Mix together the flour, 1¼ cups water, powdered milk, yeast, sugar, salt, turmeric, and spices (if using) in a medium bowl. Whisk until smooth. The resulting batter should be a little thinner than American pancake batter. Cover with plastic wrap. Let rise for 1 hour or until doubled in volume. Stir with a spoon to deflate. Stir together the remaining ¼ cup water and the baking soda and whisk into the batter. The resulting batter should be a little thicker than crêpe batter. If necessary add another tablespoon or two of water.

2. Heat a griddle or large cast-iron pan over moderate heat. Oil *very* lightly with oil. Spoon a generous 2 tablespoons of the batter onto the griddle and spread into a circle about 3½ inches in diameter. Cook on one side only until the top is almost but not 100 percent dry. Remove with a spatula. Adjust the heat as necessary so that the pancake cooks through without browning too much. The cooked side should be golden rather than brown and the resulting pancake should remain pliable. Stuff while still slightly warm.

3. Stuff: Fold together one end of the pancake and pinch closed with thumb and forefinger. Spoon in about 1 teaspoon of the stuffing (depending on the size of the pancake), then close to make a half-moon shape, pinching the edges to seal completely. Do not overstuff, particularly if using cheese stuffing. The recipe can be prepared up to a day ahead to this point.

4. Make the syrup: Combine the 1½ cups sugar and 1 cup water in a small saucepan. Bring to a boil and stir until the sugar is completely dissolved. Remove from heat and cool to room temperature. Stir in the lemon juice and rosewater or orange blossom water.

5. Heat about 2 inches of oil in a heavy, flameproof casserole to 375°F. Add the stuffed *qatayif* a few at a time and fry until crispy and brown. Drain on paper towels. While still hot, dip in the syrup. (Through not strictly traditional, it is also possible to brush the *qatayif* with butter and bake them for about 20 minutes in a 375°F oven, turning them over halfway through cooking.)

Qatayif *Cheese Stuffing*

Stir together:
1 cup unsalted white cheese, such as Nabusli or fresh mozzarella, shredded (if using fresh mozzarella, drain or blot out some of its moisture)
2 tablespoons sugar
1 tablespoon rosewater or orange blossom water

Qatayif *Nut Stuffing*

Mix together:
2 cups walnuts, coarsely chopped in a food processor
3 tablespoons sugar
1 teaspoon ground cinnamon
1 tablespoon rosewater or orange blossom water
3 tablespoons raisins or chopped dates

3

——— ∞∞ ———

SUGAR AND SPICE

❀ *Italy* ❀

BAKING BY THE CALENDAR

Each year it becomes increasingly difficult to find traditional foods in Venice. There's no market for them. All that tourists seem to want to eat is mass market gelato and döner kebaps, and the native Venetians are dying out. Until recently, baker Franco Colussi was one of the last to carry on a pastry legacy that goes back to the Middle Ages. The last time I stepped into his shop I could still smell the history of this city that once lived and breathed on profits from sugar and spice.

That was some years back. It was a couple of weeks before Christmas. The gorgeous old city stood in stark relief against the transparent winter sky. Day trippers eddied through the twisting alleys, tugging at their gift-wrapped loads. In the bakery, every shelf and every counter was crowded with the plump, golden sweet breads Venetians call *focacce*, in sizes ranging from small to jumbo, like a congress of squat Russian nesting dolls. In Venice, *focaccia* (in local dialect *fugassa* or *fugazza*) is much like Milan's panettone though broader in shape and with a veil of crystallized sugar. It is eggier and without the candied fruit of its better-known cousin.

Colussi's bakery was small, immaculate, and almost spartan in its simple furnishings. There wasn't much else there other than the fat, sweet yeast cakes and Franco, all rosy cheeks and baker's whites, planted behind his great marble slab of a worktable framed by the room-sized oven behind him. When the garrulous *pasticciere* heard of my interest in Venice's traditional pastries he almost leaped across the counter. The new generation doesn't care, he told me. "They want to make money but they don't want to work," he groused. "They want to use all kinds of artificial leavening. But yeast, yeast won't wait, it is natural, when it is ready you have to be there, be ready too." *Focaccia* dough can take as many as five risings. Franco's version was an ethereal thing, a golden confection of butter and air.

When I asked about old regional specialties like the *pevarini* that I'd read about in books, the old baker shook his head at my ignorance. "We make those in the fall," he lectured, "not for Christmas." Like many Italian bakers of the old school, Franco baked by the calendar. *Focaccia* was for Christmas and Easter, but you would never see it otherwise. For Epiphany there was *pinza*, a dessert thick with cornmeal and dense with dried fruit. *Pinza* is like a fruitcake, he explained to me, using the English word. *Pinza* has some etymological connection to *pizza*, yet like both pizza and *focaccia* it can denote something entirely different in other parts of Italy. In Bologna, a *pinza* is made by folding a rich, buttery dough around a stuffing of raisins and *mostarda Bolognese* (a quince preserve often flavored with mustard). There, too, it is traditional for the Christmas season. Vincenzo Tanara described a very similar *pinza* in the seventeenth century made by Bolognese peasants using saffron-colored bread dough, which was wrapped up jelly-roll style around a filling of raisins.[1]

After Epiphany comes Venice's favorite holiday, Carnival, celebrated with doughnuts of every description. The most traditional *frittelle* fried up by the city's *pasticcieri* are about the size of an egg and dusted with powdered sugar. They are made from a yeast dough scattered with candied fruit and spiked with a shot of grappa or anisette. The local fried food fetish is probably as old as the island republic. A fourteenth-century Venetian recipe collection gives instructions for several kinds including a sugar-dusted yeast doughnut made with almond milk. Bartolomeo Scappi, who worked for a time in Venice before relocating to the Vatican, included a recipe for *frittelle alla Venetiana* in his 1570 cookbook. These are made by deep-frying nuggets of cream puff dough rather than the yeast dough more common today.[2] This version still occasionally shows up, at times filled with a zabaglione-flavored cream. Then there are the ubiquitous crunchy fried ribbons called *galani*. Mostly, these have now migrated from Carnival to the souvenir shops where they sit regardless of season, growing stale and rancid. The Venetian fondness for doughnuts even led them to adopt the Austrian *Krapfen* despite the hatred felt toward the Hapsburg troops that occupied the city for the greater part of the nineteenth century. *Krapfen*, what Americans know as jelly doughnuts (though in Venice they're mostly stuffed with custard cream), are a favorite midmorning snack eaten year-round at coffee bars all over town.

After Carnival the bakers can briefly rest before turning to *focaccia* once more, in anticipation of Easter. Northern Italy is dotted with these sorts of yeast-leavened cakes, or sweet breads, if you will.* Milan's panettone is the most famous, but there is also the seasonal *colomba*, named after the dove it resembles, and Verona's *pandoro*, which is more like a Viennese *Gugelhupf* (and may well be descended from it). Pastry cooks all over Italy

---

* While a yeast-risen panettone fits somewhat inelegantly into the dessert category as Americans define it, Italians have no doubt that it is a *dolce* sold at the *pasticceria* (pastry shop), never at the *panetteria* (bread bakery).

breathe a little easier when Easter is over and they can make plans to head for the beach.

After the summer vacation comes another round of holidays. In Venice the feast of San Martino is a little like Halloween. Children go from square to square making a racket with pans and lids, all the while demanding small change and candy from shopkeepers and passersby. The saint, mounted on a horse with sword in hand, is consumed in the form of a giant sugar cookie, nowadays typically decorated with chocolate and sugar work. A few weeks later, the dead, or at least their bones, are eaten on the day after All Saints' Day. In Venice, *ossi da morto* (bones of the dead) take the form of crisp, yeast-leavened cookies shaped like bones and glazed with sugar. There are many versions of these seasonal cookies all over Italy.

The season's chill also finally brings out those pepper-spiked *pevarini*. These large, dense cookies are about the size of a hockey puck and typically studded with almonds and raisins. They are brown with molasses, reminding you how ubiquitous the liquid sweetener (now rare in Italian recipes) must have once been here when the city was the Mediterranean's most important sugar refiner. The pepper is a souvenir of the centuries when Venice was the spice merchant to Europe. *Pevarini* used be served in the city's wine bars, since the pepper would make the clients drink, but out-of-towners don't seem to need the encouragement anymore. Franco told me he no longer makes them much. There are still places where you can find *pevarini* in Venice today, though in most cases the bakers seem to have forgotten to add the pepper. You won't find Franco, though. He has finally retired, I am told by friends of friends. His *pasticceria* has been taken over by his sons. Perhaps they will keep up the tradition but I'm skeptical. When last I tried to visit the pastry shop it was closed. They were on vacation, a neighbor told me, spending the summer at their beach house in Greece.

Nuns' Sighs and Abbots' Ears

Of course it isn't merely in Venice or even Italy that the liturgical calendar determines the pastry cooks' work cycle. Though many of the world's religions have periods of self-denial followed by indulgence, none can compete with the roller-coaster of feast and fast traditionally called for by the Church of Rome. There are hundreds if not thousands of sweetmeats associated with Catholic holidays. Central Europe has its Christmas cookies, the French their *bûche de Noël* and *galette des rois* ("king's cake," for Epiphany). In Mexico, the Day of the Dead is celebrated with sugar skulls and *pan de muerto* (a sweet bun often decorated with bones), while in the Netherlands, Sinterklaas, St. Nicholas Day, is intimately associated with *speculaas* or gingerbread, often baked in an anthropomorphic form. Yet, as any careful examination of this list reveals, the Christian veneer on these occasions is often paper-thin. Christianity's early success as a religion can be attributed in part to the Church's willingness to absorb pagan beliefs. Thus winter solstice observations were folded into Christmas and fertility rites tamed for Easter. In many cases, the pre-Christian significance of these festivals remained.

The most symbolic foodstuff in Europe is doubtless bread. It has the same religious connotation as milk in the Hindu world. In the Christian mass it represents the god sacrificed. "I am the living bread," John quotes Jesus, "which came down from heaven: if any man eat of this bread, he shall live for ever: and the bread that I will give is my flesh, which I will give for the life of the world." But bread was sacred to European pagans as well. For them too it represented rebirth, though perhaps with less metaphysical import.

As bread rises, it swells into rotund loaves, like a belly swelling with child. In some cases, loaves take a different sort of feminine shape: round with a hole in the center. There is little ambiguity in the plaited ring (like a woman's hair) embedded with eggs that is traditional to the *tsoureki* baked for Greek Easter celebrations. Corsica has a similar bread called *caccavelli*, and Calabria has its *cuzzupa* for the holiday.[3] Central Italy too has its feminine *ciambella* or *giambella* (a large ring-shaped sweet bread), but there is also the masculine *ciambellone*, a log or thick baton, which resembles a sweet *salame*. Breads often take these phallic shapes—think of the Parisian businessman strolling home with his baguette in hand, occasionally taking a love bite out of the end.

In ancient Rome, the symbolism was much less muted. In Sicily, Demeter, the harvest goddess, was honored by a sweet called *mulloi*, made of wheat flour, sesame, and honey. It was shaped, appropriately enough for the fertility goddess, in the shape of female genitalia.[4] The Roman-era author Athenaeus described a breast-shaped cheesecake served at bridal showers in Sparta. Priapus, the god of fertility, was typically shown with a swollen phallus. His whole form, or sometimes just the god's pertinent anatomical feature, was served in the form of a pastry. Roman men ate it at the end of the meal to perk up their spirits—in a manner of speaking. Martial, the Roman poet best known for his satirical verses, suggested it could serve as a more socially acceptable stand-in for men who exhibited a taste for the flesh-and-blood version: "A Priapus of bread: / you can satisfy yourself by eating my Priapus. / Nibble at him and remain respectable."[5]

In the more prudish Christian millennia that followed, the fertility symbols remained, though the representation was a little less overt. At Christmas, the round form of the loaves, like Venice's *focaccia*, came to represent the rebirth of the sun at winter solstice while, at Easter, another rotund loaf brought to mind the first spring moon that heralded the sowing season. Naturally these couldn't be just ordinary bread. They were enriched with expensive sweeteners and with eggs, which, beyond their symbolic resonance, also add color and moistness to the dough. With the waning of the Middle Ages, sugar slowly replaced honey as the sweetener of choice and the dough became so rich with eggs and butter that it was hard to know whether to call it bread or cake.

In Bohemia, where I grew up, Christmas is represented by a *vánočka*, a long, sweet, plaited egg bread, while Easter has its *bochánek*, a briochelike cake as round as the full moon, studded with what were once expensive imported raisins and almonds. In next-door Poland you find the *babka*, typically baked in a ring pan like a bundt cake. Farther east there is Ukraine's *paska* (from the Greek word for Easter), which takes on different shapes depending on the particular region. Traditionally the *paska* would be swaddled in a ritual cloth like a newborn and carried to church in a basket, where it was blessed in a special ceremony following Easter mass. In this and other ways, the veil of Christianity seems especially transparent in Ukraine. The breads are often decorated with pagan symbols like the sun and pussy willows, with their intimations of fertility and spring.[6] These holiday breads or cakes are most likely as old as wheat cultivation in the countries of Central and Eastern Europe. They certainly predate any written recipes. Even in Italy, the oldest recipe for an enriched sweet bread can probably only be traced to 1549, to Cristoforo di Messisbugo's *Banchetti*. In it he outlined how to make sweet *pani di latte* (milk rolls) with egg yolks and rosewater.

The point of bread or cake, of course, is that you don't merely look at it, you eat it, and, presumably, as you consume it, you absorb its symbolic qualities. This is acted out as part of every Christian Eucharist. It may also explain the anthropomorphic or other symbolic shapes of many desserts. If eating the body of Christ at mass made you a better Catholic, could you not also imbibe a little holiness by crunching your way through a gingerbread St. Nicholas, or nibbling at "apostle's fingers," or gobbling up the "breasts of St. Agatha"?* There are dozens of these sweet-meats that reference saints or saintly types.

Admittedly the motivation for giving heavenly names to some desserts may have been more a matter of marketing than devoutness. Nobody ascribes any symbolic significance to angel food cake, after all. In previous centuries, many convents made their living selling sweetmeats, and giving them names like *bolo celeste* ("celestial cake") must have been a smart PR move. Portugal has an especially rich repertoire of convent sweets, which may account for its deep catalogue of ecclesiastically derived pastry names. There are nun's sighs, nun's bellies, and nun's kisses (respectively *suspiros, barrigas,* and *beijos de freira*). Saint Catherine gets to sigh as well. *Suspiros de Santa Catarina* take the form of airy meringues with a sprinkle of almonds. Not to be outdone, Santa Luzia has her own sweetmeat. This is called *pitos de Santa Luzia. Pitos* is a colloquial term for vulvas; the dessert, appropriately for a saint, takes the shape of a tightly closed package.** In Portugal you can also snack on abbot's ears (*orelhas de abade*), taste angel tummies (*papos de anjo*), and lap up seraphim cream (*creme de seraphim*). Portuguese heaven (*céu*) is full of both sweet bacon (*toucinho do céu*) and cheese (*quejinhos do céu*). Across the border in Spain, a similar collection awaits. In the case of some names it's hard to know where piety ends and black humor begins. France, for example, has its nun's farts (*pets de nonnes*). In the fourteenth century these airy doughnuts were

---

* *Dita degli apostoli* ("apostles' fingers") are a kind of ricotta cream-filled crêpe from the northern Italian province of Liguria. St. Agatha was tortured by having her breasts cut off, and she was often depicted carrying them on a plate. *Minni di sant'Aita* ("St. Agatha's breasts"), as they are known in the local Sicilian dialect in Catania, are individual-sized mounds of short pastry filled with pastry cream, covered with white or pink icing, with a maraschino cherry right in the middle.

** The tradition is that girls give boys *pitos de Santa Luzia* on December 13, her saint's day, and the boys return the favor with a present of *ganchas de São Brás* on his holiday, celebrated February 3. The *ganchas* (the word means "hooks") take the form of long sugar rods bent into a hook at the end. It doesn't leave much room for interpretation.[7]

originally known as Spanish farts (*pets d'Espagne*), which then turned into whore's farts (*pets de putain*) in the early 1700s. The nuns came into the picture soon after.[8]

Edible symbols still exist even when an ecclesiastic connection has become very tenuous or nonexistent. Catholics and Protestants alike devour decidedly pagan candy bunnies and barely Christian chocolate Santas. Thoroughly profane chocolate coins are a traditional St. Nicholas gift in the Netherlands, as they are for many Jewish children for Hanukah. Candy hearts and gingerbread lucky horseshoes no longer need any holiday to express their meaning. And is a birthday cake in the shape of a Barbie not laden with symbolism? In this respect we still have a lot in common with the Romans.

ANCIENT INFLUENCE

In Italy, as in the Middle East, the taste for sweetmeats doubtless goes back to the first glimmers of civilization. Certainly by the Roman era, Italians could avail themselves of professional cooks, bakers, and, at least in later years, specialized pastry cooks. We know secondhand that there were even cookbooks devoted entirely to pastry. Unfortunately, in most cases, we know little more than their names. In *The Deipnosophists* ("The Learned Banqueters"), written around 200 CE, the author Athenaeus's erudite guests discuss desserts at length, but the details needed by a cook are entirely missing. They mention many fritters and scores of cakes (*plakous*), which, depending on the variety, are made with milk, eggs, fresh cheese, sesame, pine nuts, walnuts, hazelnuts, poppy seeds, wine, rice, and other ingredients. They are mostly sweetened with honey, though grape must is occasionally called for too. Much of Athenaeus's pedantic discussion focused on Greek desserts, but some of these must have also been common in Rome. Other, more strictly Roman sources, tell of cheese-based pastries, fritters, and even custards.

Sugar, though known, was apparently not used as a cooking ingredient. Pliny the Elder, writing in the late first century CE, noted, "Sugar is made in Arabia as well, but Indian sugar is better. It is a kind of honey found in cane, white as gum, and it crunches between the teeth. It comes in lumps the size of a hazelnut. Sugar is used only for medical purposes." (Historians today think he was mistaken about Arabia.) With no other sweeteners at hand, Roman sweet makers had to contend with honey, grape must, and ground or chopped dried fruit, with all the limitations that brought. Sugar only began to be used by European sweet makers in the Middle Ages as a result of contacts with the Arab world.

While several ancient Roman sweetmeats seem to have later European equivalents, it is difficult to make the argument that there is a direct line that connects a Roman recipe for custard, say, to its Renaissance-era lookalike. Or take the popular Spanish doughnut called *churro*. The dough is made by stirring flour into hot water or milk, which happens to be exactly what the instructions say in a cookbook attributed to a certain Apicius in the fourth century.[9] The main difference is that the Roman recipe calls for cutting the fritters into squares before frying while the contemporary version is extruded in a star shape. So does that mean that Spaniards have been using this same technique ever since the Roman legions packed up their mess kits and headed for home? Well, maybe. Or perhaps the technique was reintroduced by the Muslims, who learned it from the Romans. There is a not dissimilar recipe in the tenth-century cookbook by al-Warrāq. Or it could be that the idea just popped up independently in late medieval Europe. There are recipes for *churros*-like fritters in a sixteenth-century German source that mirror the roughly contemporaneous *fritelle alla veneziana* noted in the Scappi book above.[10] They both include eggs though, which not all *churros* do. In cases such as this, food history turns into a guessing game.

Scholars argue about just how much Arabic or Roman influence there was on medieval European cuisine. Superficially at least, the food of the feudal elite, with its complex spicing and sweet-and-sour flavor, would seem to have a great deal more in common with the cuisine of the Arab Middle East than the funky and honey-sweetened dishes of ancient Rome. (The Romans were big into fermented fish sauce.) But of course, the Arabs themselves were influenced by the Eastern successors to the Romans, the Byzantines. They too used fermented condiments to season their dishes.

When it comes to dessert, at least, it takes a much smaller leap of imagination to see the influence of Arab confectionary on medieval Italian and Iberian food, based as it was on an intimate knowledge of sugar and other ingredients unknown to the Romans. In Europe, techniques for making marzipan, jellies, fruit syrups, rice puddings, and candied fruit and the use of flower waters, ambergris, and other aromatics were certainly adapted from Middle Eastern models. As we have seen, the technique for making Naples' beloved *sfogliatelle* has clear Arab predecesors[*] (see page 82). In Spain, a kind of almond-studded nougat called *alfajor* or *alajú* most likely dates from the era of Muslim rule. My guess is that the similar Tuscan *panforte*, strongly flavored with spices, has similar antecedents. It certainly tastes that way. The Middle Eastern connection is sometimes made explicit when medieval cookbooks pick up (and contort) Arabic names along with the recipes. For example, the *Tractatus*, an early fourteenth-century (most likely French) recipe collection, includes a recipe

---

[*] *Sfogliatelle* are made by rolling out dough, brushing it with melted fat, then rolling it up jelly-roll style. This is cut into pieces and stretched or rolled to create a container for a ricotta filling.

for something called *mistembec*, which is a dead ringer for the earlier Arab *mushabakka*, a syrup-soaked fritter. A related cookbook, the *Liber de Coquina*, includes a recipe for *ma'mūniyya*, the pudding made with rice flour and chicken mentioned in the previous chapter (see page 97). Here it is called *mammonia* but there is no doubt that it is the same dish. In England it was sometimes known as mawmenny. In most places, however, it would come to be known as blancmange (or the local equivalent). You couldn't throw a fancy meal without it.

There was one critical respect, though, in which medieval bakers were heirs to a Roman legacy. The ovens used by Europeans were direct descendants of those used in ancient Rome. If you visit the remains of ancient Pompeii, you may notice that the ovens aren't much different from the ones still used today to make the exquisite pizzas of nearby Naples. They are made by surrounding a beehive or dome-shaped core with a heavy masonry superstructure. You heat the entire construction by making a fire inside, removing the coals, and then baking in it. Once the oven gets going it stays hot for hours. The ancient Middle Eastern tandoor, by contrast, is shaped more like a jar or vase. The fire is made in the base and stays there. Critically for a region short of fuel, it heats up quickly, but then it also cools down faster because the walls are so much thinner. This divergence in technology explains, at least in part, the difference in size and shape of European and Near Eastern bread to say nothing of many baked desserts. Imagine making an apple pie or biscotti in a tandoor.

Given their size and insatiable appetite for fuel, Roman-type ovens required a considerable outlay in both capital construction costs and operating expenses. As a result they were often owned by the nobility or a town at large. The oven was seldom a domestic appliance except for the propertied elite. Moreover, given the importance of bread, it is not surprising that ovens were tightly regulated by the authorities. In medieval France, for example, a professional, the *fournier*, was charged with running to the oven and keeping it supplied with fuel. At times he was also the baker, but not always. Pastry cooks and others requiring use of the oven would be required to pay an appropriate fee to use the communal facility. All of this encouraged the formation of professional guilds of bakers and pastry cooks who, due to their differing equipment needs, were quite distinct from other dessert makers.

Once heated, large masonry ovens go through three cycles of heat. When the coals are first swept out, the oven is very hot, ideal for baking small rolls and pastries (puff pastry, for example, requires a quick heat), during the second stage the ovens were typically used for large loaves of bread, and in the course of the final long cooling period they can be utilized for slow-cooking casseroles or other meat mixtures (often enclosed in a pastry crust) but also the secondary baking required by biscotti, gingerbread, and the like. Bakers were happy to rent out their ovens during the cycles when bread couldn't be baked. Occasionally cookbooks explicitly tell you to take a filled pastry, say, to the local baker.

Nevertheless, there were many occasions when it was impractical to depend on an oven to do the baking, so other sorts of technology were developed, especially for baking delicate cakes. The most common device was a sort of improvised oven the Italians called a *testo*. To use it, cooks would rake aside coals in a fireplace, set their cooking dish on the hot ground or on a rack, cover this with an earthenware bell, and then shovel hot coals over the top. A German encyclopedia published around 1800 describes what was by this point an antiquated technique: "Formerly, cakes were baked in an earthenware pot. One placed this vessel on glowing ashes, covered it with a copper lid, and put some more coals on it and let it bake an hour. If absolutely necessary this will work, however," the author notes, "a separate oven is preferable."[11] A similar approach was sometimes used in the Near East, where baklava might be "baked" on a metal pan covered with a second pan, then piled with coals. This approach would have worked much better for a *yufka*-based dessert than a more precarious confection like a sponge cake.

Given the differences in climate and technology, the general impression you get from medieval sources is that European dessert makers imported more software than hardware from the Muslim world. Perhaps the most critical skill to be learned from the East was how to work with sugar. In this, Venice, with its fingers in both the Arab and the European pies, played the vital intermediary.

THE CONQUEST OF SUGAR

Venice's Ca' Cornaro Piscopia palace is a confection that would do any wedding cake designer proud. It is a composition of graceful columns and rounded arches that seems to hover above its reflection in the Grand Canal. It is more Byzantine than Roman, a visible reminder that the island city was once as oriental as it was European. The building was purchased by Federigo Corner and his two brothers, Fantin and Marco, in 1364 (it has been expanded since then) as a place to showcase the family's position and wealth. Not much is known of the Corner brothers' personal history. Given their later careers, it is likely they started like most young Venetian traders, employed by the city's trading elite. When they first appear in the records in the 1350s, they are on their own and already prosperous, with a growing business empire based in Cyprus and Rhodes. Federigo, at least, did well for himself. In 1379, a financial audit of Venice's business elite determined that he was the richest man in the republic, his assets calculated at sixty thousand ducats.* And the source of all this wealth? Sugar.

---

* For some sense of what that means, a representative of the Corner-Miorati bank (another venture of the extended family) earned one hundred ducats a year in 1407. The Ca' d'Oro, one of the most splendid palaces on the Grand Canal, was estimated to have cost about seven thousand ducats in the 1420s.[12]

A typical business arrangement of the time was to have one relative abroad taking care of the business while other family members took care of financing (as well as politics) back home. In the Corners' case, the brothers agreed to put Fantin in charge of the critical sugar operations in Cyprus. His first step was to secure a feudal estate appropriate for raising sugarcane from the ruling (French) Lusignan king. Though the land came with a title that conferred all sorts of aristocratic perks, the young Venetian businessman had no interest in playing at knights in shining armor. Instead he took the sugar plantation in hand in the style of a no-nonsense capitalist. To deal with a labor shortage, Fantin bought slaves from Arabia and Syria to work alongside the local serfs. He used what was then cutting-edge technology to improve the yields by investing in an expensive system of canals to irrigate the land and to power a cane-crushing mill. He built a refinery and filled it with imported equipment so that the business could produce both high-priced granulated sugar and semirefined loaves.[13] When Fantin was done he had accomplished a feat that would elude most later planters (especially in the Caribbean)—creating a vertically integrated business; that is, the Corners controlled not only the production but also refining and distribution of the increasingly desirable luxury. Eventually the brothers would export the sweet crystals to Venice and even to Syria, where the northern Italians had learned about sugar production in the first place.[14]

Europeans had first encountered the sugar plantations of the Levant during the Crusades. In 1099, Fulcher of Chartres, the chaplain to the Crusader general Baldwin of Boulogne, described how a Crusader army of twenty-five thousand men and women marched down what is now the Syrian coast near Latakia. They were hot and hungry, so when they came across a sugar plantation they fell on it like ravenous crows. "Then we found certain crops," Fulcher writes, "on the cultivated fields through which we passed, that the people called 'honey-cane,' almost like reeds ... whence came wood-honey (I think it was called), because it was ingeniously procured from this crop. We hungry people chewed these stalks all day because of their taste of honey, but with little satisfaction."[15]

Despite that first unsatisfactory impression, the Crusaders did not remain resistant to the allure of sugar for long. Once some modicum of peace was reestablished, the fields of "honey-cane" were expanded to sate the growing market both locally and abroad. The Hospitallers (later the Knights of Malta), for example, were involved in sugar cultivation from early on, sending a cantar of sugar to their hospital in Jerusalem for medicinal purposes.* It was the Venetian merchants, however, who had some of the largest plantations, "eight farms with well-watered fields" (according to one eyewitness) in the vicinity of Tyre in what is now southern Lebanon.[17] Joseph of Tudela, a Jew from northern Spain who visited the city in 1173, commented on the quality of the local sugar, noting that "people come from all lands to buy it."[18]

Eventually the Europeans were driven out of the Middle East, though not before they had acquired a taste for the local sweetener as well as the technical means needed to satisfy it. They established sugar plantations on the eastern Mediterranean islands of Crete, Cyprus, and, to a lesser extent, on Malta and Rhodes (where the Hospitallers had retreated). Venetians like the Corners, but also Genoans, Catalans, and others, provided capital for establishing these new fields of cane while immigrants from Palestine provided the know-how. At first most of the workers were local serfs, but eventually planters started importing slaves to do the hardest work. A majority of historians think that these Italian-financed operations provided the original model for the slave-operated plantation that would cause so much misery once it was adopted in the Americas.**

---

* The cantar (qinṭār in Arabic) was a medieval weight that varied from place to place. In Syria, it equaled some 495 pounds in 1233.[16]
** This view has been challenged, most notably by Marie-Louise von Wartburg. She is highly skeptical of slaves taking a major part in sugar production, citing the fact that only two sources mention "Saracen" slaves being bought but with no information about what they were used for. Her contention is that serfs did most of the heavy lifting.[19]

There were Arab precedents for this. Slaves, at least some of African origin, were used to work agricultural land in southern Mesopotamia in the Abbasid period. There is documentation of a revolt that took place in 869 in response to the harsh treatment meted out while marshland was being reclaimed in order to plant crops such as sugarcane.[20] Moroccan sugar plantations seem to have been worked by slave labor as well.

What the Venetians injected into the sugar business was a more capitalist spirit and a system of colonial exploitation. Still, there were few who could match the Corners. By the mid-1400s, the family business employed some four hundred workers (most likely a combination of semienslaved serfs and imported slaves) to produce sugar on their Episkopi estate in Southern Cyprus, a number to rival the largest tropical plantations that colonial America would see.[21]

The pattern set by the Venetians was repeated over and over in the coming centuries. In Madeira, the Canary Islands, Brazil, Barbados, and Cuba, slaves gradually replaced free laborers everywhere. Also, as in the eastern Mediterranean, American planters came to depend on the capital of far-off financial elites. The profits didn't stay in Cyprus any more than they would later stay in Barbados or Cuba. The Venetian sugar barons built their palaces on the Grand Canal, not on the eastern islands, much as West Indian merchants invested their profits in estates back in England once they had bled the colonies dry.

The Mediterranean sugar industry thrived for over five hundred years despite the fact that the region is hardly ideal for growing or even processing sugar. The season is so short there that the cane never achieves the sucrose concentration that it does in India or Brazil. But another pressing problem made its production increasingly uneconomical—mainly a lack of fuel. In the Middle Ages, sugar was produced using grindstones and presses, technology better suited to grinding wheat and extracting olive oil. Then, as numerous merchant records attest, it was boiled and often reboiled to produce sugar in a variety of grades. This required a great deal of fuel, which was much more readily available in the northern Mediterranean than in semiarid locations like Syria or Cyprus. Because of this, after being coarsely refined at the plantation, it made sense to ship the resulting brown sugar back to where the customers were and finish the refining process there. The first Italian refineries were in Venice and Genoa and even in landlocked Bologna. After 1470, Antwerp became a major destination for new arrivals of raw sugar from recently developed Atlantic colonies. This pattern of refining sugar close to the consumer rather than the producer has remained largely in place to this day.

Given the inefficiencies of growing sugarcane in the Mediterranean, it is hardly surprising that in medieval Europe sugar was rare and expensive, especially the finer grades.* It was typically sold as a spice, mostly by apothecaries who mixed it into their prescriptions to make the medicine go down. In England, sugar could cost as much as black pepper shipped from far-off India. When the fourteenth-century Venetian cookbook known as the *Anonimo Veneziano* listed a recipe for light little doughnuts of ricotta and egg whites called *Fritelle da Imperadore magnifici* ("magnificent fritters for an emperor"), what made them worthy of the name was a generous sprinkling of powdered sugar. But even for those who could afford it, there just wasn't enough sugar to go around. The demand for the sweetener proved to be insatiable no matter what the price. The more that was produced, the more it was consumed by anyone with the means.

The Portuguese were the first Europeans to expand production outside of the Mediterranean when they planted cane on the newly settled island of Madeira in the 1430s. Much of this production went to Antwerp, but even Venice took in some

---

* In 1468, for example, once-boiled sugar in Cyprus cost about thirty ducats for a cantar (about five hundred pounds), twice-boiled came in around seventy, and for the top grade the going rate was over a hundred. In comparison, wheat cost about one-tenth as much as the cheapest grade of sugar.[22]

Madeiran sugar to supplement its Mediterranean suppliers. It was, however, mostly Venice's archrival Genoa whose banks and ship owners benefited from the Madeira trade. One sailor who cut his teeth on transporting Portuguese sugar was Christopher Columbus. The Genoese mariner even married the Madeira governor's daughter. Madeiran sugar cultivation, in many ways, followed the Cypriot model. Here too there was a mix of free and slave labor, though with one difference.[23] These slaves were exclusively from Africa, as they would be in the Americas. There was one other respect in which Madeira resembled the Mediterranean islands—it too had a temperate climate less than ideal for cultivating the sweet reeds.

The first prototype of a tropical, Caribbean-style sugar plantation worked almost exclusively by African slaves came only when Portugal seized the island of Saõ Tomé. Portugal, then as now, was a little country with never enough people to colonize what would become a worldwide empire. African slaves had long been used to work sugar plantations in the Algarve, so it is hardly surprising that the planters on Saõ Tomé would turn to the African coast 150 miles to the east to supply their labor needs.

The increased sugar shipments from the Atlantic Islands (the Spanish Canary Islands were another exporter) had a dramatic impact on price in the second half of the fifteenth century. In Holland, the average price of sugar fell by half between the 1470s and the 1520s. Consequently the sweetener could be used a little more freely by cooks and confectioners, even if it still remained unaffordable for common folk. In this respect, Columbus's trip was well timed. Though he was a little befuddled about his geography, he recognized that the islands of the Caribbean were ideal for sugar cultivation. With this in mind, he brought sugarcane with him on his second trip. Not that his Spanish patrons were all that interested. Once they discovered gold and silver in the New World, that's all they cared about.

Once again it was the Portuguese, this time in Brazil, who started to produce sugar in any appreciable quantity from their American settlement. Vast plantations worked by enslaved Africans grew up around the cities of Pernambuco and Salvador. Where Saõ Tomé had produced roughly three thousand metric tons of sugar in the 1580s, Brazil exported ten times that amount a hundred years on.[24] Yet it's interesting to note that the appetite for sugar continued to keep up with production and indeed probably exceeded it if the rising price throughout the sixteenth century is any indication of supply and demand. The price dropped only at the end of the seventeenth century, when a cascade of sugar began arriving on Europe's shores from the Dutch, English, and French colonies in the Caribbean.*

What were people doing with all this sugar during the Renaissance? Was there an explosion of candy and dessert making? Well, that's only part of the story.

SPRINKLE WITH SUGAR AND CINNAMON

In 1574, King Charles IX of France, son to Henri II and Catherine de Médicis, died, leaving the throne to his younger brother, also named Henri. In his day, the young Henri III was better known for his fabulous earrings and bejeweled outfits than his prowess in battle. This didn't endear him much in Poland, where the twenty-three-year-old Frenchman had recently been elected king. Henri wasn't too fond of his Eastern European subjects either. The moment he heard the news of his brother's death, he fled his new realm for France, literally sneaking off in the middle of the night.

Since Venice was more or less on the way, the young fashionista made sure to stop by this capital of the luxe life. The Vene-

---

* The sixteenth century was a time of explosive inflation in Europe, but this only partly accounts for the fourfold price increase of sugar between about 1520 and 1600. The price of wheat, for example, also rose, but only by a factor of three.

tians were happy to play the host, reasoning that in Henri they might find an ally against both Rome and the Spanish Hapsburgs. Accordingly, they pulled out the red carpet. The renowned architect Palladio was roped in to create a triumphal gate. The city mounted a grand regatta for his majesty. There were music and fireworks and public feasts galore.[25] Henri apparently also found time to experience some of Venice's more private pleasures. He paid a visit to Veronica Franco, the city's most famous courtesan, and was so taken by her that he brought home a little enamel portrait of her.*

But whatever sweets Veronica may have offered Henri, they could not have compared to the orgy of sweet bodies that the king experienced over the next few days. At one sweet banquet, or *collazione*, a legion of sugar-paste popes, kings, cardinals, doges, gods, and beasts of every description stood guard over a feast of sweetmeats made with pistachio and almond paste. There were apparently three hundred of these figures gilded with silver and gold, as well as 1,260 sweets. At least some of the sugar sculptures were based on designs by the recently deceased sculptor and architect Jacopo Sansovino, and most were executed by an apothecary named Niccolò della Cavalliera.

In Renaissance Italy, the *collazione* or *collatione* was a sort of light meal, though records indicate that, at least in some instances, these could be quite lavish and impressive.[26] Sweets were normally a major feature of these spreads, but few were as elaborate as the feasts experienced by the young king. Perhaps the most memorable of these was another *collazione*, given in his honor at the Arsenale. Here, surrounded by Venice's famous shipyards, where the city's still-powerful navy was fitted with arms and cannons, the young royal was seated at a table set for yet another feast that promised sugary excess, though not in the way Henri expected. When the king picked up his napkin he was startled to

---

* Given his reputation, Henri's attraction to the famed courtesan more likely resembled the fascination some gay men have for Judy Garland than anything carnal.

have it crack in his hands and fall to the ground. He laughed in surprise, for it turned out that the napkin, like the tablecloth, as well as the bread, plates, knives, and forks laid upon it, were all made of sugar. The juxtaposition of Venetian wealth and artistry with its seafaring brawn was a clever, if hardly subtle, stratagem. Whether the display did them much good, on the other hand, is an open question. Henri's reign back in France is widely considered to have been a flop. He was assassinated a few weeks before his forty-eighth birthday.

In Venice, the sort of simulated sugar place setting that amused Henri at the Arsenale wasn't limited to state banquets. The sixteenth-century novelist Celio Malespini described a meal thrown by a Venetian fraternity at which "the plates, bowls, tankards, cups, gold and silver plates and other various beautiful dishes were filled with confectionary, game, fruit, fish, birds, galleys, figures and other things all composed and so perfectly made of sugar that they seemed natural."[27] We find instructions on how to create this sort of trompe l'oeil in *Secreti del reverendo donno Alessio piemontese*, a book written by Girolamo Ruscelli in 1555. The volume mostly contained pharmaceutical recipes but also included a small section on confectionary. One recipe specifically explained how to make sugar paste "from which one can make all sorts of fruit" as well as "plates, bowls, glasses, cups and other similar things." To make the sugar paste, Ruscelli soaked tragacanth (a type of tree gum) in rosewater, then added lemon juice, egg white, and sugar. All this is ground to a fine paste. "At the end of the banquet," the author ended his recipe, "one can eat all [the tableware] and break all the plates, glasses, cups and everything, because this paste is very delicate and tasty."[28]

This kind of mock tableware and the sugar sculptures were fantastically expensive. There is no copy of the bill from Niccolò, the apothecary who provided Henri's sugar extravaganzas, but another one exists from a colleague of his from 1534. This was a more modest *collatione* (also composed entirely of sweets) given in honor of Renée, the French-born duchess of Ferrara rather than the ruler of a great kingdom, but the expenses are still staggering. The invoice lists eighty-three *spongade* (as the sugar sculptures were called in Venice) for a cost of 840 lire.* There were also over a thousand pounds of assorted confectionary, about a thousand sweet rolls, and another thousand baked sweets, adding up to a food bill close to two thousand lire. To put this into context, that was double the architect Sansovino's yearly salary or, in today's dollars, into the six figures.[30] And that doesn't include the hired help and other incidentals, which added another couple thousand lire to the check. But then of course the expense was the whole point. The duchess of Ferrara was expected to be awed by the spectacle in the same way that the king of France was supposed to go home blown away by the fantastic wealth of the Venetian Republic.

The Italians were fully aware of the utility of conspicuous consumption. Paolo Paruta, a Venetian political theorist of the time, wrote: "There are few occasions when one can demonstrate one's magnificence, but during those occasions, such as weddings, banquets and in building, it is appropriate to spend without worrying about the cost but rather the magnificence and greatness of the result."[31] The sugar plates, bowls, and sculptures weren't merely amusing conceits (though they were that too), they were laden with symbolism. This wasn't the metaphysical ancient symbolism of Easter breads and candy bones, however; it was an entirely secular demonstration of raw power. Sugar was a precious material like silver and gold, and just in case its mere expense wasn't enough, it was gilded to drive the point home.

In Venice, sugar sculptures and sweetmeats were used quite regularly as an accessory to the demonstration of power. In the 1500s, private meetings in the doge's palace with the city's

---

* In and around Parma today, there is a sort of dry fruit-filled pie called a *spongata*. I doubt that there is any connection.[29]

patricians were accompanied by "*storti, buzolai pignocadi, confetti pasterelli* and other confections."* As early as 1493, Beatrice d'Este, the wife of Ludovico il Moro, the potent ruler of Milan, describes a meal given in her honor at the doge's palace "composed of diverse things all made with gilded sugar, which numbered three hundred; with infinite plates of confectionary."

The fact of state-sponsored extravagance in sixteenth-century Italy isn't especially noteworthy. This sort of behavior is common to every society. What is more interesting in the Renaissance is the form that this spending took. Late medieval Italy was a profoundly different place from feudal France or the Spain of the conquistadors. By contemporary standards, it was extraordinarily affluent. This was due in part to the trading acumen of the merchants of Venice and Genoa, in part to profits raked in by Florentine bankers and wool manufacturers. And, of course, Rome was the seat of Christendom. The Vatican, however inefficiently, sucked in income from all of Catholic Europe. What's more, Italy was more urban and densely populated than elsewhere on the continent. As a result, the people with the power and the money weren't the warrior nobility, as was the case in the north, but rather bourgeois merchants and churchmen. Since both professions needed a modicum of education, a relatively large proportion of the population was literate and cultured. Yet, even if the banker Medici ran Florence and descendants of sugar merchants such as the Corners sat in the ruling Venetian doge's chair, Italians nevertheless bought into the widely held European ideology that noble blood mattered more than a padded bank account. No Italian could boast bloodline over the king of France; after all, Henri III was anointed by God according to the belief system of the time. What they could do, however, was to wow the mon-

---

* *Storti* are presumably *torti* or sweet pies, *buzolai pignocadi* are ring-shaped pine nut cakes, and the *confetti* were most likely candied spices.

arch, not merely with their extravagance but also with their taste and artistry. On a more modest scale, this strategy of shock and awe could also be applied to their neighbors. The efflorescence of culture and learning that would later be dubbed the Renaissance had many causes, but one can be attributed to the inferiority complex of Italy's ruling class.

Renaissance patronage tends to be associated with the great artists: the Scrovegni commissioning Giotto to decorate their chapel or the Medici paying Michelangelo to design and sculpt their tombs. But the web of patronage extended to less celebrated individuals, the artisans who built the palaces, the musicians who entertained the guests, and the silversmiths who created the serving platters. The line between artist and artisan wasn't so finely drawn at the time. A noted sculptor like Benvenuto Cellini made monumental sculptures as well as salt cellars and candlesticks. Sansovino, whose designs were used for the sugar *spongade* for Henri III's sweet feast, was one of the city's chief architects. You can still see his work in Venice's chief library, the Biblioteca Marciana. Many of Italy's leading lights took part in the creation of civic feasts and celebrations.

The increased availability of sugar that came with the development of the sugar colonies in the Mediterranean and then the Atlantic gave Italian confectioners the opportunity to perfect their art. The demands of a discerning clientele gave them the motivation. Unlike in medieval Germany, or France, say, Italy's craftsmen didn't have to depend on the patronage of a single feudal lord. Instead they catered to a relatively broad class of wealthy consumers. But they also had plenty of competition. In 1569, Venice had 122 spice dealers who specialized in selling sugar, wax, and spices. They were considered a subset of the apothecary trade, which in Venice was technically not a guild. "In all parishes, every apothecary sells spice, sugar and similar items" was the comment of one government assessor.[32] A number of these apothecaries were in the sugar-refining business, and it's a safe assumption that many, like Niccolò della Cavalliera, made confectionary. Since there were so many of them, confectioners in Venice or Milan had to differentiate themselves from a crowded field, and because both civic and guild regulations often made it impossible to compete on the basis of price, there must have been pressure to innovate in other ways. A similar process took place in other cities where the climate was conducive to a blossoming of the confectioner's art; a comparably competitive milieu certainly spurred invention among the sweet makers in eighteenth-century Paris and nineteenth-century Kolkata.

The public meals of Renaissance Italy can best be understood as a sort of *Gesamtkunstwerk*, a term used by nineteenth-century Germans to describe the complete artistic experience of opera, which is created by artists and artisans of many descriptions. In the case of the Renaissance banquet, confectionary was simply the most ostentatious part of a similarly interdisciplinary event. One of the most spectacular patrons of the theatrical arts—which in this case certainly included fine dining—was Ercole d'Este and his son Alfonso at the court of Ferrara. Unlike many other Italian rulers, the d'Estes could claim a reasonable modicum of noble blood. But that wasn't of much use when their modest realm was sandwiched between meddlesome Venice and the overbearing Papal States. What the d'Estes lacked in hard power they tried to make up in the magnificence of their patronage. Alfonso commissioned Titian to paint his portraits and sustained Ludovico Ariosto, his generation's foremost poet. He also employed one of the top banquet impresarios of his day. Cristoforo di Messisbugo was the official d'Este *scalco*, a term that is sometimes translated as chef or steward but in fact has more in common with the role of general manager of La Scala. The *scalco* arranged the menus and coordinated the work of the *cucina*, which produced the hot food, and the *credenza*, in charge of the cold dishes, including most of the confectionary. But he also planned all the entertainment and the decor. Historians know so much about the d'Estes' dinner parties because Messisbugo compiled several of his banquet menus (as well as a smattering of recipes) in a volume entitled *Banchetti compositioni di vivande, et apparecchio generale* ("Banquets, Composition of Dishes, and General Presentation"). One of these feasts took place during the diplomatically critical wedding celebrations of Alfonso's son Ercole II to Renée, the daughter of King Louis XII of France.

When the young d'Este and his teenage bride arrived in Ferrara in the late fall of 1528, they were met by all the VIPs in town. Ercole's uncle, Cardinal Ippolito d'Este, was there; so were the ambassadors of France, Venice, and Mantua as well as all the notables of the city. After they had dealt with the receiving line, the wedding party proceeded to the palace down streets hung with red, green, and white draperies, led by Diego, the Spanish court jester, mounted on a camel. They were observed by crowds of ghostly onlookers, who must have observed all the pomp and fuss with mixed feelings since the city was still recovering from a deadly bout of plague.

Notwithstanding the recent epidemic, the newlyweds were fêted with dinners, plays, races, and dances in the coming weeks.[33] One banquet described by Messisbugo was thrown by Ercole at the height of Carnival season on January 24, 1529. The quantities of sugar alone involved in such an endeavor were worthy of Venice.

There were to be 104 guests seated at a long table almost a hundred feet long. The *scalco*'s staff set each place with a napkin, a sweet roll, a *brazzatella* (a sweet, ring-shaped bread boiled and baked like a bagel), a gilded, pistachio-based sweetmeat, and some *savonea* (a little like Turkish delight). But this was nothing compared with the sugary extravagance that decorated the center of the table. Here was a procession of twenty-five gilded sugar statues, each easily two feet high and "colored so that they seemed alive," representing the struggle of Hercules with the Nemean lion, a none-too-subtle tribute to the young Ercole.

Trumpets were sounded to beckon the guests to a table set with a dozen kinds of starters, divided among close to six hundred serving plates. Mostly these were salads and tarts, some sweet and others savory. Anchovy salad was served alongside sugar-dusted cream pies. Once the guests were seated, a chorus of voices, violas, and harpsichords accompanied the arrival of the first course. There were nine kinds of dishes of both poultry and fish, including a boned capon coated in blancmange and sprinkled with sugar, sweet pine nut pastries, eel in marzipan, and others. All this was divvied up between 250 plates. The second course was of a similar scale though the preparations were somewhat more elaborate, including several "German-style" recipes (German cooks were highly regarded in Italy at the time). Neapolitan-style blancmange, tinted a rich golden hue with saffron, was presented alongside roast partridge and francolins (similar to pheasants). Sweet, rosewater-scented "German-style" pastries filled with almond paste and pine nuts were placed next to fried lobster tails and claws. And yes, there was a third, fourth, fifth, sixth, and seventh course, each accompanied by more musicians. There were whole roasted goats, roasted lamprey with a sweet-sour sauce thickened with its own blood, honey and sugar syrup–soaked fritters called *fiadoncelli* made with bone marrow, marzipan tarts filled with "Turkish rice" (basically rice pudding), and more than fifty other kinds of dishes. Finally—it must have now been the next day—the table was cleared of all food and the confectionary arrived. This consisted of citron, lettuce, cucumbers, almonds, and medlars (similar to small apples), all in syrup, fruit pastes made with quinces and pears, an assortment of candied fruit "in the Venetian style," candied almonds, and perfumed toothpicks.

The banquet concluded with the presentation of a great gilded pie, which for once had no sugar in its filling. Instead, when cut

open, the pastry revealed a tangle of glittering necklaces, brace-
lets, earrings, and brooches. The guests drew lots for these party
favors, some of which were worth as much as fifty ducats apiece.
There was a brief break, another snack, and then they danced till
dawn.[34]

As the menu makes abundantly clear, Italians served sweet
dishes throughout the meal. There was no more sense that these
should be relegated to the end than in contemporary Constantinople or Delhi. But there was one way in which Italian Renaissance
cuisine was unusual, and that was in its enthusiasm for mixing
flavors that we tend to think of as distinctly sweet and savory in
the same recipe—like those eels in marzipan. Many scholars have
long been horrified at the quantity of spice called for in medieval
cookbooks, at this "spice orgy," as the great French historian Fernand Braudel called it.[35] Yet most contemporary Americans used
to Indian, Thai, and Mexican food would hardly blink at the com-
paratively modest quantities of spice called for five hundred years
ago. What we would find bizarre is the amount of sugar used.
For a fish pie filling, Messisbugo adds nine ounces of sugar and
six ounces of raisins to about a pound and a half of cooked pike
mixed with almonds. A recipe for a *sapore* (a sort of condiment
or sauce) has you grind up a pound of almonds with a few slices
of bread soaked in broth, then stir in a little vinegar, some ginger,
and a half pound of sugar. This was intended for boiled and fried
meats as well as roasts. A slightly later cookbook by Bartolomeo
Scappi is similarly enthusiastic. His instructions for a tortellini
filling include two capon breasts, a pound of cheese, and eight
ounces of sugar. This is then enclosed in a sweetened pasta dough.
Scappi makes a *suppa alla Lombarda* by layering toasted bread
with broth, meat, and cheese, seasoning each layer with a sprinkle
of sugar and cinnamon.[36] An analysis of sixteenth-century recipes makes it clear that cinnamon sugar was the favorite seasoning
of the day. It seems that nothing could be ruined—pasta, roasts,
stews—with a final sprinkling of sugar and cinnamon.

This taste for sugar wasn't limited to meat and fish. Dishes that would now be called dessert could be excruciatingly sweet. Messibugo's *sfogliata di mandorle* (a sort of double-crusted pie filled with almond paste) combines a pound and a half of equal parts sugar, dates, and raisins with the same quantity of ground almonds. This is flavored generously with cinnamon and rose-water while another four ounces of sugar is spread on top as a kind of glaze partway through cooking.[37] The cookbooks give the impression that the gradations within a meal, rather than ranging from savory to sweet, ran from sweet to very sweet.

The justification for sweetening food was, in part, borne out in medical opinion, much of which had been absorbed from Arab sources. One widely disseminated Arab text, known in Latin as *Tacuinum sanitatis*, explained how sugar is "is good for the blood." In an age when people and foods were believed to be a cocktail of the four bodily humors (sugar was moist and hot), the *Tacuinum* made the exceptional claim that sugar was "suited to every temperament, age, season, and place," no matter an individual's particular makeup. In Messibugo's day, the physician and naturalist Costanzo Felici couldn't say enough good things about the imported sweetener: "Sugar is an excellent accompaniment to everything, or one could make it such. As the saying goes, 'sugar never spoils a soup.' [It] makes eating more refined and, very frequently, drinking also, by rendering both experiences sweet and flavorful, [for] we can truly say that this is a precious food . . . and human nature finds great pleasure and delight in its sweet flavor."[38] He might have added that its cost only added to its prestige and allure. Sugar wasn't so different from the jewels that filled the concluding pie at Ercole's fantastic feast.

All that said, Messibugo's directions to shower food with sugar should be taken with a grain of salt. Another banquet bill preserved from Renée's visit to Venice in 1534 shows that the kitchen used a scant twenty pounds of sugar for a meal that used over a thousand pounds of veal, beef, and lamb, twelve goats, ninety pairs of capons, and 105 pairs of squab.[39] So maybe sugar was used with more discretion than the recipes sometimes suggest.

Today, most Italians don't use much sugar in their cooking, though there are still occasional remnants of this former sugar infatuation in some regional dishes. In the Alpine foothills, gnocchi are still sometimes sprinkled with sugar, cheese, and cinnamon as they were during the Renaissance. In the Abruzzo, ricotta-filled *ravioli* are occasionally sweetened with sugar, even when served with a savory tomato sauce.[40] In Ferrara itself, squash-filled pasta is often sweetened by the addition of crushed *amaretti* cookies. *Mostarda*, a condiment of syrup-preserved fruit flavored with mustard seed, remains commonplace in Cremona and other Northern Italian towns, where it is typically served as a condiment with boiled meat. (Messisbugo's version is no more than a spiced syrup, entirely omitting the fruit.)[41] Boar and venison are often smothered in a sweet and sour (*agrodolce*) sauce in Tuscany, and Venice has its *sarde in saor*, a dish of fried sardines mounded with onions flavored with sugar, raisins, and candied fruit, all cut with a splash of vinegar. Perhaps the weirdest sweet-savory pudding that still exists is *sanguinaccio*, a blood-thickened chocolate pudding traditionally served during Carnival in parts of the south. But these are all decidedly exceptions rather than the rule. Contemporary Italians generally reserve their sugar for their espresso and sweet pastries.*

COOKIES AND CAKE

Present-day Italians leafing through Messisbugo's sixteenth-century menus would find a great many of the Renaissance impresa-

---

* Today's Italians aren't especially sweet-obsessed. Statistically they consume a lesser quantity of sugar and other sweeteners than any other country in the European Union except for Slovenia.[42]

rio's sweet-savory meat and fish dishes utterly alien. In contrast, many of the cookies and cakes have a ring of familiarity. Even if *confetti* are no longer candied spices, sugared almonds called *confetti* are a fixture at Italian weddings. An echo of Messisbugo's *brazzatella* can be detected in contemporary Italian *ciambelle.** Sweet dry cookies, like Milan's and Naples' *mostaccioli*, were already well-known regional specialties. Marzipan was ubiquitous as a confection in its own right but also as an ingredient in other dishes. Ancient Roman cheesecakes never lost their popularity. The recipe for *torta di ricotta* found in Domenico Romoli's cookbook, first published in 1560, would hardly raise an eyebrow today. It is the epitome of simplicity, made by stirring together ricotta, egg whites, and sugar.[43] A Venetian *scalco* who was for a time in the employ of Pope Leo X, Romoli gives many recipes for cakes and cookies, perhaps due to his location at the epicenter of dessert. He also includes a recipe for meringues, here called *zuccherini*, which he apparently intended for the ill. His *biscottini* would be familiar as well, assuming that he omitted to include the step where they are baked a second time.

Just how old the idea is of cooking bread twice to make a rusk or ship's biscuit is impossible to say. William of Rubruck mentions getting high-quality biscuit (*biscoctum delicatum*) in Constantinople around 1250.[44] It must have been common by this point. Sources in France, Spain, and Germany all refer to *biscuit*, *vizcocho*, or *Zwieback*. Bakers, especially in seaports, did a thriving business baking hard, long-lasting crackers for sailors and other long-distance travelers. But nobody would mistake these for cookies. "Biscotto bread is that which is cooked two times," Vincenzo Tanara explained in *L'economia del cittadino in villa*, a kind of how-to guide for city folk weekending at their country

---

* Today, *ciambella* is a term for all sorts of ring-shaped cakes or sweet breads. The word is even used for American-style doughnuts. What Messisbugo called *brazzatelle* are now called *ciambelle scottolate*. Like the Renaissance recipe, they are first boiled before baking, and are often scented with anise.

house in the mid-seventeenth century. "Normally, after the first cooking, it is returned to the oven [having been] cut into pieces." He went on to explain how ancient Roman soldiers and sailors used to depend on a similar dried bread called *bucellatum.** He added, "Today this is often made in the form of *ciambella* or a focaccia with a hole in the center, allowing every soldier to carry it comfortably strung on a cord, rope, or belt." This neatly explains why all those holes in bagels, pretzels, and doughnuts came into being: ease of transport.

Tanara also explained that there was a second kind of *biscotto* in Italy. Having described how to make ordinary biscuits, he then provided a recipe for what would be called biscotti today:

> There is another sort of *biscotto* that is much more delicate and it is this, which is called *pan de Spagna* (Spanish bread), which is composed of twelve eggs, two pounds raw sugar which you mix together, then add in eight ounces of flour … arrange this in the form of a round loaf. Cook slowly then cut into pieces and return once more to the oven and then serve covered with sugar. Apothecaries and nuns cut them in long slices, and similarly return them to the oven. … They call these small pieces *biscottini* or in their long form, *biscotti alla Savoiarda* (Savoy biscuits).[45]

This is roughly the same recipe given by Romoli a hundred years earlier. Romoli's contemporary, Bartolomeo Scappi, also included instructions for twice-baked *biscotti*, though he called

---

* In contemporary Italy a *bucellato* is a yeast-leavened cake in the shape of a ring that varies in composition depending on the region. In Lucca it is scented with anise, while in Sicily it is chock-full of candied fruit. In Venice, on the other hand, *bussolai* aren't cakes but ring-shaped cookies. Franco Colussi told me about an obscure pastry called *bussolà di Murano*, traditional to one of the islands in the lagoon, which resembles the Sicilian version, though in this case it is spiced with pepper and cinnamon. "It is a savage thing," he told me. "But today even the Venetians don't recognize it."

his cookies *mostaccioli alla Milanese*.[46] Evidently by Tanara's day these were also called *biscotti alla Savoiarda*, which isn't entirely surprising given how close Milan is to Savoy. Today, *savoiardi* denote ladyfingers. These are, of course, baked only once, but they use a very similar batter to the *pan di Spagna* used for Tanara's twice-baked cookies.

In contemporary Italy, *pan di Spagna* is still made more or less the same way as Tanara described it. That is, it is a sponge cake based on whole eggs. It can be served plain but is often used as a base for such desserts as zuppa inglese. The French would come to know it as *biscuit de Piedmont* or *biscuit de Savoie*, which makes some sense given Tanara's comments.[47] French pastry cooks eventually enriched the recipe by adding as much butter as sugar and eggs, resulting in a *gâteau* closer to poundcake in consistency. In later years, this came to be known as a *génoise*.* Over the years, several different techniques developed for making the cake lighter. In one variation, the eggs are beaten over a gentle flame, but more commonly the egg yolks and whites are beaten separately.

Zuppa Inglese and Tiramisù

There was a time when practically every Italian restaurant in the United States had zuppa inglese on the menu. Then in the 1990s came the tiramisù invasion, which unceremo-

---

* The term *génoise*, in the contemporary sense of a light sponge cake, only dates to the later part of the nineteenth century. Incidentally, it's unlikely that the French term has anything much to do with Genoa as the name might initially suggest. In Italy, *pasta di genova* used to be what Italians now call *cotognata* or quince paste. Early French recipes for *paste de gennes* refer to the same thing. By 1750 a *génoise* referred to pastry filled with a lemon almond filling. An early recipe that comes closer to what we might call *génoise* appears in the 1791 *Il Confetturiere Piemontese*, which includes a sponge cake called *pani di santa Genevieffa*. This points to an altogether different origin for the name. Could these be the same *petits pains de sainte Geneviève* mentioned by the Duc de Luynes in 1747? He doesn't explain what they are, but the similarity to the Italian name is striking. My bet is that what we now call *génoise* is named after the French saint rather than the Italian city.[48]

niously displaced the earlier creamy favorite. Today, in restaurants and pastry shops of every nationality, tiramisù is as
unavoidable as algae in a stagnant pond.

Zuppa inglese is one of those desserts that collects
delightfully improbable origin stories. According to one, it
was invented at the court of Ferrara in the sixteenth century,
according to another in Fiesole by a thrifty housewife out of
leftovers.[49] My favorite fable takes place at an unspecified
date at the Neapolitan Bourbon court. In honor of the visiting English ambassador, the chief pastry cook had prepared
a grand cake with *pan di Spagna*, cream, and jam. Alas,
the clumsy waiter, every chef's nemesis, dropped the creation on the floor, shattering it into a hundred pieces. The
anonymous cook, with no time to remake his chef d'oeuvre,
reassembled the whole thing as best he could, layering the
cake with the cream and pouring a spiked syrup over it. To
disguise the disaster, he spread a meringue topping over it
and browned it briefly in the oven. And thus a new classic was born. The first *real* historical reference I've been
able to find to the dessert in Italy appears in an 1841 issue
of a Bolognese magazine. The casualness of the mention,
however, makes it seem like it was already common by this
point (a German novelist mentions it five years earlier).[50]
Given the name "English soup (or pudding)," the obvious
source is English trifle. (This British classic likely only took
its current form of sherry-soaked cake layered with custard
in the 1750s; before that, trifle was more like a mousse or
fool.)[51] Certainly the recipe for zuppa inglese given by Pel-
legrino Artusi in his bestselling cookbook of 1891 would
have been recognized by any Victorian. It included ladyfingers, custard, and canned fruit. The only thing that makes it
different from the English model is the use of *rosolio* (a sort

of punch) instead of sherry. Today's zuppa inglese often has a layer of chocolate custard as well as the plain, but that is assuredly a recent addition.

While it remains a mystery who first served the renamed trifle in Italy, tiramisù is another matter. Tiramisù, literally "pick-me-up," is clearly a descendant of the earlier *zuppa*. Here too are layers of sponge cake or ladyfingers, soaked with booze and layered with a creamy mixture. It's just that mascarpone is used instead of custard, and coffee is added to the mix. The dessert is relatively new, appearing for the first time in Treviso in the 1960s; the recipe appeared in print only in 1981. There are several claimants who profess parentage. Giuseppe Maffioli, who first jotted down the recipe, alleges that it was invented in 1961 at a Treviso restaurant called Alle Beccherie, by a pastry chef named Loly Linguanotto.[52] This, at least, is a more credible story than most.

Yet what are we to make of the Italian name *pan di Spagna*? Does it mean that sponge cake originated in Iberia? One of the earliest references to "*pani di Spagna*" shows up on a menu served in Rome around 1590 as part of the table setting—though it isn't at all clear that this refers to the latter-day sponge cake.[53] It is, of course, possible that the recipe was imported from Spain. There were any number of high-living Spanish ecclesiastics in Rome. What's more, a great many Jews were fleeing the Inquisition at the time, and some put down roots in Italy, though they mostly settled in Tuscany rather than Savoy, the region later associated with the pastry. In and of itself the dessert's name doesn't prove anything; French toast doesn't come from France. Frankly, I was skeptical about the recipe's Spanish origin until I came across a description of *kasutera* or "castela cake," the sponge cake introduced into Japan by the Portuguese in the sixteenth century (see page 54). Now there was a smoking gun. Given how different the names are, it is unlikely that the Portuguese adapted the recipe from an Italian source. The evidence isn't incontrovertible, but it seems likely that both Portugal and Italy learned to bake sponge cake from Spain.

Yet if sponge cake arrived in Italy from Spain, biscotti as we know them probably migrated the other way. Diego Granado's *Libro del Arte de Cozina*, published in Madrid in 1599, contains two recipes for *bizcochos* that resemble those of both Romoli and Scappi, which shouldn't come as surprise since most of Granado's recipes are no more than translations of Scappi's masterwork. It's clear that by this point the term *bizcocho* had begun to lose its original meaning since only one of the recipes is twice-baked.[54] So even if sponge cake originated in Spain, it was later popularized there under a local variant of the Italian name *biscotto*. In Spain, *bizcocho* came to mean sponge cake rather than the twice-baked confection that the name implies. There, as elsewhere in Europe, it was Italy that set the fashion in the sixteenth century.

FASHIONS OF PROUD ITALY

North and west of the Alps, the secular civilization of Italy was all the rage (religion was another matter) or, as York points out in Shakespeare's *Richard II*, "the fashions of proud Italy; / Whose manners still our tardy apish nation / Limps after in base imitation." It's not as if Italy hadn't absorbed foreign influences too, recipes included. Sixteenth-century menus are chock-full of dishes in the German, French, Catalan, and even English styles. Admittedly few of them refer to anything we might categorize as dessert; *pan di Spagna* is a notable exception. Yet despite the sprinkling of transalpine dishes, there was no question where the

trendsetters lived. The irony, however, is that the southern country's influence was as much a result of Italian weakness as it was
a sign of its genius.

Politically, sixteenth-century Italy was a mess. A web of
ever-shifting alliances maintained the balance of power among
the dozen or so city-states and principalities—but just. Until the
system fell apart, the competition among these mini-states had
encouraged the production of luxury goods like sugar, which was
poured on by each rival court to keep its competitive edge. Yet,
in the end, the Italians may have been too successful at exposing
their bling to northern guests without showing enough muscle,
Henri III's sugary feast at the Arsenale notwithstanding. When
external pressure came to bear on the delicate political arrangement on the peninsula, the diplomatic house of cards collapsed.

The first strike came from the east—where the Venetians,
and to a lesser degree the Genoans, had built their fortunes—
as Constantinople (1453), then Rhodes (1522), Cyprus (1570),
and Crete (1669) fell to the Ottomans. Then trouble came from
the north. In the sixteenth century the French kings repeatedly
marched into Italy asserting their supposed right to the crown of
Naples, which was in turn contested by the royal house of Spain.
The invaders returned at least once every decade from 1494 to
1559 under no fewer than four French monarchs. During the
same period, Rome began losing its monopoly on religion as the
Reformation ate into the Holy See's revenue. Finally, the Spaniards came from the west, eventually taking control of most of
southern Italy. Meanwhile, the Italians bickered among themselves and succumbed to French and Spanish cannons. The great
city-states withered and the lesser ones rotted into oblivion.

Venice, which had been the preeminent naval power in
the Mediterranean in the preceding century, gradually turned
inward, eventually reinventing itself as Europe's Las Vegas. Sugar
still came in, now mostly from Madeira and Brazil, but Vene-

tian refineries sent increasing quantities across the Alps. Genoa, instead of exporting hard goods, turned to exporting its sailors and bankers. A similar brain drain affected other cities and other skilled professions, from silk workers, who moved in droves to southern France, to architects, who would go on to rebuild Prague, Dresden, and Vienna in the 1600s. Seeing ever-increasing hardship and poverty back home, confectioners too spilled across the Alps in search of clients who could afford their pricey wares. In the 1500s, Italian bankers, business owners, and courtiers (some drawn to the French capital during the regency of Catherine de Médicis—see next chapter) arrived with their chefs and confectioners in tow. A hundred years later, *maccheroni* makers set up shop in Paris, and Italians opened up cafés and lemonade stands. The foreign sweet makers' influence is plain to see. Seventeenth-century French cookbooks are full of Italian cookies, cakes, preserves, candy, and sugar work. Eighteenth-century Vienna was full of Italian lemonade and almond cookie sellers. They came bearing ice cream and *Piscotten* (biscotti), which, as in Spain, were also no longer twice cooked.

⌒⌒ Ice Cream ⌒⌒

It seems that the more people love a food, the more they tell tales about it. In this respect, ice cream takes the cake. One persistent fable is that Marco Polo introduced not only spaghetti but also gelato from China. Another myth locates ice cream's origins in Sicily, where, under Arab rule, the idea of mixing flavored syrups with snow from the upper reaches of Mount Etna supposedly resulted in a sort of *granita*. Maybe, but flavored snow isn't ice cream. The Florentines, not content to give the Sicilians credit for one of humanity's finest creations, offer one of their own as the inventor. Bernardo Buontalenti was a well-known Florentine architect, set designer, and engineer who worked for the ruling Médicis. Early biographical sketches report that he was in charge of supplying the city with ice and snow in the late 1500s and reputedly worked out a way to keep them from melting during the summer.[55] Then, sometime in the twentieth century, he got the credit for inventing ice cream. An equally improbable but oft-repeated story is that the Sicilian Procopio dei Coltelli first introduced ice cream at his renowned Café Procope in Paris. While it is perfectly plausible that the Italian served some sort of frozen sorbet at his Parisian café (government regulations specifically permitted the serving of *eaux glacées*—as ice cream was then called—at cafés), there is no reason to think he was the first. These *eaux glacées* must have been relatively common by the late 1600s. The French periodical *Mercure Gallant* of 1682 mentions at least two occasions in Venice when they were served, and another in the south of France.[56]

Despite all the false leads, an Italian origin for ice cream does seem likely. Italians already had a rough idea of how to freeze the dessert in the sixteenth century, when a slurry made by mixing saltpeter and snow was used for chilling drinks. Giambattista della Porta described the procedure for cooling wine in 1558, but it seems reasonable that the popular Turkish sorbet was similarly treated. Curiously, the roughly contemporary Mogul document *Ain-i-Akbari* also explains how saltpeter was used to chill water. It's possible that Italian visitors (there were plenty of them) to northern India picked up the idea there. India certainly exported plenty of saltpeter at the time.[57]

But whatever the true source for the technique, cheaper salt was eventually substituted for the costly chemical. The first Italian recipe for a frozen "*sorbetta*" appears in the 1692 *Scalco alla moderna*, a Neapolitan collection written by Antonio Latini, steward to the chief minister of the Spanish viceroy. In his introduction to the subject of ices, Latini claimed that a certain Marina Briancesca was the inventor of the so-called *limonea*, "now called *sorbetta*." He wrote, "A great deal is used in this city due to the [local] habit of using sugar and snow." He added that his instructions were not intended for the locals, since in Naples "everyone is born with the talent and instinct to make *sorbetta*," but rather for those others who were not as fortunate. He included recipes for lemon, strawberry, and sour cherry ice as well as instructions for making cinnamon and even chocolate ice. There is also a milk ice that begins to hint at today's ice cream. (Italians would use the term *sorbetto* for both milk- and water-based frozen desserts well into the nineteenth century.) Latini's introduction notwithstanding, the recipes are pretty cryptic. "To make twenty four goblets of chocolate *sorbetta*," reads one recipe, "one needs two pounds of chocolate, two of sugar [and four pounds salt and about eighteen pounds snow.]" Presumably the chocolate is mixed with water and sugar and frozen in one dish and placed in a larger one filled with salt and snow. The final consistency is a little unclear. Perhaps it was a little like today's granita? In another recipe, the chocolate mixture is frozen into a solid tablet, resembling a semifreddo.

Meanwhile, in Paris, French confectioners were already in on the secret. The first comprehensive description of ice cream making in French appeared in *La maison reglée*, published the same year as the *Scalco alla moderna*. Tellingly, the French cookbook spells out on the front cover that the volume contains instructions on "the true method for making all sorts of water essences and liqueurs, strong and refreshing in the Italian style." Its author, Nicolas Audiger, claimed he had learned the art in his youth, some thirty years earlier in Italy. Afterward, he would work for some of the most notable members of Louis XIV's court, including Colbert, the king's powerful first minister, before opening up his own confectionary shop. Audiger was much more explicit in spelling out just how to make his *crème glacée* as well as his many *eaux glacées*. They are made by placing one bucket inside another, filling the space in between with ice and salt, and stirring the interior until it reaches "snow" consistency.[58] The French mostly called ice cream "*neige*" until the mid-1700s, even while the contraptions used to make it continued to be called by the Italian name *sorbetier*. Though, just to make things confusing, in France, a "sorbet" continued to be a drink. Audiger's *eaux* or syrups are, to all intents and purposes, Turkish sorbets, flavored with everything from flowers and spices to those Middle Eastern favorites, musk and amber. The author made it clear that they could be served either chilled or frozen.

In Vienna too, confectioners picked up the method of making ice cream from Italian sources, as did the English and the Germans. By 1770, an Italian, Giovanni Bosio, had even set up an ice cream shop in New York City, where the frozen confection was still somewhat of a rarity—if not for long.

By the eighteenth century, if not earlier, the Parisians and the Viennese had adapted the imported techniques to local tastes. By this point, Italy was no longer setting the fashion. In Naples,

Venice, and Turin, the upper classes were increasingly aping the manners of France. By the nineteenth century the French finally succeeded in their conquest of proud Italy, even if this was limited to the dining rooms of the elite. Count Cavour, the first prime minister of a united Italy, would send his chef to be trained in France, while the Italian royal family was eating "macaroni à la Parisienne."

PAVÉS DE VENISE

In Venice, the Pasticceria Tonolo proudly displays the gold medal it won in 1909 in Paris for its sweet focaccia. The pastry shop is in the same neighborhood as Colussi's old workshop, an easy ten-minute amble across two squares and two bridges. Yet in other respects it is a world apart. Where Colussi's shop was spare, even ascetic (if such a term can be used for a pastry shop), Tonolo sports a long refrigerated counter with three stories glistening in shades of chocolate brown and custard gold, all devoted to variations on crispness and cream. Behind the counter, fat glass jars spill over with gaudy candy, while glass shelves that reach to the ceiling display fancy packets of cookies and chocolates. At ten o'clock on a weekday morning the *pasticceria* is packed. Businessmen refill on an espresso and a jam-filled *cornetto* (croissant) while mothers in Prada order birthday cakes for their *bambini* between cell phone calls. In the background, ladies of a certain age linger and chat over a macchiato and *Krapfen* (filled doughnuts), burying their teeth carefully into the gently yielding dough so that the cream doesn't spurt onto their Fendi scarves and the powdered sugar doesn't disturb their morning's laboriously applied maquillage.

Everything is a little daintier here. The *bussolai* are crisp little circles the size of a doll's wristband. "Ours are more *rafinati* [refined]," the owner, Franco Tonolo, assures me. Franco gives the impression of a lab technician charged with handling volatile explosives. As soon as he is introduced, he flits off to ward off any potential disaster, leaving me to his affable cousin Giuliana Tonolo Piarotto to tell the family story. The *pasticceria* dates to 1886, when Giuseppe Tonolo opened a shop in Mirano, a small town on the mainland scarcely a dozen miles from Venice. Wealthy Venetians used to spend the autumns there hunting, and the little café became a gathering spot for the local gentry. Giuliana tells me that it was one of these *nobili* who took her great-grandfather's focaccia to the Paris show in one of their newfangled automobiles. "A poor *pasticciere* could never have afforded the trip," she explains. In 1953, part of the family (a shop still exists in Mirano) moved the business to the current location in Venice. "My grandmother was *famosissima* for her pastry cream," Giuliana boasts. The comment says a great deal about the French influence here. Parenthetically, it also points to the very different role played by professional women in Italy and France.

Though Tonolo makes all the traditional Venetian desserts for the holidays—the *fritelle* for carnival, *pinza* for Epiphany—what it is really known for is desserts like cream puffs and Paris Brest (the same idea but in the form of a large ring) filled with a very French *crème pâtissière*. Perhaps their most delicious dessert is something called a "creme," which resembles a Napoleon made of layers of custard cream and marsala-soaked *pan di Spagna* contained by ineffably thin layers of puff pastry top and bottom. Franco tells me the French refer to these as *pavés de Venise*. It is arguably equal parts France and Italy, much like Italian pastry today.

The other point that Giuliana inadvertently makes underlines how central women are to Italy's culinary tradition. It was her grandmother, not her grandfather, who was famous for the pastry cream. This was true in the next generation as well. Franco stops by to briefly explain: "My father made the pastry, but my mother made the cream." In Paris, the pastry profession has long been an almost exclusively male enterprise. (This is also true for cities as disparate as Vienna and Kolkata.) Women may be in the front of the shop selling the wares, but it is the master (not mistress) *pâtissier* who is in the back. Which is not say that Frenchwomen have not been baking, or even selling, pastries since time immemorial, it's just that their creations were traditionally not as valued as those produced by professional male artisans. In Italy, where the lines between the home and professional kitchen are much more blurred than in France, women tend to get more credit.

When it comes to pastry, Venice wasn't the only Italian city to come under French influence. This was especially true close to the French border. Given its proximity, it's hardly surprising that pastry shops in Turin (the capital of Piedmont) are sometimes hard to distinguish from those of nearby Lyon. Turin's *pasticcieri* are justly renowned for their *sfoglia di pere* (a puff pastry tart with pears), *torte di frutta* (fruit tarts with a base of pastry cream), *Saint-Honoré*, *profiterole* (when fried, also known as *bignè*, from the French *beignet*), *troncheto* (aka *bûche de Noël*), *crème caramel*, and many other stalwarts of the Gallic repertoire. This is nothing new. In the late eighteenth century, *Il Confetturiere Piemontese* ("The Piedmontese Confectioner") was packed with French sweets. Though written in Italian, the book is full of French kitchen jargon. There are recipes for "*gatteau*" and "*maroni glacé*" (candied chestnuts), but even desserts of Italian origin were reimported under strangely miscegenated names. The *Confetturiere*'s "*pasta di maccheroni*" has nothing to do with noodles; it is simply a mutation of the French almond cookie, the *macaron*. Even his *biscottini* are little cakes, the French *biscuits*, rather than the twice-baked cookies long familiar to his countrymen.

Yet even far from the frontier, in Naples, that bastion of pizza and *maccheroni*, you find French desserts. The *sfogliatelle* (discussed above) is probably the city's most identifiable sweet, but the local version of a French baba comes a close second. Every pastry shop has its *babà al rum*, every tourist shop its jars packed with baby *babà* bathing in syrup. The dessert's arrival can be traced to the nineteenth-century fad for all things French that swept European dining rooms, including those in the ancient city. Here too, every fashionable family needed its *"monsù"* chef imported from France making his signature *crèmes*, *gateaux*, and *baba au rhum*. Somewhere in the process of adoption, the French, ring-shaped baba turned into the mushroom-shaped confection featured in every Neapolitan pastry shop. Today, it is vastly more popular here than in France, where it doesn't quite fit into contemporary ideas of confectionary. Neapolitans are so fond of the dessert that the name is used as an endearment. *"Si nu' baba,"* you are a baba, is an expression that means, more or less, "you're the real deal" or "you're hot stuff," depending on your intentions.[60]

Fast Lives, Slow Food

In the twenty-first century, Italians continue to celebrate the two great Christian festivals, Christmas and Easter, with sweet yeast breads, with the *colomba*, the *pandoro*, but most especially the panettone. More than likely, these come in a cardboard box, packaged and produced in some large factory. Although artisanal producers still produce some, these holiday cakes have become a huge international business dominated by enormous industrial bakeries, especially Verona's Bauli. The company got its start in the 1920s producing Veronese specialties in an unlikely place: Argentina. Like so many Italians searching for a better life abroad, Ruggero Bauli in 1927 boarded a ship to Argentina, where the young *pasticciere* made a success of himself. A decade later, having picked up the entrepreneurial ways of the New World, Ruggero returned home, where he was soon cranking out five thousand pastries a day. But it was really only with the return of peace in the 1950s that the enterprise was set on track to become the behemoth it is today. In 2009, the company bought two major competitors, Motta and Alemagna, making it the unchallenged leader in the sweet bread market. In 2007, Italian bakers produced 117 million panettone and *pandoro* cakes worth 579 million euros for the Christmas season alone.[61] The industrial confections are cheap and readily available. An artisanal focaccia or panettone can set you back fifty euros, but the shrink-wrapped ones sold in suburban hypermarkets can often been had for less than ten. As a result, most pastry shops don't even bother to compete.

But does this mean that panettone has entirely lost its symbolic value? I don't think so. It's just that its significance has shifted a little. Though hardly anyone would associate it with the return of the sun at winter solstice, it has picked up other meanings along the way. To Italians, this formerly regional pastry is now a marker of Italian identity. The supermarket cart with its boxed seasonal sweet cuts across regional and class barriers. That it is affordable to everyone is a sign of national prosperity, something that many Italians still do not take for granted.

Like Italy itself, Italian food is changing, but that has always been the case. Italians are relatively conservative in their eating habits; they do travel widely, however, and inevitably pick up some foreign tastes to bring home. *Cucina Italiana*, the country's preeminent cooking magazine, regularly features recipes for such things as roast beef with mango, and "cheese cake allo yogurt e frutta." In Venice, Tonolo now sells brownies as well as Paris Brest and *fritelle alla veneziana*. Society is transforming as well. The Italian family has been radically downsized, which does not bode well for the future of home cooking. Venetians and Romans alike complain that it is only the grandmothers who now cook—everyone else reheats or goes out for dinner. As elsewhere in the developed world, cooking is now increasingly in the hands of professional chefs and test kitchen directors of multimillion-euro companies.

Of course pastry has always been largely in the hands of professionals, but even for the pros it is now ever easier to cut corners. Franco Tonolo complains that many bakeries now buy their *Krapfen* frozen and then simply fry them as needed. "It is so much more convenient for them," he grumbles. During the prime baking seasons before Christmas and Easter, he gets up at six or even four in the morning and may not finish until nine at night. The medal-winning focaccia needs to be handled every four hours; the dough must rise four times to achieve the right consistency. No wonder the bakers would rather buy their doughnuts frozen and resell panettone made in a factory. Certain segments of Italian society became so outraged by the trend toward factory-made food that they started the now worldwide Slow Food movement. That they even found this necessary (in Italy!) may mean that the war has already been lost.

Yet when it comes to dessert, at least, I am not despondent. Even average *sfogliatelle* in Naples shatter into exquisite shards, confectioners in Siena, Pisa, and Florence make *panforte* as they have since the Medicis were in the banking business, and just about every Italian city seems to have an artisanal *gelateria* where the ice cream mix doesn't come from a factory. And even in tourist-overrun Venice, Tonolo is packed with customers who can tell the difference between a frozen doughnut and the store's cloudlike *Krapfen*.

Focaccia Pasquale
Venetian Easter Cake

Enriched yeast cakes, or breads—if you will—are likely the oldest pastry on the planet, dating back to at least ancient Sumer. (See page 84.) The tradition can be traced through ancient Greece, ancient Rome, and right through today's brioche. More often than not the cakes had some sort of religious tie-in. This is certainly true of the Milanese panettone and its Venetian equivalent, focaccia, or "*fugassa*" and "*fugazza*" in the local dialect. The latter is typical for Easter (and sometimes for Christmas as well). Unlike panettone, it does not usually contain candied fruit. It is also squatter in shape. Nonetheless, as with all Italian recipes, the ingredients do vary. Many contain lemon rind, for example, instead of the orange rind called for here. This particular version is very loosely adapted from Giampiero Rorato's *La grande cucina veneziana*. Along with the Asian spices once so typical of Venetian cooking, the recipe lists iris root, which was once used to simulate a violet smell in perfumes and even wine. In Venice, this is now as obscure as it is here. It is sometimes sold as an herbal supplement, so if you want to experiment, go ahead. Just be careful you don't come up with something that smells like an old lady's boudoir.

Makes a 2¼-pound cake

½ ounce active dry yeast (2 packages)
⅔ cup tepid milk
14 ounces (about 4 cups) unbleached all-purpose flour
3 tablespoons grappa
1 teaspoon vanilla extract
½ teaspoon ground cinnamon
Large pinch ground cloves
2 teaspoons grated orange rind
6 egg yolks
5 ounces (10 tablespoons) unsalted butter, softened
3½ ounces (about 1 cup) bread flour
¾ cup granulated sugar
¼ teaspoon salt
1 egg white, lightly beaten with 1 tablespoon water
Slivered almonds
Coarsely granulated sugar

1. Stir the yeast into the milk. Let stand until dissolved. Stir in 5¼ ounces of the all-purpose flour. Cover with plastic wrap until the mixture doubles in size, about 30 minutes. Combine the grappa with the vanilla, spices, and orange rind. Cover and set aside.

2. Using the dough hook attachment in the bowl of a stand mixer, stir 3 egg yolks and half the butter into the risen yeast mixture. Stir together 3½ ounces of the all-purpose flour with the bread flour and half the sugar. Gradually add to the yeast mixture and mix on low speed until smooth and elastic, about 5 minutes. Cover with plastic wrap and allow to rise until doubled (about 2 hours). Stir together the remaining flour with the remaining sugar and the salt. Stir together the remaining egg yolks and the grappa mixture. Add both of these to the risen dough along with the remaining butter. Knead once again until smooth and elastic. Cover once again and let stand until doubled (3–4 hours).

3. In the meantime, prepare an 8-inch springform pan by lining the sides with a 4-inch-wide strip of parchment paper. You can "glue" the parchment to the pan with softened butter. Also lightly butter the bottom of the pan.

4. Once the dough has risen, form it into a smooth ball and transfer it to the prepared pan. Cover with plastic wrap. Allow to rise one final time until doubled (4–6 hours). Very carefully brush the top with the egg white and sprinkle with slivered almonds and coarsely granulated sugar.

5. Preheat oven to 350°F. Bake until golden and a tester comes out clean, about 1 hour. Cool completely before serving. Focaccia lasts for several days loosely wrapped at room temperature.

4

LET THEM EAT CAKE

❋ *France* ❋

ALI BABA AND OTHER TALES

Rue Montorgueil doesn't rank very high on most Parisian tourists' itinerary. It's a plain, rather ordinary commercial strip running due north from Forum Les Halles, the grubby shopping mall that replaced the French capital's wonderful old wholesale market. The street does, however, boast a monument that no dessert lover should miss: at No. 51 is Patisserie Stohrer, the city's oldest pastry shop.

The road didn't have much more charm in 1730 when the twenty-four-year-old Nicolas Stohrer opened his patisserie on what was then called rue du Mont Orgueilleux. But the location, though hardly fashionable, saw many of the city's well-coiffed trendsetters pass by its front window. Across the street was the auberge du Compas d'Or, the terminal of stagecoaches from the north, and right next door was a depot where the dusty aristocrats fetched their sedan chairs to conduct them to their gilded townhouses. In this respect the pastry shop was perfectly placed for picking up a snack for the long stagecoach voyage out or a little something to take home. Young Nicolas wasn't just depending on the handy location, though, to draw in the leisure class; he was also banking on his reputation as a former cook to Louis XV and his Polish queen, Marie Leszczinska. At Versailles, the story goes, he had become known for a sweet, yeasty cake called a baba. The French baba, in case you're only familiar with the Italian version, is today typically made in the form of a ring cake and heavily soaked with rum syrup. Stohrer continues to have a reputation for the finest version in town.

Nicolas owed his start to Marie's father, the exiled Polish king Stanislaw Leszczynski. The monarch had been deposed in 1709, following which he had spent the next ten years in Germany just across the Alsatian frontier. Then, with financial help from the French royal family, he moved a few miles south of the border into Alsace proper. There, in the town of Wissembourg, he set up house with his family and a half-dozen or so retainers in a comfortable chateau.[1] It was here that a local boy, Nicolas Stohrer, got a job scrubbing pots and scraping carrots for the grand meals that were expected of even a has-been king. I can't imagine that Stanislaw suffered too much in exile. The king, now in his fifties, was a devoted bookworm and must have relished the time he could spend in his library. He was, according to later reports, also known as a gourmet and even an amateur cook. The noted food journalist Grimod de La Reynière claimed that it was the Polish king himself who invented the baba. (Admittedly the reporter was an infant when Stanislaw died.) Not unexpectedly, the owners of Patisserie Stohrer assert that it was young Nicolas who created it, though they give credit to the aging king for its name. According to their delightfully implausible story, the king took a bite of the cake, which was supposedly soaked in fortified wine, while reading the recently translated *Thousand and One Nights*. In his enthusiasm for the new confection, he christened it "Ali-Baba," later shortened to baba.

The French love to tell anecdotes about their food, and if some eminent person can be attached to a dish, so much the better. Some of the tales happen to be true, many are made up, but in most cases the stories are like a napoleon or *millefeuille* made up of layers of crisp fact and frothy fiction. Pulling it apart neatly is almost impossible. What's more, once you've scraped away all the fluff, the truth you are left with can be a little dry.

Baba, as more credible French authorities point out, is nothing more than the Polish name for a *Kugelhopf*, or what Americans call a bundt cake.* In Alsace today, a *kouglof* or *kougelhopf* (as they spell it) is a magnificent tall thing, like some towering medieval crown. It belongs to that Europe-wide tradition of baking enriched yeast breads for weddings and baptisms, and especially for Easter, that dates back to at least the Middle Ages. It's unclear whether it was already made in Alsace when Stanislaw arrived, but it was certainly commonplace in other parts of the German-speaking world. In Augsburg, these decorated ring cakes were so ordinary that they were listed on a 1690 menu at a Lutheran orphanage. Eleanora of Lichtenstein included a recipe for Kugel-Hopff in a popular medical guide and cookbook first published in 1697. Eleanora was the duchess of Troppau and Jägerndorf in Silesia, then on the Bohemian–Polish frontier, so it's safe to assume the recipe was also familiar in next-door Poland.[2] The only thing that Stanislaw had to do with its invention was that he made it popular in France under its Polish name, "baba" being so much more amenable to

---

* The name *Kugelhupf* (also *Gugelhopf* or *Gugelhupf*), from the German meaning "ball-head," probably originates from the term for a hairdo of tightly coiled braids, which the cake resembles. The early ones weren't always made in a ring mold but rather in a decorated pan that does indeed look like an elaborate hairdo. In this, the cake is related to all those braided loaves common in the Mediterranean. The term "bundt cake" or *Bund* (also *Bunt*) *Küche* comes much later, most likely in the mid-nineteenth century. *Bundt* means circle or collar, an obvious reference to the cake form. The cake may have been introduced into the United States by German Jews. One of the earliest recipes appears in *"Aunt Babette's" Cookbook*, a Jewish collection first published in 1889.

the Gallic tongue than the Germanic original. The king's pastry cook, however, may have played some part in introducing it to the French court, since he tagged along when the exiled monarch's twenty-two-year-old daughter, Marie, married the fifteen-year-old Louis XV and moved to Versailles. It's altogether plausible that Nicolas's "baba" featured on the queen's breakfast table.

In another mythical retelling of the baba's royal conception, Stanislaw accidentally spills his favorite sweet Malaga wine on the dry cake (or alternatively dips it in). Of course, there is no reason to think that people didn't dip slices of *Kugelhopf* into wine, hot chocolate, or any other beverage, but soaking it beforehand was most definitely not part of the early recipe. Wine does occasionally appear, but as an ingredient in the dough; it was not bathed in syrup as it is today. Grimod de La Reynière, in this case writing of what he knew firsthand, pointed out in 1808 that "the principal flavoring of the baba is saffron and Corinth raisins [dry currants]." Contemporary cookbooks bear him out.

Just when soaking the cake in rum, or any liquor, actually became part of the recipe is hard to pinpoint. *Baba au rhum* only begins to show up in the mid-1800s, most likely as a belated consequence of the vogue, in the earlier part of the century, for English-style punch made with Caribbean rum. Before the French Revolution of 1789, there was never much of a French rum industry because of prohibitive trade barriers designed to protect mainland brandy producers. "Le punch," a journalist noted in 1805, "is a drink that became fashionable first in England and then France, especially after 1789. . . . All the Parisian cafés now serve *punch au rhum*."[3] It took until the 1840s for rum to became a popular flavoring in desserts, showing up in recipes for jellies, frostings, and of course Stanislaw's baba.

In most cases, the French penchant for associating dishes with famous men (and, less frequently, women) is obscured by the shadows of time, but the story of baba's first cousin, the sava-

rin, sheds light on how this might work. In 1845, one of Paris'
most highly respected pastry shops was located on the place de la
Bourse, right next door to the Paris stock exchange. It was run by
three brothers with the family name Julien. Presumably inspired
by the recent success of the rum-soaked baba, the youngest
brother, August, decided to do his own spin on the trendy dessert, replacing the raisins with finely chopped candied orange
rind and soaking the dessert with a syrup based on kirsch instead
of rum.[4] (In later years the ring would be filled with cream, but
this wasn't the case at first.) The idea that any culinary "invention" appears out of the blue is nonsense. Most new dishes are
really no more than a variation on a previously familiar theme.
Over time, an accumulation of changes really does transform
a cuisine, but it doesn't happen overnight. But no matter how
original it really was, the Julien brothers needed to figure out
what to call the new dessert. There is no way of knowing how
many names the brothers debated at the brainstorming session
that came up with "savarin" in honor of Jean Anthelme Brillat-
Savarin, France's most famous food writer and gourmand, but
the name stuck. In a similar vein, they named another cake after
the renowned diplomat and bon vivant Charles-Maurice de Talleyrand. If the savarin weren't so well documented, it's easy to
see how people might begin to think that Brillat-Savarin was the
dessert's inventor rather than just its namesake. This doubtless
occurred with many more obscure foods. At least where the baba
is concerned, the connection between the dessert and the celebrated Polish gourmet is more plausible than the wacky assertion made by one writer in 1899 that the *Kugelhopf* was created
by a prelate named Gérard Kugelhopf![5]

At Stohrer, the original saffron-tinted baba is now available
only by special order, but that doesn't come as too great a hardship since three other babas are regularly in stock: a baba rum,
another filled with pastry cream, and a third filled with whipped

cream. The shop doesn't just specialize in eighteenth-century desserts; there are additions from the following century as well. You can buy old-fashioned treats like the *puits d'amour* ("wells of love"), which in this case are tarts filled with caramel-flavored cream, as well as the *religieuse*, a sort of teepee of éclairs and cream that is meant to resemble a nun's habit.* There are modern sweets too, like the now ubiquitous filled *macarons*. Nicolas and his successors did well by his business, making it through a baker's dozen of wars and revolutions. The stories about his baba may be no more than fanciful confections, but the hard fact is that his shop is still there almost three hundred years after he first fired up his ovens.

MEDIEVAL FRANCE

The world that Nicolas Stohrer was born into was in many ways much closer to the Middle Ages than it was to the present. In his day, French society resembled a finely crafted model of the pre-Copernican universe, composed of separate worlds, each with its own rules and order, all rotating around a fixed center, the king. When Nicolas quit working for the queen and set up shop in Paris, he automatically left the sphere of the aristocrats and relocated to the planet of the town dwellers. He now had a different status and had to follow other rules. Whereas, in ancien régime France, a pastry cook in private employ could make whatever he pleased, once he opened up his own shop he had to join the pastry makers guild and abide by its regulations. These allowed him to make pastries both sweet and savory—not only babas and sugared cheese tarts but also meat pies filled with lark, pigeon, capon, ham, and the like, as well as fish pies for Lenten days.

---

* According to the nineteenth-century pastry chef and author Pierre Lacam, the *religieuse* was originally created at the Frascati patisserie in 1836.

Guild members could also sell *gaufres* or waffles and thin wafers rolled into cylinders or cornets called *oublies*.[6] Sugar work, on the other hand, was strictly off-limits.

Four and Twenty Blackbirds Baked in a Pie

The Middle Ages were the golden age of pie. No Italian banquet was complete without its *torte*, and no French fête could do without its *pastés*. But these were hardly our idea of pie. Admittedly, there were custard tarts and cheese tarts, the ancestors of *tarte au citron* and cheesecake. Fruit pies were not unheard-of. Mostly, though, pies were filled with meat—or fish for fast days. However, don't imagine that these were like contemporary English meat pies, or French pâtés *en croute*. In many cases the pastry enclosed whole beasts or their chopped-up bits. Occasionally the casing would be baked blind (empty) and filled with live critters, such as blackbirds, to amaze the diners once the lid was removed. More often than not, the dough was no more than a paste of (cheap) rye flour and water, as tough and inedible as papier-mâché. The 1653 *Pastissier françois* instructs readers to make it one or two inches thick, especially if the pie was to be transported any distance. There were also occasionally more delicate crusts made with wheat flour that incorporated butter. The butter was either worked into the dough, much as you would for a cookie, or alternately layered with a flour-water paste to make puff pastry. The traditional English technique (that Americans use to make pie dough), where fat is cut into flour before adding water, didn't use to be common in France.

Where the French picked up the puff pastry idea isn't entirely clear. The *Pastissier françois* contains the first recipe for *pâte feuilletée* as it is known today. It instructs the reader to make a dough of flour, salt, and water, cover this with an equal layer of butter, fold it in half, roll it out again, then repeat this five times. There's an earlier Turkish recipe for a kind of simple puff pastry to be used in making baklava in a manuscript from around 1600 that is made by folding over the dough twice and then re-rolling it, but there's no reason to think that there is any relationship with the French recipe. More plausibly, the French version may have been an adaptation of the old Arabic technique (common in both Renaissance Italy and Spain), where fat-smeared dough was rolled into a cylinder before being flattened again. This is the recipe Lancelot de Casteau included in his cookbook fifty years earlier, calling it "pour faire pastéz d'espaigne fueiltéz" or how to make Spanish puff pastry. Or was the folded version a purely French creation? There is a reference to something called a *gâteau feuillé* as early as 1311, though any assumptions about how it was made are pure speculation. We are probably on safer ground with the menu given in honor of Catherine de Médicis's coronation; it included "Quarante plats de petits feuilletage," or forty plates of little puff pastries.[7] Though whether they were made "in the Spanish style" or the French, we'll never know. What is certain is that the technique of folding the dough won the day.

There are several texts that document the medieval French approach to food in general and pastry in particular. When it comes to the realm of the medieval bourgeoisie, a much-quoted source is a volume of advice and recipes from the end of the four-teenth century known as the *Ménagier de Paris* (Goodman of Paris). In it, an upper-middle-class husband of some experience gives his wife exhaustive advice on everything from menus to sexual guidance to gardening tips. The book was written in troubled times. Paris had been devastated by repeated bouts of the plague ever since the Black Death visited the great city in 1348, causing the demise of more than half of its population to disease. During this period, France was also embroiled in the Hundred Years' War against England. Then there were the popular uprisings that periodically wrenched the capital, most recently in 1382. Yet, as the *Ménagier* makes clear, there continued to be weddings as well as funerals.

The book includes several menus for marriage feasts with exquisitely detailed shopping instructions that, handily, even include prices. Much of the food for these sorts of events was catered by local suppliers who, as in most other European towns, were divided up into guilds, each of which had a legal monopoly in its own specialty. To replicate the menu of one wedding, the *ménagier* sends his wife (or her servants) to the bread baker, the butcher, the poulterer, the sauce maker, and the *oubloier* (waferer). At this last stop she is to buy several varieties of wafers as well as sugared *galettes*, small cakes. These were apparently intended as a special treat for the maids of honor.[8] Given how cheap they were, they must have been really small or not very sweet. Sugar was even pricier here than in Italy. In Paris, the sugar imported from the Mediterranean cost almost as much as the cinnamon and ginger that had traveled half the world to get there. According to the *Ménagier's* numbers, the price of a pound of sugar could have bought you eighty capons or a couple of whole pigs! Other contemporary sources bear this out. Nevertheless, it wouldn't do to have a wedding feast without sugar and spices, so the young wife also drops by the *épicier* or spice seller, who also sold candy and such. (The term "spice" had a rather broad meaning in those days.) Here she is told to pick up some candied orange and citron rind, sugared almonds, rosewater, candy, and sugar-coated anise.[9] You served these so-called *épices de chambre* or "parlor spices" at the conclusion of a meal.

The *Ménagier* includes plenty of sample menus for his inexperienced bride to consult, and not just for weddings. The bills of fare usually consist of three or four courses, each one made up of an assortment of dishes. Sweetened preparations show up with some regularity and generally toward the end of the meal. Crêpes and *rissoles* (sweetened fritters) are fairly common; the most frequent sweet item, however, is blancmange (or "blanc mangier" as the *Ménagier* writes it). This, you will recall, is the spiced, sweetened pudding we've met in Italy and the Middle East made by cooking down poultry and almond milk. In France, blancmange (also called a *brouet*) was sometimes tinted different colors and carefully arranged to make a pattern. We know, for example, that during his visit to France in 1377, the Holy Roman Emperor Charles IV was served a *brouet* striped with green and white at a multicourse state banquet. Dishes based on fresh cheese, or curds as the British call them, were popular too. The soft cheese was folded into batters and used in tart fillings. *Lait lardé*, or a similar concoction called *tourtes de lait*, was made by cooking egg yolks in milk until they curdled or alternatively curdling hot milk with wine and sour grape juice. This was then drained and pressed much like Indian *paneer* before being fried in slices and sprinkled with sugar.[10] It's tempting to see in these sorts of sweets the later French affection for creamy custards and mousses, though they were still some way off from crème caramel.

Still, one would be hard-pressed to call any of the *Ménagier*'s sweet dishes dessert in the modern sense. As in Italy, they are served right beside the meat and fish dishes, which were themselves sometimes showered with sugar. Yet even while there is seldom a course made up entirely of sweet dishes, the term *dessert* (here spelled "desserte") does show up a couple of times. The French noun *dessert* originates with the verb *desservir*, or unserve, that is, to remove what has been served. In other words, *le dessert* was set out once the table had been cleared of the dishes that made up the main part of the meal. In the *Ménagier's* menus it is mentioned as a penultimate course, before the so-called *issue*. In one case, it consists of frumenty (a wheat-based pudding) and venison, neither one of which is apparently sweetened; in the second menu where the word is used, it is made up of a preserve (probably made with honey), candied almonds, fritters, tarts, and dried fruit. This, finally, does begin to approach our idea of dessert, though it would be centuries before the expression came to signify what it does today.[11] The only consistently sweet course at this time was the *issue*, served once the meal was done. It typically consisted of wafers and *hypocras*, the sweet spiced wine served in medieval times as a digestif. Those candied "spices" bought at the *épicier* were common too, as were fruit and nuts.

Even if there wasn't a dessert course per se, the taste for sweetness was increasing in France as in the rest of Europe. As elsewhere, using sugar was surely a sign of wealth and influence in medieval France, though its use was still quite limited at the end of the fourteenth century. You would expect this in the *Ménagier*, which was, after all, addressed to the merely affluent, but even at the pinnacle of society, sugar was a sometime thing. In the 1392 version of the *Viandier*, a recipe collection attributed to Taillevent, chief cook of Charles V, there are, if anything, even fewer sweetened dishes. If any deductions at all can be made from the royal cookbook, it is that, at the time, sugar was predominantly used as a seasoning for fish or as an additive to foods intended for invalids. In both cases, this may have sprung from the medieval medical theory of the four humors. Supposedly sugar had heating properties and thus would balance the cold nature of fish

and warm up those who were suffering from "colds." To make
a Lenten "flan" or "tarte," Taillevent ground up three kinds of
freshwater fish with some almonds, saffron, and wine. This was
then baked in a pastry shell and finished off with a sprinkle of
sugar. (The *Ménagier* has virtually the same recipe.)

Did medieval Parisians just not have a sweet tooth, or was it
simply a matter of supply determining demand? No hard numbers exist on how much sugar actually made it to Paris, but, given
the sweetener's extraordinary price, it couldn't have been much.
Later, when Venetian and then Portuguese sugar flooded into
the market in the fifteenth century, the French turned out to be
almost as enthusiastic as the Italians in showering their dishes
with the sweet crystals. You can track this growing infatuation
because a set of related recipes under the title *Viandier* exists as
early as 1300 and keeps reappearing right through the seventeenth century. The cookbook's first version has no sugar whatsoever; a hundred years later there are a score or so sweetened recipes. But by the 1450s, there are sweet recipes in every course.[12]
Sugar is stirred into every form of *brouet* and *blancmange*; used
to season soups, stews, and galantines; added to a roast mutton
stuffing, sprinkled on roast poussins, and stirred into a sauce for
pheasants and peacocks. There are also sweetened recipes that
we would recognize as dessert: a bread and a rice pudding, an
almond custard, cheese tarts and pear tarts. However, the line
between sweet and savory is as yet fuzzy. The majority of the
Viandier's tarts and pies are still mostly filled with meat and fish,
and, yes, these too get their helping of sugar.

Compare cookbooks across Europe on the eve of the Renaissance and certain universals become clear: the ubiquitous use of
spice, the everpresent pies, the meat, fish, and almonds beaten to
a mush, into the *brouet*, or *Mus* as the Germans called it. Which
is not to say there weren't national differences. The French liked
a little more acidity in their food than their neighbors and used

a wide variety of spice. Central Europeans kept their food a little simpler. Italy, in the meantime, became increasingly infatuated with sweetness, a vogue that they exported along with their sugar loaves. Admittedly, whether the northerners followed suit in the sixteenth century because they were emulating Italian fashions or simply because they now had access to Venetian and Genoan sugar is difficult to prove with any confidence. What is incontrovertible is that the 1500s would prove to be a century of sweet food all across Europe, and one way or another, the Italians were the source.

CATHERINE DE MÉDICIS

Poor Caterina de' Medici! Or Catherine de Médicis as the French called her—even as they cursed her name. After her death, the Italian-born queen was pilloried for having too much political sway in her adopted land. In more recent years, her alleged influence on French food habits has been ridiculed by food historians who (correctly) point out that neither artichokes nor ice cream arrived in France with her retinue. But that was hardly her fault.

Catherine didn't have it easy from the start. Her mother, a French countess, died a fortnight after her daughter's birth, and her father, a golden boy of the Medici banker clan, succumbed to what was most likely syphilis a few days later.[13] The little girl was subsequently shuttled between relatives and convents, a pawn of family and dynastic politics. At the age of fourteen, she was married off to the French prince Henri, second in line to the French throne and the same age as his bride.

The two were united in Marseille in 1533, with appropriate pomp and circumstance, at a wedding presided over by Catherine's uncle, Pope Clement VI, and the French king Francis I. No details remain about what was served at the banquets, but they were surely as grand as anything seen in Venice at the time. According to one legend, Italian ice cream makers first introduced the frozen dessert to France at this time. Given that ice cream didn't exist yet in Italy, this is highly improbable. It can, however, be safely assumed that Italian confectioners were part of the pope's party. Visiting northern French aristocrats (and their cooks) must have been exposed to an endless parade of Italian sugar sculptures and sweetmeats during the banquets given by the pontiff and his Italian entourage. How could they *not* be impressed by all this Médicis splendor?

It's worth remembering that in the glory days of the Italian Renaissance, France and its capital were a bit of a backwater, caught up in the fighting of the Hundred Years' War with the English in the first half of the fifteenth century and largely abandoned by the French kings in favor of their country estates in the second. In northern Europe, the only cities that came even close to Florence and Venice were the wealthy Flemish towns, which, under the rule of the Dukes of Burgundy, became the cultural centers of the French-speaking world. Not that they were especially French. The courtiers at the ducal palace in Brussels were as likely to have grown up speaking Flemish or German as the language of Joan of Arc, and the merchants who assembled in Bruges and Ghent to trade German silver, English wool, and Russian furs for Genoese alum, Portuguese oranges, or Venetian sugar made the multilingual empire even more cosmopolitan. This multicultural influence persisted well into the sixteenth century as Flanders passed to the Hapsburg crown and Burgundy proper was absorbed into France.

This is apparent as late as 1604, with the publication of *Ouverture de cuisine*, a cookbook printed in the southern Flemish city of Liège. The author, Lancelot de Casteau, was apparently chief cook (or more likely steward) to several generations of local potentates and had absorbed influences from across Europe. Many of his recipes called for Italian ingredients like Parmesan and Bologna sausage. He also described how to make pasta dishes like "*rafio-ules*" (ravioli) and "*maquaron*" (*maccheroni*). This has led some scholars to speculate that he may have spent time in Italy. Yet, given the number of references to dishes from elsewhere—Spain, England, Ireland, Portugal, Catalonia, and even Hungary—isn't it just as likely that he was the inheritor of the worldly Flemish approach and that Italy was simply the trendiest influence on his cuisine? Certainly cinnamon, the spice so ubiquitous in Scappi and Messisbugo, is here in spades. And so is sugar, appearing in some ninety recipes from boiled Irish-style duck to Hungarian pancakes.

Admittedly, the influence of Catherine de Médicis and other Italians on French cuisine during the sixteenth century may have been overstated in the past, but that doesn't mean there was none whatsoever. Across Europe, the zeitgeist was decidedly Italian. Shakespeare knew where the action was when he set his plays in glamorous Venice and Verona. The first printed cookbook to be extensively disseminated internationally was a Roman collection of recipes and diet advice named *De honesta voluptate* in its original Latin. Subsequently it was translated into French in 1505, German in 1541, and Dutch in 1560. The dozens of Latin editions must have also circulated widely as well. Perhaps an even greater runaway success was Girolamo Ruscelli's *Secreti del revendo donno Allessio piemontese*, which is more a compilation of medical and alchemical prescriptions than a cookbook but nevertheless contains numerous confectionary recipes. French-language editions were printed in Antwerp (1557) and Lyon (1564). But even Italian cookbooks in the original must have been consulted in foreign courts. Today, France's Bibliothèque Nationale has many more copies of Bartolomeo Scappi's comprehensive opus than the Italian national library. Tellingly, one of these is imprinted with Catherine's coat of arms.

The method of cultural dissemination wasn't always so benign. The reason that Catherine had been married off to Henri was because of French ambitions in the Italian peninsula. Starting in 1494, and for the next fifty years, French kings kept crossing the Alps to make their various dynastic claims stick. As a result Charles VIII, Louis XII, Francis I, and Henri II and their courts all spent time in Italy. And war wasn't always hell. At any given time it seemed like half the Italians were inviting the invaders over for dinner even if the other half were showering them with cannonballs.

Henri wasn't the only French royal to be married to an Italian. Later in the century, Henri IV would marry Catherine's distant cousin Marie de Médicis. This meant that for all but a dozen years, between 1547 and 1617, an Italian-born queen (or queen mother) resided at the pinnacle of French power. Needless to say, both women wielded enormous influence at court, though it is generally Catherine who is credited with bringing the Italian Renaissance to France. That is probably an overstatement. Equal billing should be given to her father-in-law, Francis I, who collected Italian artists like they were going out of style. Leonardo da Vinci was only the most famous of his acquisitions.

Initially, the young Italian bride mostly remained in the shadows. Certainly Francis didn't have much use for his daughter-in-law when it seemed like she would never get pregnant. It was only once she bore her first child, ten years after the Marseille wedding, that she was grudgingly acknowledged. (She would eventually bear ten children.) Her status improved even more when first Henri's elder brother and then his father died. In 1547 she became queen of France. When her husband was killed in a jousting accident a dozen years later, she was in a position to take charge, initially as regent and then as the young king's overbearing mother. It was during those thirty years between 1559 and 1589 when she effectively ruled France, rather than when the teenage orphan first arrived in her adopted country, that the Italian influence became unmistakable. Just like her late father-in-law and her Médicis ancestors, she spent to impress, expending royal revenue on art and architecture. She became renowned for throwing spectacular festivals, complete with music and that new dance sensation, ballet. The queen mother was also, apparently, no wallflower at the dinner table. "Her appetite is enormous," the Venetian ambassador reported in 1561. "She is already a stout woman." A posthumous assessment by the chronicler Pierre l'Estoile made much the same point. "She ate heartily," he wrote, "feeding herself well."

From the 1550s onward, Italian nobles and financiers flocked to Paris, attracted by her patronage. Her chancellor (first minister) and chief marshal (war minister) were both Italians, but they were only the most notable among a growing gaggle. Hundreds of other well-born Italians snagged military or episcopal appointments, or were given pensions by the monarchy, much to the frequently expressed dismay of French noblemen. Given Catherine's spending habits and the crown's ever-inadequate revenue stream, the state's budget increasingly depended on bankers from Florence, Lucca, and Milan, all of whom set up shop in Paris.[14]

What's more, the Italian presence wasn't limited to the French court. One result of the French wars on the peninsula was that a steady stream of displaced Italian artisans emigrated north in the wake of the upper-class carpetbaggers. In Marseille and Lyon, the wealthiest bankers and merchants were Italian, but they were just the tip of the iceberg. One contemporary estimate put the number of Italians living in Lyon at twelve thousand. Even if that number is a little high, it's possible that as much as 20 percent of the town's population came from northern Italian city-states, drawn, in part, by Lyon's state-sponsored silk manufacture. In the second half of the sixteenth century, Italian entrepreneurs

and craftsmen were instrumental in setting up the manufacture
of satin, stockings, cotton, ribbons, silk faience, glass, mirrors,
and other luxury goods in France.

And what of that other artisanal luxury good, confectionary?
Here the evidence is skimpier. There are no records of how many
Italian cooks, bakers, and confectioners worked in the households of their wealthy countrymen, but surely the numbers must
have been considerable.

It is a fair guess that Italian confectioners introduced the
idea of grand sugar sculptures to the French court as well as the
fruit preserves so beloved south of the Alps. But can the French
adoption of the *biscuit*, especially the sponge cake called *biscuit
de Savoie*, be dated to this period? And what of *macarons* and
meringues?

When it came to confectionary, Paris was no Venice. This
is made clear from a bill from a banquet given by the burgers
of Paris to celebrate Catherine's coronation.[15] The meal, held at
the bishop's palace on June 19, 1549, was a catered affair. More
so than any cookbook, this bill reflects the state of the art of
French cuisine before the Italian influence took hold. Game was
still an obsession. The itemized receipt includes more than six
hundred game birds, forty hares, and eighty rabbits, as well as
scores of chicken, turkeys, and other expensive meats. The pastry
was supplied by a certain "Pierre Moreau, called Bridon, master *pâtissier* residing in Paris." His ovens must have been blazing day and night with the hundreds of pies and cakes ordered
for the occasion. Master Bridon's order is interesting for both
what it includes and what it omits. As one would expect for the
time, there are a half-dozen kinds of meat pies but also cream
tarts (*darioles de cresme*), date tarts, marzipan, choux pastry
rings, crescent-shaped cakes, stirrup-shaped cakes (*estris*), various wafers, little puff pastries, and "*tartres de Millan*" (a sort of
shortbread moistened with curds), as well as a couple of pastries

I can't identify.* Equally old-fashioned was the order for "spices, dragées, hippocras, wax and other drugs furnished for the feast" from Pierre Siguier, apothecary and spicer. In passing, it's worth noting the decline in the price of sugar. Now cakes of Madeira sugar cost about a quarter of the price of ginger (and less than a fifth of cinnamon) and were accordingly bought in much larger quantities, approximately fifteen pounds for this feast alone.** Nonetheless there were very few pastries and confections here that the wife of the *ménagier* would not have recognized over a century ago. There were none of the fruit preserves or the *biscuits* that would be popular in fifty years. Equally absent was the sugar work that characterized the fabulous feasts of Renaissance Italy. But that would change, and Catherine, Marie, and their courtiers surely had some hand in it.

Compare the feast given on the occasion of Catherine's coronation to a meal given in honor of Anne of Austria, the Medici queen's new daughter-in-law, in 1571. This, like the banquet twenty-two years earlier, was given by the wealthy burgers of Paris. The evening began with dinner, followed by dancing, and finished with a meal of sweetmeats (here referred to as a *collation*), all attended by the queen's son (now King Charles IX), his brothers, and other high-ranking nobles. It's revealing that the guests are said to have admired the novelty of the *collation*. In Catherine's native Florence, it would have barely merited notice. The spread included all the ingredients of a typical Italian *collazione*: preserves, both dry and liquid, sugared nuts, fruit pastes, marzipans, *biscuits*, and "every kind of fruit in the world." There

---

* The list includes *cheineaulx*, which may be a sort of curved wafer, but also *lésardeaux*, perhaps a zigzag-shaped cookie?[16]
** This, interestingly, is very close to the amount bought for an only somewhat smaller feast given in Venice for Renée of Ferrara fifteen years earlier. (See page 148.) Clearly the French taste for sweet-savory combinations wasn't too different from their southern neighbors. The confectionary was another matter.[17]

were even the sort of sugar sculptures for which Venetian apothecaries were famous. The main table was decorated with sugar
work representing the story of Minerva and how she brought
peace to Athens; tragacanth paste was also employed for trompe
l'oeil meat and fish.[18]

Thirty years later, Lancelot de Casteau's *Ouverture de cuisine*
is full of references to these sorts of Italian-inspired desserts.
Among them are *biscuit* and *grand biscuit succré*. The simple *biscuit*, mentioned in one of the book's sample menus, was presumably a cookie, while the *grand biscuit* noted elsewhere was likely
a sponge cake. As used here, the French word *biscuit*, which first
begins to refer to dessert in the sixteenth century, appears to have
migrated from the Italian. By the seventeenth century, the French
tend to use the term *biscuit* for various small and large cakes,
all based on *a pan di Spagna*–type sponge cake batter and never
require a secondary baking.* The Italian origin of these cakes is
made explicit in some cookbooks. The first guide ever devoted
to pastry, the 1653 *Le pastissier françois* (attributed to François
la Varenne), gives instructions for *biscuit de Piedmont*, made like
today's ladyfingers, as well as *biscuit de Savoie*, which has similar dough but is made in a mold a little like a madeleine. (Italians continue to call ladyfingers *savoiardi* after the Piedmontese
kingdom of Savoy.) A contemporaneous cookbook, written by
Nicolas de Bonnefons, makes the claim that *biscuit de Savoie* was
invented forty years earlier, a comment that probably shouldn't
be taken literally.[20] It may, however, point to a date when the Italian cake was likely adopted—and adapted—in northern France.

De Casteau, la Varenne, and Bonnefons all include a scattering of other Italian names and methods. One curiously named

---

* In medieval France (as elsewhere in Europe), *bescuit* and *becuit* had referred to a hard,
twice-cooked cracker or ship's hard-tack, and while this sort of *biscuit de mer* (sea biscuit)
continued to exist, it never appears in the post-Renaissance cookbooks.[19]

cookie that begins to appear in mid-seventeenth-century cookbooks is the *macarron* or *maccarron*. In technique, this seems
to be a descendant of Italian *mostaccioli*. These, according to a
late-sixteenth-century Venetian source, were made by baking
nuggets of spiced marzipan.[21] A similar recipe for "*monstachole*"
appears in de Casteau's 1604 opus, though he included flour
and eggs, which must have made for a texture closer to biscotti.
The later French recipes are much simpler and quite close to
today's *macaron*, instructing cooks to fold beaten egg whites
into almond paste flavored with rosewater. But why the peculiar
name that French dictionaries insist comes from macaroni? Part
of the explanation may be that the macaroni of the time often
resembled little dumplings rather than what we think of as pasta.
As Pierre Richelet's 1694 *Dictionnaire françois* defined it, macaroni were "little pieces of dough divided up and cut in slices." La
Varenne explicitly said that the cookies should be made "in the
shape of a macaron."[22] In other words, the reference was to the
shape of the Italian item, not to what it was made of. The *Dictionnaire* makes the incidental point that, in Paris, these macaroni
were made by the city's predominantly Italian *limonadiers* or soft
drink vendors.[23] Even before this, a treatise on chocolate from
1643 recommends *biscuit* and *macaron* as a suitable accompaniment to hot chocolate, later sold by those same *limonadiers*.[24] So
perhaps they sold both the almond cookies and the pasta, which
may explain where the linguistic confusion set in.

One indication of the Italian sway was just how much the
southerners were resented. In 1575, anti-Italian riots wracked
Paris. In 1588, just months before Catherine's death, the property of Italian magnates in Lyon and Paris was seized. Following
her demise, Italian bankers were gradually forced out and Italian
prelates lost their hold on the French Catholic church.

Nonetheless, the Italians would have an Indian summer
when Marie de Médicis arrived in France in 1600. Unlike the

earlier Italian queen, Marie came to France as an adult and never quite mastered the language. She sought comfort in surrounding herself by her countrymen.[25] This became especially apparent when she ruled as regent between 1610 and 1614 (and in reality until 1617). That said, Marie de Médicis would never hold the reins of power with quite as much aplomb as her kinswoman. Her foreign courtiers were, if anything, resented even more than they had been earlier.

If a single date can mark the end of Italian influence at court, it is April 24, 1617. That was the day Concino Concini, the Médicis queen mother's war minister, and her favorite, was murdered by members of the royal guard in the outer courtyard of the Louvre. The assassination had been ordered by Marie's fifteen-year-old son, Louis XIII. Soon after, Concini's wife was tried for sorcery and beheaded. The Italian queen was forced out of Paris a few weeks later. When she was finally allowed to return to the capital in 1621, her political role was much diminished—though her lifestyle continued in grand Médicis form. She tried to seize power one more time in 1630, which led to her definitive expulsion. As she fled to Holland, the era of the Italians at the French court was, to all intents and purposes, over. In manners of fashion and food, it was France that would dominate Europe for more than two hundred years.

SUGAR AND SALT

When it came to cuisine, a newfound obsession with indigenous French food first became evident in an outpouring of cookbooks that occurred during the long reign of Louis XIV (1643–1715). La Varenne's *Le Cuisinier François* ("The French Cook") of 1651 was the first of a new nationalistic breed, but many others followed. Chefs and their publishers competed for readers with claims that their books were the latest and greatest even as they disparaged the other guy. Niche markets were even developed, especially for pastry and confectionary.

The recipes of this new foodie generation gradually abandoned the tropes of medieval cooking. Spices and other exotic flavors were sidelined, if not pushed right out the door. But perhaps an even bigger change was the growing gap between sweet and savory, between what today would be called the main course and dessert. As elsewhere in Europe, the trend of medieval French cooks adding sugar to meats and fish had only increased as the sweetener became more available by the 1500s. Yet by La Varenne's day, this once popular aristocratic seasoning was now hardly ever sprinkled on fish pies or stirred into fricassees. The transformation didn't happen overnight, of course. The *Cuisinier François* had its sugared salmon soup, roasted sweet sole, and lamprey in sweet sauce. The 1660 *Le cuisinier méthodique* ("The Methodical Cook") included recipes for pigeon "compote," preserved oysters, and fish fritters that were all sweetened. The 1662 *L'escole parfaite des officers de bouche* ("A Perfect School of Instructions for the Officers of the Mouth" in its contemporary English translation—in print as late as 1742) still contained a salmon ragout with sugar, cinnamon, and cloves as well as a sweetened veal kidney tart. But these old-fashioned dishes were decidedly the exception.[26] This is clear not only from the cookbooks but also from the occasional traveler's missive that complained about food outside the French heartland. In a 1691 visit to Spain, the Countess d'Aulnoy had much the reaction of a Victorian matron confronted with the curries of India. She was repulsed at the quantities of spice and even more disgusted by a sweetened ham served to her in Madrid. "[It was] covered with candies of the sort that we in France call nonpareils," she wrote with horror, "whose sugar melted into the fat." Seventeenth-century French visitors to Flanders, Germany, Poland, and even Ireland were similarly aghast by the still largely medieval use of spices and sugar.

This new French culinary idiom must have predated La Varenne's cookbook by at least a generation. In 1630, Jean-Jacques Bouchard—a writer best known for his soft porn—was traveling in Provence where he noted, very specifically, that the food was prepared "in the Italian style, with abundant spices and . . . sweet sauces [made] with Corinthian grapes, raisins, prunes, apples, pears, and sugar."[27] The implication is that by this point the (northern) French manner of seasoning was different.

La Varenne made the Frenchness of his cooking explicit when he called his book "The French Cook" as if to distinguish it from all those other, foreign, approaches. This national self-consciousness is evident in other fields too: politics, religion, and language. Is it mere coincidence that the Académie française, charged with safekeeping the French language, was established in 1637, a dozen years before the publication of La Varenne's manifesto? Nonetheless, the rules of cuisine, much like the strictures of grammar, are often inconsistent. Even if there was now a Maginot line between sweet and savory, it was a leaky one at best. Sugar may have been banned from predominantly salty dishes, but the likes of crème brulée and sweetened apple fritters kept on being served right beside joints of roast venison.

However imperfect this new dividing line, it had a decisive influence on encouraging the creation of new pastries and confections. First, the segregation of sweet and savory encouraged specialization, something that often leads to improvements in technique. This was true on both the savory and the sweet side of the wall. After all, French cuisine is defined much more by technique than by its ingredients, a trend that already seemed to be in full force by 1700. Second, as sweet dishes migrated to a separate course, or were even served as their own meal, there was an increasing need to expand the repertoire. Hosts couldn't just keep serving the same old thing to their guests when everything on the table was sweet. Soon enough, everything was in place for the invention of something we might recognize as dessert.

THE SUN KING

In the gray winter months of early 1700, Versailles glittered with candlelight reflected in a firmament of mirrors. It was Carnival season, and the bright stars of the highest nobility competed to outshine one another at the blazingly decadent court of the Sun King. In January the jaded aristocrats were titillated with costume balls of ever-increasing theatricality. The king hosted a party in which the chateau was transformed into an imperial Chinese palace. Two weeks later, Marie-Adélaïde of Savoy, the Duchess of Burgundy and the future mother of Louis XV, threw a ball where the female guests came attired as nymphs and goddesses. The following evening the theme was shabby chic as the ladies came dressed as country wenches.

The undeniable hit of the season, however, was a fête organized by the Comtesse de Pontchartrain, the wife of the powerful chancellor. She set the scene by transforming her gilded residence into a replica of the Saint-Germain fair.[28] This fair was held annually in the newly fashionable Paris faubourg of Saint-Germain and attracted the highest levels of society to browse its booths selling paintings, ribbons, toys, and sweets. At least one contemporary British visitor was impressed by the "Many Shops of Confectioners, where the Ladies are commodiously treated."[29] But why make the trip to Paris when you could have the same experience chez Pontchartrain while avoiding the mud and the hoi polloi? It was like a Disneyland version of the fair, but better, because the guests could collect their souvenirs without having to pay a sou.

"There were Chinese shops, Japanese shops, and so forth, selling all manner of the most refined, beautiful, and unusual goods," reported the twenty-five-year-old duc de Saint-Simon, the inveterate gossip of the Versailles court. "And the shopkeepers would take no money: all the merchandise was presented as gifts to the Duchesse de Bourgogne and the other ladies." Then there were the refreshment stands: the confectioner, the pastry shop, the citrus vendor with his sunny produce, and even a *limonadier* who would prove to be no other than Procope, who took the night off from his renowned Saint-Germain café to complete the evening's experience. This spread was the Comtesse's clever answer to a *collation*, a word still in vogue for mostly sweet meals. The guests were invited to partake of the sugary snacks, before dancing through the night. A party at Versailles was a world apart from the festivals of Catherine de Médicis. It was all so, in a word, French.

To appreciate how French cuisine, especially its sweeter side, was invented, you need to understand Versailles. Unlike unkempt, complicated Paris, Versailles was a rarefied never-never land with its own culture, its own rules, and its own particular value system, a little like an upper-class boarding school with balls and concerts instead of lessons and cricket matches. In this milieu it was perfectly normal to devour one's fortune by throwing dinner parties, to blow more money on a gown than a whole village of peasants would earn in a year.

When Louis XIV definitively moved the court to his suburban palace in 1682, he also instituted a regular schedule of entertainments. His aim, in part, was to prevent the once-independent magnates from getting too restless in their gilded cage, so he served up a rarefied program of bread and circuses—or brioche and Molière as the case might be. Theater troupes were brought in from Paris on a weekly basis, but there were also evenings of dance and music. After the show, the privileged audience was typically treated to supper. At one such soirée an Austrian visitor noted two tables had been set up to accommodate about eighty guests. These dinner parties occurred several times each week.[30] It was all part and parcel of the Sun King's strategy of keeping his kingdom's elite at his beck and call.

Yet the meals themselves became less theatrical than they had been at the Renaissance courts. There were no pigs encased in pastry castles paraded through the hall as there had been at the wedding of Lucrecia D'Este in fifteenth-century Bologna; no banquets interrupted by jousting knights à la Catherine de Médicis. To understand the change in style, it's important to remember that those feasts of yore were hardly quotidian events. They were infrequent, special, no-holds-barred extravaganzas staged to astonish and amaze. In between the feasts, there was relative famine. There would not have been enough spice in all of medieval Europe to shower the food of even the elite with sugar, cinnamon, and ginger every single day. Compare that to the court of Louis XIV and his successors. Their banquets, served by and to France's power elite, were practically everyday affairs.

In this milieu, the exercise of political power required a carefully crafted social strategy. In the old feudal system, aristocrats were mostly judged by their martial prowess, but now a courtier's success depended almost exclusively on getting into the king's inner circle, or even its periphery. Points could be scored just as well at dinner as they had once been on the battlefield. In those olden days, the nobility used to be spread out all over the country and accordingly occasions for entertaining their peers were few and far between, but now the opportunity presented itself every evening. This must have put enormous pressure on every host and hostess, to say nothing of their chefs, who had to deliver impressive meals day in and day out. It was now part of the cook's job to innovate, to keep the jaded palates of the guests from succumbing to boredom, yet at the same time not to overwhelm them to such a degree that they couldn't be back for more a few hours hence. This may be part of the explanation for the relatively bland (or subtle, if you wish) yet simultaneously ever more inventive cuisine of the new age.

When it came to the internal structure of the French meal, it began, albeit very gradually, to resemble something we might recognize today. Sometime in the late 1600s, the number of courses, and what was served at each, became more routinized.

Still, each course consisted of multiple dishes that were set out more or less at once. At a large meal, there would be several platters of the same dish distributed around the table so everyone could get a taste. Savory dishes may have no longer been finished with a dusting of sugar, but they continued to be placed next to sweet preparations. Thus great roasts might be surrounded with smaller plates of vegetables, pies, fritters, and even the occasional crème brulée.

François Massialot's *Le cuisinier roïal et bourgeois* ("The Royal and Bourgeois Cook," published in several editions starting in 1691) offers a sneak peek at the meals served in Versailles' early days. Massialot had made a name for himself running the kitchens for Louis XIV's brother and other similarly illustrious personages and was only too pleased to show off his bills of fare. His book lists more ordinary meals (of a mere dozen dishes per course), but he also gave the order of service for grander occasions. One of these is a banquet hosted by the marquis de Louvois, the king's eminent war minister, on August 25, 1690.[31] The guest list was a who's who of France, including the king's son and heir apparent, Louis, the monarch's nephew Philippe d'Orléans, and other members of the royal family. Massialot didn't bother to specify the names of the other invitees, indicating them simply as "all the rest of the court."

The guests sat down to a table loaded down with the first "service." Lined up in the center of the tables were great steaming tureens of thick soup (potage), twelve kinds split up among twenty-two serving containers. Carefully lined up on either side were a dozen sorts of smaller dishes referred to as "entrées," which could include anything from pâtés to roast beef. To complete the symmetrical arrangement, there were thirteen smaller plates of so-called hors d'oeuvres. These were not the appetizers of today; rather, they were literally "outside the work," that is, separate from the larger dishes. This arrangement ensured that de Louvois's guests could nibble on hors d'oeuvres such as sausages and braised squab with basil if they grew weary of the turkey potage with chicory or the grand entrée of roast veal garnished with fried veal cutlets.

For the second "service" (oh yes, this was just the beginning), there were twenty-two platters of roast beef, mutton, suckling pig, and "all sorts of poultry," along with salads. There were also the *entremets*, then a vaguely defined term that encompassed pastries both sweet and savory as well as, occasionally, vegetables. (In present-day French, *entremet* is more or less synonymous with dessert.) Here, the marquis' guests could select among not only *entremets* of ham or pheasant pies but also blancmange, doughnuts (*beignets*), or apricot marmalade–filled tarts. For those who weren't yet stuffed, there were another eight kinds of hors d'oeuvres. These too were a medley of sweet and savory. The guests had the choice of *foie gras*, poached truffles, crème brulée, or perhaps a sweet omelette.

Unfortunately, Massialot didn't say what the princes, dukes, and marquises indulged in for the third course, which he called the "fruit and confectionary." The reason for the omission was that, as he pointed out in his introduction, it did not belong in a book devoted to cooking. It was a matter for the so-called *office* or pantry rather than the *cuisine*. But the chef didn't leave his readers guessing for too long; his confectionary manual *Nouvelle instructions pour faire les confitures* ("New Instructions for Making Confectionary") came out just one year later. In it, Massialot included an illustration of the sort of dessert table that would have greeted the marquis' eminent party. It is a construction of dizzying magnificence. A steep mountain of fresh fruit towers in the center surrounded by precariously piled pyramids of candied fruit. Ranged round is a landscape of carefully stacked marzipan and *biscuits* interspersed with porcelain basins of stewed fruits. Careful compositions of flowers and leaves complete the bucolic scene.[32]

Reading between the lines of Massialot's two books, you get the impression that a lively rivalry had developed between the kitchen and the *office*. Much like dessert chefs today, confectioners worked to a different rhythm than cooks preparing roasts and fricassees. Their work was more methodical and precise, with an increasingly specialized battery of tools to make jellies, ice cream, candy, and other sweet delights. They also became much more critical to a banquet's success now that fully one-third of the meal was devoted to their creations. Amid the social shenanigans of Versailles, dessert was no mere afterthought.

The somewhat mysterious author (known only as L.S.R.) of another entertainment guide of the time gave a delightful rendition of the purpose of dessert. "It is undisputed that dessert is the reveille of the meal," he wrote in 1674, "without which we would sink into melancholy and deep reverie; it dissipates most pleasantly our sorrow and relieves us of that dull numbness into which we seem so often to be plunged by our affairs; with the raised glasses and toasts it sends us into a more joyous state. . . . As the saying goes, it is between the pear and cheese that one invents a thousand pleasantries to pass the time and sustain the gallant society that is the charm in our lives."[33] L.S.R. was still a little old-fashioned; his dessert still included "fragrant tongues" and sausages. More commonly the word *dessert* was now used with its modern sense. The 1690 *Dictionnaire Universel* defined it as "the last course placed on the table. . . . Dessert is composed of fruits, pastry, confectionary, cheese, etc."* But it had already meant this for some time. The writer of the 1662 *L'éscole parfaite* made the point that the fruit course was commonly called *dessert*.[35] Though a simple bowl of strawberries is hardly what the author had in mind. His fruit course included candied fruit and chestnuts as well as fruit preserves;

---

* The pastry, in this case, was always sweet; the 1701 edition of the *Dictionaire* cites the following usage: "One sweetens the pastry (pâtisserie) that is served as dessert."[34]

pears, plums and walnuts in syrup; fruit jelly; marzipan; *biscuits*; and cheese.

By 1700, French confectioners undeniably outshined their Italian masters. An explosive burst of invention is palpable leafing through the 1692 edition of Massialot's confectionary guide and the much expanded and revised version of 1716. Virtually every category has been greatly enlarged. The earlier book had included nine recipes for *biscuit*; the latter had over twenty. There are dozens more compotes and preserves, many more custards and creams, jellies, *macarons*, and meringues.

The peculiar atmosphere of Versailles that promoted entertaining to a competitive sport undoubtedly pushed cooks both savory and sweet to outdo themselves, but there were other impulses specific to dessert chefs that propelled them toward ever-greater innovation.

After about 1650, the world sugar price collapsed as the international center of sugar exports shifted from Brazil to the Caribbean. There, the English learned to squeeze ever-increasing amounts of the sweetener from their slave-operated plantations in Bermuda and Jamaica. The French followed suit when they took control of Saint Domingue (Haiti) in 1697. In Amsterdam, where a good portion of the colonial sugar first made landfall on the continent, sugar was trading for half the price in the last decade of the seventeenth century than it had been fifty years earlier. Not that sugar was cheap—in Paris, an unskilled worker could buy close to ten pounds of beef for a day's wage but only a pound of sugar—but there was now plenty of it. This meant that it could be used with abandon, at least by those who catered to the constellation that circled the Sun King.[36]

Much of this new supply of sugar wasn't beaten into cakes. Rather, it was stirred into the bitter, stimulating beverages that had become so *à la mode*. But that too created new opportunities for serving sweet snacks to accompany the newly trendy coffee, chocolate, and, to a lesser extent, tea.

Coffee and Cake

Chocolate, of the drinking variety, arrived from Spain sometime in the early years of the seventeenth century. Cardinal Richelieu, Louis XIII's chief minister, had apparently picked up the habit from Spanish priests. (He drank it for his health—naturally!) It was reported that Marie Thérèse, the Sun King's Spanish wife, liked it too.[37] But no matter who popularized it initially, the exotic (and expensive) beverage was thoroughly naturalized by the time the gilded gates first swung open on Louis XIV's hyperchateau.

Coffee came a little later, introduced from Turkey. Adrien Perdou de Subligny, writing for his gazette, *La Muse de la cour* ("The Muse of the Court") in 1666, still called it the "Turkish liqueur" and recommended it to men needing a little lift.[38] Writing in 1685, Philippe Sylvestre Dufour claimed that it had only been served for the last twenty-five years in France.[39] Certainly by that point it was commonplace. In a letter from 1690, the Marquise de Sevigné mentioned that she mixed coffee with milk and sugar, adding that her doctor quite approved.[40] Coffee also became an occasion to eat out.

The original Parisian coffeehouses were little more than wooden booths and were as well known for their lemonade and other cold drinks as for their mochas. This is why café owners were known as *limonadiers* well into the nineteenth century. One of these early lemonade sellers was the Sicilian-born Francesco Procopio dei Coltelli, whom we met at the Carnival ball of 1700. The Italian barista had opened his own coffee bar sometime in the 1670s in the trendy Faubourg Saint-Germain. By 1686 he had moved to much larger premises and outfitted his new establishment in ultra lux style with mirrors on the wall and marble-topped tables.*

---

* Though much redecorated, the café still exists on what is today the rue de l'Ancienne Comédie.

By this point, London and Amsterdam had coffeehouses too, but these were more like smoky, rowdy taverns and accordingly attracted a similar mix of clientele. No woman of high society would set a single silk-clad slipper into such an uncouth atmosphere.* In Paris, however, Café Procope and its equally elegant imitators oozed elegance and style. An anonymous pamphlet from 1700, *Le Portefeuille galant* ("The Portfolio of Style"), noted them as "places frequented by well-born people of both sexes." And this seems to have been true of much of the eighteenth century. In 1759, the *Dictionnaire universel du commerce* ("Universal Dictionary of Commerce") noted, "almost all Parisian cafés are magnificently decorated." They were a runaway success; according to official estimates, by 1715, there were already between 300 and 350 cafés in Paris.[42]

An early image of one of these trendy spots shows up in a print reproduced in Louis de Mailly's 1702 *Entretiens sur les cafés* ("Conversations About Cafés"). Here ladies dressed to the nines sit in carved armchairs sipping what is probably coffee from porcelain goblets. Seated with them is a curé, to underline just how respectable it all is, though a quick glance at the premises would make that clear enough. The high walls, illuminated by an elegant chandelier, are hung with fine tapestries and grand canvases. At the other two tables, well-dressed gentlemen play at cards and backgammon. The ladies aren't just drinking coffee though. There are little plates on the table too. It is impossible to identify the food, but chances are it is sweet.

From early on, cafés served snacks to go along with their beverages. Nicolas de Blegny, in his 1691 guidebook to Paris, gave the addresses of two pastry shops that sold wholesale to large households, to inns, and to the *limonadiers*. So we know

---

* Even in the late 1800s, at a high-society tea salon like London's Gunter Tea Shop, the waiters delivered the establishment's famous ice cream to the ladies who remained in their carriages, while the men lounged at the outdoor tables.[41]

that *biscuits*, marzipan, and *craquelins* (a large cracker) could be had with your lemonade or hot chocolate, as well as sweet wafers, waffles, or any other snack produced by the *pâtissiers*.[43]

As the comment in the *Dictionnaire François* highlights, some of the *limonadiers* may have been running (probably unauthorized) catering operations on the side. Primarily though, the cafés sold all sorts of mostly sweetened drinks, not only the newly popular drug beverages but also various flavors of lemonade (raspberry, pomegranate, peach, etc.), including versions spiked with wine and eau de vie. One popular drink that they also served was sorbet, which, like coffee, came from Turkey. This, of course, wasn't the frozen dessert, it was the drink. The 1696 Dictionary of the Académie française defined *sorbet* as not so different from lemonade: "a very pleasant beverage made of the flesh of lemons and sugar and which came here from the Levant. It is very commonplace among the Turks."[44] This is the meaning the word had well into the nineteenth century. But did coffee shops also sell ices? The answer to that depends on just how you read a document that gave royal approval to their guild in 1676.[45] In it, the *limonadiers* are permitted to sell a wide variety of beverages as well as candied and preserved fruit. But there is also a reference to something called "*eaux de gelées, et glaces de fruits et de fleurs*," the second part of which seems to translate as "fruit and flower-scented ices." We have recipes for these from Massialot and other contemporary sources. So perhaps a sort of sorbet (as we know it) was on the menu as well.[46]

Tea, the third of the newly fashionable beverages, never gained the same sort of traction in France as it would in England or Russia. It had its moments though, as the elaborate silver and porcelain tea services from the ancièn regime make clear.

Of course the affluent could not only afford the expensive beverages (even lemonade had to be made with costly imported lemons) sweetened with pricey sugar, they could also spare the time to linger over their refreshments. At Versailles, meals, or at least occasions at which food was present, ate up large chunks of the day. Not only did the highborn have more time in general, they had a totally different rhythm to their day than the working classes, who had to follow the dictates of the sun. Dining hours moved progressively later and later in the day as the eighteenth century progressed. Typically there were two meals. The more substantial *dîner* was in the mid-afternoon; the lighter and briefer *souper* took place in the later evening. Whereas in the early days of Versailles the two meals were served around one and eight o'clock respectively, by the eve of the Revolution the haut monde sat down to dinner closer to four, and supper might not start until eleven in the evening or even later.[47] These late dining hours meant that there were prolonged stretches between meals, both in the morning and in the hours that stretched into supper. These lengthy intervals might make even a languorous marquise a tad peckish. The new beverages fit handily into these meal-less lacunae. They got the courtiers going in the morning and perked them up before the evening's entertainment.

One popular way that women of intellectual bent filled their late afternoons was to invite a circle of friends and acquaintances to their salon for a few hours of cerebral excercise—and gossip. This genteel and relatively informal get-together would become a French institution for at least the next two hundred years. Naturally the likes of coffee and tea were more likely to keep the conversation sparkling than the brandy and eau-de-vies that were also increasingly in vogue around 1700.[48]

But not even the blazing beacons of the Enlightenment who were frequent guests at the salons—on break from constructing the intellectual foundations of the modern world—could live on caffeine alone. Nor could less enlightened aristocrats who had to wait until three or later for their first proper meal. But what do you serve with chocolate and coffee? An early book on the vir-

tues and deficits of the new beverages suggested that the French
should follow the oriental example and eat *biscuits* or other patisserie with their coffee.[49] It also notes in passing that some people
were wont to dip a *biscuit* or two into their chocolate. But a couple
of cookies would hardly suffice to keep the bons mots aloft. What
was needed for this new caffeinated age was a new sort of repast,
not quite a full-blown meal but more than just a sweet nibble.

∼ Chocolate ∼

Many volumes have documented the long and colorful
history of chocolate, from its beginnings as an exclusive
beverage of Aztec emperors to the elite beverage of first
Spanish and then other European aristocrats, to the more
democratic drinking chocolate of the Walter Baker company, and then finally to the mass-marketed chocolates of
Cadbury, Hershey's, and Lindt. What has received somewhat less attention is the role of chocolate as a flavoring for
desserts.

It didn't take long for sweet makers to start using chocolate in their confections. Italian cookbooks contain chocolate recipes as early as the 1600s, and the country continued
to be known for its chocolate makers into the next century.
As late as 1803, the French pastry authority J. J. Machet noted
that Italian chocolatiers working in France had an excellent
reputation.[50] A few years later, the first great Swiss chocolate entrepreneur, Francois-Louis Cailler, learned his chops
in Italy.[51] Yet no one quite took to the new flavoring with
the enthusiasm of the French. As early as 1685, the French
author of *The Manner of Making of Coffee, Tea, and Chocolate* noted that one might take chocolate in its solid form (as
opposed to a beverage), adding that it is made into "dragées

(that is candy), biscuits, marzipan, and many other sorts of sweetmeats (*friandises*)."[52] The cookbooks took their sweet time catching up. Massialot's 1692 cookbook only included a single chocolate dessert, a *biscuit*.[53] It was only twenty-four years later—in a heavily revised and expanded edition—that chocolate desserts got that attention they deserve. There were now recipes for a chocolate crème (a little like a runny pudding), a kind of chocolate fudge (*conserve*), and candy (*pastille*) as well as the chocolate-flavored marzipan already mentioned more than thirty years earlier. A generation later, the 1751 *Cannameliste* included recipes for chocolate truffles, chocolate-covered nuts, even chocolate mousse.[54] In less than a hundred years, chocolate went from being a beverage drunk with dessert to something eaten as dessert. French confectioners would never look back.

Into the breach came the *collation*. In medieval France, this had simply been another name for a meal, much as it is in English, but by the late 1600s its meaning was closer to the Italian *collazione*, more like an elaborate snack or high tea, both of which it prefigured. It fell to the *office* to provide it. Was this because it was just too impractical to fire up the kitchen ovens for yet another meal? Or was it because the pantry was in charge of the beverages anyway so why not have them whip up something to go with it? L.S.R. gives advice on what to serve for a late-night *collation*. His menu includes fresh and dried fruit, marzipan, and biscuits, but also a venison paté, tongues, sausages, and cheese.[55] Incidentally, the list doesn't differ much from what he suggests for dessert.

Just as it had become increasingly less common in early seventeenth-century France to mix sweet and savory, it only followed that at cafés as well as salons, sweetened beverages—whether hot or cold—would be served with sweet foods. Until very recently, when the American habit of drinking cold, sweet, caffeinated beverages with meals has caught on, the French couldn't stomach the taste of sugared tea, coffee, or even lemonade with their meat or fish. This seems to have been the case from the start. As these drinks became ever more popular during the Sun King's reign they required a much expanded pastry repertoire. But then so did the last dessert course, which was becoming evermore copious.

One source on the ever-growing list of new and improved recipes is a volume written by the chief confectioner to the expatriate Polish king Stanislaw Leszczynski. The book's author, Joseph Gilliers, boasts of the connection with the famed gourmet on the title page of his 1751 ode to confectionary, *Le Cannameliste français* (the term derives the French term for sugar cane). Here, once again, the old categories expand. There is now a score of *biscuit* recipes. Ice cream (called *neige*, or snow) comes in more than thirty-one flavors—including artichoke! Many of these were likely served as both dessert and as a *collation*, and in some cases for breakfast too. Menon, one of the bestselling cookbook authors of the eighteenth century, included plenty of sugary entremets in his *La science du maître d'hôtel cuisinier* ("The Techniques of the Steward-Chef") in 1749. His sweet pastries and fritters reflected an earlier tradition, but the fashion for ever-creamier dessert is evident too. The custards (here called *crèmes*) are now smoother too, since recipes now specifically refer to cooking them in a bain-marie, or a hot water bath. There are dozens of these creamy puddings, with minor variations of texture. There are chocolate *crèmes* and ones flavored with coffee and tea, but there are also others scented with parsley, chervil, and celery. In one interesting development, a rice-thickened pudding (*crème de ris souflée*) has beaten egg whites folded into it, one of the first French soufflés to use the term.[56] In another shift that may be more linguistic than culinary, *gâteau* is now used to refer to a large sponge cake.* These large sorts of cakes are also now occasionally baked in "turk heads" and other metal molds, which seems to reflect contemporary innovations in mold making. Naturally all of these would have been served right along with the meats, fish, and vegetables. Menon did not forget about dessert, however. His next book, published the following year, was a no-holds-barred celebration of the sugary arts. In *La science du maître d'hôtel confiseur* ("The Techniques of the Steward-Confectioner"), the confectioner is a showman, creating fabulous follies out of an all-but-inedible sugar paste. It's as if the ghosts of the Italian Renaissance had once more come to life, even if the style was different. The table decorations reflected French rococo sculpture of the time. The style had largely been inspired by the Italian baroque masters, though the French version was decidedly more froufrou.

According to Menon, these sorts of centerpieces were the height of good taste, certainly compared to those tacky productions of Massialot and his generation. In the book's introduction he had this to say about changes in confectionary fashion:

> The art of the *office*, the same as every other, has been improved through gradual changes; in so much as the earlier work is almost useless to today's pantry.... Whatever happened to all these pyramids built with so much more work and effort than with taste and elegance that we used to see on our tables? Whatever happened to those confused heaps of fruit, more an explosion of excess than of intelligence and delicacy? In a word, there is between today's modern pantry and that of the past almost the same difference as between modern architecture and

---

* The French word *gâteau* is even less specific than the English "cake." It can refer to small cakes or cookies like madeleines, large iced layer cakes, or even pastry confections such as a *gâteau des rois* or a *gâteau Saint-Honoré*.

gothic architecture. What a pleasant sight we see [now-adays] in the diverse decorations which are born each day of the imaginations of our intelligent confectioners. See the parterre [simulated lawn] decorated with sugar figures, the figure of the Saxon, decorated with pow-dered sugar of different colors, trees, dried fruit, flower pots, cradles, garlands, with compartments in chenille of diverse colors. What intelligence! What taste!

The confectioner's art always required a degree of precision and craft that had at least as much in common with the silver-smith and his precious liquid metal as with the cook simmer-ing his ragout or the pastry cook rolling out his puff pastry. The implements that stocked the pantry could almost have been mistaken for those of a foundry: equipment for refining sugar, specialized pans for melting it, devices for carefully calibrated heating and cooling, and dozens of molds for the creation of edi-ble gems. Gillier's *Cannameliste* devoted a page to mold illustra-tions: scalloped and triangular molds for chilled custards, frozen mousses, and ice cream; molds for caramels, jellied fruit, and candied fruit. The last of these could take the shape of the fruits themselves, but others resembled hog's heads and pig's legs as well as crayfish and sea fish.

The way an eighteenth-century food authority like Menon saw it, confectionary was as much a branch of the decorative arts as it was of cuisine. The confectioner shared techniques that would have been familiar to the decorative painter, a fine furni-ture maker, or even a milliner, especially when it came to those sculpted sugar centerpieces that catapulted from the imaginations of all those "intelligent confectioners." Moreover, his noble clien-tele demanded the same level of perfection (at any price) as from those other artisans. These elite standards persisted even after the Revolution had ripped the old aristocratic order to shreds.

If anything, the arrivistes needed to prove they were just as grand as the previous generation. By the late 1700s, Menon's relatively small-scale tragacanth-paste tableaux had been transformed into set pieces of architectural dimension. When Antonin Carême, history's most famous pastry cook, said, "I believe architecture to be the first amongst the arts, and the principal branch of architecture is confectionery," what he was surely thinking of were the multistoried temples and pagodas that were his first claim to fame.

ANTONIN CARÊME AND THE FRENCH INFLUENCE

Marie-Antoine Carême was an offspring of the French Revolution, a poor slum child who at the age of eight was abandoned by his father with the words, "Nowadays you need only the spirit to make your fortune, and you have that spirit. *Va Petit!* With what God has given you."[57] Happily, leaving home would turn out to be a better alternative than staying home in a fleabitten corner of the Left Bank with a gaggle of siblings. In the interim, however, what Marie-Antoine most needed for God to give him was a bit of dumb luck. For the year was 1792, three years into the fury of the French Revolution. Paris was in the bloody grip of Robespierre's terror. Versailles had been pillaged and looted by angry mobs. Louis XVI and Marie Antoinette were confined to the Tuileries palace and would soon join the long line of nobles marched to the guillotine by the Jacobins. That the eight-year-old even survived was remarkable; that he happened to be picked up by a caterer in need of extra help was nothing short of miraculous.

So, with a heavy-handed shove from Providence, Carême was on his way to becoming the most famous chef in Europe. Four years later, as post-Revolutionary Paris finally settled down to some degree of normalcy, Antonin (as he now called himself) apprenticed with Sylvain Bailly, a *pâtissier* with a shop on the rue Vivienne, just behind the Palais Royal, then, as now, one of the tonier sections of town. Nearby, underneath the palace arcades, the chefs of former aristocrats had set up eating establishments, now called by the trendy new name *restaurant*. It's reasonable to assume that Antonin delivered pastries to these new dining rooms and mingled with their apprentices.

◟ Marie Antoinette ◞

The answer is no. The almost universal opinion among contemporary historians is that there is no proof that the queen consort of Louis XVI ever said "Let them eat cake" when she heard that the populace had no bread to eat. Of course the translation is imperfect to begin with. The phrase would have been "*Qu'ils mangent de la brioche*." But "let them eat lightly sweetened enriched bread" doesn't exactly roll off the tongue. And, to be fair, brioche was typically referred to as a *gâteau* rather than a bread at the time, and was eaten in the context of other sweets.

Despite the fact that Marie Antoinette may not have been the brightest star in the royal firmament, she was not known to be callous. In the decadent twilight of the ancien régime, the Austrian-born queen did, however, become the focus for every sort of scurrilous rumor. The pamphlets that circulated around Paris painted a picture of intimate royal feasts turning to orgies where the queen indulged her lust with men and women alike. This was highly unlikely; the queen was, by aristocratic French standards, a bit of a prude. Her real passions seem to have been for music and gardening. Moreover, the cake story predates Marie Antoinette's arrival in France by close to a hundred years. Louis XIV's Spanish bride, Marie Thérèse, apparently grumbled that if they had no bread, the peasantry should eat the crust from meat pies. The earliest mention of the famous phrase in print seems to come from Jean-Jacques Rousseau, who recounted the story of "a great princess" hearing that the peasants had no bread and responding "let them eat brioche." Rousseau wrote this twenty years before Marie Antoinette was born! And at least one other princess was credited with the phrase before the royal bride ever left Austria.[58]

Perhaps the "let them eat cake" myth was merely wishful thinking on the part of Parisian sweet makers, who dreaded the passing of the old regime and the annihilation of their clientele. The luxury good makers were so distressed at Marie Antoinette's imprisonment that they plotted to free her. In the so-called Wigmakers' Conspiracy of 1793, a faction of Parisian luxury goods makers, including pastry cooks, lace workers, and *limonadiers* as well as the eponymous wigmakers, schemed to liberate her highness. Alas, they were betrayed. But they need not have worried. The coming ruling class was as happy to eat cake as their beheaded predecessors.

The Revolution brought any number of changes to the French dining scene. The beheading or dispersal of the old ruling class caused wholesale unemployment among its chefs and pastry cooks. Some followed their employers into exile, while others sought employment with foreign noble houses abroad. Many, however, turned to the public and opened restaurants where any commoner (with the necessary cash) could dine like a viscount. Another seismic shift shook up the centuries-old structure of the guilds. Even as the revolutionaries tore down the Bastille prison, they tore up the old legal system. In ancien régime France, birth, position, and membership in often-hereditary corporate bodies defined one's position before the law. Members of the nobility—the so-called second estate—had different rights and legal privileges than townspeople. Analogously, a confectioner who belonged to the requisite guild had held monopoly rights based on his guild membership. But no more. Now, under the new republican regime, each individual citizen was (at least on paper) equal before the law, with the result that guilds were tossed into the dustbin of history along with the institutional perks of gentlemen.* Theoretically this meant that anyone could hang up a shingle. Moreover, the ancient rules that had divided cooks, bakers, *pâtissiers*, and confectioners finally broke down. (These barriers had always been permeable in private employment even as guild monopolies were zealously—but not always successfully—protected in the public marketplace.) Now it became commonplace to be both *confisseur* and *pâtissier*, to sell candy, pastries, and even meat pies under the same roof.[59] Certainly Carême's exuberant *pièces montées* (as the decorative centerpieces were called) combined both pastry and sugar work, something that was practically illegal under the old regime.

Antonin's employer happened to be located across the street from the largest collection of books in the world, the Bibliothèque Nationale. Like everyone in the profession, Carême began his day well before dawn, but he was often done by mid-afternoon. With time on his hands he was drawn to the library, especially the exhaustively illustrated volumes on architecture. He must have been an incongruous sight, the little pastry cook in his flour-caked clothes smelling of butter, caramel, and sweat. Before 1789, it's unlikely he would have even been let inside, but now citizen Carême had the luxury to make extensive drawings, copying designs by architects the likes of Palladio, Tertio, and Vignole as well as the exotic architecture of India, China, and Egypt. Back at the patisserie he would build temples and pyramids, crumbling castles and sculpted fountains, Romantic landscapes, all made

---

* To be strictly accurate, the abolishment of the craft guilds anticipated the storming of the Bastille by over a decade. They were disbanded in 1776 by Louis XVI's radical controller general, Anne-Robert-Jacques Turgot, as part of a package of reforms meant to ward off the winds of revolution.

with pastry and marzipan, with spun sugar and tragacanth paste. By all accounts, he was brilliant at it, even if his creations probably have more in common with theatrical set design than architecture. In his *Le Pâtissier royale parisien* ("The Royal Parisian Pastry Cook"), first published in 1815 but considerably expanded in 1828, the now-famous chef gave directions for fifty-two of these *pièces montées*. The four-hundred-page tome includes extensive illustrations and detailed instructions for how to make the centerpieces. There are globes, vases, and lyres; hermitages, grottoes, and waterfalls; a Chinese summer house, a Venetian pavilion, and a Turkish mill. The level of detail is remarkable, especially in a profession known for its paranoid secrecy.

One of the simpler pieces, "a fountain with palm trees," is a sort of fanciful pavilion held up by twelve columns in the shape of palm trees, their trunks made of tragacanth paste covered with pale green sugar, while the leafy capitals are made of puff pastry tipped with pistachios. Beneath the white roof of the pavilion, a fountain ejects a tall spray of spun sugar. But that's just the top third of the edifice! The fountain and its enclosure sit on a base of wafers *d'allemande*, which is supported by free-form mock-stone arches made of *petits pains à la duchesse* (glazed with rose-colored sugar), bordered by a circle of almonds *mirlitons*. Underneath this, the bottom-most base is made of sugar-dusted "*canapés*" with yet another border of coarse sugarcoated meringues.*

To twenty-first-century eyes, these assemblages can appear like kitsch exploded to an operatic dimension—all that's missing is a miniature chocolate Aida belting out "Ritorna Vincitor." But, to the nineteenth-century sensibility, this sort of runaway fabulousness was supremely tasteful precisely because if its rich ornamentation. Simplicity was not considered a virtue. Much more

---

* Wafers *d'allemande* are spiced with cinnamon, cloves, and nutmeg; *petits pains à la duchesse* are éclairs filled with apricot or peach marmalade; almond *mirlitons* are small round tarts lined with puff pastry and filled with a sort of frangipane (almond and egg) filling, the "*canapés*" refer to strips of sugar-dusted puff pastry.

important was the evident fact that these fantastical *pièces montées* were visibly the result of enormous time and effort expended by an artiste unparalleled in his craft. Carême's sheer technical bravado (and his efforts to share and publicize it) set the bar very high indeed for generations of French pastry chefs—to say nothing of wedding-cake decorators of the next two centuries.

Carême's talents were quickly recognized. Providence smiled once again on the young Antonin because, as it turned out, rue Vivienne, where he served his apprenticeship, was also home to the noted gourmand and, not inconsequentially, one of Europe's greatest statesmen, Charles-Maurice de Talleyrand. Talleyrand was a brilliant politician and a savvy opportunist (though that may be redundant). He was a nobleman who made his career through the overthrow of the aristocracy. An early supporter of Napoleon, he also helped manage the restoration of Louis XVIII to the throne in 1815. What's more, the former bishop combined a prodigious appetite for women with a taste for fine dining. One Englishwoman who was none too pleased by his advances noted, "During the whole repast the general conversation was upon eating. Every dish was discussed, and the antiquity of every bottle of wine supplied the most eloquent annotations. Talleyrand himself analysed the dinner with as much interest, and seriousness as if he had been discussing some political question of importance."[60] Of course, to Talleyrand, French cuisine *was* a weapon of diplomacy, and eventually he would deploy the young Antonin Carême as a marshal in his culinary conquests.

Most likely it was Talleyrand's *maître d'hôtel*, Boucher, who first noticed Antonin and began to commission the teenage pastry cook's flamboyant *pièces montées*. Many of these were assembled in the basement kitchens of the Hôtel Gallifet when Talleyrand moved across the river to the foreign minister's palace (today the Italian cultural institute) in the ever-fashionable Faubourg Saint-Germain. (Talleyrand was Napoleon's foreign minister at this point and, accordingly, a prodigious entertainer.) By 1804 Antonin had accumulated enough capital to set up his own pastry shop, though just how much time he spent there is questionable, given the effort he devoted to shuttling between Talleyrand's city and country residences, to say nothing of free-lancing for Napoleon and his family.

The ambitious pastry cook also made a conscious effort to seek out catering jobs that would put him next to the best chefs of the day. "It was under Monsieur Richaut, the famous sauce cook of the house of Condé [a preeminent family of the ancien régime]," he would later recall, "that I learned the preparation of sauces . . . and under the orders of Monsieur Lasne that I learned the best part of cold buffet preparation. . . . I saw a great deal, I made valuable observations and I have profited by them."[61] These freelance apprenticeships allowed him to make the relatively rare transition from *pâtissier* to chef.

All this was occurring at the same time as Napoleon marched his men toward a vainglorious doom. Yet even as the French troops perished in the east, Paris bubbled with a revived social scene (almost) worthy of Versailles. Then, in 1812, European power politics were turned upside down following Napoleon's disastrous foray into the Russian winter. By 1814 it was the Russian emperor Alexander I who marched into Paris. He boarded with Talleyrand, who, in the interim, had nimbly switched sides. The tsar was so impressed by the wily old diplomat's celebrated chef that he requested his services for the duration of his stay. "My cooking," Carême would boast, "was the advance guard of French diplomacy."

Nonetheless, when it came to the following year's Congress of Vienna, where Talleyrand was sent to negotiate peace with the victors, Carême was absent. Instead, he opted to stay home to put the finishing touches on his first book. *Le Pâtissier royal parisien* came out in September 1815 and sold well enough to warrant a second edition by December. Over the next forty years, scores of editions of Carême's books would be published, in Paris, mostly, but also in Leipzig, London, and Barcelona.

By this point, the wunderkind of the Parisian slums was renowned across Europe. Royalty vied for his services. For a time, he cooked for the Prince Regent (later George IV) in London. Then he left for Vienna in the employ of the free-spending British ambassador. He accepted an invitation from Tsar Alexander I to come to St. Petersburg, but he did not find the Russian capital or the semifeudal organization of the Romanov kitchens to his taste. After just a few months in St. Petersburg, he returned to Paris, and then once again to Vienna, and then back to Paris.

By the 1820s, French cuisine had succeeded in conquering Europe much more successfully than had Napoleon. Antonin Carême was simply the most famous chef among the foreign legions that labored abroad. English lords, Austrian counts, and Russian princes all employed French or at least French-trained cooks. After the Revolution, they were a dime a dozen.

Admittedly the fashion for all things French long predated Antonin Carême. As early as 1687, a German commentator groused, "nowadays everything has to be French with us. French clothes, French dishes, French furniture . . . to such an extent that even French diseases are exclusively in fashion."[62] It all started with Louis XIV. Few European monarchs could even aspire to reproduce the magnificence of Versailles, but many tried to emulate as much of it as their pocketbooks allowed. They got news of the latest French dining fashions from a continuous stream of diplomats, spies, and courtiers who flowed back and forth across the continent. When Anna Amalia, duchess of Saxe-Weimar in the mid-1700s, began to hold salons *à la française*, she imported a French pastry chef to bake the appropriate accompaniments. In Paris itself, the food was a tourist attraction. As early as 1670, Savinien d'Alquie boasted in the first gastronomic guide to France that foreigners visiting Paris declared that "the thing they want most in the world is to have a hundred stomachs so that they could eat everything that is put in front of them, since they've never before had anything so good."[63] There is no doubt that some of this can be put down to chauvinism evidenced by many French food writers; however, foreigners did concur. French cookbooks were translated into every major language. By 1815, English-, German-, Italian-, Spanish-, even Czech-language cookbooks were riddled with French jargon. Here you could learn how to make "French *biscuit*," "*Zitronem Gelee*" (*gelée au citron*), "*Meringhe*" (*meringues*), "*compotas*" (*compôtes*), or "*krem ze smetany*" (here, literally a *crème* made of cream), in each respective language.[64] Still, Versailles' culinary influence before the Congress of Vienna shouldn't be overstated. Eighteenth-century cookbooks outside of France have plenty of Italian and even English recipes too. The French culinary conquest of Europe really only began once the little emperor was safely removed to St. Helena.

You would think that with the collapse of Napoleon's empire, Europe would turn its back on the font of all that destruction, but in fact just the opposite happened. If, on the eve of the storming of the Bastille, French models in dance, fashion, theater, and food were widely emulated abroad, after Waterloo, Paris could claim no rival as the world's tastemaker. In the case of food, this happened in part because of all those unemployed French cooks who trained generations of foreign chefs to cook *à la française*. But there may have been another reason too, which stemmed from the fundamental changes in French society caused by the Revolution. Previously, the foreign fashion victims who emulated the styles of the Bourbon court tended to belong to the same highly restrictive aristocratic clique as the crowd at Versailles. But that model was now gone, replaced by a less exclusive social order. For most of the nineteenth century, France would be the only place in Europe with a republican form of government (albeit fitfully) and the sole country where the bourgeoisie unmistakably had the upper hand, in politics as in style. Europe's middle classes now had a fashion plate that they could imitate. Admittedly, the wealthy burgers of Leipzig, Vienna, and Turin had much ambivalence about all those violent Gallic revolutions, but at the same time France symbolized enlightenment, a place where they, the untitled classes, could call the shots. In Paris the future was now.

When Antonin Carême returned to Paris from Vienna in 1822, he was fully aware of the changing times—even if he didn't always approve of them. Although a descendant of Louis XIV now sat on the throne, real power was spasmodically but inexorably flowing from the old landed aristocracy to the haute bourgeoisie created by revolutions both industrial and political. By the 1820s, the richest person in France wasn't the king; it was a banker by the name of James Mayer Rothschild. In 1823, he offered Antonin Carême a job. If, after a career spent cooking for Europe's royalty, the chef hesitated accepting a position with a commoner (and a Jew to boot), he kept quiet about it. He would only graciously comment: "If the nouveau-riche man shares the good life with his friends at table, he finds nobility of character and his soul is happy." Carême's new employer's vast resources couldn't have hurt the decision either. Without doubt they both knew that the financier wasn't just hiring Carême for his meringue know-how. Despite their money, the Rothschilds weren't initially accepted in Parisian society, but who would refuse to dine at their house where the great Carême presided over the kitchen? Soon enough the great German poet Heinrich Heine would note, "all society meets at their parties." Needless to say, the Parisian banker's evenings were in a league of their own. The age-old strategy of entertaining to impress didn't apply to millionaires alone, however; it would increasingly by employed by the growing ranks of a more modest middle class seeking to ennoble its character.

The Sweet Life of the Bourgeoisie

Visitors to France after the 1816 restoration noted how much things had changed since 1789. One tourist was the Irish novelist Sydney Morgan. Lady Morgan, as she was known despite her bohemian pedigree (her father was a theater impresario), wrote unabashedly romantic novels laced with a heavy dose of Irish nationalism. Her politics didn't endear her much to the English ruling class, though they seemed only to increase her sales. She liked visiting France, where she felt free to air her opinions, and wrote about her trips there on at least two occasions. Lady Morgan had a delightfully perceptive eye when it came to the everyday. She wrote, for example, about the invention of the *déjeuner*, a late breakfast or lunch. "The Revolution," she said about her 1816 stay,

> has effected a considerable change, particularly by introducing a custom hitherto unknown on our side of the Channel, that of taking a *déjeuner à la fourchette*. Before the Revolution, few persons of any rank took a regular breakfast; even their dinner was not always the most substantial or luxurious meal. . . . The supper, on the contrary, combined all that was brilliant in society, and elegant in display. . . . Of these once elegant and fashionable entertainments, not a trace now remains.

These new *déjeuners* were apparently served at noon and consisted of a substantial buffet. Visiting the château of the noted liberal and American Revolutionary War veteran General Lafayette, she was greeted with a lunch table "profusely covered with roasts, ragouts, dressed fish, pastry, salads, fruits, and sweetmeats, with all sorts of wines, while tea and coffee were served round, *pour la digestion.*" Dinner was now served in the early evening instead of the afternoon. What Lady Morgan does not mention is the reason for these changes.

Whereas among the old idle aristocracy, leisure had ordered the day (including when meals were served), for the ascendant bourgeoisie, it was their office hours that set the schedule. Bankers, merchants, and civil workers could not devote their entire afternoon to dinner—thus the delayed dining hour. This also meant that the salon (still very much in vogue) had to be shifted later into the evening. Here the bill of fare stayed as it had been earlier. It still depended as much on the confectioner as it had in the era of Marie Antoinette. One minor change was that in Lady Morgan's day, tea briefly became the dernier cri in beverages. The novelist asserts that every "woman of condition" had one of these soirées once or twice a week when tea and pastry were served. "The most usual, and indeed the most fashionable evening collation," she wrote, "is 'le thé,' which, without being strictly the English tea, or the French goûter, formerly taken between dinner and supper, combines much of what is best in both—the exhilarating beverage of souchong and hyson, with confectionary and ices, found only in France." She added that this is often served a little before midnight.

Much to Lady Morgan's approval, women and men mingled at these evenings at home, discussing politics, philosophy, art, and fashion. "There is perhaps no country in the world," she wrote, "where the social position of woman is so delectable as in France." Yet even as the genteel bomb-thrower was relishing the unbounded status of her continental sisters, Frenchwomen were increasingly fenced into ever-narrower confines. One of the less-noted corollaries of the Revolution was the increasing divide between the roles of men and women in society, at least among the trendsetting classes. Though this took place in every corner of the industrializing world, it took distinct forms in every society.

The French bourgeois was a somewhat different creature than the German burgher and an altogether different breed from a middle-class American. In France, the new plutocracy didn't discard everything from the ruin of Versailles. What they did was to pick selectively through the wreckage, in the process refashioning the ancien régime's old tools to the new context. In the old days, what mattered most was your bloodline. In an aristocratic society a person could compensate for a lack of breeding by lavish spending and behavior that imitated the elite, but that only got him or her so far. Now that barrier was gone. Individuals were increasingly judged on their actions rather than their pedigree. Class still mattered, but so, increasingly, did gender.

Ironically, as wealthy men succumbed to an ideology of work, the upper-middle-class women who had traditionally helped their businessmen husbands run their shops were gradually restricted to a life of leisure. This was a slow process. In one study of northern France, the shift took place only with the generation that grew up around 1850.[65] What these women found was that leisure, or at least socially acceptable forms of leisure, had to be learned. The model of Versailles provided some guidance, but no bourgeois woman could really give herself over to pleasure for pleasure's sake in the style of Marie Antoinette. Pleasure had to be rationalized and explained. Even in France, pleasure needed a reason. Dessert, for example, became a useful accouterment to that holdover from the monarchy, the salon. Serving lavish desserts was also a way of demonstrating the taste and discernment that now substituted for an aristocratic bloodline as a sign of breeding.

It's instructive to compare the tastes and consumption habits of the French middle classes to those of England. It goes far in explaining the continental predilection for fine, expensive artisanal confectionary rather than the widely affordable but relatively low-quality offerings on sale across the Channel. Here a few words of explanation about the structure of post-Revolutionary France are in order. Despite the fact that barely a decade seemed to pass without some revolution, and republics alternated with kingdoms and empires with a rapidity that would give later generations of schoolchildren palpitations at exam time, there was actually one continuous trend from 1789 to 1914. Gradually but inexorably, the role of the aristocracy, whether as power brokers or tastemakers, withered and eventually disappeared. This was not the case in England, where the gentry held onto power well into the twentieth century, in part by co-opting rich merchants and industrialists into its exclusive club. In France, the tastemakers were decidedly bourgeois—and often female, at least when it came to such things as fashion, home furnishings, and dessert.

The difference in national attitudes came starkly into focus during the first world's fair, held in London in 1851 in the purpose-built Crystal Palace, that vast ornate cathedral to industry.[66] Here, there were affordable, machine-made English dressers and exquisitely expensive, handcrafted French sideboards. There was cheap Manchester muslin and costly Lyon silk. Wallpaper from northern English factories was exhibited beside wall coverings from Parisian ateliers. The reaction from the French press was unequivocal: the French products were vastly superior in both taste and quality. Never mind that only a small elite could afford them. For, you see, a Frenchwoman of taste wasn't supposed to worry about cost; what was important was the product's perceived aesthetic worth. In England, by contrast, middle-class women were more likely to focus on thrift and perceived value. This difference can be explained in part by the fact that the French bourgeoisie usurped the tastes of the beheaded aristocracy (though admittedly at a more modest magnitude), while in England the middle classes developed their own class-specific set of tastes and consumer expectations. Certainly a tin of mass-produced biscuits was a better value, calorie for calorie, than a single, artisanally crafted *millefeuille*, but try telling that to the fashionably dressed Parisienne shopping on the rue Saint-Honoré.

That said, many French industrialists salivated at the success and scale of British biscuit (cookie) factories. In a report from the

1867 fair (this one held in Paris), the authors were happy to note
that there were now two hundred factories producing *biscuits
de Reims* (a sort of dry, mold-baked ladyfinger) in France, up
from three in 1820.[67] The largest of these employed 260 people.
They were less pleased to point out that in England, it was not
unusual to find a biscuit factory of a thousand employees, with
steam providing the power.* British manufacturers like Huntley
& Palmers cranked out hundreds of tons of dense butter, sugar,
and flour cookies per week, compared to twenty or thirty tons
for the largest French factories. Nonetheless, the writers of the
report judged their countrymen's products as of "excellent quality," while the British ones get a grade of merely "very satisfactory." They were certainly satisfactory enough to be imported en
masse into France, where middle-class ladies of more modest
means served them with that other British import, tea.

Even while many Frenchwomen bought these new industrial
pastries, they never gave up their attraction to the artisan-made
confectionary. One reason was that serving these edible objets
d'art indentified a woman's social status as much as the silverware
on her table and the knickknacks on her mantel. Naturally the
expectations had to be scaled back a little from the old aristocratic standards. When it came to furniture, instead of a solid
silver dressing table (exhibited at the Crystal Palace), an artistically carved mahogany one would have to do. Similarly, precisely
crafted pastries would take the place of Carême's multistoried
pièces montées. But they had to live up to a similar level of crafts-
manship and "artistic" standards.

It is telling how often the French food critic and contemporary of Carême, Grimod de La Reynière, used the word *artiste*
in connection with pastry and confectionary.** The chocolatier

---

* The writers made the incidental point that, in at least one large English factory, almost half
the workforce consisted of children younger than twelve years old.
** *Artiste* has a somewhat broader meaning than its English equivalent, encompassing both
artist and artisan. In either case it is a compliment, indicating someone of great talent.

Bucéphale is a chocolate *artiste*. Monsieur Duval is an *artiste* of sugar work. The pâtissier Benault deserves the title for his *gâteaux de Savoie* but especially his pistachio cream tarts.[68] Later in the century, Carême's pupil François Gouffé outlined the talents needed to become such an *artiste*:

> In order to succeed in the art of pastry, a youth must be quick and intelligent—twin qualities which by imperceptible degrees transform a workman into an artist. He must have a lively and inventive fancy, one able to originate ideas . . . his taste must be good, to enable him to grasp intuitively the proper proportion of ingredients to be mixed to make a palatable whole; he should have that *artistic feeling* which imparts to everything, great and small, that harmony of style which captivates the eye.
>
> A pastrycook must have a rudimentary knowledge of drawing, of sculpture, and of architecture . . . he [must] bring to his work artistic tastes and habits, that he should know how to design an ornament, and carry out his design without violating the most elementary rules of art.[69]

All this artistry came at a price. The French *artistes'* confections were nowhere near as cheap as those English biscuits. But neither were they out of reach for a woman of taste. This penchant for luxury, even in small doses, still characterizes French attitudes to food. In the course of research, I had the good fortune to interview Pierre Hermé, widely considered France's top living *pâtissier*. His stores resemble expensive jewelry boutiques more than sweetshops. He readily concedes that what he sells are luxury goods, but he emphasizes that they are "*affordable* luxury goods." "We have a lot of schoolboys who come in and buy just one *macaron*," he told me. "Here you can have a small pleasure, for just two euros." In today's Paris, a Pierre Hermé *gâteau* is just as impressive, just as indicative of "good taste" as a Cartier choker—but, at six euros a slice, for vastly less cash.

In the nineteenth century, one sign of feminine refinement was to like things that were ornate yet delicate. This was certainly true in women's fashion. As men gave up the tights and fancy shirts of the old order for somber suits and monochromatic overcoats, women usurped the role of the preening peacock, enrobing themselves in layers of crinoline and delicate lace. In a similar vein, it was thought that women should like foods that were frilly and decorative but also delicate and dainty. It was widely assumed that the weaker sex was especially fond of sweets.

It is unclear just how far back the association of sweetness with femininity goes in France. In England, the writer John Evelyn makes the connection as early as 1699. In the context of discussing that era's new fashion of using less sugar in savory dishes, he noted, "now sugar is almost wholly banish'd from all, except the more effeminate Palates."[70] English attitudes don't always hold across the Channel, but in this case there seems to be a consensus. In *Émile*, his 1762 treatise on educating children, the French philosopher Jean-Jacques Rousseau devoted many pages to arguing that girls should practice controlling their urges, not the least of which was their inborn desire to eat sweets. As Sophie, his model student, grows up, she is expected to give up the inborn childish inclination. When she was younger, this led her to steal into her mother's cupboard to taste the *dragées* and *bonbons* hidden there. The exemplary mother caught her in the act and punished her. Eventually, Sophie is persuaded that *bonbons* spoil the teeth and that eating too much makes you fat. "In this way Sophie reformed," Rousseau wrote. "Sophie has preserved the characteristic taste of her sex: she likes milk, butter, cream, and sweetmeats; is fond of pastry and dessert, but eats very little meat; she has never tasted either wine or intoxicating liquors. Moreover, she eats very moderately of everything."[71]

This idea that women (and children) have a more developed sweet tooth becomes commonplace in the nineteenth century. Dessert, Carême suggested in the 1815 edition of the *Pâtissier royal*, was the reward at the end of the meal, "especially for young ladies and children at table." In 1825, Brillat-Savarin, the great French philosopher of the kitchen, noted that the appreciation of gastronomy also includes the love of sweet delicacies (*friandise*). He said that these "light, delicate dishes of little substance such as preserves, pastries and so on" were included in his philosophy of taste specifically "for the benefit of the ladies and those men who resemble them."[72] By the second half of the century, even working-class women had acquired the taste for sugar. Tholomyès, the hedonistic student in Victor Hugo's *Les Miserables*, expresses what was by then a cliché: "but my beauties, remember this: You eat too much sugar. Women have only one fault, nibbling sugar. Oh, consuming sex, the pretty, little white teeth adore sugar."[73]

But, as Rousseau makes all too clear, the well brought up Frenchwoman wasn't just supposed to gorge on sweets, she was to choose them with a taste and discernment that made up for any lack of breeding. Now that sugar was widely affordable, just having sweets on your table was no longer a status symbol. The dessert had to be artistically made, naturally, but it also had to be au courant. Menon had made this point long ago when he disparaged his predecessors for their passé pastries. If keeping up with the latest styles had always been a marker of the leisure class, it now became practically a full-time occupation as the pace of fashion quickened in the nineteenth century.

New flavors elbowed aside the old, none more so than the once exotic and rare vanilla. Like chocolate, vanilla originates in tropical America. It is the long seed pod of a type of orchid native to New World jungles. The Aztecs used it to flavor their spicy hot chocolate, and when the Spanish took up the beverage, they adopted the sweet-scented spice as well. The French followed suit. Given that it was foraged in the wild, vanilla was fantastically expensive. In his treatise on the new drug beverages, Dufour noted that a half-pound of good vanilla cost twenty livres in the 1690s (the equivalent of about three weeks' wages for a skilled craftsman).[74] Up until the late eighteenth century, it was used almost exclusively as a partner for chocolate. There were the occasional recipes for vanilla ice cream and vanilla custard, but it did not become ubiquitous until much later. Grimod de La Reynière listed a mere half-dozen vanilla-flavored sweets and beverages in his 1810 *Almanach des gourmands* even as he waxed poetic on its delights. He also went to great lengths to expose all the counterfeit vanilla on the market. There was plenty of motivation to make ersatz vanilla, given that it cost two hundred francs a pound in his day (dinner in a fine restaurant cost about fifty).* Due to its price, only the best pastry shops could afford to use it with any regularity. Pastry chef Pierre Lacam, writing as late as the 1880s, wrote how in his youth (some thirty years back), he had worked in a pastry shop where vanilla was never even used. Instead, orange flower water was the most common flavoring. He added that cheaper shops still continued the practice. Vanilla only became more affordable once it began to be cultivated in the French colonies in the Indian and Pacific oceans, where it was introduced in the first half of the nineteenth century.[75]

Sweetshops ignored new trends in flavoring at their peril. What's more, there was pressure not merely to keep up with the competition but to outdo it with ever-newer creations. In 1810, Grimod de La Reynière was already writing of confectioners coming up with gimmicks to generate buzz. He described how the former royal (and now imperial) confectioner Duval set up an exhibit of sugar work of the "triumphs and amusements of the Emperor" to attract customers. The publicity stunt apparently

---

* Today, vanilla is hardly cheap, but even the most expensive Tahitian vanilla costs no more than about seventy-five dollars per pound (in 2010).

attracted a large crowd of curious onlookers. Like fashion design-
ers, sweet makers came up with new lines of bonbons, especially
for the busy winter holiday season. The confectioner Des Roziers
came up with at least two brand-new confections that year for
the annual New Year's ritual of candy giving. As a result, Des
Roziers claimed that he had a turnover of forty thousand francs
on December 30 alone! Of course there had been a thriving, if
not always especially competitive, retail market for sweetmeats
in Paris since the Middle Ages, but in the new bourgeois century
the dynamic of supply and demand was fundamentally altered.
Simply put, there was much more of both. By the 1870s, there
were around four hundred pastry shops in Paris serving a population of a little less than two million. Sweet makers needed to do
something to stand out from the crowd.[76]

One reliable source on the waning and waxing of fashions
in patisserie is the nineteenth-century pastry chef and cookbook
author Pierre Lacam. He wrote that pastries made with Italian
meringue had a vogue after 1873. Linzer tortes were à la mode in
Paris in the 1880s. *Sablés*, the French answer to shortbread cookies, were practically unheard-of in the 1850s, but by the 1880s
no pastry shop could do without. (Lacam claimed they were
invented in Lisieux in Calvados in 1852.)[77] Presumably their
popularity benefited from the marketing of the imported British
biscuits they resembled.

Many desserts, like the savarin, were created by novel rework-
ings of the classics or by a new combination that had never been
tried before. The same brothers Julien who had come up with the
savarin are credited with that other nineteenth-century classic of
French patisserie, the *gâteau Saint-Honoré*. What they came up
with is a study in crispness and cream. A brittle crust of pastry
forms a base for gently crispy cream puffs covered with crunchy
caramel, while pastry cream and whipped egg whites provide a
cloudlike contrast. None of these individual elements was new,

but the idea of assembling them together into a crown and filling the center with *crème Chiboust* (pastry cream lightened with whipped egg whites) was original. If Carême's labored *pièces montées* were a little like the solid silver dressing table of the 1851 World's Fair, the *Saint-Honoré* was the well-padded Second Empire sofa, highly ornate, of course, and almost aristocratic with its crownlike design, but in the end much more practical. A *gâteau* for the bourgeoisie if there ever was one.

If, in France, the *gâteau Saint-Honoré* was "the emperor of cakes"—as one food historian described it—it was another, simpler cake, the *gâteau moka*, that would have the greatest influence beyond the borders of its birthplace. The cake, created according to Lacam by a pastry cook by the name of Guignard in 1857, is little more than a *biscuit* made in a style that had been familiar to French cooks since the time of Marie de Medici. What broke the mold was its frosting of coffee-flavored buttercream. An 1872 recipe instructs you to slice the cake in thin layers and fill it with a buttercream made by beating a coffee-flavored Italian (cooked) meringue into softened butter (an egg yolk–based filling is now more common).[78] Unlike in central Europe, cakes, in the sense of large round frosted disks, weren't particularly important to the French repertoire. There isn't even a specific French word for it like the German *Torte* (see the following chapter). *Gâteau*, like the English "cake," is nonspecific. *Biscuit* was equally vague since these could be small or large, cookies or cake. Prior to the *gâteau moka*, what we would call cakes were typically either dusted with sugar or occasionally glazed with royal icing made by stirring together sugar and egg whites.

Curiously, this sort of buttercream-filled layer cake never really took off in France. By the time Lacam mentioned it in 1888, it was already on the out list. Where it really captured the imagination was in Austria-Hungary, where it begat hundreds of layer cake offspring.

Perhaps buttercream was just too heavy for French tastes accustomed to a panoply of custards and creams, piped into cream puffs or piled onto pastry. In France these sorts of desserts were everywhere. Pierre Lacam recounted how in Lyons, the pastry shops would have a strainer of sweet, vanilla-scented whipped cream set beside the unfilled cream puff shells. Each would be filled to order so that the pastry would remain crisp. In Rennes, he wrote, each Sunday afternoon, a parade of young women carried basins full of whipped cream to pile on the country *echaudés* that they also sold.* There is still a penchant for a combination of crisp and creamy in French patisserie, rather than the denser, chewier textures that characterize many other European desserts.

Where you do find these heavier desserts is in the countryside, especially in the border regions like Franche Comté, where, instead of the fluffy *charlotte russe* of the capital (lined with ladyfingers and filled with "whipped cream, Bavarian cream, blancmange or any jelly" according to Antoine Gogué's 1855 *La Cuisine française*), there is the apple charlotte, made by lining a mold with leftover bread and filling it with stewed apples. Alsace has its rustic apple tarts, Brittany its crêpes. Yet when these were adapted by the professional urban pastry chef, they were inevitably transformed into something daintier for their customers.

Teatime on the Rue Royal

In France, bourgeois women were the pastry shop's primary clients. This was in part a result of the transformation of French

---

* *Échaudés* vary by region; some are very buttery and sweet while others are savory. In either case, they are made with a yeast-leavened dough that is boiled before being baked (like a bagel or Messisbugo's *brazzatella*).

society after the collapse of the monarchy, in part due to the changes brought about by industrialization. Paris in particular became increasingly unmanageable (at least as far as the middle class was concerned) in the period between 1779 and the founding of the Third Republic in 1870, decades when deadly street protests alternated with revolutions. In the first half of the nineteenth century, the capital's population roughly doubled. The city's poor crowded into dark fetid tenements, their untreated sewage flowing into the Seine, which also became their primary source of drinking water. The streets were rough, filthy, and dangerous throughout the city. The upper classes, as yet, weren't segregated by district, or even by building, so that "respectable" women had no choice but to mingle with fishwives when they opened their front door. Cafés, which, even in the days of Napoleon's empire had welcomed women, became no-go zones except for men and for women you wouldn't bring back home to mother. Consequently a kind of fortress mentality took hold in the thick-curtained apartments of the middle class, where even the type of entertaining described by Lady Morgan became more constricted. The salon did not quite melt away, but it was no longer the sort of intellectual sparring ground where both men and women could talk politics. Now the important decisions were made in smoky cafés by men with fat cigars, while the salons were ever increasingly places to chat about matters of taste rather than affairs of state.

Meals were changing too. The grand dinners and even the exclusive salons once held at Versailles had existed in a world somewhere between the public and private spheres, a little like an exclusive restaurant or club. That was no longer the case. In the bourgeois century, dining at home increasingly became a private event presided over by the woman of the house rather than a professional maître d'hôtel. The cook, but most especially the confectioner, needed to make a new, more modest kind of product, more nibble than show. Pastry shops proliferated to supply small-scale desserts like savarins and baba rums, *religieuses* and charlottes for the nuclear family dinner table and other intimate get-togethers. Certainly the sort of dizzying desserts deemed necessary for Talleyrand's table would have been all too ostentatious for an afternoon visit where coffee, chocolate, or (less likely) tea were offered by women to women along with sweet snacks from the *pâtissier*. All that was left of the splendid eighteenth-century aristocratic *collation* was the unassuming afternoon *goûter*.* In an early-twentieth-century shopping guide to Paris, the American writer Frances Sheafer Waxman described the city's habits a generation earlier: "All French people, men, women and children, were wont to break the long wait from a twelve o'clock lunch until an eight o'clock dinner [with the *goûter*]. The French society lady would stop in the midst of her shopping or calling at one of the innumerable *pâtisseries* where are sold such delectable tiny tarts, *éclairs* and *petit fours*. One or two of these cakes with a glass of Madeira constituted the *goûter*."[79] She may have added that women oftentimes partook of a similar snack at home.

By this point, women were no longer quite so restricted to their well-upholstered prisons. In the 1860s and '70s, Paris was transformed when Baron Haussmann, Napoleon III's city planning czar, bulldozed great swaths of the city to put in his boulevards. In the process the slums were razed, sanitation improved, and Paris became a much healthier, airier city, at least for those who could afford to live there. The grand avenues were now lined with expensive apartment buildings even as the poor were shunted to the outskirts. This meant that respectable women dared to go out, to go shopping to the new gaslit department stores, stopping by the *pâtissier* for a little pick-me-up. Pastry shops, at least the few that had tables, became the respectable feminine alternative to cafés.

---

* Today, the after-school *goûter*, often a *pain au chocolat* or a baguette smeared with Nutella, is mostly associated with children.

To get a sense what these places looked like, go visit the original branch of the famous Parisian confectioner Ladurée on the Rue Royal, a few steps from the exclusive boutiques of the Faubourg Saint-Honoré. The company traces its origins as a pastry shop to 1871, when the former bakery was transformed into what would later be called a tea room. The last time I was there, the place looked decidedly shabby. Still, if you look past the incongruous disco-era spotlights tacked onto the ornate gilded woodwork and a century's worth of nicotine stains, you can see what once appealed to its well-heeled clientele. The place is meant to evoke the age of Versailles, though a shrunken Versailles of Victorian propriety. The ceiling is decorated with a profusion of tubby angels in a pseudo-rococo style reminiscent of the old monarchy. Like the famed mirrored rooms of the old palace, the walls are lined with mirrors, giving each guest opportunity to preen and be seen. Here, elegant ladies swathed in yards of crinoline and silk could sip their Madeira and close their lips around sweet cream-filled éclairs—all out of public view. For unlike the typical Parisian café, which is open to the street, Ladurée is shut in behind curtains, ensuring that the ladies within are shielded from any immodest stares. This discreet alternative to the male café would become a model for what would later be dubbed the *salon de thé.*

The solution to where Frenchwomen at the turn of the twentieth century could modestly congregate outside of their homes came from an unlikely source, the English tea room. "For some years now," the author of *Les consommations de Paris* ("The Foods and Beverages of Paris") wrote in 1875, "Parisians have picked up the English habit of eating out at [pastry] shops." Some, at least, had also started drinking tea *à l'anglaise*. Less than a generation later, afternoon tea was the new vogue.* Apparently the people

---

* Up until this point, *le thé* was more like an after-dinner cocktail party. In 1884, even as the new fashion was taking hold, the etiquette authority Louise d'Alq recommended serving the tea at eleven P.M. With the beverage she suggested serving a large soft *gâteau* such as a brioche, biscuit, or baba, then a plate of "so-called tea cakes" as well as a platter of "sandwichs."[80]

who introduced this particular Victorian ritual to Paris were a pair of English brothers surnamed Neal who ran a stationery and book shop, the *Papeterie de la Concorde*, on the Rue de Rivoli in the 1880s. They arranged a couple of tables at the end of the counter, shielded by a screen, and put up a sign advertising "afternoon tea." This consisted of tea with biscuits. The idea took off, though with some Parisian alterations. Mary Abbot's guide from 1900, *A Woman's Paris: A Handbook of Every-day Living in the French Capital*, explained: "Tea, if one requires it,— and it is the rage now in Paris to *"feeve o'clouguer"*—[from five o'clock] may be had at many places, principally at cake-shops." By this point the Neal brothers had set up a proper tea shop above their bookshop. Ladurée was now considered a little dowdy. "Among the shops, near the Madeleine," Abbot tells us, "is Ladurée's, which had a vogue once, and is still moderately patronised, especially on Sunday afternoon, after vespers." The in place to take tea was the Ritz Hotel. Novelist Jeanne Philomène Laperche (writing under the pseudonym Pierre de Coulevain) had no illusions as to the style and purpose of the new vogue:

> [D]uring the last five years, [tea rooms] have sprung up like mushrooms. They are to be found everywhere now, in the Rue Cambon, Rue de Rivoli, Rue St.-Honore, on the road to the Louvre and to the Bon Marche. Paris has gone beyond London in this respect. Does that mean that the Frenchwoman has become a tea-drinker? Not at all, and what is more, she never will be. She neither knows how to drink it, how to prepare it, nor how to serve it. She swallows it in an absent-minded way, like any kind of infusion. It excites her nerves without making her gay. She is too fond of talking, and of showing off to advantage, to give the necessary attention to the teapot, samovar or kettle. She is incapable of repeating several times

over the prescribed questions: "Strong or weak? How many pieces of sugar? Cream or lemon?" And when she does ask the questions she never listens to the answers. The tea-room where, if she is not afraid of appearing too *bourgeois*, she takes her chocolate, makes a pleasant halting-place between her shopping and her trying-on. It answers two purposes—her wish to be sociable and at the same time exclusive.

There was still something of the old *salon* in these get-togethers, even if the electrically illuminated surroundings made for a very different atmosphere. The need for dessert had shifted some too. You still needed a sweet snack to go with the chocolate or tea, but there was little of the showiness of the eighteenth century. Now that sugar was cheap, instead of the sweetmeats being posed in elaborate set-pieces to demonstrate wealth and power, the tarts and cakes were arranged more in the manner of sales displays, a little like couturier gowns in shop windows. The clientele still demanded a high level of artistry, but the cakes now resembled jewelry more than furniture. For purely practical reasons, the *salon de thé* reinforced the need for smaller individual portions. The individual tart, the napoleon, the éclair, the baba made in an individual mold, the *opéra* (essentially a *gâteau moka* with a chocolate glaze) served as a small rectangle were specifically created to serve just one customer at a time.

At home, the so-called *service à la française* (the custom of serving numerous dishes simultaneously) was being replaced by *service à la russe*, where one dish followed another. This change in service, which had been introduced in the early 1800s, was adopted very, very gradually in France. Carême, for one, was unenthusiastic about the change. There were still writers in the second half of the nineteenth century who objected to it, in part because they thought it cheap.[81] Yet it came to dominate nonetheless, and when it did, it was the final death knell for the age-old habit of serving a selection of sweet entremets along with the roasts and stews. Dessert itself was no longer a buffet of mostly sweet dishes with the odd savory mixed in. In her 1883 etiquette guide, *Le nouveau savoir-vivre universel* ("The New Etiquette for Everyone"), Louise d'Alq explained how, for the dessert course, cheese is followed by fruit, then cakes, confectionary, and finally ice cream. Not that this meant the towering sweetmeats of old were abandoned quite yet. For dinner, our nineteenth-century Miss Manners specified three vases of flowers and two *pièces montées* interspersed with plates of cakes, *dragées*, pyramids of fruit, and compote dishes filled with jelly. It wasn't quite Versailles (Madame D'Alq emphasized that she was writing for families of "modest" wealth), though the echo was still there. But just. Her approach was now increasingly old-fashioned. Other authorities suggested little more than flowers and fruit for a centerpiece.[82]

So here, after our long journey, we finally arrive at the modern sense of dessert; that is, one or more exclusively sweet dishes served to finish a meal. By 1900, the contemporary definition, which had so long been in flux, was now set. It hasn't changed much since then.

This is not to say that, in the hundred-plus years that followed, French pastry hasn't been immune to innovation. There have been new desserts invented and foreign (especially American) desserts incorporated into the repertoire. It's almost impossible to find a *pâtissier* without *les brownies* or *les cookies* for sale. *Le crumble* became a cliché of casual dining spots in the early years of the twenty-first century. The term *salon de thé* has become largely meaningless as every other restaurant seems to advertise itself as a café/*salon de thé*. There are still those old-fashioned places frequented by women of a certain age, discreetly set above pastry shops in the provinces, but in Paris you are more likely to hear Japanese than French in institutions like Ladurée. Frenchwomen no longer need such places to be sociable and exclusive. Dessert is no longer integral to ideas of gender—or class for that matter. Well, almost.

The Picasso of Pastry

When I ask France's most famous pastry chef about the subject of dessert and femininity, he is unequivocal. "It's very feminine, sensual, emotional," Pierre Hermé says of dessert, "because when you taste a cake, or another pastry, it provokes the emotions."

"[It is] because the first flavor is sugar," he continues, echoing a theme more common to distant India, "because it is the flavor of mother's milk. In France, I've never seen that men would be interested in sweet things. Yes, I think that pâtisserie carries values that are decidedly feminine."

Admittedly, Hermé is not an anthropologist or a psychologist, but he knows his pastry. He has received France's highest honor, the Légion d'honneur, for his contributions to the art. If there is a contemporary heir to Antonin Carême, it is he.

I met Pierre Hermé in his little office above his Lilliputian sixth arrondissement boutique located only a few minutes' walk from Hôtel Gallifet, where Antonin Carême constructed his fabulous *pièces montées* for the insatiable Talleyrand. Downstrairs, the little gem of a confectionary shop is so small that the customers wait in a line that stretches halfway down the block. The window makes it look like a trendy jewelry shop or an art gallery more than a pastry shop vitrine, completely opaque except for four small transparent squares that frame the almost austere desserts. Two of the openings contain a pair of practically monochrome éclairs, while the other two feature slightly oversized shot glasses filled with what the shop owner calls "emotion vanille," a sort of postmodern baba rum made by layering King Stanislaw's favorite cake with strata of mascarpone cream infused with three types of vanilla.

Some years back, *Vogue* magazine dubbed Hermé the "Picasso of pastry." Though the appellation is a little silly, there is something to it. Despite the evident mastery of the confectioner's craft that his desserts display, Hermé himself doesn't have the meticulous, almost scientific demeanor of many pastry chefs. There is something unruly about him. He really does come across with the intensity and deep curiosity of an artist. In more ways than one, he is the very personification of how creative and robust French confectionary remains to this day. And influential too.

Hermé is not only a whiz in the kitchen, he is a master of marketing. In one inspired publicity stunt, he made the unspoken parallel between the couturier and *confiseur*, fashion designer and confectioner, crystal clear. For several years running, he would introduce new collections of pastry by staging a fashion show where models carried the season's confections down the runway.

What he is best known for, however, is launching the *macaron* craze that swept through Europe in the first decade of the twenty-first century. Of course *macarons* had been common enough in France since the 1600s. The recipe hasn't changed much since then. They are still little more than egg whites, ground almonds, and sugar, though today they are mostly sold in pairs with a layer of buttercream in between. Even the idea of filling *macarons* is not especially new. During Marie Antoinette's 1792 internment by the revolutionaries, hollowed-out *macarons* were used to smuggle in contraband. In a more mundane vein, late-nineteenth-century recipes sometimes called for a filling of apricot jam.[83] Nonetheless, the kind of buttercream-filled *macaron* popular now probably only dates from the post–World War II era. Ladurée claims that they were invented by Pierre Desfontaines, a distant cousin of the shop's first owner in the mid-twentieth century, but this is difficult to corroborate. It is true, however, that Ladurée was well known for the confections in conventional flavors of chocolate, vanilla, and coffee when Pierre Hermé worked for the company in the 1990s. Hermé's epiphany was to bring in a whole new world of wacky flavors, from relatively normal ones like green tea or rose to off-the-wall ideas such as wild rose, fig, and foie gras. The idea took off to such an extent that in 2009 Picard, France's giant frozen food chain, was selling a selection of *macarons* with flavors that included basil-lime, white peach–rose, and yuzu praline!

The decorated *pâtissier* has no false modesty about his influence, but neither is he willing to rest on his laurels. Hermé welcomed me with one of his new signature vertical parfaits layered in individual glasses. This one began with a wee disk of génoise covered with a layer of ever so slightly spicy wasabi yuzu gelée (made with fresh wasabi, he assures me), a muddle of chopped-up grapefruit, and a dollop of wasabi-flavored custard cream. A couple of green tea marshmallows about the size of sugar cubes sat jauntily on top. It was altogether refreshing, playful, and just weird enough to make you stop and question what dessert is really supposed to be. Yet, except for the unexpected flavor, there was nothing here that a nineteenth-century chef wouldn't recognize. The classical technique, the penchant for creaminess, were there. A slight grin flashed across the great chef's face before he plunged a spoon into his own serving. The future of French dessert is in good hands.

Gâteau Saint-Honoré à l'orange
· ·

Today the *Saint-Honoré* is typically filled with pastry cream lightened with whipped cream, but this wasn't necessarily the case in the 1800s. Pierre Lacam, writing in that century's last decade, noted that there were numerous variations of the crown-shaped confection. One version was made all of brioche, some were filled with whipped cream only, others with a Bavarian cream (set with gelatin). Some years earlier, Jules Gouffé in his 1873 *Le livre de patisserie* listed eight variations on the *Saint-Honoré*, including the classic one filled with *crème Chiboust* and flavored with vanilla, chocolate, coffee, or orange zest, and another four filled with strawberry, chocolate, apricot, and pineapple bavarian cream. The following is adapted from his orange one, using the classic *crème Chiboust* rather than the whipped cream–enriched pastry cream more common today. If you are concerned about the risk of using raw egg whites, use the pasteurized kind. Gouffé also calls for the traditional *pâte à foncer* (lining paste), used almost exclusively for these sorts of confections in his day, though a more contemporary *pâte brisée* or even store-bought puff pastry could be used. Classic French tart dough was made using a fundamentally different technique than English or American pie dough, using soft rather than hard butter. The result is more like a cookie dough rather than being flaky. Today many French cooks make a *pâte brisée* (one type of *pâte à foncer*) using cold butter. The following recipe is a lot of work, which is why most reasonable people left it up to the *pâtissier* to do the work for them.

Makes 8 servings

½ pound *pâte à foncer* (see recipe following)

Choux *pastry*

1 cup water
¼ cup unsalted butter, cut into pieces
½ teaspoon salt

3½ ounces (about 1 cup) all-purpose flour
4 eggs

Superfine granulated or castor sugar

Crème Chiboust

6 egg yolks
2 cups whole milk, divided
Pinch salt
1⅓ ounces (about 6 tablespoons) all-purpose flour
1 teaspoon orange zest
1 tablespoon orange flower water
6 egg whites
1 cup sugar

For the oranges

1 cup sugar
¼ cup water
2 medium seedless oranges, divided into sections

1. Roll the *pâte à foncer* into a round ⅛-inch thick. Cut out a 10-inch circle, set this on a baking sheet lined with parchment or very lightly buttered cookie sheet, and place in the refrigerator. Once cold, prick the center in several places with a fork.

2. Preheat oven to 400°F.

3. To make the *choux* pastry, combine the water, butter, and salt in a heavy saucepan over moderate heat. Bring to a boil and then, all at once, add the flour. Stir well with a wooden spoon until

the dough no longer sticks to the sides of the pan. Remove from heat, transfer the dough to a bowl, and then stir in 1 egg at a time, making sure each egg is fully incorporated before adding the next. It is much easier to use a food processor or heavy-duty mixer to incorporate the eggs. Let the dough cool briefly.

4. Partially fill a pastry bag fitted with a ½-inch plain tip with the *choux* pastry and pipe a 1-inch-wide ring around the edge of the puff pastry circle. Bake in the center of the oven, about 25 minutes. Remove and let cool. When cool, dust the surface of both the pastry and the "crown" with castor sugar. Using a blowtorch, caramelize the sugar. Set aside to cool.

5. Prepare the *crème Chiboust*: Stir together the egg yolks, ¼ cup milk, and pinch of salt in a medium bowl. Whisk in the flour until smooth. Bring the remaining milk to a boil. Gradually pour the hot milk into the yolk mixture, stirring continually, then return all of this to the saucepan over moderately low heat. Cook, whisking continually, until the mixture is as thick as pudding and just barely begins to boil. Strain through a fine sieve if lumpy. Stir in the orange zest and orange flower water. Cool until tepid (about 100°F), stirring occasionally. With an electric mixer, beat the whites until they form soft peaks. Gradually beat in the sugar and beat until they are very firm and glossy. Fold the egg whites into the custard in two additions. Cover and refrigerate.

6. Make the sugar syrup by combining the sugar with ¼ cup water in a heavy saucepan over moderately high heat. When the sugar has melted and reached the crack stage (about 300°F), set aside. Using a skewer or long fork, dip the orange sections in the melted sugar and arrange these on top of the *choux* pastry "crown."

7. Mound the cream in the middle of the crown or use a piping bag to pipe it decoratively around the middle.

Pâte à foncer (Pastry Dough)

Any remaining pastry dough can be used for making quiches, tarts, etc. You can refrigerate it for about a week or freeze it for several months.

Makes a little more than 1 pound dough

9 ounces (about 1½ cups) bleached all-purpose flour
½ cup ice water
6 ounces (1½ sticks) unsalted butter, at room temperature
¾ teaspoon salt

1. Sift flour onto a work surface, forming a little mound. Make a well in the center. Pour in half the water, add the softened butter, and sprinkle with salt. Using just your fingertips, break up the butter into small pieces, then slowly begin to stir in the flour—once again, using just your fingertips. With a rubber spatula, clean the butter from your fingers and incorporate back into the dough. Continue to incorporate the flour, gently squeezing the dough together. You will need to use up all the flour. If it seems to need a little more water, add it before all the flour is used up. You can't add any more water once all the flour is incorporated, but if the dough is too soft you can mix in a little more flour.

2. Once you have a relatively soft dough, proceed to work it in the following manner. Gather the heap of dough in front of you. With the heel of your hand push off small pieces the size of a

walnut from the far side of the dough away from you, flatten-
ing them as you do so. Once you have done this once, gather
the dough in another heap and do this two more times. Wrap
in plastic wrap and allow to rest for two hours. This is essential
so that the gluten in the dough can relax.

5

SCHLAG AND STRAUSS

✳ *Vienna* ✳

DEMEL'S

It is unlikely you'd peg Kurt Nitsche for a pastry chef. He is a man of compact stature and liquid eyes, looking for all the world like a retired chemistry professor rather than someone who devoted his life to the sugary arts. Appearances notwithstanding, Herr Nitsche spent the better part of his career working for Vienna's most renowned pastry shop, Christoph Demel's Sons. Demel's is to Vienna what La Scala is to Milan, or Wrigley Field is to Chicago. (Well, perhaps not quite so democratic.) I figured that if there was anyone who could give me insight into the life of the confectioner in this, the most dessert-obsessed city in the world, it was this modest, meticulous maestro. He rose graciously from his bentwood café chair when I recognized him, introducing his friend and colleague Karl Schuhmacher, another one of the profession's more influential luminaries. (More on him later.)

I had been a little surprised when Herr Nitsche suggested that we meet at Café Griensteidl rather than at Demel itself. Griensteidl is a bit of an imposter, though an awfully successful one: all dark wood and a vast expanse of windows overlooking the Hofburg, the old imperial palace. It's located on Michael-erplatz, a charming round "square" that was once home to the original Demel's. There was also a Café Griensteidl here once, but that closed in 1897. This incarnation is a mere twenty years old, a blink of an eye as far as the Viennese are concerned. Yet the locals have grudgingly adopted it, in no small part because they know that the café shares the same owners as Demel, so the cakes are impeccable. And you don't have to fight the tour bus hordes that descend on the more famous pastry shop. As we sit down, I order a *Maroni-Torte*, a four-layer affair of chocolate and chestnut cream robed in an infinitesimally thin coating of marzipan and an overcoat of chocolate glaze. A little "kiss" of chocolate-dipped chestnut cream sits jauntily on top. As I tear into the cake I notice that the pastry chefs have only ordered cof-fee. Herr Nitsche waits politely as I clean my plate before launch-ing into his tale.

The trajectory of a Viennese pastry cook's life hasn't changed much since Ludwig Dehne, the founder of what is now Demel's, first opened his doors more than two hundred years ago. "My career at Demel's began in 1968," Kurt Nitsche begins, "after my apprenticeship at a little pastry shop in the eighteenth district." Unlike in France, where the guilds were blown to bits by the same winds that did away with the monarchy, in Austria the old guild system is alive and well, and duly regulated by the government. You can't just open up a shop here and call yourself a pastry chef. Still, a suburban apprenticeship hardly prepares you for the rig-ors of Demel's. Herr Nitsche started at the bottom, making tea biscuits (*Theebäckerei*). "We made a hundred and fifty different kinds in the early days," he murmurs nostalgically, adding that the varieties have dwindled down to just a few dozen.

"Women just don't entertain at home the way they used to," he explains.

After his stint in cookies, the young pastry chef graduated to the yeast dough department, and finally the chocolate station. Demel's still has a dozen of these highly specialized units or *Posten*, each focused on a single type of dessert. There is the cake *Posten*, ice cream *Posten*, pastry *Posten*, meringue *Posten*, and another station entirely devoted to Sacher torte. It all sounds very rational, but to hear Herr Nitsche tell it, the kitchen resembled a freemason's lodge as much as a modern business.

Each *Postenchef* used to have two assistants and a little stained book of his own specialties he would share with no one. "If he called in sick, his cakes wouldn't get made," the veteran confectioner recalls with a suspicion of a smile. "When journalists came, the count (Demel was owned for a time by the Hungarian count Berzeviczy-Pallavicini) wouldn't even let us speak to them. If you handed over a genuine Demel's recipe, your career would be over.

"Sometimes when someone asked for a recipe, we would alter it so it wouldn't work," he chuckles. "But this too was propaganda for the firm. People just became more curious about how the desserts were really made."

Herr Nitsche's final stop was in the decorating *Posten*. "The best cake decorator in Vienna," Herr Schumacher interjects, even as the Demel's alum pulls out a portfolio worthy of Antonin Carême. He shows me pictures of cakes as delicate as a Strauss waltz, while others are as bombastic as a Verdi opera. There is a nine-story cake he baked for an Indian wedding for four hundred guests. The sweet skyscraper towered over nine feet above the table. The recipe called for twenty-five pounds of butter, twenty-four pounds of flour, ten pounds of sugar, 342 eggs, and another twenty-seven pounds of almonds and dried fruit—and that was only for the bottom layer, which was the only one that was edible. It cost €11,000 (about $15,000) in 2007, or about half a year's salary of the average Austrian worker.

In some ways, today's Demel's is a little less quirky and a bit more transparent than it used to be in Herr Nitsche's youth. The recipes now reside in computer files, and the decorating *Posten* is in full view of the customers. The pastry chefs work their magic behind glass walls, a little like Disney's animators were once put on display. Yet, despite the updates and the numerous changes in ownership in the last two hundred years, the standards have remained high. Even under the new corporate owner (Demel was acquired by the multinational catering concern Do&Co in 2002), the whipped cream for its famous Sacher torte is still beaten by hand.

The first sweet maker in the Demel line was actually named Ludwig Dehne. He opened up an ice cream salon on the ground floor of a rococo palazzo on Michaelerplatz in 1786, the same year that Mozart premiered his *Marriage of Figaro* at the nearby Burgtheater. The confectioner was perfectly located to capture the well-to-do theatergoers, directly across the street from the imperial palace and surrounded by the old aristocratic quarter of the city.

Not much more is known about Dehne. He was evidently not from Vienna, because he married his wife, Antonia, the daughter of a well-to-do tailor, at least in part to gain the privileges of citizenship. Given the then-current fashion among his aristocratic clients for all things French, he changed his name to Louis. He seems to have specialized in ice cream and candy rather than cakes. Sadly, his success didn't protect him from this disease-ridden age, and he succumbed to tuberculosis before he could celebrate his thirtieth birthday.

And what of Antonia? She was now saddled with small children and a thriving business in a profession in which women weren't allowed to work. Her solution was decidedly practical. Within six months, the twenty-three-year-old widow married a talented confectioner named Gottlieb Wohlfahrth. Gottlieb had a shop a few blocks away on the Mehlmarkt (today's Neuer Markt), a decidedly less ritzy location. A dozen years later, though, they had returned to Michaelerplatz, as it happened, right next door to Dehne's original spot. In 1813, they distributed handbills to let tout Vienna know:

> Gottlieb Wohlfahrth has the honor to notify the nobility and the worthy public that he has relocated his shop from Mehlmarkt to his own premises at No. 4 Michaelerplatz, where one will find every kind of delicious pastry [*Backereyen*] and refreshments, along with preserved fruits, the finest liqueurs, etc. These are served promptly at the cheapest price. As of June 27th of this year, every afternoon after 2 o'clock, our clients will be able to avail themselves of ice cream of various kinds, served by the portion, in slices, or molded (for the last category one need order in advance) which our guests will no doubt honor with their approval.
>
> The comfort and spaciousness of the premises in the new shop has inspired the proprietor to open a type of lounge—and to this end to supply it with newspapers—providing a pleasant social setting for spending one's leisurely hours.
>
> Decorative pieces, "plateaux," plates for confectionary, cake stands [*Tambours*] and the like are available for sale or rent, as before, in the greatest variety and the latest styles.[1]

The timing was good. In the autumn of 1814, the city filled up with a vast gaggle of European aristocrats assembled for the Congress of Vienna, which had been called to remake Europe after the Napoleonic Wars. Across the street from Gottlieb and Antonia's shop, the imperial residence was turned into a lodging house for two emperors and empresses, four kings, one queen, two crown princes, three princesses, and two grand duchesses. And in their train came great crowds of nobility, to say nothing of all the worthy public.

For most of the visitors, the diplomatic negotiations didn't seem to be very high on the agenda. "Doubtless, at no time of the world's history had more grave and complex interests been discussed amidst so many fêtes," one attendee remarked. "A kingdom was cut into bits or enlarged at a ball: an indemnity was granted in the course of a dinner; a constitution was planned during a hunt."[2] For the nine months that the Congress lasted, Vienna was abuzz with a never-ending series of balls and banquets, outings, and concerts.

What an opportunity for the best-placed confectioner in the city! Some of the attendees traveled with their household staff—most notably the chief French negotiator, Talleyrand, who had brought his chef—but most relied on the local caterers. A surviving banquet menu for one large gala gives a sense of the quantities involved. The list included hundreds of hams, hares, and game birds followed by great numbers of tarts and pastries as well as almond, pistachio, chocolate, and Seville orange cakes and puff pastry "*gateaux*." There were also some twenty-five hundred biscuits, one thousand *Mandl Wandl* (almond cakes), sixty *Gugelhupf*, and many other cakes and sweets.[3]

Gottlieb Wohlfahrth must have done roaring business over the next few months, which set the sweet maker on the road to success for many years to come. A decade later, a foreign visitor was most impressed by the Michaelerplatz premises: "A magnificent shop, where, in the background, thirty six people can't do enough to satisfy the customer's every need. For sweets we recommend that strangers visit the establishment from eight to ten at night when it is beautifully illuminated, the light cascading down through cut crystal."

Unfortunately, it would turn out that Gottlieb was a better confectioner and showman than a businessman, because when he died in 1826, he left Antonia groaning with debt. Widowed a second time, she didn't rebound as easily as when she was young. She did what she could to help her first husband's son, August Dehne, run the family business, but the workload was just too much for her. She died in 1832 at the age of fifty-six; the church register noted the cause of her death as "exhaustion." Perhaps she felt some satisfaction before she passed away from seeing her son August married to the daughter of a rich linen merchant.

The younger Dehne had more luck than his father and more sense than his stepfather. Early on, he acquired a monopoly on confectionary and beverage sales at the Burgtheater, then the city's top theater and opera house. Because the pastry shop was virtually next door, uniformed waiters could shuttle drinks and treats through an underground corridor. In 1848, he picked the right horse when revolution swept through the capital. That year, as the city's working classes took to the barricades to topple the emperor, Dehne rallied to the side of the regime, leading a company of guardsmen to help suppress the rebellion. Like the Paris confectioners who tried to rescue Marie Antoinette from the guillotine, he dreaded what might happen to his high-class confectionary business if the archdukes and baronesses were ditched into the dustbins of history. Unlike his French colleagues, however, Dehne chose the winning side and did well by it. He was also sensible when it came to money. Not wishing to repeat his stepfather's fiscal ineptitude, he ploughed his money into land, figuring it was a more precious commodity than cakes in a city that was exploding in population. By the 1850s, Dehne was comfortably well off and ready to call it a day. In the meantime, his son had gone into law and had no interest in beating eggs from dawn until dusk. So, in 1857, showing his mother's practical streak, August sold the business to Christoph Demel, the shop's head confectioner. A decade later, the new owner's sons took over and named their shop Christoph Demel's Sons, the name it retains to this day.

When Dehne handed his sweetshop over to his assistant, he also gave him a well-worn recipe book of the sort Kurt Nitsche remembers from his early Demel's days. The little volume provides an only slightly faded snapshot of the sweets and treats sold 150 years ago. There are various types of simple cookies like *Zimtringes* (cinnamon rings), *Anisscharten* and *Mandelscharten* (card-shaped almond wafers flavored, respectively, with anise and almonds), and crisp fritters called *Hobelspänen*. You find fruitcakes, almond cakes, French brioche, and Spanish "Marzeban." There are more complex confections too, like the *Windtorte*, an ornate shell of baked meringue filled with whipped cream or ice cream.* The *Nelson-Torte* was a multilayered extravaganza with a lemon glaze.** The *Russische-Torte* was, incongruously, flavored with orange. (Given the names, these last two probably dated from the 1815 Congress of Vienna.) There are fancy bonbons and *dragées* too as well as all sorts of liquid and semiliquid sweets: sorbets, liqueurs, jellies, punches, and the like.

Nonetheless, the greatest legacy bequeathed by August Dehne wasn't his well-worn cookbook but rather his exclusive clientele and the exceptional location. In certain ways the Demel brothers' Vienna was a very different city than it had been when the elder

---

* The *Windtorte* seems to be an oversized descendant of a meringue cookie called a *Spanische Winde* popular in the eighteenth century. The name most likely comes from the contemporary German name for a morning glory, *Spanische Winde* (did the cookies resemble the open flower?), rather than having anything to do with Spain.

** The *Conditorei Lexicon* ("Confectioner's Lexicon") of 1898 gives two entirely different recipes for the cake, both of which would require the organizational skills of an admiral to complete. In one version, four different cake layers—hazelnut, chocolate, pistachio, and meringue—sandwich apricot, maraschino, and raspberry preserves. All this is coated with a lemon glaze. In the second, you pipe a tall almond meringue border onto a partially baked almond cookie crust. The resulting well is filled with an almond cake batter. Once baked, the center is iced with lemon glaze as well.[4]

Dehne had set up shop on Michaelerplatz. The city had grown, and now wealth was no longer restricted to a narrow aristocracy. Yet despite the changes, power and prestige still emanated from the imperial court. Accordingly, when the Demel brothers finally moved in 1887, they made sure to remain within sight of the entrance of the Hofburg. Even now, though the owners have changed and the menu has evolved, the location remains the same.

In the days of the Hapsburgs, the court may have needed Demel's as much as the confectioner needed the royals. Throughout its history, the imperial kitchen couldn't produce everything the palace wanted. Sometimes it was just better to turn to a specialist. Dehne had been delivering his sweets to the Hofburg for years. In 1836, little Franz Josef, who would grow up to be emperor, made sure his baby brother Maximilian knew what he had missed at his birthday party. In a letter (I imagine he had some help in this), the six-year-old crown prince wrote: "At half past five, during afternoon snack time, we sat down and had coffee served with lots of pastries [*Bäckereien*], then came the doughnuts, ice cream, almond milk, and bonbons from Dehne." Notwithstanding the multiyear relationship, official recognition eluded August Dehne. That only came under Christoph Demel's watch. Finally, in 1874, the new owner could post the prestigious k.u.k. (*kaiserliche und königliche*—"imperial and royal") in front of his name.[5] This was more or less equivalent to the British "by appointment to her majesty the queen," a seal of quality, and a huge PR coup in its day. The relationship with the Imperial house continued until the bitter end. In 1915, in the early days of World War I's destructive fury, the aged Franz Josef still sent Demel's chocolate candy to the women and children in the imperial family. Perhaps in memory of the Dehne bonbons of his youth? Demel's still boasts its Imperial Good Housekeeping seal, even though Austria hasn't had a monarch for close to a hundred years.

SWEET EMPIRE

Foreigners often remark about the peculiar fixation the Viennese have with an imperial past that vanished more than three generations ago. But then, Vienna is an unusual city. It has spent its modern history as the outsized capital of the little republic of Austria, yet in some ways it remains less a part of Austria than a glowing remnant of the old Hapsburg crown. The fantastically rich dessert tradition is a direct product of the ethnically diverse empire that used to sprawl across the heart of Europe. Vienna was the place where German sweet dumpling vendors competed with Venetian biscotti sellers, where French courtiers rubbed shoulders with Turkish diplomats. To further their dynastic interests, the Hapsburgs imported Spanish princesses and Burgundian princes who typically arrived with their own foreign retinues. In the eighteenth and nineteenth centuries, Vienna had the most multinational population of any city in Europe, and possibly the world.

Vienna's beginnings were not especially auspicious. In the 1300s, the Hapsburgs started out with a raggedly shaped and discontinuous realm that consisted of torn bits and pieces of Alpine valleys and a broad swath of rolling countryside mostly to the west and south of Vienna. It wasn't until Ferdinand I moved to Vienna in 1521 that it became the dynasty's permanent capital, but even then it wasn't especially impressive. With barely twenty-five thousand inhabitants, it was about one-tenth the size of Paris. Moreover, Vienna wasn't especially safe. The Ottoman Turks under Suleiman the Magnificent had almost taken the city in 1529; Turkish troops remained uncomfortably close for the next 150 years. (This was probably good for dessert but bad for the citizens' frayed nerves.) It was only after another aborted Turkish siege in 1683 that the city would be safe from the eastern superpower.

Given the fortress city's small size, the imperial court entirely dominated it. In the earlier years especially, many of its members were more comfortable speaking French or Spanish than German. Ferdinand I, for example, had been born and raised in Spain, and both his son and grandson spent their formative years there. A Madrid–Vienna axis remained for years; two more emperors would marry Spanish royalty. The imported empresses brought with them households that could number in the hundreds and included many Spanish but also Italian artisans.[6] Undoubtedly there were confectioners among the staff arriving from Spain, where sugar processing was well established. Nevertheless, the first official record of a *Hofzuckerbäcker*, or court confectioner, only dates to 1576. His name was Matthias Voss. He came from the Netherlands, most likely from Flanders, where most Portuguese sugar was refined. Other confectioners are noted in Vienna in the 1500s as well, and, given the court's limited resources, the habit of turning to town sweet makers to provide the Hofburg's fitful needs must have started early. This was a distinctly different situation than in France, where the high aristocracy typically had their own servants to cater to their sweet tooth.

Presumably these early Viennese confectioners made the candied spices and fruit preserves found elsewhere in Europe at the time, though if the Austrian term *Zuckerbäcker* is any indication, they were just as likely to be in the sugar refining business. *Zuckerbäcker* (also written *Zuggerpacher* or *Zugherpacher*), which today means roughly "confectioner" or "pastry chef," originally meant someone who packed sugar or processed it into the characteristic cones, certainly not someone who baked cakes. By the time the *Zuckerbäcker* finally received imperial recognition in the form of their own guild in 1744, their job had become very precisely defined. According to paragraph nine of the ordinance, they were permitted to make "biscuits [*Pisquiten*], zwieback, almond and other sweetmeats, white and colored confections, candy and other [things] made with sugar, and both candied fruit and preserves, and . . . ice cream, jellies and other refreshments."[7]

It's worth noting that these are specialties that any Venetian confectioner would recognize, which is hardly surprising given how many Italians had settled here. After the Hapsburg acquisition of the Duchy of Milan in 1714, the numbers of southern migrants only kept increasing. By the late 1700s the streets echoed with cries of "*Letti-Mandoletti! Bombiletti! Commandi, signore?*" as Italian vendors wandered the streets selling their almond cookies.* In 1783 the writer Johann Pezzl reported the remarkable increase in these sweetmeat hawkers. "Flitting everywhere with their trays," he noted, "they occupy the street corners, the paths, the gardens and the theaters. Six years ago, there were only two such Italian sweet peddlers, now there are a good forty, both Italian and German."

Writing twenty years later, the satirical journalist Joseph Richter complained that he could barely walk a step down the Kohlmarkt without running into a *mandoletti* vendor. He added, only partly tongue in cheek: "But where would we be without them? What would the millers do with their spoilt flour and the spice sellers with their unsold enema sugar if there were no customers for the *mandoletti*?" (Sugar, presumably of inferior quality, was a frequent ingredient in enema recipes.) There were many complaints against the Italian sweet peddlers, and not just because they were suspected of using inferior ingredients. The confectioners despised them not merely for their foreign origin but because their guild was supposed to have a monopoly on this kind of sweetmeat. Eventually the *Zuckerbäcker* had their way and the *mandoletti* sellers were confined to the city's periphery.

---

* Presumably these were much the same as Italian *mandorlini*, which are a sort of dense, chewy cookie made with an Italian (cooked) meringue, ground almonds, and flour. Later Austrian recipes for *mandoletti* are more like French *macarons*, sometimes adding hazelnuts to the mix. *Bombiletti* (perhaps a variant on *bombolette*, meaning little pitcher?) is a little obscure but may have referred to cups of chilled beverages.[8]

It took a couple of tries though. Italian vendors sold ice cream and lemonade as well. In fact it could be argued that Italy had a much greater influence on music and confectionary—those arts in which the Viennese excel—than did France, despite all the imported *biscuits* and *crèmes*.

Nonetheless, at least for the upper reaches of the aristocracy, the style magnet of Versailles was already beginning to exert its irresistible attraction. Dynastic politics played into this as well. When the Habsburg empress Maria Theresa married Francis, the Duke of Lorraine (now a part of France), in 1736, the duke brought the French style of his youth right into the Hofburg. Under his staff, meals began to be served in the French manner, *à la française.*[9] In 1770, Maria Theresa's fifteenth daughter, Maria Antonia—the ill-fated Marie Antoinette—was married off to the French king Louis XVI to create yet another family link.

During Marie Antoinette's lifetime, and with even greater intensity after her untimely end, French literature, French design, French fashion, and most notably French food became all the rage in the Hapsburg lands as elsewhere in Europe. Though just how deeply any of it sunk in is another matter. Austria shares with Bohemia and Bavaria a style of cooking that is usually lumped together as South German cuisine (*Süddeutsche Küche*). The recipes are mostly of the stick-to-your ribs variety, with a lot more meat and dumplings than fish and vegetables. Certainly the Austrian emperors themselves tended to have plain Austrian tastes no matter the *ragouts* and *pièces montées* that became de riguer at state functions. According to Michael Kelly, a tenor who sang at the *Marriage of Figaro* premiere, the reigning monarch, Josef II, dined almost exclusively on boiled bacon—though he also apparently liked his chocolate candy.[10] His grandson Franz Josef had a well-documented fondness for boiled beef. Moreover, it's sometimes hard to distinguish between genuine French imports and the French names given to indigenous meals and rituals. When the six-year-old Franz Josef reported on his after-

noon birthday party, he called it by the French word *"goûter,"*
but did that mean that the Viennese had picked up the habit
of a mid-afternoon sweet snack from the French? Were all the
ragouts, bouillons, fricasées, bonbons, biscuits, gelées, and *crèmes*
that litter German-language cookbooks of the early nineteenth
century simply slavish copies of French originals or just very
loose translations? Were they just masquerading under French
names to make them sound trendier, in the way Ludwig Dehne
called himself Louis? Most likely there was a wide spectrum of
influence, from a great deal to almost none at all.

Certainly the Vienna of Mozart and Dehne was no mere
reflection of Paris. The once-modest capital of the early Hapsburgs now contained a quarter-million inhabitants. The aristocracy who lived there, or just came into town for the season from
their vast Bohemian and Hungarian estates, built extravagant
baroque palaces and dressed the part. Karoline Pichler, a novelist (and sometime student of Mozart), described noble ladies
swept off to Sunday services draped in great black capes trimmed
with Polish fur, edged with red satin and blue fox, glistening with
clumps of gold. The bewigged and powdered men were no less
fabulous in their black velvet coats lined with pink satin over
vests made of cloth of gold, their feet encased in red-heeled slip-
pers with diamond buckles. The city was full of cafés and dance
halls. In 1809, a visiting German journalist noted with amazement that every evening fifty thousand Viennese were out dancing.[11] Surely an exaggeration but it gives you a sense of the place.

∽ Sugar Beet ∽

In the gray months of late autumn, the railway sidings in
suburban Vienna are often backed up with long brown
trains mounded with homely, light brown lumps. Sugar
beets look like rutabaga, large tan turnips promising noth-

ing so much as pig feed. Yet it was these unglamorous bulbs that made sugar cheap and available to anyone and everyone. This is the most prosaic but influential cause for the ascent of sugar in Viennese cooking and baking.

One of the twisted ironies of the old sugarcane industry is that, although slavery did bring down the cost of sugar in the 1700s, it wasn't by all that much. It wasn't until the technological innovations of the following century, but most especially the introduction of the sugar beet in continental Europe, that sugar got cheap. By that point, many of the Caribbean sugar colonies simply couldn't compete with European sugar. It would be simplistic to say that in and of itself the sugar beet caused the downfall of slavery in the Caribbean, but it did play a role. By 1900, sugar beets produced two-thirds of the world's sugar. (Today that proportion has once again been reversed.)[12]

The idea of producing sugar from beets wasn't especially new. The French agronomist Olivier de Serres noted that the syrup produced from beets resembled sugar syrup as early as 1600. It wasn't until 1747, however, that Andreas Sigismund Marggraf, a Berlin chemist, managed to crystallize this syrup into something resembling cane sugar, and it took a student of his, Karl Franz Achard, to make the process economical. Achard published his results a little before 1800 in France, where the authorities were as yet lukewarm to the idea. Meanwhile, in Silesia (then part of Prussia), two sugar beet refineries were built in 1801 and 1805 under his direction. A French newspaper reported in 1811 that Achard's partner, Baron de Koppy, "is very well satisfied with the quantity of sugar, rum, spirits, and vinegar furnished by his beets, and with the ready and lucrative sale he had for these different staples." No wonder. Sugar prices had skyrocketed due to Napoleon's blockade of continental ports, which had cut off most colonial goods. The French were nonetheless reluctant to pick up the technique from the Germans, turning instead to their indigenous grapes to try to produce a sugar substitute. Napoleon finally gave the thumbs-up to the sugar beet in 1811. With four years to go to Waterloo, however, the industry barely got started before the ports reopened to the tropical crystals.

With the return of peace, the sugar beet industry largely collapsed in both France and Prussia. It was not revived until after about 1835, when both Prussian and Austrian government policy began to favor its cultivation and manufacture. Local consumption was taxed even as exports were subsidized. As a result, production skyrocketed. By 1900, Germany and Austria-Hungary led the world in sugar production, followed by France and Russia.[13] Finally, dessert was for everyone.

It wasn't just the aristocrats who were transforming Vienna; it was also the bankers and businesspeople, manufacturers of silk and paper, "the worthy public" addressed by Gottlieb Wohlfahrth's handbill. They too wanted to live the high life, to go to the theater and stop at Dehne's or Wohlfahrth's salons for a dish of ice cream. Many, like Dehne, were immigrants. People of every social rank and occupation—numberless Hungarians, Slovenes, Slovaks, and Poles—crowded in from the multinational empire. By the late 1800s, it seemed like every middle-class Viennese household had a Czech cook. Around 1840, Johann Georg Kohl, a north German travel writer, noted that many sweetshops across the Hapsburg Empire were run by emigrants from Grisons (Graubünden), a Swiss canton wedged into the Tyrol. He also points out that it was generally reckoned that about a thousand Turkish citizens lived in Vienna, not primarily ethnic Turks but rather Sephardic Jews, Greeks, and Armenians.[14] As a result of the mixing and blending of all these nation's sweet-making traditions, Vienna became a sort of primordial batter from which arose today's multifaceted dessert repertoire. Though "dessert" is perhaps too limited a term for all the sweet foods eaten by the descendants of the Hapsburg imperium.

SWEET SUPPER

When I was little, I spent my summers and holidays at my grandmother's house in Choceň, a town of little consequence in eastern Bohemia. My grandmother, Marie Mrázová, was born a couple of years before 1900, to a family of rural gentry. As I sat on her lap she would tell me stories of visiting the Hapsburg capital as a child with her father, who was a sometime member of the Austro-Hungarian parliament. Like many women of her class and generation, Marie was sent to finishing school, where she was supposed to learn the fine arts of cooking and embroidery—neither one of which interested her in the least, and neither one of which she needed much after she married my grandfather, a prosperous industrialist. That's what the cook and her helper were for. But Marie made an exception for cakes and other sweets, as evidenced by a family cookbook handed down from her. It's almost entirely devoted to pastry.

By the time I arrived, my grandfather was gone and all the money and land had been expropriated by the communists. Marie was left with a cramped apartment and a spartan kitchen. In her case, though, necessity wasn't the mother of invention. She still wasn't much of a cook—at least when it came to the savory dishes. Sweets, however, were another matter and, luckily, these weren't just limited to dessert. On many weekday evenings, she would start up her coal-fired stove and take down the ancient

cast-iron pan from the wall to make *lívance*, yeasty pancakes that
we spread with homemade prune butter. On Sundays she might
bake *buchtičky*, little pillows of Danish-like dough that were then
drowned in sweet custard sauce. Other times we sat down to a
supper of hot semolina porridge stuck with a dollop of liquefying
butter and thickly dusted with sugar and cinnamon. Depending
on the season we ate dumplings filled with blueberries, apricots,
or plums smothered with breadcrumbs or cottage cheese, sugar,
and melted butter.

None of these was considered dessert; they were a meal. In
much the way Americans would categorize pancakes and waffles as breakfast rather than dessert, there are numerous sweet
foods that central Europeans would never think to eat after a full
meal. It's just that we ate our pancakes for supper instead of in the
morning. This is still true elsewhere in the old Hapsburg Empire.
I recently visited a ski resort in Innsbruck where the goggled
diners happily made a meal of *Kaiserschmarrn* (an airy pancake
cut into pieces) with applesauce, or a *Dampfnudel* (a large, plain,
steamed dumpling) with custard sauce and a topping of sugar
and poppy seed. When I explain this habit to French acquaintances they blink in fascinated horror. In contemporary France,
such a *collation* in lieu of lunch or supper would be unthinkable.

On Austrian menus today, the term *Mehlspeise* is used more
or less as Americans use the term "dessert" or the English, "pudding." This is not, however, what it meant in earlier Hapsburg-
era cookbooks. Two hundred years ago, it signified, loosely, food
served on fast days made with some sort of dough. Literally, *Mehlspeise* means "flour food." The *Neues Saltzburgisches Koch-Buch*
("The New Salzburg Cookbook"), a seminal cookbook written
by Conrad Hagger around 1700, includes a vast section devoted
to these *Mehlspeisen*. Hagger, according to the fulsome curricu-
lum vitae with which he introduced his book, worked his way
up in the kitchens of princes and bishops. His stints took him to
Belgrade and Innsbruck, Vienna and Milan. Mostly, though, he

cooked in what is now south Germany, finally settling down for a long gig with the archbishop of Salzburg. The cookbook occasionally reflects some of his early peripatetic career, but in most respects the recipes are solidly south German, none more so than the *Mehlspeisen*. Many of these aren't sweet at all, and some have barely any flour in them. His "flour foods" include recipes for frittatalike egg dishes, strudels filled with spinach or cabbage, sweet puddings, unsweetened doughnuts, and a "Goglehopff" as well as dishes that belong more appropriately to the confectioner, the likes of lemonade and fruit preserves.

A hundred years later the *Mehlspeise* category had narrowed, but it still included many foods no one would consider dessert. One popular south German cookbook that saw many editions, Maria Neudecker's *Die Baierische Köchin in Böhmen* ("The Bavarian Cook in Bohemia"), does indeed include such things as pancakes, strudels, *Gugelhupfs*, baked apples, rice pudding, and doughnuts in her *Mehlspeise* section, but the author also included potato dumplings and noodles. In more modest households, supper might consist of no more than soup followed by one of these *Mehlspeise*.

In part, the *Mehlspeise* can be explained through religion. The identity of the central European Hapsburg Empire was forged in wars fought against heretics and infidels. On the one hand, the realm was the easternmost Christian bulwark against the Turk, having stopped the westward surge of the Ottoman Empire in the 1600s. On the other, it was the citadel of staunchly orthodox Catholicism. Earlier in the seventeenth century, the Hapsburg emperors had wiped out the Protestants in Bohemia and their other domains. They saw themselves as the heirs to the Holy Roman Empire and took their mission as the titular rulers of Catholic Europe very seriously. That certainly included enforcing the church's dietary rules, especially the cycle of fast and feast that demanded abstention from meat practically one day in three. As a result, central European cookbooks were divided into meat and fast sections well into the nineteenth century, a practice that had been long abandoned in France.[15]

Unlike the other great Catholic nations of Europe, the Hapsburg imperium was almost entirely landlocked. There were freshwater fish, of course, but they were never as abundant (or cheap) as sea fish. This may be part of the reason the central Europeans turned to dumplings and strudels. For those who could afford it, these were often sweetened. The Renaissance habit of adding sugar to everything—not only dessert-type dishes but meat, fish, and vegetables—was alive and well in south German cooking right through the eighteenth century. As late as 1810, Neudecker instructed readers to put sugar in a dish of crab strudel, in baked calves liver, in braised beef, and in meat sauces—though admittedly the fashion for sweet-savory foods was on its way out.

Whereas in more modest homes, a *Mehlspeise* might take the place of a main course, among the aristocracy it functioned more or less as the entremets did in eighteenth-century France. At the Hofburg, as at Versailles, each course consisted of numerous dishes that landed on the table all at once, the sweet preparations interspersed with the savory. Dessert was another matter altogether. In this case the term, as well as the idea of a final sweet course, was largely a French import, and the same sort of dishes were served as in France, mainly cookies, candy, ice cream, compotes, and other—mostly flourless—sweets. In the imperial kitchens a different department was responsible for the sweetened *Mehlspeisen* (doughnuts, *Gugelhupfs*, and strudels) and the sweets that belonged to the *Zuckerbäcker* or confectionary department. As the guild rules outlined, the latter was supposed to be in charge of such things as jellies (hugely popular at the time), meringues, custards, and compotes.

The distinction between *Mehlspeise* and dessert remained even after the fashion for so-called *service à la russe*, where food was served sequentially rather than all at once, caught on in the Hapsburg domains in the 1800s. Now soup was followed by "entrées," fish, meat, and then finally the sweets, or at least certain types of sweets. Czech cookbook author Karolína Vávrová gave numerous sample menus in her *Pražská Kuchařka* ("Prague Cookbook") from 1881 that largely follow the imported French model. The sweet *Mehlspeisen* are the one exception. These warm "flour foods," she instructed, are to be served either before or after the roast, adding that among these are understood to be baked puddings, strudels, soufflés, doughnuts, and similar. Stewed fruit, creamy desserts, cakes, ice cream, and cookies were always to be served after the roast and in that express order.[16] But then who could object to doughnuts at any point in a meal?

JAUSE

Religion may also explain, at least in part, the Austrian tradition of the *Jause*, or snack. The Viennese are great snackers, happily stopping midmorning or afternoon for a *Krapfen* (doughnut) or a *Wurst* (sausage). In Mozart's Vienna, the *mandoletti* sellers competed for customers' attention with vendors hawking doughnuts and the Bavarian *Dampfnudeln*. But of course you couldn't nibble on a *Wurst* if it happened to be Friday, or Lent, or any one of a number of other fast days. A slice of strudel, though, or in later days, a piece of cake, could be had any day.

⌒ Doughnuts ⌒

Austrians, like all good Catholics, have a tradition of over-indulgence before the long fast of Lent. Admittedly, Carnival is more low key here than in Rio or New Orleans. In the Tyrol, where old traditions live on, Fat Tuesday, or *Fasching*, is celebrated with a parade of townspeople hidden behind grotesque masks straight from a Hansel and Gretel nightmare. But mostly the imminent arrival of Lent is marked by an Alpine-sized avalanche of doughnuts, or *Krapfen*: *Krapfen* filled with jam and cream, chocolate *Krapfen* and vanilla *Krapfen*, but also the eggy, boozy *Eierlikor Krapfen* filled with an egg-based liqueur. The explanation for this orgy of fried dough balls is simple. Doughnuts are an indulgence that used to depend on animal fat: clarified butter if you could afford it but lard for most. But in either case, great cauldrons of animal fat, something that used to be forbidden for the next forty days and forty nights.

Of course doughnuts are hardly limited to the Catholic world, or even to Europe. They are probably as old as frying. The ancient Greeks had their doughnuts, as did the Indians and medieval Arabs. Spanish speakers in both the Old World and the New eat several kinds of *churros*. The Dutch relish their *olie bollen*, which eventually turned into American doughnuts according to most historians. And of course we mustn't forget Italian *zeppole* served on St. Joseph's Day, right in the middle of Lent, proving once again that Martin Luther was right about the Italians.

Roughly speaking, there are historically two ways of making fritters. In the case of *churros*, and at least some of the fritters that go by the name *bignè* (from the French *beignet*) in Italy, the dough is made by mixing flour into hot water. You often find egg in there too. There's a recipe for this sort of thing in the ancient Roman cookbook of Apicius. Scappi, the Renaissance maestro, called a much-enriched version of the same thing *frittelle alla Veneziana* (sic). The other kind of fritter is essentially made with an enriched bread dough, leavened with yeast. This is the category to which the much-beloved *Krapfen* belongs. In the

United States a third, cakey kind of doughnut was developed in the mid-1800s that depends on baking soda or powder for its lift.

In central Europe, the origin of a fritter called *Krapfen* probably goes back to the Middle Ages. *Das Buch von guter Speise*, a collection of recipes from around 1350, has several recipes for *Krapfen*, though these only give directions for making the filling, omitting instructions on how to make the dough. Savory fillings such as meat, fish, and even sauerkraut show up in German-language doughnut recipes over the years, but there are many sweet versions as well. A recipe from 1531 has you mix honey and wine into the dough as well as the usual eggs, flour, and yeast.[17] In many cases the *Krapfen* were unfilled. Instead, there is some evidence that they were dipped in honey or possibly some sort of fruit butter (apples and plums were traditionally boiled down in central Europe without the addition of expensive sugar).

Jam-filled *Krapfen* seem to have come along only when they moved to the big city. (It's hard to remember today that jam used to be an exclusive product to which the confectioners had a monopoly.) In Vienna these filled doughnuts came to be called *Faschingskrapfen* because of their association with Carnival (*Fasching*), though *Krapfen* were by no means limited to the holiday. The Florentine *Gazetta Universale* reported that, in 1790, Leopold II distributed three hundred pounds of ham, three thousand pounds of roast veal, three thousand bread rolls, and two thousand *Krapfen* to the Viennese street after a ceremony during which vows of allegiance were exchanged between him and the representatives of his domains.[18] Rather skimpy if you ask me, but the Hapsburgs were known to be skinflints. And *Krap-*

fen weren't cheap. They ran one to two *Kreutzers* unfilled and double that with a filling. That would have cost an ordinary worker one or two hours' wages. The really fancy ones cost even more. You could tell a good-quality doughnut by the telltale ring around the edge, a sign that it was light enough not to sink in the cooking fat. In Vienna, calling a girl as pretty as a *Krapfen* was a high compliment. And when a gentleman was so intimate with a lady that they would share a doughnut, there had better be a proposal in the works.

Jelly- or cream-filled doughnuts were—and are—popular throughout central Europe. The Poles, Czechs, and Germans all have some version of these fried dough balls. Nineteenth-century Ashkenazi Jews often celebrated Hanukah with jelly doughnuts. Now, ironically, this Germanic specialty is eaten with abandon on the streets of Tel Aviv and Jerusalem for the holiday. Even the Italians picked up the taste for these doughnuts. In Venice, *Krapfen* were simply added to their already extensive fritter repertoire. In Florence, the local *bomboloni* (a little smaller but made following the same recipe) are most likely derived from the northern original. In America, the Pennsylvania Dutch have retained the carnival doughnut habit into the twenty-first century. They call the fried dough balls *fastnachts* (after the German name for Shrove Tuesday), though theirs are mostly of the unfilled variety. For the rest of America, doughnuts have no season.

The local snacking habit conveniently aligned with one of those imported fads that swept central Europe at the dawn of the nineteenth century, mainly the French *thé* with its accompanying *collation* of sweetmeats. As in Paris, this was a "meal" served more often in the evening than in the afternoon, typically before or after a night at the theater. The actual drinking of tea was almost incidental to it. In dance-mad Vienna they seemed especially fond of the *thé dansant*, a sort of semiformal ball.

For those not quite in the know, books were published to explain just what was to be served at these functions. It helped if the author had a French name. François Le Goullon, chef to the trendsetting Anna Amalia, duchess of Saxe-Weimar-Eisenach, put together a popular little volume with the long title *Der elegante Theetisch oder die Kunst einen glänzenden Zirkel auf eine geschmackvolle und anständige Art ohne grossen Aufwand zu bewirthen* ("The Elegant Tea Table or the Art of Giving Brilliant Parties in a Tasteful and Respectable Manner Without Great Expense").* The book, first published around 1800, remained in print for over a generation. Listed were the sorts of things the duchess presumably served to the likes of Goethe and Schiller when they dropped by for tea.

Anna Amalia was by all accounts an extraordinary woman: a competent ruler during her son's minority, an accomplished amateur composer, and a great patron of literature. I imagine her teatime resembled the brilliant *salons* of the Parisian intelligentsia more than the sweaty dance parties of Vienna. The menu, however, was surely a blending of both. Given Le Goullon's origins, it's hardly surprising that chocolate mousse, cream puffs, madeleines, and other sorts of French tea cakes were served,

---

* The issue of expense must have been a considerable one. A German writer writing in Leipzig, where the prices couldn't have been vastly different from nearby Weimar, noted the costs of various pastries the mistress of an upper-crust household might expect to pay. Cakes could be had from anywhere between twenty to a hundred *groschen* depending on the variety. Ice cream ran from thirty to thirty-six *groschen* per *quartl* (a third of a liter). A modest *collation* for a "few" friends included two cakes, two German pounds (a *pfund* weighed 560 grams) of cookies, another pound of pastries, and two pounds of *macarons* at a total cost of 120 *groschen*. A skilled worker earned about five *groschen* a day at the time.[19]

but, remarkably, many of the snacks in the chef's cookbook were much more local. There were Bohemian *Mandel-Kollatschen* (almond butter cookies) and German *Krapfel* (doughnuts), and plenty of *Kuchen* (baked sweets of various shapes) as well as *Torten* (though Le Goullon spelled it "Tourte").

In Vienna, social climbers needing assistance in these French dining fashions found another guide in the books of F. G. Zenker, one-time chef to the princely Bohemian family of the Schwarzenbergs and a prolific popularizer of aristocratic foodways. "Tea-drinking has probably never been in vogue as it is now," Zenker wrote in his 1824 *Der Zuckerbäcker für Frauen mittlerer Stände* ("Confectionery for the Middle Class"), "when no gathering or get-together can be held without being entertained with this drink." He explained the concept further in a how-to entertaining book published three years later:

> The *Thee-Zirkel* (tea party) describes an amiable gathering of the upper classes. The term "tea" refers [not so much to the beverage] as to the type of society, the hour of the day, the toilette of the ladies and the entertainment that is to be expected.
>
> It is worth mentioning the tone that should govern these occasions, for these gatherings are solely a matter for the ladies. Consequently, if men are invited, they should consider it a special privilege. The well-known beverage is prepared by the lady of the house herself. The confectioner delivers the iced tea, not to be confused with tea ice cream, a couple of types of ice cream, several sorts of fruit, especially oranges, and assorted iced cookies; coffee and chocolate are only [served] on special request.[20]

For the Viennese, these occasions were at least as much about the sweet snacks as the beverage. Certainly tea drinking was never more than a passing vogue.

In the provinces, they had only begun to hear about the trendy beverage a decade later. In an 1845 cookbook devoted to coffee and all the sweets appropriate to serving with it, the best-selling Czech cookbook author Dobromila Rettigová was skeptical of the new potion. After explaining at length how to make coffee and hot chocolate, she turned somewhat grudgingly to tea: "Besides coffee and chocolate, even here there is now a habit of serving tea instead of coffee at afternoon get-togethers—it is a new fashion; it is not up to me to decide how healthy this beverage is, however experienced physicians claim that it does not benefit our sex."[21] The author, though, was a tolerant soul. If people wanted to drink tea, that was their own business, just as long as they kept the suspect brew away from children.* No matter the beverage, what is abundantly clear from Rettigová's little book is that the habit of taking a hot drink with dessert in the afternoon was well established.

Like Zenker's tea circle, these at-home gatherings had a decidely feminine and, to some degree, bourgeois association. They allowed women to socialize while their husbands were at work or at male-dominated coffeehouses. In Germany they called these coffee klatches *Kaffeekränzchen*. A 1715 encyclopedia for women defined the word as "a daily or weekly gathering and assembly of a few intimately acquainted ladies . . . where they drink coffee and divert themselves playing l'Ombre [a card game]."[22] The book makes no mention of it, but it is certain that some sort of sweet snacks would have been served with the beverage.

As Zenker pointed out, in the Hapsburg lands this *Jause* or afternoon *thé* gained in popularity in the 1820s and '30s, in what is now called the Biedermeier era. This was, arguably, the

---

* Interestingly Czechs would later take to drinking tea as a way to associate themselves with their Slavic Russian brothers in the national revival that swept Bohemia and Moravia in the second half of the nineteenth century. Drinking tea differentiated them from the coffee-drinking "Germans."

first time in Austrian history when the middle class influenced current fashion, much of which focused on domesticity and the decisively unaristocratic virtues of child rearing and mother-hood. As in Paris, Viennese middle-class women were expected to exert their influence within the household, not in business or any other public sphere. When women met women, it was most often in the home. Given the aspirational nature of the middle class, a cup of coffee turned into a competitive sport where points were scored for the best silver and the greatest variety of snacks. These, even more than in France, were inevitably sweet.

Rettigová's cookbook, with its one hundred recipes, under-lines the popularity of the many *Theegebäck* and *Kaffeegebäck* (tea and coffee pastries). This new breed of sweet snack seems to have found the ideal climate in the prim salons of the Biedermeier and multiplied exponentially as the century progressed. By 1900, the pastry trend was given a boost by the new fashion for taking tea *à l'anglaise*, which gave confectioners and home bakers alike yet one more reason to make cookies and cakes. The 1906 edi-tion of Katharina Prato's popular *Die Süddeutsche Küche* listed more than 120 recipes for *Theegebäck* as well as some 70 for hors d'oeuvres–type snacks appropriate for the afternoon meal. Like many cookbooks, there are numerous suggested menus. Curi-ously, breakfast and *Jause* are combined under the same heading. Though they are not identified as such, some of the dishes do seem more like breakfast than others, but what's notable is that the same items might be deemed appropriate for both. A typical recommendation includes a coffee ice cream float or hot choco-late, served with *Kipfel* (crescent rolls), *Hohlhippen* (tube-shaped wafers), *falsche Butter-Schnitten* (chocolate nut slices), candied fruit, and a *Dobostorte* (see page 297).[23] Whether most people woke up to this sort of meal on a regular basis is hardly rele-vant here; what's important to point out is that it would not be considered peculiar. This is still the case today. *Gugelhupf*, fruit tarts, and even cakes are a common feature of Austrian breakfast buffets.

Given that it was normal to make a meal of sweet foods for breakfast, lunch, teatime, or supper, is it any wonder there was such a vast repertoire of sweet dishes?

THE KAFFEEHAUS AND THE ZUCKERBÄCKER

Though women in Biedermeier Vienna tended to entertain at home, they weren't entirely shut-ins. In the decades following the Congress of Vienna, the Hapsburg capital was a much more congenial city than Paris. It was about half the size, which helped, but there was also a culture of leaving behind the grubby streets and taking walks in nature, especially Prater Park by the Danube. This Biedermeier fashion for taking the air was noted by the travel writer Johann Georg Kohl around 1840 when he visited Brno, the chief city of Moravia. Describing a scene in Franzensberg (the region's first public park), he wrote: "Here are music, sunshine, gaiety; well-dressed citizens with their wives and children, drinking coffee under the trees, and wandering among the shady walks, enjoying the beauty of the evening." When he visited Vienna's leafy suburbs, the setting was much more theatrical:

> In the Sans-souci gardens at Mödling, there are nine tents of tastefully draped red and white cloths, pitched in a meadow, each of which is dedicated to one of the Muses, whose names, embroidered on flags, flutter over the tops. In the centre stands a tenth, wherein a Vienna leader flourishes as Apollo, and regales the Muses with Strauss's waltzes. These muses are young maidens and old women, attended by cavaliers and children, who

resort to those nomadic airy temples to drink coffee. Taking refreshments in this poetical style is quite in the taste of the Vienna people.[24]

Naturally there were other refreshments than coffee. The itinerant *mandoletti* sellers, banished by this point from the inner city, wandered through the crowd. The confectioners also set up booths or tents where they sold lemonade, almond milk, and wine punch as well as their sweetmeats. An early one of these outdoor lemonade huts was set up just outside the city bastions in 1789 by Giovani Milani, the Italian owner of the popular Café Milani on Kohlmarkt. Here he could sell coffee as well as lemonade and ice cream.* Men, women, and children alike dropped by to sip the oriental beverage. In contrast, within the city walls, the cafés were a strictly masculine affair and, early on at least, only had a tentative connection to dessert.

The Viennese picked up the coffee-drinking habit from the Turks beginning sometime in the mid-1600s, though the first real *Kaffeehaus* (café) was only opened in 1685 by an Armenian named Johannes Diodato. Though he had obtained a royal privilege to be the sole vendor of the "Turkish drink" for twenty years, by the turn of the coming century he had plenty of competition. Cafés never just served coffee. Diodato served lemonade and that other Turkish drink, sherbet, from the beginning; a competitor served tea and chocolate too.[26] After a bitter dispute with the brandy distillers—whose guild members were selling illicit coffee—Maria Theresa declared in 1747 that both guilds could sell the other's beverages.

Seventy years later, the menu grew more extensive. Johann Pezzl noted the changes in 1812:

---

* A writer describing the scene a generation later wrote: "This coffee tent got the nickname of the Ox mill, because the gentlemen and ladies promenading in the limited space of the bastion kept having to make the rounds in front of and through this tent, which had the semblance of the repetitive workings of such a mill."[25]

The purpose of coffee houses has been infinitely expanded since they first emerged. Not only can you drink coffee there but you can also have tea, chocolate, punch, lemonade, almond milk, 'wedding soup' [presumably meaning *Chaudeau*, a sort of zabaglione], Rosoglio [a sweet cordial], ice cream, etc. all things that, a couple of centuries ago in Germany, we couldn't even name.[27]

By that point, many cafés were beginning to serve meals. They had been permitted to serve small warm dishes twice a day as a consequence of Britain's continental blockade during the Napoleonic wars, which cut off the supply of coffee beans. They had to offer something to their customers, and, given the central European penchant for sweet meals, pancakes, strudels, and all sorts of other warm *Mehlspeisen* must have featured prominently on the menu. The cafés largely retained the privilege even after Napoleon was safely exiled to St. Helena.

By the 1820s, there was a great deal of overlap between what the coffeehouses and the salons of the confectioners were serving. Fundamentally, though, the coffeehouses weren't about food, they were about community. There were cafés for every social class; cafés for Armenians, Czechs, Hungarians, Italians, Jews, and Turks; cafés for bureaucrats, butchers, musicians, and lawyers. Women were generally not welcome until the late nineteenth century, when some of the more respectable cafés created separate salons for ladies.[28] In one crucial sense, the *Kaffeehaus* still serves the same function as it did three hundred years ago. "People go out to communicate," one café owner told me. He was even sanguine about the intrusion of cell phones. "Mobile phones enable a café to function as an office," he laughed. "It used to be that people would interrupt their office routine by going to the café, now they interrupt their café routine by dropping by the office." In Vienna's coffeehouses, the cakes, and even the coffee, are incidental.

Not so at the salon of the *Zuckerbäcker*, where the cake's the thing—to say nothing of the ice cream, bonbons, jellies, cookies, and a hundred other sweet nothings. Even while cafés were able to sell pastries and ice cream, the confectioners were forbidden to sell Vienna's favorite beverage. As late as 1873, a guidebook warned that "at these establishments besides pastry, ices and liquors no other beverage is served." And that wasn't the only restriction. The confectioners' guild was perennially in dispute with the so-called fine bakers who made fruit tarts, croissants, enriched yeast breads, and the like. In theory, the confectioners were restricted to making sweets with no more than 50 percent flour, while the bakers were to limit their sugar. In 1899 it was stipulated that the bakers were entitled

> to make fine pastry only from dough containing flour, made with milk, butter, eggs, yeast and salt. Sugar may only be used on the exterior for sprinkling or dusting on top. As for the interior [of the dough] sugar is permitted only insofar as it is necessary for fermentation or color. The bakers are not allowed to use ingredients that fall under the competence of the confectioners' guild such as jams, preserved fruit, chocolate.[29]

Of course every bureaucratic regulation begets subterfuge, and not everyone interpreted the rules in exactly the same way. Both the bakers and the *Zuckerbäcker*, for example, managed to get away with selling *Faschingskrapfen* (jelly doughnuts).

By the last decades of the 1800s, the confectioners didn't just have the bakers to worry about. New competition arrived in the form of industrialized confectionary companies that could produce the candies, bonbons, and wafers that had been the *Zuckerbäcker's* mainstay for hundreds of years. Moreover, they could do it on the cheap and by the millions. Desperate for more business, the confectioners' guild petitioned the authorities to be allowed to serve coffee, tea, and such. They were finally granted permission in the 1890s—though every shop had to obtain a special license. Later they were also allowed to serve light savory snacks, but, again, only after applying for the privilege. This is the origin of today's *Café-Konditorei*, a hybrid of the sort of confectioner's salon run by Dehne and his successors and the *Kaffeehaus*.*

Ironically, the Kafkaesque rules that limited what a Vienna confectioner could make or sell may have spurred the profession to ever-greater innovation. I wonder if the vast profusion of nut-based pastries, for example, can be attributed to the limits imposed on using flour? Could the dozens of almost flourless *Torten* that were invented in the second half of the nineteenth century be an unintentional by-product of the arcane Hapsburg legal code? When you compare Europe's two great dessert traditions, it is clear that the French are artistes of pastry while the Austrians are maestros of cake. The bureaucrats may have had some small role to play in this.

Let Them Eat Torte

The *Torte* or cake is as much part of the Austrian national DNA as baklava is to the Turkish genetic code. It has been subjected to scholarly research, government regulation, and vituperative lawsuits. On the banks of the Danube, cakes matter.

In Linz, not unexpectedly, the locals are obsessed with the linzer torte, a buttery hazelnut or almond tart most often filled with raspberry jam that peeks through a lattice top. The dessert is unquestionably old—but just how old? This is a question that Waltraud Faißner, chief librarian of the local museum, has spent years trying to answer. Her job has allowed her to indulge her

---

* The German term for confectioner, *Konditorei*, gained ascendancy over the Austrian *Zuckerbäcker* after the country's toxic tryst with Nazi Germany between 1938 and 1945.

obsession, with the result that she has compiled a vast collection of linzer torte recipes that go back well over three hundred years.

⌒ Gingerbread ⌒

In the Mediterranean world, the idea of making molded or shaped honey cakes goes back to ancient Roman times. You can still find a distant echo of these in Calabria, where in the town of Siriano they make hand-shaped honey cakes locally called *mustaccioli* (or *mustazzoli*) out of flour, water, and honey and occasionally with that ancient Roman sweetener, grape must. Local sweet makers traditionally make these for the holiday of San Rocco as votive offerings. Often they are shaped in the form of an arm or another injured part of the body, with the afflicted part highlighted with tinsel. In other cases the whole family might be depicted in honey bread. On the saint's day, these ex-votos are rubbed against the statue of the saint to bring relief before being deposited in a large basket. Next day, the cakes are auctioned off for a worthy cause, which in this case is mostly to pay for the entertainers and fireworks hired for the occasion.[30]

Just when spiced honey cakes traveled to northern Europe is unclear. According to one theory, these sort of votive breads were brought back to Germany from the Holy Land after the Crusades. Added spices, which were thought to carry the smell of paradise in those days, would have made the cakes more precious. In England, gingerbread cost on the order of two shillings a pound in 1285, enough to buy twelve pounds of cheese. These sorts of spice cakes were certainly common enough in central Europe by the 1400s. In Prague, Celetná street (from *calet*, a pleated bread made by the gingerbread makers guild) was named after the guild members resident there as early as 1348. In Germany, the spice merchants of Nuremberg were supplying ginger-bread to the Basel city council by 1370. The Dutch town of Deventer was exporting a sort of honey spice cake as early as 1417.[31]

The gingerbread was often pressed into intricately carved wooden molds. The resulting shapes have long had a sort of totemic significance. There were the saints, of course, brought back from religious fairs as mementos of piety (and souvenirs). In the Netherlands, large *specu-laas* (gingerbread) men are still made in the shape of St. Nicholas for his holiday. Other designs had more worldly meanings. In Germany, a mounted lionman or cock-rider represented virility.[32] Naturally, hearts represented love. In Alsace before World War I, both brioche and gingerbread hearts were given as tokens of affection by would-be lovers. Some had a mirror in the center in which the lover could admire herself. Street fairs in central Europe still sell gaud-ily decorated hearts imprinted with schmaltzy messages like "I'm crazy about you" and "you're my dream girl."

In 2005, Frau Faißner was invited to a meeting of Austrian librarians at the grand baroque abbey of Admont nestled among the brawny peaks of the eastern Alps. The scenery was lovely but the meeting wasn't exactly scintillating, so, during one of the breaks between discussing digitization and electronic catalogs, Frau Faißner decided to poke about the gilt-encrusted book-shelves of the old library. Given her passion for baking, her eye was drawn to a manuscript cookbook from 1653 that used to belong to Anna Margarita Sagramosa, an Austrian noblewoman who had married into an Italian family and moved to Verona.

Leafing through all those Austrian recipes, Frau Faißner got the impression that Anna must have been homesick for the tastes of her homeland. But then the librarian saw something that caught her breath. Atop one yellowed page was a neatly penned heading that read "Linz Turdten." And that's just what it was—despite the idiosyncratic spelling—a linzer torte filled with jam and covered with a lattice top. The only difference was that it called for quince or pear preserves instead of the raspberry more common today. In the end it turned out that the book contained a total of four linzer torte variations, attesting to the dessert's popularity at even that early date. Frau Faißner's ruddy complexion was even more aglow that day as she rejoined her fellow librarians in the cavernous refectory.[33]

Since that time, the single-minded librarian has collected more than eighty recipes for the *Torte* predating 1858. Common to almost all of them are lemon rind, jam, and almonds (hazelnuts don't appear until 1900), though only about half have a lattice top.[34] No doubt there are others gathering dust on forgotten shelves. I bet we haven't heard the last of Waltraud Faißner's discoveries yet.

The origin of what the Austrians call a *Torte* probably goes back to Italy, to the round medieval *torta*. The sixteenth-century cookbook of Bartolomeo Scappi shows a half-dozen illustrations of the straight-sided cake pans—much like today's layer cake pans—intended for baking *torte*. Nevertheless, what was typically baked in these pans weren't cakes but pies with a pastry shell. In Marx Rumpolt's roughly contemporary *New Kochbuch* (1581), many of his *"Turten"* are made more or less like a linzer torte, with a buttery crust that encloses fillings that range from figs to plums to strawberries. When Rumpolt wrote the book he was working for the Elector of Mainz on the banks of the Rhine, but he was born in what is now Hungary. He included several banquet menus from the Hapsburg court of Ferdinand I (or possibly Maximilian), so it is likely he learned his chops in central Europe. Interestingly, there is a recipe for Hungarian *Turten* that is reminiscent of a *Torta ungaresca* found in the fourteenth-century Italian collection mentioned in chapter 3 (see page 82), made by stretching and then layering the dough. Here, it is filled with apples much like an apple strudel. Other recipes call for rolling and layering thin sheets of dough much like baklava, but these are referred to as Spanish recipes.[35] Other German-language cookbooks of the time tend to follow a similar pattern, though occasionally the *Torte*, instead of being a filling enclosed or topped with a crust, is more like a pudding that is spread out in a *Torte* pan.[36]

Presumably anything baked (or presented) in one of these round cake pans came to be called a *Torte*—in much the way a casserole or paella refers to both the dish and what is cooked in it.* At some point in the seventeenth century, central Europeans mostly lost the crust, and the meaning of *Torte* migrated to a cake cooked in a round pan and typically iced with a sugar glaze. The batter was usually made with eggs and ground nuts, though a sponge cake wasn't out of the question. The first identifiably Austrian cookbook (printed in Graz in 1686) has a recipe for *Piscotten* (from the Italian *biscotto*), yet even though it is baked in a cake pan the author did not call it a *Torte*. Much more typical is a recipe for a *Mandel-Dorten* (here spelled with a "d"), made by beating together ground almonds, butter, eggs, and sugar. The author instructed readers to bake the cake in embers and then to ice it.[37] The Graz cookbook included five other variations, including an unsweetened spinach *Dorten*.

But that was nothing compared to the almost four dozen *Dorten* recipes in Conrad Hagger's 1719 cookbook, *Neues saltz-*

---

* As ever, there are exceptions to every rule. Illustrations in eighteenth-century cookbooks also show clover-leaf-shaped *Torte* pans and others that resemble the petals of a flower.

burgisches Koch-Buch, or the almost sixty *Torten* recipes in the *Wienerisches bewährtes Kochbuch* ("The Reliable Viennese Cookbook"), first published in 1785. Hagger's book includes over three hundred engravings, almost all devoted to fantastically shaped pastries and templates for decorating *Dorten* that would do any baroque ceiling painter proud. Hagger's cosmopolitan experience shows, not least in his cake recipes. Many of these *Dorten* depend on nuts (mostly almonds but also pistachios) to give them substance. Some still resemble tarts of the linzer torte variety while others are more like sweetened frittatas, where the main ingredients are freshly ground fatback mixed with eggs. We also find, for the first time in a German-language source, not one but three recipes for a chocolate *Dorten.* In one recipe the chocolate seems to be added merely for color, but another includes enough of the ingredient to make a dense, almost brownielike chocolate cake.* (The third doesn't specify quantities.) Of course, France already had its collection of chocolate-flavored desserts, but there was nothing resembling a cake. The chocolate *biscuit* recipe that appeared slightly earlier in Massialot's 1692 cookbook results in a chocolate-colored meringue cookie.[38]

As with many cakes today, the visual appeal of Hagger's cakes was more crucial than their taste. Color was important. To make a green *Dorten,* he added pistachios or even spinach; saffron yielded a golden dough; dye derived from sunflowers would tint the batter red; cinnamon produced light brown; and chocolate dark. One recipe instructs the cook to layer five or six colors to create a kind of rainbow cake.

It's important to visualize these cakes in the context of what else was going on the table. They were intended, after all, to decorate the bare spots between other dishes. They were also, in a

---

* The recipe tells you to beat together 4 *Loth* (2.5 ounces) butter, 4 egg yolks, 1 *Pfund* (20 ounces) ground almonds, 3/4 *Pfund* (15 ounces) sugar, and 6 *Loth* (3.7 ounces) chocolate, or more to taste.

sense, supporting players for the showy sugar sculpture center-pieces that decorated the dining rooms of German princes. As at Versailles, these figures rose like so many glittering Venuses out of a sea of ragouts and fricassees. Here too the tables were turned into a veritable Eurodisney of fjords and fountains, pagodas and palaces, surrounded by sugar sculptures that were supposed to personify such things as wisdom and honor, justice and virtue. It must have been magnificent—but it cost a mint. By the mid-eighteenth century the Hapsburgs, who never enjoyed the same sort of expense accounts as the Bourbons, gradually did away with these fleeting tableaux, replacing them with rococo porce-lain. It was as ornate as the sugar works it was made to resemble, but it could be reused over and over. The confectioners now had to content themselves with filling towering china display pieces with glittering candy, radiant molded jellies, and ornate sweet-meats, which would remain on the table throughout the meal. Mostly, though, the *Zuckerbäcker*'s decorating urges were trans-ferred to the *Torten*. By the nineteenth century, these became the main centerpiece, especially for the middle classes. The form of these cakes was very different from *gâteaux Saint-Honoré* and savarins served on the Boulevard St.-Germain, but they occu-pied the same position on the dining table, a modest substitute for those fantastic sugar sculptures of old. As late as 1881, Kar-olína Vávrová would still instruct her readers to arrange flowers in the center of the table, then dispose around them "two bas-kets of fruit, whatever the season offers, two cakes with a variety of cookies and two bowls of stewed fruit." In this context, looks were everything.

Though the dense nut-torte never entirely went out of style, the fashion for all things French in the 1700s brought another type of cake, the *biscuit*, to central Europe. Not that sponge cake was exactly a new discovery; it was the same thing as the earlier *Piscotten*, but the trendy name gave it new panache. The batter was naturally much lighter than the indigenous nut-based recipes and was often baked in a paper ring rather than a cake pan. As in France, many of these pastries were basically cookies along the lines of the *biscuits de Savoie* or ladyfingers, but there were cake-sized *biscuit* too. In the German-speaking world, when these were baked in a *Torte* pan, the resulting sponge cake was occasionally called by the awkwardly conjoined term *biscuit-Torte*.

But no matter what the dough, both the *Torte* and the *biscuit* were finished in much the same way, with an icing tinted with a painter's palette of colorings. Given this penchant for color, the tea tables of Duchess Anna Amelia and her contemporaries must have been a rococo decorator's fantasy come true: gleaming with silver and gold and stacked with jewel-like disks of pink, red, green, and brown hiding cakes flavored with lemon, almond, raisins, and the increasingly popular chocolate and vanilla.

Chocolate reached Vienna from Italy and Spain at roughly the same time it became popular in Paris. The intimate connection the Hofburg had to the Spanish court throughout the sixteenth and seventeenth centuries must have introduced the luscious liquid soon after it was taken up in Madrid. As elsewhere, it was originally Vienna's pharmacists who prepared chocolate, but, by the eighteenth century, chocolatiers, many of them Italian, had a guild of their own.

This chocolate was very bitter and noticeably scented with vanilla if we are to believe the recipe from Giuseppe Antonio Sala, the chocolate maker to the Imperial court in 1760. To make a little over six pounds of prepared chocolate, Sala started with approximately 6½ pounds cocoa beans and added only about 5 ounces sugar and 1½ ounces vanilla. According to the Imperial records, he charged the court an extravagant price of thirteen gulden for a batch of this size. (There were repeated complaints about his prices.) In those days, that would have been enough to buy more than 500 pounds of ordinary bread or 350 gallons of cheap wine.[39] Fifty years later, Viennese chocolate makers had a profitable business exporting almost ten tons of chocolate a year.[40]

Presumably the vast majority of this was used for drinks, though chocolate desserts were becoming increasingly common. By 1806, Maria A. Neudecker—hardly a trendsetter—listed a half-dozen chocolate-flavored recipes. There are chocolate cookies, a strudel, a mousse, a torte, a soufflé, and even a "mock chocolate soup" that has no chocolate in it—presumably for her readers on a budget.[41] Some, like the mousse (*Chokoladecreme*), were clearly French imports, but the tortes go back at least a hundred years, as Hagger's books makes clear. There's even an early recipe for chocolate soufflé (*Auflauf*) that appears in an aristocratic cookbook as early as 1701.[42]

Eighteenth-century chocolate torte recipes contained more or less the same ingredients as today's flourless chocolate tortes. They were based on a batter of ground almonds, sugar, grated chocolate, and eggs and often flavored with a little cinnamon and lemon rind. In some cases the eggs were added whole, though in other recipes they were separated, a technique more common in later recipes. The bakers' apprentices who made these cakes must have had arms of steel. Le Goullon instructs his readers to beat his "*Tourte*" batter one hour, and that's *before* beating the egg whites and adding them in. In comparison, his chocolate *biscuit* is a breeze, requiring a tolerable fifteen minutes of initial beating. Once the batter was ready, the cook poured it into a brass pan (these occasionally had legs), set it in the embers, covered it with a dome, and piled more embers on top. Alternatively, the embers might be swept aside, the cake pan would be placed on the hot ground and covered with a specially shaped earthenware bell (much like the earlier Italian *testo*), and once again covered with embers. The cooled *Torten* were then coated with a kind of royal icing based on egg whites and sugar. Occasionally the instructions say to return the iced cake to the oven briefly to harden the surface and make it shinier. Between the effort and the expense of the sugar, the eggs, and the imported almonds, no wonder these cakes were intended for an aristocratic audience.

Franz Sacher's Cake

Undoubtedly the most famous of the steel-armed baker's apprentices was Franz Sacher, remembered for giving birth to Vienna's renowned Sacher torte.* The linzer torte may be older, but let's face it, it's from Linz. There is something rustic and homemade about even the fanciest linzer torte. The Sacher, on the other hand, is an edible manifestation of an urban, cosmopolitan Vienna, as smooth and fitted as a little black cocktail dress. Given how central it is to the Viennese self-image, it is perhaps not surprising that this legendary cake has led to numerous court cases, hundreds of imitations, and an ever-flowing fountain of misinformation.

At the risk of being the target of another lawsuit, let me try to work out how the legend was created. First, a few words of definition for those who haven't tasted the real thing. The Österreichisches Lebensmittelbuch, the regulatory Austrian food codex, devotes over 250 words to defining the cake in painful bureaucratic detail. Briefly, it is a chocolate sponge cake with both an apricot and a boiled chocolate glaze. The latter can only be made with chocolate, water, and sugar. I much prefer the description given in the 1894 *Appetit-Lexikons* (Food Encyclopedia): "What is called the Sacher Torte is a chocolate cake of a higher order," wrote the editors in delightfully purple prose,

> distinguished from her companions by wearing beneath her lustrous chocolate gown an undergarment of apricot jam. The Sacher seems destined to preserve the name of its creator in the memory of generations to come, for it is a Viennese specialty, one of those "sweet follies" found in the Imperial city of sweet abandon which, elsewhere,

---

* In Austria spelling on the Sacher torte varies. The Sacher Hotel prefers "Sacher-Torte," while more generically it is referred to as "Sachertorte."

can never be fully replicated. The Sacher Torte is imitated quite well by all of Vienna's confectioners and restaurants, but those enchanting, charmingly graceful originals made by Eduard Sacher's company are inimitable. [Franz's son Eduard had run one of the most prestigious hotels in the Hapsburg capital until his death in 1892.] On the tongue, it is pure poetry. No wonder that more than 20,000 are exported each year to the whole world.

As for the inventor, it is known with some certainty that Franz Sacher was born on December 19, 1816. In those days, Vienna was still dominated by the imperial court and the beneficiaries of great aristocratic estates; however, it was also increasingly a place where a young man of modest birth but outsize ambition could move up in the world. Franz knew the aristocratic milieu from day one. His father was the Vienna castellan (estate manager) to the imperial chancellor (prime minister), Prince Klemens Wenzel Nepomuk Lothar von Metternich, the most powerful man in Austria and arguably the most influential European politician of the Biedermeier era. Historians have mixed views of Metternich. Some see him as a ruthless reactionary who created the modern police state, while others credit him for creating a system of alliances that held Europe back from a continent-wide conflagration for close to a hundred years. I imagine the young Sacher flitting around downstairs even as upstairs the movers and shakers of the world dropped by for coffee and cake. Seemingly the boy showed some talent in the kitchen, because he was eventually apprenticed under Metternich's chef, *maître* Chambellier. Franz must have done what all apprentices do: cleaned the fireplaces, turned the spits, stirred the ice cream, and beaten the eggs for the *Torten* and the *biscuits*. Mostly, the menus would have been French, given the chef and the style du jour. As the story is told, in 1832, two years into his training, the young apprentice (Franz must have still been fifteen given his late birthday) was asked to make dinner for the chancellor and three of his friends. The rest is the stuff of legend, a legend that was put to good use by his son, Eduard Sacher, in promoting his hotel later in the century. Here's the tale as told by Eduard in a letter from 1888:

> The Sachertorte is an invention of my still-living father. He created the cake as a young apprentice chef, in the kitchens of old Metternich, where my father had learned the culinary art. When he set it on the table 56 years ago it was met with acclaim from those present and earned him much praise from the prince. Since that time, my father's cake has been continually produced, and no cook or confectioner has been able to imitate it. The proof is that, each day, the table of his majesty, as well as of the crown prince and his consort, is set with this cake. One finds it all over Vienna, in all the largest cities, on menus everywhere, as a renowned specialty. Four people work for me in a specially designed kitchen, day and night the whole year long, and many a day 200 to 400 cakes costing from 1 to 6 Gulden are sold and shipped. Our Sacher-tortes go to Paris, Berlin, London and even overseas.

It is a good story: the wunderkind pastry chef whipping up an instant classic for the empire's eminence grise; the legendary cake emerging fully formed, like Athena from Zeus's head. It's just that parts of the narrative don't quite add up. The first bit of damning evidence comes from Austrian food historian Ingrid Haslinger. She alerted me to a 1906 newspaper interview in the *Neues Wiener Tagblat* with Franz Sacher himself, on the occasion of his ninetieth birthday, where he says he invented the eponymous torte in the late 1840s.[43]

It turns out that Franz (or François as he now liked to be called) left the employ of his father's boss soon after 1832 to work for another expat French chef, Monsieur Impère, who directed the kitchens for the Countess Rosine Esterházy. (The Esterházys were prominent Hungarian magnates.) The countess, however, couldn't quite afford her lavish lifestyle, and so, soon enough, Impère took off for a more lucrative contract in St. Petersburg. He offered to take "François" along, but the young cook declined, taking instead a job with Count Nikolaus Esterházy, a less profligate member of the same Hungarian family. This involved spending winters in Vienna and summers at his employer's Slovakian estate, where the young chef had a captive audience for his talents. There his cooking captured the fancy of Count August Breuner-Graffeneg, an enterprising aristocrat who owned a casino in Bratislava. This gave Sacher a chance to strike out on his own, which the still twenty-something did with a flourish, not only running the casino's restaurant but also catering events all around Bratislava. Which brings us back to the Sacher torte, which the ninety-year-old Sacher said he invented at this time, not in 1832.

To those who didn't grow up with it, the appeal of the Sacher torte can be somewhat elusive. Even when well made, many Americans find it too dry and insufficiently sweet, while for the French it's too sweet and not chocolaty enough. What's more, the apricot-chocolate combination isn't to everyone's taste. But what the Sacher torte has is amazing durability. A chocolate *biscuit*, on which the Sacher is modelled, would dry out in a day or two with the old-fashioned egg white and sugar glaze, but the jammy undergarment in combination with the fudgy glaze keeps the famed cake moist for weeks with no need of refrigeration. It's a caterer's dream. In an era before refrigeration, the success of Sacher's cake was almost preordained. It was this very durability that later allowed Eduard Sacher to ship the cakes halfway across the world. So it should come as no surprise that when Franz/ François Sacher finally settled down in Vienna after 1848 to run a catering business, he would have a steady clientele for his sweet folly.

So what of the legend? Could it be that the chocolate-begowned sweetheart of Viennese confectionary was actually invented in Bratislava to answer the logistical needs of an ambitious young caterer? Perish the thought! The myth is so much sweeter than the bitter truth.

For lack of any other evidence, my best guess is that the Metternich creation story originates with Eduard Sacher. I doubt that, were it not for his hotel, the Sacher torte would have ever achieved its fame. Supposedly, the hotelier's letter was in response to a column in the *Wiener Zeitung*, the official government newspaper. According to at least two books sanctioned by the Hotel Sacher, the feuilleton (as opinion columns were known in Austria) appeared in the May 1888 edition of the newspaper.[44] The article's author had apparently listed all the great culinary specialities of Vienna but neglected the Sacher torte, prompting the younger Sacher's indignant response. The trouble is that no such feuilleton exists in the *Wiener Zeitung*, neither in May nor April nor June. Moreover, there seems to be no original of the letter either. So what are we to believe, the word of an old man a few months before his death, or a putative letter in response to a nonexistent feuilleton? Could it be that Franz Sacher did indeed make some sort of chocolate cake for old Metternich but it wasn't the cake he would develop later for his catering business? As is evident from the cookbooks, chocolate cakes were common enough in those days. It was the combination of the jam and chocolate icing that was original.

Yet I, for one, am almost less interested in the shifty (and unprovable) facts of the invention of the Sacher torte than in the birth and robust life of the legend. Whether it is a myth or not, the Metternich tale beautifully illustrates the Viennese zeitgeist and how it has changed over the years. In the late nineteenth century, associating a cake with the old chancellor had a political dimension; it aligned you with the conservative parties of the royal court, just the sort of people Eduard Sacher wanted as clients for his hotel. In the post-Hapsburg era, the specifics of Metternich's more unsavory acts lost most of their potency. To the Viennese nostalgic for their imperial past, he was the symbol of a time when the Austrian capital mattered. The cake picked up some of that patina. Even today, the cake is no ordinary confection; it is an edible national symbol, and I wonder if the Metternich connection doesn't have at least something to do with it.

In the late 1800s, as the entry in the *Appetit-Lexikons* makes clear, the *Torte* was mainly associated with Eduard Sacher's hotel. It was its calling card, a chocolaty advertisement that could be sent all around the world due to its remarkable durability. It would seem that initially it was the hotel's renown that led to the cake's celebrity, not the other way around. But that would change.

Eduard was nothing if not entrepreneurial. His first Viennese venture, which he opened in 1866, was a tony restaurant across the street from the old opera house. The following year, he would run a Viennese "beer hall" at the Paris World Exposition, an event attended by almost all the aristocracy of Europe. Many of these titled tourists apparently dropped by Sacher's Parisian establishment and kept coming even when he relocated back to Vienna. By 1876, he had a hotel, widely acclaimed as one of the best in the city. Sacher's establishment was at the top of its game for decades. In 1891, an American visitor confirmed that "every night, after the opera is over, all that the Austrian capital contains of titled and noble personages flock to his restaurant to partake of the gastronomic curiosities, which he prides himself in setting before his guests." What's interesting, though, is that even while this source gave an exhaustive list of Sacher's specialties, he didn't mention the torte. Was it not quite so legendary in those days, or did our reporter just not have a sweet tooth? Certainly an 1895 guidebook to the city recommended tourists stop by the hotel for a slice of "the famous Sacher Torte with its chocolate-brown dress, which is the delight of gourmets the world over." The travel guide makes it quite clear that the restaurant wasn't just for likes of the King of Serbia and the Prince of Wales (who made the hotel their regular hangout), but that even "the little people" could afford to eat there, at least for lunch, which cost a gulden.[45] It wasn't exactly cheap but, accounting for inflation, was roughly equivalent to the cost of lunch at the five-star hostelry today.

By 1930, the hotel needed its chocolate-robed celebrity more than the cake needed the hotel. When Eduard Sacher's widow, Anna, died in 1930, the hotel was in the same shabby state as imperial Austria—denuded of its wealthy aristocrats and subject to a vicious inflationary spiral. Its facilities may have been state-of-the-art in the 1870s, but by the 1930s people expected central heating and running water in their hotel rooms. This point, at least, was addressed by the new owners after 1934, when they bought the company after it declared bankruptcy. Given that the investors were led by Hans Gürtler, one of Vienna's preeminent lawyers, it isn't surprising that they soon turned to the courts to safeguard the hotel's preeminent asset.

By this point the Sacher torte was ubiquitous. The recipe had first been popularized by the bestselling cookbook author Katharina Prato, who first included a chocolate torte "à la Sacher" in the seventh edition of her canonical *Süddeutsche Küche* in 1870, and in scores of subsequent editions.*

By the 1930s there were dozens of versions of the cake. Some were as thin as a linzer torte, "no more than two centimeters

---

* Several writers have claimed that she included the recipe in the first (1858) edition, which is not true. The next four editions do not contain it either. It doesn't show up until the seventh edition of 1870 (or possibly the 1867 sixth edition, the only one I have not been able to track down). Unlike the cake served at the Sacher Hotel today, Prato's recipe is made in a single layer. It's noteworthy that the recipe doesn't appear in print until after Eduard Sacher reopened his restaurant in Vienna.

high" according to an 1896 French-language guide to Viennese pastry; or two to three fingers in height, as a popular Viennese cookbook confirms. This is undoubtedly the oldest version of the cake since the early Prato recipe calls for thirty minutes' cooking time "at moderate heat." Thicker cakes would have needed more time; later sources suggest forty-five minutes to an hour. Over the succeeding decades, recipes appeared for Sacher tortes made with potato flour, breadcrumbs, or almonds and others soaked with rum. Some were split and filled with the jam or even hazelnut buttercream.[46]

When the bankrupt Hotel Sacher was sold, Anna and Eduard's son, also named Eduard, gave up the right to run a hotel under the family name, but he hadn't, as far as he was concerned, sold off the rights to the cake too. Those remained a valuable asset, which he quickly cashed in by selling the original recipe and the right to use his name to Anna Demel. As of July 24, 1934, the "Eduard Sacher-Torte" became a marquee headliner of Vienna's most famous *Zuckerbäcker*.[47] Now there were two "original" Sacher tortes: Demel's served a version made in one layer, while the Hotel Sacher featured a *Torte* that sandwiched apricot jam between two layers. In Vienna this was cause enough for a lawsuit. In point of fact, the case brought by Hans Gürtler on behalf of the Hotel Sacher wasn't about who made the better cake but about the bragging rights, about who was allowed to call their cake "the original." So even as the country was collapsing around them and the Nazis were marching into Vienna, the Sacher's owners sued. And on September 29, 1938, they won. Austria had ceased to exist, but the Sacher owners could claim that quintessentially Austrian icon, the "original" Sacher torte, as theirs.

That wasn't the end of it, however. If the first Sacher–Demel conflict was a desperate gambit for desperate times, the next confrontation, what Viennese wags would call the seven years *Torten-Krieg* (cake war), was a very modern battle about corporate branding. The argument that began to wend its way through the

judiciary in the 1950s once again had to do with the jam between
the two layers of cake. Demel's lawyers claimed that the "original"
had only one layer, while the hotel's attorneys insisted that it had
two. Both sides brought in experts and famous chefs. After years
of back-and-forth arguments in the Vienna Commercial Court,
the case eventually went all the way to the Austrian Supreme
Court. And the final verdict? The court made the Solomonic
decision that, though the cake originally sold at the Hotel Sacher
had indeed had only one layer (the cake was apparently split
under the rule of Anna Sacher in the 1920s), the hotel had the
right to keep calling their version the "original" since the recipe
did originate with the Sachers.[48] And thus we have the "Original
Sacher-Torte" sold by the Hotel Sacher and all those other Sacher
tortes, including Eduard Sacher's version sold at Demel's. Which
is better? You'll need to judge for yourself. Just watch what you
say. The hotel is ever vigilant for any infraction on the cake's
trademarks, and its lawyers sue regularly to keep it that way.

At the Hotel Sacher, the recipe is a jealously guarded secret,
locked up in the owner's safe. Only she, her children, the manag-
ing director of the hotel, and the pastry chef know all the details
of making the cake, which they would divulge at their legal peril.
Everyone else who works in the bakery has only one restricted
task. For example, there is just one person who breaks and sepa-
rates the eggs, another who makes the icing. The cake remains
big business. In 2006, around 360,000 cakes were made by the
forty-one employees of the company's pastry kitchens.[49]

HAPSBURG TORTE

Cities have their cycles of boom and bust, short storms of creativity and long doldrums of stolid repetition. You see this
inventive zeitgeist among the artists, musicians, and architects

of sixteenth-century Venice. A burst of imagination in literature and religion accompanied the Bengali Renaissance in colonial Calcutta. In both of these cases the sweet makers followed suit, redefining their art for a new age. In Vienna, the genius of the age settled on the Hapsburg capital for a couple of decades on either side of 1900. Literature, music, and art all flourished, but so did the applied arts, especially design, architecture, and confectionary. The Viennese joke that Germans consider them to be Italians while Italians think them German. Like many clichés, there is a kernel of truth to this. There is something deeply sensual in a Klimt painting or a Mahler composition, but there is also an element of Germanic precision. You could say the same about any number of Viennese tortes.

By the second half of the nineteenth century, Vienna was a large, thriving metropolis at the heart of a rapidly industrializing empire, gathering up people from every corner of its multiethnic domain. Between the censuses of 1869 and 1910, the city's population more than doubled to two million (a number it would never regain). Starting in 1857, the small inner city finally burst the bastions built to keep out the Turks. The walls were razed, to be replaced by a grand boulevard, which was lined not with aristocratic palaces but rather with such bourgeois institutions as the parliament, city hall, and university. Increasingly it was doctors, professors, lawyers, bankers, and business owners who set the tone of the city rather than the imperial household and the Schwarzenbergs and Esterházys. But, that said, well-to-do commoners coexisted in a precariously balanced power relationship with the crown. Austria-Hungary remained much less democratic than did republican France. Nevertheless, the middle classes of both countries had something in common. In both cases, despite their political ascendancy, the bourgeoisie had a deep-seated inferiority complex vis-à-vis the old ruling classes. As a result they tried to replicate as many aspects of the aristocratic lifestyle as they could. One avenue open to them was sponsorship of the arts. Certainly it was a lot easier to acquire a reputation of connoisseurship than a thousand-acre aristocratic estate.[50]

Of course "good taste" wasn't limited to fine art and the opera. It extended to cuisine as well. This explains, in part, the outpouring of cookbooks in the late nineteenth century. These were not only full of instructions on how to make the latest cookies and cakes but also implicitly promised to reveal the recipe for climbing a rung or two up the social ladder. I wonder, though, whether they did more to increase than assuage women's insecurities. How many must have measured themselves against the perfect housewives depicted in the books and found themselves all too inadequate? No wonder that the wives of the burgeoning middle class had many new needs. Sigmund Freud seemed to answer some of them. Demel's, Gerstner, Heiner, Sluka, and other nineteenth-century *Zuckerbäcker* fulfilled others.

The chef d'oeuvre of these Viennese pastry cooks was the *Torte*. In some ways, their elaborate confections were comparable to the large orchestral works that Austrian composers wrote in order to assure their reputation. Like the symphonies, the cakes of this era were showy, complex, and intended to impress a picky audience.

In this fecund age, it seemed like a new torte was born every day. There were, of course, the quotidian cakes with their humble names: the poppy seed cake, the chocolate cake, the hazelnut, walnut, and almond cakes. On the model of the Sacher torte, they also now bore the names of their inventors, so there were the Demel-, Dobos-, Dommayer-, Kauber-, Kofranek-, Lotti-Richter-, Pischinger-, Rokitansky-, Schneider-, and Seleskowitz-Tortes. There were cakes that trumpeted the modernity of the industrial age. Revolutions in transport were honored with a railroad, an automobile, and even a bicycle torte. It is claimed that the Panama cake was named to mark the opening of the canal.* Naming a cake after a famous person was always a good PR move too. Dozens of celebrities—now mostly forgotten—had cakes named after them. There were tortes à la Andrássy, Esterházy, Habsburg, Hunyadi, Kneipp, Nelson, Malakoff, Napoleon, Radetzky, and Sonnenthal. The Metternich-Torte consisted of five layers of almond dough filled with coffee whipped cream and topped with coffee ice cream.[52] And for those who ran out of better ideas, they looked to places and cities, so there were Brabant, Brazilian, Dutch, French, Greek, Italian, Polish, Russian, and Tyrol tortes, alongside cakes named after Bad Ischl, Berlin, Budapest, Genoa, Gmunden, Merano, Milan, Paris, Prague, Schladming, Schönbrunn, Traunkirchen, Trieste, and Vienna. Cookbooks included scores of these recipes. Bestselling author Louise Seleskowitz listed some eighty tortes in her 1908 *Wiener Kochbuch*, but her colleague Sophie Meissner—if you will pardon the expression—takes the cake, with 121 cake recipes in her 1901 *Modernes Kochbuch*.

Many of these new cakes depended on chilled creamy fillings, some based on butter, others on cream. These came in dozens of formulations and scores of permutations. Buttercream came into its own after the Budapest baker and delicatessen owner Lajos Dobos created his multistoried extravaganza in the 1880s. The *Dobostorte* is a virtuoso example of turn-of-the-century design, with five or more svelte sheets of sponge cake, each nestled between layers of chocolate buttercream, the whole finished with a mirrorlike finish of caramel. The Hungarian delicatessen owner seems to have picked up the idea in France. The *Dobostorte* is very clearly based on the multilayered French *gâteau moka*, with its buttercream made with egg yolks, hot syrup, and butter,

---

* The still-popular *Panamatorte* is an almond sponge cake originally filled with chocolate buttercream, though *Pariser Creme* (a chocolate frosting made with whipped cream) is also sometimes used. You often read that it got its name after the opening of the Panama Canal in 1914, which is doubtful, since the name appears at least at least three years earlier. Perhaps it got its name when they started digging?[51]

though in the Hungarian version chocolate replaces the coffee in the original.* Whether Dobos introduced the idea of buttercream to the heart of the Empire is hard to say, but he certainly popularized it when he served his cake at his booth at the 1896 Millennium Exposition in Budapest.[53]

But the pastry cooks' imaginations were hardly limited to buttercream. Mousses, jams, icings, and even ice cream were piled one upon the other as the pastry cooks tried to titillate consumers' sweet senses in ever-newer combinations. Like a sweet tower of Babel, the Viennese torte rose up higher and higher on the foundations of its multilingual, multicultural empire. But the end was at hand. By 1914, the Hapsburg crown was as brittle and insubstantial as a *Spanische Windtorte*. The gunshots in Sarajevo shattered it to pieces. Vienna's golden age had passed.

Empire Collapses

In the last prewar census held in 1910, the great metropolis of Vienna was the dominant city of an empire of over fifty-one million souls. By the end of World War I, it was the capital of a Lilliputian Austria of six million. Practically a third of the new country's population resided in the city itself. The transformation was nothing short of apocalyptic, even if visitors may not have immediately noticed much change. The war itself hadn't come anywhere near the empire's heart, and, initially at least, Vienna's ecosystem was large enough to maintain the opera and the coffeehouses. In fact, the cafés and especially the *Café-Konditorei* may have been even busier as a result of the social changes of the 1920s, which allowed women greater freedom to chat and nibble in pub-

---

* There are at least a half-dozen ways to make buttercream, utilizing both cooked and uncooked egg whites or yolks. Some use a custard base and others use no eggs at all. All this results in frostings of varying texture and density. By 1900, most of these variations were in use both in France and in central Europe.

lic. The government still patronized Demel's; whether republican or monarchist, the rulers could hardly hold a reception without a spread of tortes. But it soon became abundantly evident that all this was little more than glistening icing over a hollow core.

The famed Hapsburg bureaucracy could hardly justify its gargantuan carcass. The aristocrats finally ran out of credit. As in Germany, hyperinflation wiped out the savings of the middle class. Then came the depression, a fascist government, and, in 1938, absorption (with considerable Austrian support) into Hitler's Reich. Vienna's large Jewish population, who had included some of the most brilliant minds of their generation, were murdered or sent into exile. Even as it drew to a close, World War II was not as kind to Vienna as World War I had been. Allied bombers severely damaged the opera house, the gothic cathedral, and thousands of other buildings.

The postwar period was a troubled time for both the *Zuckerbäcker* and the café owners. People had no money or time to linger over coffee or dessert. Butter, sugar, and eggs were expensive luxuries to be hoarded for special occasions, not lavished on a casual afternoon *Jause*. It was at this time that the line between the male-dominated *Kaffeehaus* and the feminine *Café-Konditerei* began to blur as many of the old smoky cafés now began to feature desserts to draw in the crowds. Numerous coffeehouses also turned into full-fledged restaurants to make ends meet. But the hard times didn't last forever. In 1983, with the return of prosperity, a celebration of the tercentenary of the Vienna café brought on a kind of café renaissance. It may have had something to do with the cakes.

NEUER MARKT, c. 2010

Vienna's Neuer Markt is a relatively quiet square, given its location right near Kärntnerstrasse, Vienna's main shopping drag. It's about five minutes' walk to the Hotel Sacher in one direction and another five to Demel's in the other. This is where Anna Dehne's second husband had his confectionary shop two hundred years ago before moving to the much tonier Michaelerplatz.

Today, the northeast corner is taken up by Oberlaa, a branch of one of Vienna's newest and most innovative *Zuckerbäcker*. On a sunny Sunday afternoon the café spills out into the square, the tables packed with a mixture of locals and a smattering of foreigners. True to the café's reputation for novelty, the table menu features the "neu, new, nuovo, Mango-Schokolade Torte," a flourless almond cake layered with *Pariser Creme* (chocolate mousse), mango puree, and a thin layer of whipped cream. It's light and fruity, a nice balance of creamy chocolate and bright, tropical intensity. There's a bit of Paris there in the mango—maybe even a little Guadeloupe—but in other respects it is utterly Viennese, yet altogether modern.

Visitors sometimes get the impression that the Vienna they see today is a charming relic of a golden, imperial past where glittering, uniformed viscounts and duchesses in confections of satin and crinoline spent their adult lives whirling through neverending waltzes, only pausing occasionally to sip coffee and nibble on Sacher torte. And many Viennese do nothing to discourage this gilded delusion. But in fact Vienna has seen numerous cycles of revolution and reaction, not least in the case of dessert.

In the twenty years or so that followed World War II, the future of Viennese dessert seemed in doubt. But then came the sixties generation. In Berkeley that meant flower power and hash brownies; in Paris it resulted in burning barricades and nouvelle cuisine. Vienna wasn't entirely immune from the spirit of 1968, though here the revolution took more subtle forms.

When I met Kurt Nitsche, Demel's retired cake maestro, at Café Griensteidl, he introduced me to Karl Schuhmacher, a colleague of many years. The two friends are both storied veterans of Vienna's pastry firmament, though they come from very different constellations. Herr Schuhmacher is tall, courtly, and a little otherworldly. He has the air of a theoretical astrophysicist more than a bomb-throwing pastry chef. Yet according to his friend, it was Schuhmacher who helped shake Vienna's pastry world out of its postwar lethargy. In 1968, as Nitsche went to work for Vienna's most venerable pastry shop, Schumacher headed for Paris. He had followed the usual pastry chef's career of apprenticeship and long training, eventually rising to the top position at Gerstner's, another iconic Viennese *Zuckerbäcker*. But he was bored. "We started at seven and finished by ten," he says with a bittersweet grin, "and then we would spend the rest of the day playing cards." Looking to France, with its innovation-driven cuisine, Gerstner's head pastry chef thought: why couldn't we do the same thing with pastry? "I was interested in everything new, bringing in new influences," he reminisces, adding without any false modesty, "and I was very famous for it." So he traveled widely, picking up ideas in France and even the United States, filling his cakes with lighter mousselike creams, introducing foreign flavors to the tradition-bound craft.

It was he who founded Oberlaa in 1973 and worked night and day, tweaking, updating, and modernizing the traditional Viennese repertoire. His little shop was located in the eponymous spa town just south of the capital. Culinary revolutions are generally not noisy affairs, but slowly, gradually his influence was felt. Yet in the end his lucky break came in a very Viennese, almost Hapsburg fashion.

In those days, the little town was a bit of a backwater, so to draw attention to it, the Vienna Parks Department had asked Princess Caroline of Monaco and her sister, Stephanie, to attend the launch of a new rose variety in 1975. (Their mother, Princess Grace, was passionate about the flower.) Sensing an opportunity, Karl Schuhmacher made a large oval cake decorated with a bouquet of sugar roses that was presented to the princesses during their visit. As quickly as possible, Oberlaa printed a brochure featuring a picture of their cake and the famed royals. It wasn't quite the same thing as getting the imperial seal of approval that decorated Demel's boxes, but in the 1970s it was about as close as a confectioner could get. Success didn't come overnight, but with a little helping hand from royalty, the Oberlaa brand prospered. Today the company has more than a half-dozen branches across Vienna. They are perhaps a little less edgy than when Herr Schuhmacher was at the helm, but neither are they sitting on their laurels.

In many respects the Austrian capital is as modern as any city in Europe. There are ecohotels that promise zero environmental impact. There is a vibrant arts scene, and cutting-edge restaurants dish up the most up-to-date global-inflected cuisine. Yet in some ways the city of Franz Dehne and Franz Sacher is still the most traditional of Europe's old capitals. Today's pastry shops may be filled with hot pink *macarons* flavored with roses, and "peach cobbler" and "lemon drop" cupcakes, but in many of its habits Vienna remains Vienna. The *Apfelstrudel* is still freshly baked and the Hotel Sacher lawyer is still busy making sure no one dares transgress the Original Sacher-Torte®. But, most important, both cake and strudel still come with a generous helping of whipped cream.

Kávový dort s griliášem

Mocha Torte with Hazelnut Praline

• •

By the time Marie Janků-Sandtnerová came out with her bestselling *Česká kuchařka* ("Czech Cookbook") in 1924 (the book is still in print), the French *gâteau moka* was not only thoroughly acclimated in central Europe, it had multiplied into numerous variations. Janků-Sandtnerová herself includes three. This is the best one, in my opinion. Given the local penchant for nut-tortes, many of the cakes included almonds, hazelnuts, and walnuts.

This particular rendition adds a hazelnut praline to the mix, a stroke of genius if there ever was one. Make the cake a day ahead and refrigerate overnight before serving. Leave it out about an hour or so, though. It is best a little below room temperature.

Makes 12 to 16 servings

Praline

6 tablespoons granulated sugar
2 tablespoons water
2 ounces (about ½ cup) peeled, toasted hazelnuts

Cake

6 egg yolks
¾ cup granulated sugar
1 tablespoon dark rum
1 teaspoon vanilla extract
4 ounces (about ¾ cup) fine semolina flour
3 ounces (about ¾ cup) walnuts or hazelnuts, finely ground
7 egg whites
2 ounces (4 tablespoons) unsalted butter, melted and cooled

Frosting

½ cup milk
3 tablespoons espresso
2 egg yolks
3 tablespoons all-purpose flour
4 tablespoons granulated sugar
1 teaspoon vanilla extract
9½ ounces (2 sticks plus 3 tablespoons) unsalted butter, slightly
    softened
9½ ounces (about 2 cups) confectioners' sugar

1. Make the praline: Combine the 6 tablespoons sugar with 2 tablespoons water in a small, heavy saucepan. Cook over moderate heat until amber colored. Do not mix. If you need to stir the mixture, swirl the pan. When the sugar is caramelized, add the nuts, stir briefly, then pour onto lightly buttered or nonstick aluminum foil. Cool completely, break into pieces, and crush moderately fine in a food processor.

2. Make the cake: Preheat oven to 350°F. Butter and flour a 9-inch springform pan. Beat the egg yolks and ¾ cup sugar with an electric mixer until thick and creamy. Beat in the rum and vanilla. In a small bowl, stir together the flour, nuts, and half of the crushed praline. In a separate bowl using clean beaters, beat the egg whites until firm and glossy. Fold the whites into the egg yolks, then fold in the flour mixture, and finally the butter. Transfer to prepared pan and bake 45–60 minutes until a tester comes out clean. Cool to room temperature, then refrigerate at least 4 hours or overnight.

3. Make the frosting: Combine the milk, espresso, 2 egg yolks, all-purpose flour, and granulated sugar in a small saucepan. Whisk until smooth. Set over low heat and cook, stirring continually, until it is the consistency of thick pudding. Remove from heat and whisk in the vanilla extract. Press plastic wrap onto the surface and chill. Using an electric mixer, beat the butter until light, then gradually beat in the confectioners' sugar. Beat in the custard mixture.

4. To assemble the cake, cut into three layers. Use about one-half of the frosting to sandwich the layers together. Use the remainder to frost the outside. Dust the sides with the remaining praline and decorate the top with rosettes of frosting and/or toasted hazelnuts or chocolate-covered coffee beans. Refrigerate at least 4 hours before serving.

6

A DEMOCRACY OF SWEETNESS

❋ *United States* ❋

THE SWEETEST PLACE ON EARTH

I wanted to hate the place, I really did. Every Eurotrash, Slow-Food-proselytizing, Sacher torte–weaned sinew and tendon in my body strained to despise Hershey, Pennsylvania. But I just couldn't do it.

I began to melt even as we drove into town, even as the smell of run-over skunks and manure that filled the toffee-thick summer air was overlaid by the distant whiff of chocolate. Once in Hershey, I couldn't help but be charmed by the kiss-shaped tops of lampposts and the kiss-shaped topiaries lining Cocoa Street and Chocolate Avenue. By the time I stumbled through the revolving doors of Hershey's Chocolate World, my guard was down. I was completely overcome by the chaotic swirl of candy and humanity—and even of the paranormal blending of the two. How else to explain the fact that I shoved my seven-year-old daughter into the arms of the two-legged, six-foot-high Kit Kat with its preternatural grin? All this as I ogled with saucer-eyed wonder the hovering balloons in the shape of Hershey's kisses, the Hershey's Bars as big as mattresses, the giant bags of Reese's Pieces, the corkscrew chutes that shoot candy from a height of three stories to the awaiting silver buckets emblazoned with the Hershey's logo held by open-mouthed children. I felt like Augustus Gloop, the fat kid in Willy Wonka's chocolate factory.

But of course that's the whole point. I was completely seduced by a multibillion-dollar megacorporation that spews out more than eighty million of those miniature foil-wrapped confections along with millions of tons of other sweet effluence each and every day.[1] The folks at Hershey's know exactly what they're doing. The appeal of what they make and how they sell it goes right for the child in each and every one of us. There is the shiny foil packaging designed to catch the eye in much the same way as the shiny mobiles parents hang over cribs. The flavors, primarily sugar and milk, are formulated to satisfy our inborn taste preferences. Jean-Jacques Rousseau would be horrified. Hershey's caters precisely to that very primal, childlike urge that the French philosopher insisted children must be taught to control. Here, there are none of the class referents you find in a *gâteau Saint-Honoré*, none of the nuanced social meanings of a Sacher torte. Candy bars and Hershey's kisses require no plate, no silverware, no café, no salon. In this, they are like many quintessentially American desserts such as cookies, cupcakes, and brownies, all meant to be eaten by hand, yet without any of the pinky-raised delicacy demanded of a madeleine or any of the challenging esoteric flavors of a modern day *macaron*. Though Hershey's may be a candy company, its success tells us a lot about the American idea of dessert.

Anyway, here the distinction between the two food categories is often a moot point. Unlike in candy-obsessed England, say, where the line between what they call "sweets" and "pudding" (candy and dessert in American English) is firmly drawn in the sand, or in Austria, where a chocolate bar is fundamentally a different kind of food than a piece of *Schokoladentorte*, on this side of the Atlantic the distinction is as fuzzy as a Hostess Sno Ball. Our desserts come in convenient little packages: as cookies, brownies, cupcakes, and ice cream sandwiches. Like the Austrians, we find occasions to eat sweets from dawn till dusk, though here they tend to take the form of sweet snacks rather than a sit-down meal. We like dessert for breakfast in the form of Pop Tarts and Cocoa Puffs. The diet-obsessed are encouraged to drink chocolate or piña colada shakes for lunch or chow down on the likes of Slim-Fast Chocolate Cookie Dough Flavored Meal On-The-Go Bars for supper. Bodybuilders eat protein bars in flavors hyped as "black forest cake" and "double fudge brownie." Sweet "snacks" fill aisle after aisle of our grocery stores. And can you really distinguish between what to call a product such as an Oreo (a cookie) and a Mars Bar (a candy bar)? And does it matter? We eat almost all of our sugar in some sort of processed form, whether in the shape of Froot Loops, M&Ms, Pepperidge Farm, or Krispy Kremes. And if you're not convinced, look at the statistics: for every pound of sugar sold in a grocery store, another six end up in foods produced by factories and other commercial enterprises.[2]

But who's to say this is bad? Mass production has given us an enormous variety of both candy and dessert at a very economical price. In the United States, sweets have long been available to everyone, not just to upper-crust ladies and their lap dogs. There is, perhaps, a certain lack of subtlety and complexity in the thousands of sugary snacks in an average American supermarket, but even that is changing as premium brands of mass-manufactured confectionary come on the market. If food snobs can't abide the Almond Joy, there is always Scharffen Berger 82% Cacao Extra Dark—both owned by Hershey's. If they aren't happy with Good Humor, they can turn to Ben & Jerry's, both divisions of Unilever.

But wait, you say. What about homemade cookies and cupcakes? What about motherhood and apple pie?

Of course there are mothers who peel their own apples and roll homemade dough to make pie. But how many more of us reach for the canned pie filling and the Sara Lee? After all, isn't Sara Lee "made with the goodness of home"? And if you really insist on freshly baked pie, supermarkets have installed bakeries so the smells of homemade freshness waft through the bakery aisle. Which is not say that the myth of mom and apple pie isn't still with us; it's just that the treat is more likely to resemble a Moon Pie.

The myth shouldn't be dismissed out of hand, however. Up until the industrialization of the nation's food supply, just about every dessert was homemade in America. Moreover, here, unlike in the Old World, it was mostly mom doing the baking. Then, in the mid-nineteenth century, mass production began to intrude into the home kitchen. Ever since the advent of coal and steam, American desserts have existed along a continuum stretched between industrially produced and homemade. During the Civil War era, most desserts were made in domestic kitchens. But then the balance began to shift. Imagine an old-fashioned baker's scale. One side is weighed down with pudding and pie, with pound cake and gingerbread, with molasses, butter, and eggs. As the nineteenth century approaches the twentieth, the other side of the balance begins to slump, first loaded down with refined sugar, cornstarch, and baking powder, then Hershey's Bars and Jell-O, then an avalanche of Ho Hos and Ring Dings, Chips Ahoy and Entenmann's. Some of the old-fashioned pastries cling on to make it into the new era while others change with the times. Many, however, fall by the side. Obviously there are many desserts that fall somewhere on the spectrum between a handcrafted shoofly pie and a factory-produced Reese's Peanut Butter Cup. American classics like pecan pie (now invariably made with Karo corn syrup, introduced in 1902)[5] and carrot cake with its Philadelphia-brand cream cheese frosting are obviously more "homemade" than s'mores or Rice Krispies Treats.

In the United States, though, what's missing along this continuum between manufactured and homemade is the professional, artisanal pastry cook with his or her specialized repertoire. Oh, sure, there are places that sell cannoli and *millefeuille*, but they are the haute couture of the pastry trade. At American bakeries you expect to find doughnuts and cupcakes, and—though the shops are invariably run by full-time professionals—the owners typically put a big sign in the window that says HOMEMADE, as if mom were still in the back whipping up a batch of oatmeal cookies. Compare that to Europe: nobody in Vienna goes to their neighborhood *Zuckerbäcker* because they want "homemade." They shell out their euros for the work of a full-time artisan, not a surrogate mom catering to their childlike sweet tooth. Here it's different. Which is why, in the United States, the story of dessert is very much about mothers and factories. Needless to say, the mothers came first.

PUDDING AND PIE

Let's step back for a moment and look at an American kitchen well before Hershey's and Sara Lee, a time when iron horses had just begun to roar across the Kansas plain and children still worked in barns, not in coal mines. As yet this is Jefferson's America, an agricultural country of independent and often isolated homesteaders. There is no village baker as there is in Europe, mostly because there are few villages that would support him. Most women bake their own bread in often primitive or improvised ovens. As in the old country, for all but the wealthiest households, dessert is decidedly a sometimes thing, made mostly with locally grown flour, the fruit that can be picked out back, the eggs from your own chickens, the lard from the winter slaughter, and a little semirefined sugar or molasses stocked up for special occasions. The cash economy is pretty rudimentary.

You can get some insight into the preindustrial American lifestyle in the Little House books that describe the author Laura Ingalls Wilder's pioneer childhood. Not surprisingly, since on the frontier getting enough food was a full-time job for everyone in the family, food is often at the center of the narrative. As they arrive in Kansas in the 1870s, Laura watches her father build a log cabin and a stone fireplace where her mother cooks mush from homegrown cornmeal, prairie hens and deer shot by her father, and more cornmeal mush. The occasional salt pork and pancakes with store-bought molasses come as an all-too-infrequent respite from the dull, repetitious diet. The family buys little because they have no cash. Occasionally "Pa" trudges many miles to the store, only to return with a tiny satchel of white sugar, which "Ma" immediately squirrels away for those special occasions when company might call.[6] Life probably wasn't too different for the great majority of Americans who lived off the land.

Things may have been different among the very wealthy planters in the antebellum South with their abundant kitchen slaves and aristocratic pretensions, and for the silk stocking crowd in New York and Philadelphia—but these were decidedly the exception. Even relatively rich farmers shared the rural isolation of Laura's youth. Listen to the description of life in the early 1900s recounted by William Weeks Hall, the son of a sugar planter family in rural Louisiana:

> During the first half of the last century, the land was cheap and the plantation houses, their dependencies and their quarters, together with their sugar mills, were surrounded by immense tracts of land, fields under cultivation, primeval forests, and swamps of cypress. Each plantation was a community in itself, and was self-supporting.
>
> Very little food came in from the outside, and the cost of it came not from the buying of it, but from the labor and the hazards of raising it. The receipts [recipes]

of each plantation, therefore, were the result of what you had raised yourself. . . . There was no going around the corner to the A&P for something; when you ran out of it, you simply ran out.[7]

It's worth pointing out that he's describing a family that was solidly upper class. The Weeks had thrived from the brutal sugar plantation system that supplied America with its sweetener for coffee and pie before the Civil War. By the 1830s, David Weeks owned three thousand acres of land and 160 slaves in and around the town of New Iberia. You can still visit the mansion he built in 1832. It sits on the banks of the muck-brown Bayou Teche surrounded by grand old oaks dripping with Spanish moss. The colonnade in front makes for a grand impression, but frankly, this is no Tara. Inside, it consists of four cramped bedrooms and a modest dining room and parlor. As was typical of the South, there was a pantry in the house, but the kitchen was in a shed to one side not far from where the house slaves, who did the cooking, were quartered.

David died even as the house was being finished, but his daughter-in-law Mary Palfrey Weeks, who lived there until her death in 1888, offered a glimpse of Southern country cooking and baking of the time. A photo of Mary from around 1880 shows a woman who looks like she could have used a little less trouble and a tad more dessert in her life. She had married into the family in 1846, a prosperous time for the slave plantation owners. But then came the Civil War, and for a time her world was turned upside down. Her husband took most of his slaves to Texas, where he hoped his "property" would be safe from the Yankees. In the meantime New Iberia was overrun by both Confederate and Union armies. Atrocities were common on both sides. Things got so bad that at least one planter's family reportedly resorted to eating owl gumbo.[8] But by the 1870s, prosperity had returned. Mary's African American servants were no longer

slaves but were still the ones lighting the morning fire, pluck-
ing the chickens, and beating the batters for puddings and cakes.
There was decidedly no owl on the menu.

We can get some sense of what Mary Weeks and her hard-
working staff made for dinner in those days since we know that
she owned two cookbooks by Eliza Leslie (the Martha Stewart of
her day). She also subscribed to *Godey's Lady's Book*, a popular
women's magazine that was a little like a weepy *Good Housekeeping*. Even more telling of what she actually cooked is a scrapbook
of carefully hand-copied recipes. Given the fact that sugarcane
was all around them, you would expect there to be plenty of desserts in her collection, and indeed there are, but this was common in receipt books north and south. The desserts are typical
of the era. Both sides of the family were originally from Virginia,
and, despite the fact that her Louisiana neighbors often spoke
French, the puddings and pies that were shuttled between the
pantry and the outdoor oven reflect the family's Southern heritage. The recipes were mostly descended from English originals,
something that was true of the majority of American desserts.

Leafing through the yellowed pages of Mary's notebooks
you find loads of fruit pies, jellies, blancmanges, and puddings.
Lemon is a popular flavoring in the desserts, as are some spices—
especially nutmeg and cloves. The penchant for old-fashioned
flavorings such as rosewater appears to be waning by the 1870s
though it isn't entirely gone. Coconut seems to be experiencing a
vogue and vanilla has become commonplace.*

Turning to Mary's copies of Eliza Leslie's *Lady's Receipt-Book*
(1847) and *Miss Leslie's New Receipts for Cooking* (1854), you
notice such extinct nineteenth-century sweets as syllabub and

---

* In the early 1900s, vanilla had been associated with French patisserie. To get the flavor,
home bakers had to track down expensive vanilla beans, but by Mary Weeks's day the availability of vanilla extract, produced by companies such as Oliver's of Philadelphia and promoted by famous food writers like Eliza Leslie, made it less exotic, if not exactly cheap.

Sally Lunn (the first is a kind of mousse, the second a sweet buttery bread), but other recipes in the collection are more familiar. There are instructions for making doughnuts. We would also recognize the jumbles in the cookbooks as sugar cookies, and the gingersnaps as—well—gingersnaps. The pound cake isn't all that different from today's version even if Leslie's version is scented with rosewater and iced with a pink sugary icing. And then there were all those familiar pie recipes.* In certain cases some of the names in the collection are a little misleading. Take "cookie," for example. The word derives from the colonial Dutch *koekje*, or "little cake," and that is what Leslie's recipe resembled. The result is more of a dense scone than what we would call a cookie. Nothing resembling a drop cookie batter existed until the turn of the century; up until the 1890s virtually all cookies were of the rolled variety. Another seemingly familiar treat is the cupcake. These were common enough in the 1800s, but they bore little resemblance to the generously iced muffins ubiquitous today. The "cup" in the cupcakes referred to the measurement of the ingredients that went into the batter—a cup of butter, two cups sugar, three cups flour, and so on. At times these were literally baked in cups, which, by the end of the century, led to purpose-made cupcake tins. Still, cupcakes baked in regular loaf pans were just as common.[9]

The United States was largely settled by British immigrants and as a result shared many of the food attitudes of the motherland. And the migrants kept coming well after the Revolution. Moreover, upper-class Americans wishing to buff their social graces still looked for their polish across the Atlantic. Even so, the two food cultures began to split well before the War of Independence in a number of ways. Part of the divergence can

---

* The medieval European passion for putting anything and everything between two layers of piecrust survives here as nowhere else. Americans though, unlike the French and English, have long preferred sweet fillings.

be explained by America's native ingredients (England had no huckleberry pie, no Indian pudding) and part by our distinct settlement patterns and demographics. Social expectations were different too. In spite of their best efforts, American plutocrats couldn't achieve the same sort of social position that centuries of tradition reserved for the upper tiers of English society.

What's more, the Industrial Revolution hit Britain early and hard. At a time when America was still largely rural, Albion's smoky slums were filling up with an underclass that had neither time nor even a place to cook. Mostly, they bought what they could on the street. Itinerant vendors sold prepared food of every description.* Increasingly, though, England's working poor came to depend on cheap, industrially produced bread, jam, and biscuits for their calories. (In America, industrially produced desserts didn't come into their own until the twentieth century, by which point the technology had vastly evolved.) Meanwhile, as the British proletariat was suffering from malnutrition due to a surfeit of sugar, the Victorian ruling classes, much as the rest of Europe, increasingly went in for French food. French chefs were (relatively) cheap and available, at least if you were an aristocrat. The middle classes were lost somewhere between. Food historian Stephen Mennell has convincingly argued that one cause for the downfall of English cooking in the nineteenth century was this very split that occurred between the trendsetting elite who employed professional foreign chefs and a middle class that

---

* In a book with the self-explanatory title *London labour and the London poor: the condition and earnings of those that will work, cannot work, and will not work*, journalist Henry Mayhew listed the desserts that were for sale in London in the 1860s: "The pastry and confectionary which tempt the street eaters are tarts of rhubarb, currant, gooseberry, cherry, apple, damson, cranberry, and (so called) mince pies; plum dough and plum-cake; lard, currant, almond and many other varieties of cakes, as well as of tarts; gingerbread; nuts and heart-cakes ; Chelsea buns; muffins and crumpets . . ." He also noted with some surprise the "novel and aristocratic luxury of street-ices." Clearly the Industrial Revolution hadn't entirely wiped out all decent English food—as yet.

couldn't hope to keep up. Thus innovation was stifled. As the wealthy finished their meals with *gâteaux* and *biscuits* that emulated Carême, the bourgeoisie of Bristol and Manchester made do with trifle, plum pudding, and a fancier grade of factory-made biscuits.

Given the prodigious British sweet tooth noted as early as the Elizabethan era, it is surprising how spare the repertoire of indigenous desserts is in the United Kingdom today, at least when compared with the continental dessert superpowers of France and Austria, or even the upstart United States. (Candy is another matter—here Britain does rule the waves.) In *British Food*, a work that seeks to revive the much-maligned cookery of his native land, former *Guardian* food editor Colin Spencer can come up with only two score desserts as traditionally English. Even so, over half of these are puddings or puddinglike. Little wonder that in British English "pudding" is synonymous with dessert. And indeed, other than its puddings (and perhaps shortbread), which experienced past vogues in both America and mainland Europe, most foreigners would have a hard time identifying a typical British dessert.

In the colonial era, the variety of distinctively English desserts was undoubtedly much greater than it is today. Yet even then pudding ruled, in England as in the colonies. Here, the taste for pudding remained well into the nineteenth century, though Americans tended to prefer theirs baked rather than boiled or steamed, as was the British custom. Marion Harland, Virginian food writer and novelist, included fourteen boiled and forty-five baked puddings in her 1873 cookbook, *Common Sense in the Household*. In contrast, Mrs. Beeton, her British contemporary (and the reigning culinary empress of Victoria's world-spanning realm), included a comparable number of baked puddings but almost double that number—some eighty recipes—for boiled or steamed puddings in her sixteen-hundred-page tome. Not

included in either of these numbers are all the puddings baked
in crusts that were also common on both sides of the Atlantic.
The British tended to refer to these as baked puddings, or tarts,
whereas in America they came to be increasingly referred to as
pies. Today these crust-enclosed puddings are relatively rare in
the United Kingdom; treacle tart being a notable exception.*
In the United States they not only retained their popularity but
propagated. There are dozens of these custard pies in the American repertoire, from pumpkin to lemon meringue to all those
pudding-filled, cream-topped pies that flew across the backlots
of Hollywood. Some, like the pecan pie, are clearly American
inventions, created as cooks experimented with local ingredients. The recipe originates with British "transparent pudding,"
a custard made with sugar, melted butter, and eggs and baked
in a crust. In the United States, this was renamed chess pie by
the 1860s. Then someone had the brilliant idea to add pecans,
probably only in the late 1800s.[10] With certain other dishes it's
sometimes hard to tell whether the English or the American version came first. Some recipes traveled both east and west. Witness Mrs. Beeton's version of Washington pudding and American bread (cornbread). The fact that she calls a recipe lemon
meringue "pie" rather than a tart or baked custard also implies
that it was an American import, as presumably was her version
of pumpkin pie.[11] Not that using pumpkins in pies was anything
new in the British Isles. "In England," wrote Thomas Mawe in
1778, "they mix [pumpkin] with sliced apples, milk, sugar, some
grated nutmeg, etc. and thus make a kind of pudding, prepare
in the shell and bake it in an oven, which is commonly called
pumpkin pye, and for which purpose the plants are cultivated
by the country people in many parts of England."[12] A somewhat
more elegant recipe with raisins and sherry had already appeared

* Treacle tart is made more or less in one of two ways. In the first case it is much like shoofly
pie, in which syrup is thickened with crumbs; in the second it resembles a chess pie, though
made with sugar syrup rather than brown sugar.

more than a hundred years earlier in Hannah Woolley's *Queen-Like Closet*.[13] Of course these weren't what we think of as pumpkin pies. The pumpkin custard–filled version we're familiar with made its debut in the first American cookbook, written by Amelia Simmons in 1796. It wasn't much different, however, from numerous earlier English recipes for potato, chestnut, quince, and even yam custards baked in a crust.* So just how American is pumpkin pie? Let's give it the benefit of the doubt.

Apple pie, of course, is only American in the same sense that most of us are descended from immigrants. Apple pies (or tarts) go back to the Middle Ages in England. The *Forme of Cury* (1390) contains instructions "For to Make Tartys in Applis." By the late 1500s, recipes for apple pie appear that are practically indistinguishable from those of today. In his 1664 diary, the English naval administrator Samuel Pepys declared a supper of pease porridge and apple pie most excellent. That suggests where it fit into English cooking: good enough for a civil servant but hardly cuisine. That this rural and profoundly unaristocratic dessert reached its iconic status in America says at least as much about Americans' image of themselves as the Sacher torte does about the Viennese. The apple pie is profoundly egalitarian—any homesteader could grow an apple tree—and requires few fancy ingredients or citified techniques. It is also firmly associated with home and the domestic realm. (More on that later.) Like many of the myths Americans like to tell about themselves, it was especially associated with New England, and thus there was a certain puritan stolidity about it. Contrast this to Old England, the land of the pudding eaters, where apple pie, or tart, was hardly something that would ever grace the table of a chic lady or posh gentleman.

But King George's kingdom didn't give us just pudding and pie. There was also cake. There too, the English cake repertoire

---

* The yams used were presumably the true yams of African origin rather than sweet potatoes, so that, while this may be a progenitor of the sweet potato pie or "pudding" recipe first published in Mary Randolph's *Virginia Housewife* of 1828, it is not identical to it.[14]

of the colonial era was much broader (at least in technique if not in flavorings) than it is today. There were dense fruitcakes, pound cakes, adaptations of French *biscuit*, and various sorts of yeast-leavened cakes not unlike a baba or *Kugelhopf*. Many of these must have been very heavy and sweet given how much butter, sugar, and dried fruit there is in them. One English dessert called Portugal cake, for example, has the familiar proportions of a pound cake (that is, a pound each of flour, sugar, eggs, and butter) but adds a half-pound of currants and sweet fortified wine for good measure.* There are recipes for it on both sides of the Atlantic, including in Mary Weeks's beloved *Godey's Lady's Book*.[16] Some American recipes for this confection are simply verbatim transcriptions of earlier English sources, but more often the recipe drops the expensive European sack and increases the currants. The cakes were baked in little pans, a little like French madeleines. Yet compared to American fruitcakes, the Portugal cake was a lightweight. Cakes baked for special occasions could be huge. Amelia Simmons gave a recipe for "Election Cake" that calls for thirty quarts of flour, ten pounds of butter, fourteen pounds of flour, and twelve pounds of raisins.[17] In cookbooks of this time, these cakes were often leavened with yeast, though, increasingly, beating eggs for an hour or two became the normal way of getting air into the dense batters.

By the late nineteenth century, this British penchant for fruit-rich baked goods slowly abated in the New World, though fruitcakes continued to be the traditional wedding cake of choice well into the 1960s. Mostly they became the butt of jokes in America, much like British cooking as a whole. A fruitcake was more likely to refer to a weirdo than to anything you might want to eat.

---

* The name, Portugal cake, presumably refers to the ingredients: the imported dried grapes and "sack" or fortified wine from Portugal or Spain. An early recipe from 1727 recipe calls it "Lisbon or Portugal-Cakes" and calls for ground almonds and "Canary wine" as well as orange-flower water.[15]

⌒ Wedding Cake ⌒

Today, the wedding cake is just about the only confection that still conjures up the glory and folly of the baroque confectioner's art. Weddings are one of the few occasions when wealth and power are still calculated in layers of sweet fondant. At a fancy society event, the cake can run into thousands of dollars.

The idea of the wedding cake as we know it originates with the British, who served an iced fruitcake for the ceremony since at least the eighteenth century.[18] In England, these earlier cakes were known as "bride's cakes," while, according to Noah Webster, the term "wedding cake" was more common in nineteenth-century America. Among the English ruling classes, who had imported the French penchant for elaborate *pièces montées*, the cakes grew in ornateness and complexity. Like Antonin Carême's multistoried monuments, they resembled architecture or perhaps furniture more than what we would think of as a wedding cake. There was little of the master's whimsy though. Moreover, expense was no guarantee of quality. The overwrought wedding cake created in 1863 for the wedding of the future King Edward VII and Princess Alexandra of Denmark, for example, gives the unfortunate impression of a gothic tower fused with a rococo cuckoo clock.

Caught up in the fury of the Civil War, Americans didn't pay much attention to that particular pastry edifice. It was the next royal wedding cake that caught their notice. This was one of two giant cakes created by Queen Victoria's chief confectioner for the wedding of Edward's sister Louise. (The cakes were likely the work of Alphonse Gouffé, the brother of one of Carême's star pupils, Jules Gouffé.)[19] One of the cakes was widely reproduced in popular publications. Newspapers reported that it was over five feet high and weighed in at 225 pounds.[20] It was surmounted by a miniature classical temple topped off with an image of a vestal virgin, while allegorical figures of Agriculture, Fine Arts, Science, and Commerce stood round the base. What it lacked in romance, it made up for in classical tastefulness. Every American bride who dreamed of being a princess now knew just the kind of cake she should have for her wedding. These sugary monuments, along with the white gowns popularized by Victoria's princesses, became all the mode in the mansions of Fifth Avenue and Beacon Hill. In fact, the cake and the dress came to resemble each other: both white, both virginal. A contemporary description of Princess Louise's wedding dress could easily apply to the multi-tiered wedding cakes of the coming generations: "The bride was dressed in white satin . . . with ornaments of orange blossoms and green leaves and a cloud of . . . lace." About a dozen years later, American cookbook author Estelle Woods Wilcox explained how bride's cakes should be placed on lace paper, adding, "It is not imperative that you use orange blossoms in the decorations of a bride's cake, still it is usually done."[21] By this point the term "bride's cake" had been revived in the United States to describe a white cake that might be served alongside (or increasingly instead of) the old-fashioned wedding fruitcake.

Earlier bride's or wedding cakes (or dresses for that matter) didn't used to be white. One popular English cookbook of the early nineteenth century specifically advised dyeing the icing red (or pink) with cochineal.[22] Writing in post–Civil War America, Mrs. Wilcox insisted that only white icing was now permitted. Then, as now, it was often inedible. An American trade journal around the turn of the century took this in stride, noting that the sugar curlicues were there for decorative purposes, adding, "bride cake icing is hard and unpleasant to eat."[23]

Wedding cakes are so packed with symbolism that it is hard to know where to begin. A writer for *Godey's Lady's Book* commented in 1831 how, as in marriage, the sweet exterior was only camouflage for the "crusty humour beneath." A contemporary English writer expressed the sentiments in slightly different words: "The bride cake is composed of many rich and aromatic ingredients, and crowned with an icing made of white sugar and bitter almonds, emblematical of the fluctuations of pleasure and pain which are incidental to the marriage state."[24]

The significance of the Victorian era's virginal white is all too obvious, yet the ceremonies surrounding the cake didn't always used to be so chaste. One ritual common in eighteenth-century Britain took place after the cake had been cut up. In this "idolatrous ceremony" (as *The Gentleman's Magazine* dubbed it in 1832), the bride holds the ring between the forefinger and thumb of her right hand while the groom repeatedly thrusts small pieces of cake through the opening. These are then distributed to the bridesmaids. As British anthropologist Simon Charsley has pointed out, the ritual of the newlywed husband and wife plunging the knife through the virginal exterior symbolically consummates the marriage. But that isn't the end of it. Like marriage, the cake was supposed to last forever, and accordingly brides would save a fragment for posterity. Unsurprisingly, many of these stale crumbs have outlasted the marriages, or in some cases even the brides. In 2009, a slice of Princess Louise's famed wedding cake hit the auction block for an asking price of £145. The seller warned that it was not safe to eat.[25]

But even nineteenth-century Americans probably didn't eat these sorts of cakes on a regular basis. They cost a mint and required way too much work. Mind you, so did French-style sponge cakes. These were considered very elegant but must have been hit-or-miss for occasional home bakers. And they were expensive, even if they lacked the imported fruit. Consider the dozen eggs called for in a sponge cake recipe from Catharine Beecher's 1850 *Domestic Receipt Book* (Miss Beecher was another household oracle of the Civil War era.) If you didn't have hens and had to buy the eggs, it would have cost you roughly twenty of today's dollars.[26] And just try baking a sponge cake in a wood-burning oven. This would explain why Miss Beecher's directions for making a cake bring to mind a surgeon suiting up for a triple bypass. It is a two-person operation: one to prepare the batter, the other to beat the egg whites. "Tie up your hair so that none can fall, put on a long-sleeved apron, have the kitchen put in order, and then arrange all the articles and utensils you will have occasion to use," she instructed. To determine the oven's temperature, she told you to put your hand in it and count: "If you cannot hold your hand in longer than to count twenty moderately, it is *hot enough*." No doubt an experienced baker would eventually get the hang of this, but even talented home bakers didn't make fancy cakes all that often. Their abilities could never compare to the skill set acquired by a professional pastry cook through years of everyday repetition.*

Given all the fuss and bother, these fancy cakes tended to be reserved for special occasions. The more usual cake of that rural antebellum era was a sort of sweet, yeast-risen loaf or "common cake." Since bread baking was a weekly—if not more frequent—

---

* It's interesting to compare Miss Beecher's instructions on testing heat with the empirical approach of a French professional like Jules Gouffé. Rather than depending on your pain threshold, he tests temperature by placing pieces of paper in the oven, identifying the correct heat by their color. For a sponge cake, he recommends cooking it at "dark paper temperature."[27]

activity in most households, you could always fold a little sweetener into the dough to make a kind of coffeecake. "Very fine common cake is also easily made, at every baking," Miss Beecher noted, "by taking some of the dough of bread and working in sugar, butter, and eggs. . . . These can be made more or less sweet and rich at pleasure."

Yet even while most of the new nation's desserts can be traced to England, some arrived with Dutch and German settlers. Dough-nuts, as they were first called, are likely the offspring of Dutch settlers' *Oliekoecken* ("oil cakes"). Washington Irving, writing in 1809, described these as "balls of sweetened dough, fried in hog's fat called dough nuts or oly koeks—a delicious kind of cake at present scarce known in [New York] excepting in genuine Dutch families."* The early recipes all call for a yeast dough. By at least 1845, though, cooks started using saleratus, the precursor to baking soda. It was only then that we got something resembling Dunkin' Donuts. However, when the dough balls got their hole is hard to pinpoint, though it must have been before the Civil War.** (Miss Leslie, for one, instructed her readers to cut her "dough nuts" into diamonds.) The June 29, 1861, edition of the *Baltimore American* reported on a New England doughnut fiesta that included the holey version. The bill of fare might have convinced even Homer Simpson to enlist:

---

* There is broad consensus among American food historians that doughnuts are descended from their Dutch ancestors, yet fritters of various descriptions certainly existed in England since medieval times. There was even something called a "dough-nut" made in Herfordshire (just north of London). These were made for Shrove Tuesday just as in Catholic countries, as William Hone reported in 1831. He described them as "small cakes fried in hog's lard." It is perfectly plausible that, while doughnuts in the Hudson Valley could claim Dutch parentage, those in New England may have been descended from old England.[28]

** In 1916, the *Washington Post* interviewed a retired eighty-five-year-old sailor, Captain Hanson Gregory, who claimed that he was the one to invent the doughnut hole in 1847 while working on a schooner. Whether this was no more than a sailor's yarn is impossible to corroborate, though the fact that he came from Camden, Maine, not far from Augusta, makes the story not entirely implausible.[29]

The ladies of Augusta, Me., some time ago distributed over fifty bushels of doughnuts to the Third Volunteer regiment of Maine. . . . Never before was seen such an aggregate of doughnuts since the world began. . . . Every breeze sighed doughnuts—everybody talked of dough-nuts. The display of doughnuts beggared description. There was the molasses doughnut and the sugar dough-nut—the long doughnut and the short doughnut—the round doughnut and the square doughnut—the rect-angular doughnut and the triangular doughnut—the single twisted doughnut and the double twisted dough-nut—the "light riz" [risen?] doughnut and the hard-kneaded doughnut—the straight solid doughnut and the circular doughnut, with a hole in the centre. There were doughnuts of all imaginary kinds, qualities, shapes, and dimensions.[30]

The predominantly British repertoire of cookbook writers like Miss Leslie and her colleagues also suffered the occasional French incursion. Here and there they include recipes for such exotic confections as charlotte russe and éclairs. In some loca-tions Americans may have tasted the real thing. Mary Weeks, like many of her planter neighbors, did make the three-day trip to New Orleans a couple of times a year and no doubt tasted the fancy creations sold at continental patisseries. These shops pro-liferated in New York, Philadelphia, and New Orleans after the upheaval of the French Revolution, which sent many aristocratic pastry chefs overseas to avoid unemployment or the guillotine. No doubt there were devoted American amateurs who scoured cookbooks for recipes for "French puff paste" and "*tartelletes à la Chantilly*" (both contained in the 1856 *American Family Ency-clopedia of Useful Knowledge*), but they probably made them at home as seldom as we do today.

What with all the planning, labor, and expense involved, dessert was surely not eaten with the casualness of a fudge bar eaten at the corner Starbucks. Moreover, except for an occasional foray into the big city, for people like Mary Weeks, going out for dessert wasn't even a possibility. Except for the very largest metropolises, there was nothing remotely equivalent to Vienna's Demel or Ladurée in gay Paris. For the vast majority who lived in the countryside, entertaining at home was the only option. Every hostess no doubt did her best under the circumstances; still, it's hard to know just how elaborate some of these get-togethers really were. I can't quite see even someone as affluent as Mary Weeks serving the kind of "plain, substantial dinner" in her cramped Louisiana dining room that Catharine Beecher called for in her *Domestic Receipt-Book* in 1850.

"Such a dinner as this cannot usually be prepared and served easily," she lectured, "without two to cook and serve in the kitchen, and two waiters in the dining-room." Beecher then goes on to describe a sit-down affair for twelve involving a soup and fish course, then a half-dozen main courses. Dessert followed in the form of pudding, pastry, fruit, and coffee. Twenty years on, in the mid-1870s, cookbook author Marion Harland's suggestions were even more demanding, especially when it comes to the sweets: "Pastry is the first relay of dessert, [then come puddings]. Next appear creams, jellies, charlotte-russes, cakes, and the like; then fruit and nuts; lastly coffee, often accompanied with crackers and cheese."* Recognizing that some households lacked the resources for such elaborate shindigs, the lifestyle guides recommended more casual soirées. Marion Harland was a great proponent of the "the social standing supper"—as these cocktail-free cocktail parties were then called—where the emphasis was much

---

* It's interesting to note that she observes the British habit of ending a meal with a "savory" as opposed to the Continental or, later, American habit of finishing on a sweet note.

more on desserts. In this they were very much like the earlier European *collations* or *thés*. In a typical menu, ice cream, jellies, and cake received equal billing with oysters, chicken salad, and sandwiches. There were of course other, even more informal, occasions when desserts were consumed: at light luncheons but especially at teatime, when the menu consisted almost entirely of baked goods and ice cream.

There is an odd disconnect between the Jane Austen–like social scene that Harland and dozens of etiquette books of the time described and the grubby routine of the actual cooking and baking. But something similar exists today in the fantasy world of Martha Stewart, with its nostalgia for Suzy Homemaker (admittedly Suzy on steroids and Botox), and the real-life day-to-day of Boston Market. Like the women who watch Martha create improbable meals, the ladies who aspired to fulfill Harland's prescriptions lived in a changing world where the fairer sex was conflicted about her place in the world. By the late nineteenth century, quotidian existence was becoming very different from the agricultural ways of Mary Weeks's generation.

THE TASTE OF PROGRESS

The service provided by Beecher's and Harland's cookbooks and the advice columns in *Godey's Lady's Book* was to give formerly rural, now upwardly mobile women a model of what was expected of them as they negotiated the new urban middle-class lifestyle that accompanied the Industrial Revolution. As they looked around them, everything was changing: where food came from, where people lived, what they bought, how they got their information. When it comes to dessert, these were all deeply interconnected.

Cheap, fast rail transport equalized the price of commodities across the United States, whether it was sugar, flour, or even lard.

This meant that candy manufacturers were able to set up shop in Chicago even though most sugar was refined in New York. Wheat could be shipped from Ohio and Kansas and milled in Minneapolis before the flour was sent east. Somewhat later, the synthetic fats necessary for many shelf-stable products could be cooked up in Cincinnati, loaded onto freight trains to New York City, and then shipped right back in the form of Oreos.

This had implications for cookbook writers and manufacturers alike. When it came to baking recipes, they could finally include standardized measurements that meant something. Unlike in the olden days, when every product varied by region, now a cup of flour was a cup of flour, whether in Massachusetts or Missouri. Sugar especially became more and more the same. The sweet cane juice had long been used in many forms, from the lumpy brown jaggery of India to the triple-refined crystals of Paris's high-class *confisseurs*. Eliza Leslie, for example, called for a wide variety of sugars, including loaf sugar, white sugar, "best brown," and molasses in her antebellum cookbooks. In her day, confectioners had to refine their own sugar to get a sufficiently pure product. By 1873, though, Marion Harland would warn: "Except for gingerbread, use none but white sugar." Due to technological advances, refineries were producing sucrose that was virtually pure, and, due to the efficiency of the operation, there was almost no difference in price between brown and white sugar.[31]

In the first fifty years of the Republic, the price of sugar had hovered at around fifteen cents a pound. A bricklayer might have to work more than half a day to buy a five-pound bag; a stevedore could barely afford it after a full (ten-hour) day's work.* By the 1840s, improvements in refining machinery were quickly followed by a rapid fall in price. In the 1850s, sugar cost half of what

---

*Other ingredients were expensive too. To make a batch of some three dozen jumbles (sugar cookies) as described in Eliza Leslie's 1832 cookbook, *Seventy-Five Receipts for Pastry, Cakes, and Sweetmeats*, would have cost on the order of fifty cents, or half our stevedore's daily wage!

it had two decades earlier. By the 1880s, when you adjust for the cost of living, the sugar Hershey's and other manufacturers were buying had plummeted by 75 percent in fifty years; moreover, they didn't need to spend any money on additional refining.[32] The price of sugar only stabilized when, in 1887, Henry O. Havemeyer corralled together most of the East Coast's sugar refineries into the monopolistic American Sugar Refining Company. But by this point it was cheap enough that Americans continued to consume ever-greater quantities of the sweet crystals despite the flat price.[*]

Technological progress didn't merely affect the purity of sugar. The culinary industrial complex found new uses for long-familiar chemicals like citric acid even as it added new products to the food scientist's pantry. Cornstarch, for example, was invented by a New Jersey–based chemist in 1842 as a laundry starch but soon found its way into puddings and sauces. However, the chemicals that transformed the American dessert scene the most were the so-called chemical leaveners such as sodium bicarbonate that came to be used as substitutes for unpredictable yeast and fiddly, expensive eggs. The chemicals just got better and better. In her 1850 cookbook, Catharine Beecher went to great lengths to differentiate among saleratus (sodium bicarbonate), pearlash (potassium carbonate), and, her favorite, sal volatile (ammonium carbonate). She gave in-depth instructions about where they should be bought, how they should be stored and used, and how to concoct your own baking powder. By 1900 those instructions were no longer necessary. Our familiar and reliable baking soda and baking powder were almost universal.

---

[*] Roughly speaking, per capita consumption rose more or less steadily from about nine pounds in the 1820s to over seventy pounds after the turn of the twentieth century. By the turn of the millennium, we were consuming a yearly 150 pounds of sweeteners (sugar and corn syrup) for every man, woman, and child.

⌒ 31 Flavors ⌒

Like many other American desserts, the history of ice cream in America follows a trajectory that takes it from a home-made, special-occasion treat to an everyday snack made in factories. Once upon a time, as in Italy or France, it was an artisanal product available to the young country's small urban population. The cheaper versions were sold on the streets of Boston and Baltimore to anyone with a few pennies to spare, while the hoity-toity retired to ornate pleasure gardens to enjoy their scoops of vanilla, lemon, or strawberry ice cream in cut-crystal parfait glasses. Incidentally, in the early days the scoops were minute—about two tablespoons' worth—as an 1819 ad for Philadelphia's Columbian Garden shows.[3] The difficulty of securing a supply of ice as well as the labor and expense involved in making ice cream by hand meant that only the wealthiest homes could afford homemade. George Washington had an ice cream maker, as did Jefferson, Hamilton, and Madison.[4]

The nineteenth century saw the pleasure garden morph into the ice cream saloon and finally, by the 1890s, into the soda fountain. Yet for the majority of Americans who lived in the countryside, ice cream was a rarity. This only began to change after the hand-cranked patented ice cream maker was invented in 1846 (by Nancy Johnson of Philadelphia) and when commercial ice production (along with fast rail transport) made it feasible to make ice cream at home. By the 1880s, Mrs. Lincoln's *Boston Cookbook* pronounced, "A good ice-cream freezer should be in every kitchen." At this point middle-class homemakers could depend on regular deliveries from the iceman. Ice cream parties became a popular way to entertain, and many churches raised money at ice cream socials.

Today, the idea of smashing up all that ice, mixing it with salt, and turning a crank for forty-five minutes seems like a god-awful hassle, but compared to preparing and cleaning a wood- or coal-fired stove and then beating a cake batter for an hour or two by hand, it's a downright breeze. The wide availability of cheap ice made homemade ice cream a democratic treat in the United States, whereas in Europe it remained the preserve of fine confectioners.

After World War II, people could buy freezers, making it possible for the first time to sell ice cream in grocery stores. And what better way to break up the trip to the mall than to stop at a Dairy Queen or Howard Johnson? Howard Johnson opened his first shop with just three flavors in 1925. By the 1950s, the company's four hundred restaurants offered twenty-eight flavors. Then, in 1953, Baskin-Robbins came up with thirty-one. Nowadays, hardly anyone makes ice cream at home, but we sure eat enough of it, some twenty quarts per capita, or about four times the European average.

Confectioners and home bakers alike also benefited from kitchen gadgets great and small. As in Europe, great bellowing factories of the early industrial age didn't merely roll out railroad track and steam engines—they made whisks and teakettles too. You no longer had to give precise and elaborate specifications to the neighborhood tinsmith to get yourself a hand-cranked ice cream maker in the way Miss Beecher explained. Or follow her meticulously detailed instructions on constructing an oven. You could just buy one. Just read Marion Harland, who was a great enthusiast of Victorian gadgetry: "I take it for granted that you are too intelligent to share in the vulgar prejudice against labor-saving machines. A raisin-seeder costs a trifle in comparison with the time and patience required to stone the fruit in the old way. A *good* egg-beater is a treasure. So with farina-kettles, syllabub churns, apple-corers, potato-peelers and slicers, clothes-wringers and sprinklers, and the like."[33] It's not that these devices hadn't existed before; they used to be expensive because they were custom-made. The new mass-manufactured contraptions made it possible for fine ladies of modest means to contemplate fancy home baking for the first time.

The advent of the same machine age that churned out egg-beaters and cast-iron stoves created opportunities far from the bucolic countryside. The period between the Civil War and World War I—the very period when American sugar consumption exploded—saw immense population shifts. St. Louis went from 77,860 people in 1850 to 310,864 in 1870; Chicago more than tripled in size in the twenty years following 1880. As people across the country threw down their scythes and hopped the train to the big city, a country of farmers was transformed into a nation of factory and office workers. In 1840, one in ten Americans lived in a city; by 1910 it was one in two. For his part, William Weeks Hall was unsentimental about the urban-bound migrants leaving the nearby sugar plantations:

> [In the city] they have found, not only higher pay, but also the choice of more manifold opportunities, as well as for the promise of their children more varied occupations in which to be trained. [They] are freed from the seasonal hazards of the fields. [Here] there are only two or three months of regular sugar-making activity, and if a freeze should occur, even that is blotted out. The good old days, as sentimentalists call them, are gone. In their place, we have rapid transportation, preservation, refrigeration and complete electrification in the service part of the house.[34]

Those who weren't flocking to the burgeoning cities were often relocating their nests to a different rural outpost. A substantial minority headed west from exhausted East Coast farms to settle on land recently cleared of native peoples and Mexicans. In less than a generation, many of these western pioneers went from subsistence farming to producing cash crops. Laura Ingalls Wilder provided a textbook example of this. When she got married in 1885 she moved to South Dakota and, on arriving at her new home, discovered her pantry was already stocked with industrially produced goods: "There was a wide drawer that already held a whole sack of white flour," she wrote, "a smaller one with graham flour, another with cornmeal, a large shallow one for packages, and two others: one already filled with white sugar and the other with brown. Underneath the drawers was an open space to the floor and here stood the stone cookie-jar, the doughnut jar, and the jar of lard." Laura finds she has a large cast-iron coal-burning stove instead of a fireplace and soon enough even a "hired girl" to help around the house.[35]

But what does she know of cooking? This was a new world in which farmers sold what they grew and ate what they bought at the general store. Laura hadn't grown up with Uneeda biscuits or Quaker oatmeal. In many ways, she was just as culturally dislocated from a culinary tradition as the poor Irish, Slovak, Italian, and Jewish women who flooded American shores at this time, or the rural Pennsylvania Dutch families who crowded into Pittsburgh tenements. They too were struggling to adapt. In the new industrial age, people may have now had iceboxes, but they increasingly didn't have much connection with what they put in them. Instead of growing and eating their own apples and corn, they spent their wages in grocery stores—on flour from wheat that might have been raised by the Ingalls in South Dakota or sugar from Cuba. What both migrants and immigrants had in common was that they didn't know how to eat or cook, or at least felt insecure about it.

Into this arrived a revolution in communication. In the nineteenth century, a tsunami of information was made possible by the introduction of cheap wood pulp–based paper (paper used to be made out of relatively expensive cotton rags) and steam-powered presses that allowed for mass-market, recipe-filled magazines, popular cookbooks, and even new ways of selling crockery. When we first meet the newlywed Ingalls at their new South Dakota house, they are poring over a Montgomery Ward catalog, picking out china. "They needed it for the table," Ingalls wrote in the third person about her youth, "and there was such a pretty set advertised, a sugar bowl, spoon-holder, butter dish, six sauce dishes, and a large oval-shaped bread plate." (Ingalls still had the bread tray when she died, at ninety, in 1957.) Popular women's magazines were so full of ads they might have been mistaken for catalogs. Even recipe collections were chockablock with product placements. In many cases the cookbook itself was little more than a multipage advertisement. Food manufacturers printed promotional pamphlets by the millions, often hiring well-known cookbook writers and magazine editors to do the writing.

There were many reasons why advertising-laced publications and premium cookbooks found such a ready audience here in a way they never could have in Europe. Perhaps the most important was simply that American women could read. At 90 percent, the female literacy rate was almost double that of France at the time.[36] This enabled women at all levels of society to discover the joys of Argo cornstarch and come to realize how their life was incomplete without Fleischmann's yeast. In the case of recipes—whether penned by bestselling authors or corporate hacks—women could learn in great detail just how to use these new wonders of the industrial age. What's more, the cookbooks and advertisers now had a national audience, largely due to the same transportation revolution that made sugar, flour, chocolate, and baking powder standard nationwide.

Needless to say, industrialization wasn't a uniquely American phenomenon. Certainly Britain had a head start of several decades on their transatlantic neighbors. Society was in flux across Europe as well, what with wars, revolutions, and the rise of the bourgeoisie. However, American prosperity created a much larger middle class than in the Old World. This, in turn, created a labor shortage at the bottom. Accordingly, a middle-class woman in Philadelphia or Akron would have, at most, one servant to do the cooking and housework (despite Beecher's recommendations to the contrary). A household of similar income in Germany or Italy was used to employing a full-time cook as well as a maid or two. Moreover, the American domestic was increasingly likely to be an Irish immigrant girl with no cooking experience whatsoever, while the European cook typically had years of training. Is it any wonder that the American household manuals are full of advice on training servants? And that post–Civil War cookbooks hardly ever instruct readers to beat a batter, say, for an hour, as contemporary Austrian cookbooks commonly do?

The transformation from a rural to an urban society happened on both sides of the Atlantic, but in continental Europe, the connection to the home village was typically much easier to maintain. European women still learned to cook from their mothers and aunts rather than from professional authors. In the United States, one of the relatively few jobs open to middle-class women was teaching cooking, and a sure way for a woman to advance culinary credentials (to say nothing of her income) was to write for the increasingly popular women's magazines or work for the food industry to promote their products.

In Europe, too, there was a flood of cookbooks targeted at the bourgeoning bourgeoisie. But society was fundamentally different over there. In France and Austria, cookbooks often presented a peek into the lifestyles of the ruling classes, explaining how to set an aristocratic table on a more modest budget. Many were written by chefs who had worked for noble families—or at least claimed they had. Even when authors who had not worked in professional kitchens presented dessert recipes, they were often adaptations from well-known confectioners, perhaps simplified a little for the home cook. The books were often aimed at readers in the provinces since in Paris or Vienna most households had no need to do their own baking. In the United States, the upper classes didn't lead profoundly different lives from those a step or two down the social ladder. There was no need for American authors to explain how to lead a pseudoaristocratic lifestyle. What women desperately needed was advice on how to live in the new urban setting once they had moved up in the world. Dessert recipes were not intended to emulate a professional's repertoire; instead, they were aimed to be as foolproof as possible for women of variable skills and means. Most American women were much more dependent on home baking since few had the luxury of a *pâtisserie* or a *Zuckerbäcker* down the block.

And even if they had, there was a stigma attached to buying baked goods rather than making them. No doubt this was due to America's more isolated rural heritage. There was also an increasingly justifiable fear of adulterated baked goods that were sometimes sold by city slickers. But America's almost religious attitude about home baking also came out of the patriarchal Protestantism that dominated nineteenth-century thinking. According to the then-current ideology, women had a narrowly circumscribed role. Their job was to nurture the family both literally and figuratively. Men, in the meantime, had the run of the world. Under these circumstances, home baking became a marker for moral womanhood—perhaps even more so in this changing world.

Morality was especially tied up with bread, but it insinuated itself into all home baking. "A woman should be *ashamed* to have poor bread," preached Miss Beecher in 1850, "far more so, than to speak bad grammar, or to have a dress out of the fashion. It is true, that, by accident, the best of housekeepers will now and then have poor bread, but then it is an accident, and one that rarely happens. When it is very frequently the case that a housekeeper has poor bread, she may set herself down as a *slack baked* and negligent housekeeper."

This idea persisted well into the twentieth century. When cake mixes were first introduced in the 1920s, they had little success, in part because they didn't work that well. But even when General Mills introduced a foolproof mix in 1948, there was consumer resistance. The company hired psychologists to look into the matter, and they discovered that many women resisted the mix because they felt that the resulting cake wasn't sufficiently "homemade," that they hadn't adequately fulfilled their roles as homemakers (a loaded term if there ever was one!). In the original formula, all you needed to do was add water. The psychologists suggested the company's food technologist leave out the powdered eggs so that women felt like they were contributing something to the process. Television commercials explained how "you'll get a cake with that home-made goodness because you add the eggs."[37] Who would doubt the word of Betty Crocker?

FLAVOR SENSATION

Chocolate makes for an interesting case study of how information and culture were transmitted in the United States compared with the much more gradual trickle-down process that occurred in Europe. In America, this twentieth-century flavor sensation was little more than a drink before the industrialists and media mavens got a hold of it. It bears repeating that chocolate as we know it—that smooth and silky blend of sweetness and earth—is as much a product of the Industrial Revolution as steam kettles and newsprint. It couldn't have been made without the first and, at least on this side of the Atlantic, it derived much of its popularity from the second.

In the days before Hershey's made its candy bars as American as apple pie, chocolate had decidedly French, and accordingly somewhat louche, associations. In the 1820s, the fancy Philadelphia confectioners Henrion and Chaveau hyped their goods in their native tongue as "Confitures de France et des Colonies." Baker's, the most successful American chocolate manufacturer, trademarked the use of a chocolate shop waitress, "La Belle Chocolatière," for use in its promotional materials. Though the inspiration for Baker's corporate face was a pastel of a young Viennese waitress, created by a Swiss artist, it was the French name that mattered. As late as 1866, Stephen Whitman, who brought boxed chocolates into the mainstream, touted the quality of his chocolates by the fact that he used machinery made in France, which was "not excelled by any other establishment on this side of the Atlantic."[38] Even Hershey's caramel company had a "Le Roi de Chocolate" line for its more hoity-toity clientele.

Of course French was sexy, and chocolate had been associated with sex all the way back to Aztec times. In Victorian America, however, even while boxed chocolates were very much part of the mating dance, drinking chocolate was increasingly marketed as a healthful and wholesome beverage to be served by mothers to their children (rather than by perfumed French mademoiselles to their bewigged Casanovas). This was the first step to taking it mainstream.

⌒ Sex and Chocolate ⌒

In post–Civil War America, sweets such as bonbons—much like fancy truffles today—became part and parcel of

the mating ritual: the male of the species presenting elaborately wrapped nuggets of flavored fat, sugar, and chocolate
to the choosy female. "The young man who has spent many
pleasant moments as a boy with nose pressed to the candy
counter, seems to know by instinct that his surest weapon
as a suitor is a box of candy," a contemporary remarked.[39]

Naturally there were rules to be followed and etiquette
to be observed. Mrs. Oliver Bunce, who trafficked in the
advice racket in the 1870s, offered the following words of
wisdom: "A gentleman may send a bouquet, a box of bonbons, or a souvenir of any sort, to a lady with whom he
is well acquainted." But not, she made clear, the other way
around. The ladies could return the favor with "embraces
and tokens of tenderness" but only if "well acquainted."
While it was permissible for a woman to tempt a man with a
bonbon or two from her box, to give a man a gift of wrapped
chocolate was sign of forwardness. In later years, the rules
were relaxed a little, though confectionary packed in fancy
boxes was still classified with jewelry, perfume, and other
intimate gifts that signified romantic intent.

Those in the bonbon business knew full well the sexual
implications of a well-placed sweet. "When once the gallant would indite a sonnet to his mistress' eyebrow, he now
purchases a box of bon-bons addressed to a destination a
few inches lower. Instead of singing [to or of] her cherry
lips, he fills them," one confectioner enthused. There was an
intriguing similarity between the elaborately enrobed boxes
of candy and the layers of lace, crinoline, and silk that concealed the wooer's presumed prize. Yet here, it was up to the
woman to disrobe the objects of her affection. To reach the
sweet and creamy center she needed to take off the lace and
silk-trimmed box, remove the tissue paper doilies, and then

finally use her lips and tongue to remove the outer candy coating.

That women should be actively engaged in this sort of foreplay in the presence of a prospective husband was risqué enough; that they should do it without any male involvement, and in private, was something else altogether. Victorian Americans looked askance at any act of solitary female pleasure. It was a slippery slope from the indulgent reading of novels and eating of bonbons to self-pleasuring and gratuitous sex. Since women were supposed to be chaste and nurturing mothers, supportive wives, indeed the moral guardians of every family value and the backbone of social decency, the only logical consequence to the eating of bonbons was the collapse of the entire Victorian moral order. Nevertheless, despite the many admonishments for women to abandon their wicked, bonbon-eating vices, chocolate candy has remained an enduring cliché of the American dating dance. The sale of boxed chocolate still skyrockets around Valentine's Day. Moreover, the association of chocolate and self-gratification still endures in the popular idea that women eat chocolate to lessen the pangs of sexual rejection.

The popularity of chocolate-flavored desserts (as opposed to just a drink) can be credited to the promotional savvy of the Walter Baker Company. The company James Baker (Walter was his grandson) founded in Dorchester, Massachusetts, in 1765 was in the business of making drinking chocolate. In those days, chocolate could be made only in the cooler months, and accordingly, the company shared its millworks with a paper-, grist-, and sawmill. As the market for drinking chocolate slowly expanded, the firm started shipping its "Best Chocolate" to coastal destinations from Halifax to New Orleans. By 1869, when the Transcontinental Railroad finally connected the East and West Coasts, the company's products could be whisked to every major city across America.

Though Walter Baker had started advertising his brand in the 1840s, the marketing push did not really come into its own until after the Civil War, when the company was under the leadership of Henry L. Pierce. Pierce was an especially hyperactive tycoon in an era swarming with that particular breed. He was an activist in the antislavery movement. In later years, Pierce was the mayor of Boston (twice) and served as a Republican congressman in the Reconstruction-era Congress.

Young Henry was the stepnephew of Walter Baker, but despite this his early internship at the company did not end well. Apparently, he couldn't abide the boss's views on the slavery question. Walter had no interest in rocking the political boat, especially since some of his best customers were Southern slave owners.* So Henry left town and got a job with a newspaper in Milwaukee.

When Walter passed away, Henry Pierce returned and, at the tender age of twenty-eight, convinced the board of directors to let him run the place. The young abolitionist quickly took the company into the modern age. He merged and acquired. He expanded production. He hawked Baker's chocolate at those nineteenth-century lovefests of progress, the world's fairs, winning the silver medal in Paris in 1867, the gold in Vienna in 1873, and another gold in Philadelphia in 1876. But, most important, the one-time newspaperman spent loads and loads of money on advertising.

---

* Early on, Baker's sold three grades of drinking chocolate: the so-called Best Chocolate, a lesser grade named Common Chocolate, and their cheapest offering sold as Inferior Chocolate. Prior to 1865, the cheaper grades were mainly supplied to American and West Indian slaves. This chocolate, which sold at almost half the price as the top product, contained so much ground rice that it produced a very thick and muddy chocolate drink.[40]

By 1872, his company was running ads in over 150 regional, mostly New England, papers. By the end of the next decade, this had increased to 530 daily, weekly, and monthly publications across the country. By 1896, Baker's was reaching housewives in eight thousand newspapers nationwide. That same decade, the company went after the predominantly female fiction-reading public by buying full-page ads on the back covers of over six million novels. The ad campaigns were reinforced by posters in streetcars, billboards along train routes, and lithographed cards and signs in grocery stores.

This, of course, got women thinking about chocolate as a flavor for wholesome homemade desserts rather than risqué bonbons; still, to get them to cook with it required a baking lesson or two. Instructions soon came in the form of recipe booklets. The first of these was a twenty-four-page pamphlet distributed at the Philadelphia Centennial Exposition. Then, in 1880, came *Choice Recipes*. In the next five years, a million of these forty-page recipe collections rolled off the presses—that's one pamphlet for every thirteen adult women in the United States.* Six years later the company produced a larger, 179-page book with not only recipes but also a concise chocolate history. In 1893, the company enlisted Miss Parloa, a nationally renowned cooking instructor (and one of the original teachers at the vastly influential Boston Cooking School), to pen several of Baker's cookbooks. It would be hard to make a direct causal relationship between Baker's marketing blitz and the vast increase in chocolate-flavored desserts in America, but it is surely more than coincidence that in pre–Civil War cookbooks chocolate dessert recipes are few and

---

* It's worth noting how far the American chocolate dessert repertoire still had to go. The 1886 pamphlet devoted most of its contents to testimonials. They had clearly barely figured out how versatile chocolate could be. Though there are numerous recipes for chocolate-based drinks, almost none of the chocolate cake recipes have any chocolate in the cake itself, only in the frosting.

far between (chocolate drinks are fairly common), while by the 1870s, chocolate cakes and ice cream begin cropping up, and by the end of the century they are commonplace.* Many of these call for Baker's cocoa by name. Yet even a paid flack like Parloa was nowhere near as brazen as Fannie Farmer (Farmer started out as a student of Miss Parloa's school), whose wildly influential *Boston Cooking School Cookbook* of 1898 would contain sixteen chocolate desserts—specifying Baker's brand chocolate in each and every case! That said, the most popular way to consume the seed of the cacao tree remained a beverage. It would take Milton Hershey to change that.

Baker's strategy of advertising, printing cookbooks, and product placement in the recipes of well-regarded celebrities was mirrored by many other manufacturers of newfangled dessert ingredients, most notably by the makers of baking powder such as Royal and Rumford, by the Jell-O Company, and by Proctor & Gamble Company when it introduced Crisco brand shortening. P&G even produced a kosher cookbook in 1933. They must have thought this a public service since, according to Rabbi Margolies of New York (an authority quoted in the cookbook), "the Hebrew Race has been waiting 4,000 years for Crisco." A great many of the American desserts popularized in the last 150 years owe something to the hype machine of the culinary industrial complex.

TREATS FOR TOTS

Of course factories didn't just produce the raw ingredients that went into sweets. By the early years of the twentieth century,

---

* A rare exception here is Eliza Leslie, who outlined a half-dozen chocolate recipes in her early books. However, she too specified Baker's brand cocoa as early as 1847.[41]

they were making the sugary snacks from start to finish. A great many of them—the likes of Life Savers, animal crackers, Oreos, and Hershey's Bars—were treats primarily intended for children. As the success of chocolate in the twentieth century reveals, our childhood tastes in candy and other packaged sweets influence our adult preferences for dessert. It all started with penny candy, with cheap sugar and machines.

In 1847, Oliver Chase, a Boston druggist, adapted a printing press to stamp out his sugary medicated drops. Next thing you know, regular candy makers were stamping out candy in red, white, and blue and every other color of the rainbow. Initially it was only the machines used by small-scale confectioners that were industrially made, but by the 1870s the candy itself was issuing in great streams from steam-powered factories. Milton Hershey picked up on the trend early, advertising his first (unsuccessful) caramel business in Philadelphia with cards imprinted with his name and "manufacturer of Pure Confections by Steam." The transformation brought about by the new candy factories was noticed as early as 1864 by the periodical *Once a Week*. A writer noted, "what was once an article of luxury for the use of the rich, has now become an article of necessity almost for the children of the very poor."

When Hershey came on the scene, it was mostly chocolate candy that was pricey, but it used to be that all candy cost a mint. That exclusive little shop run by the French confectioner Sebastian Henrion in Philadelphia was typical of the antebellum era. In the early days, Monsieur Henrion had mostly sold nuts, syrups, and candied fruits, though imported chocolate and bonbons were eventually added to his offerings. In 1826, he charged an astonishing thirty-one cents a pound for raisins and almonds and a dime for an orange, or something like fifty and seventeen dollars, respectively, in today's wages.[42] By the 1830s, when the firm was renamed Henrion and Chaveau, the proprietors expanded

the selection of French bonbons and started making their own
marshmallows, gumdrops, and jujubes—the first of their kind in
the United States—and sold them at boutique prices.*

Whether in Philadelphia or New York, the confectionary
business was an exclusive, labor-intensive operation almost
solely run by gentlemen with mustaches and funny accents. The
mustaches would remain, but the accents would soon change. By
the middle years of the nineteenth century, candy would become
a much more American and democratic treat. In Philadelphia
alone, there were eight times as many candy makers in 1860 than
there had been when Monsieur Henrion opened his fancy shop.[44]
By the time peace was signed at Appomattox, Yankees were selling candy for a penny a piece.

This was perhaps the greatest change, for with the advent of
cheap sweets, children could buy them with their own pocket
change. The post–Civil War generation was the first to grow up
eating candy, a taste they would retain for the rest of their lives.

The birth of the child consumer, the progeny of the Industrial Revolution, may explain dessert flavor preferences more
than any other event in the history of American sweetness. In
continental Europe (though not in Britain), children were mostly
incidental to the confectionary industry at this time, but on the
streets of Boston and Baltimore, candy became a child's game.
(Dessert would come later.) No doubt the explanation for this is
complex. Certainly the fact that food was cheap here, and wages
relatively high, meant that even normal folk, children included,
could afford such superfluities as the occasional candy. What's
more, the industrializing cities offered children paid work,

---

* It is unclear whether the marshmallows were a kind of throat lozenge made of the marsh
mallow plant or the confection the French called *pâte de guimauve*, made by whipping up egg
whites, sugar, and the sticky extrusion of the same plant. The latter resemble the fluffy little
pillows we think of as marshmallows today. Later, when these were made industrially, gelatin
replaced the root extract.[43]

whether as factory hands, newsboys, bootblacks, or street peddlers. The 1880 census reported that a third of all twelve- and
thirteen-year-old boys worked for wages, and this didn't include
the kids who worked at home or on the farm.[45] The early capital-
ists often preferred to hire children since they were seen as more
manageable, cheaper, and less likely to strike. Federal child labor
laws did not come into force until 1938. The poorest of the poor
made a little spare change by collecting vermin, they begged, or
they just scoured the floors of trolley cars. But no matter how
they came by their pennies, they would inevitably have one or
two to spare. The people who made and sold candy took note.

Though many items of the Industrial Revolution were
designed to fulfill an existing need—mass-produced chairs
and frying pans come to mind—for many other products, the
manufacturer had to create a market where none had existed.
American food producers were especially good at this. And the
unformed minds of children were the ideal raw material from
which to mold a regular customer. It was widely and not improbably assumed in Victorian America that children have little control over their mental and physical impulses, which led them to
desire things that were neither necessary nor practical. Nobody
needed penny candy—any more than they would later need
Coca-Cola or Twinkies—but as soon as such sugary treats could
be manufactured, the undiscriminating palates and greedy eyes
of children beckoned. In Main Street candy shops, little boys and
girls looked up in awe at the towering jars of jewel-like treats
glistening behind the transparent wall. Even children with empty
pockets could ogle and dream of the day their fantasies would
come true.

The candy itself was mostly some variation of sugar boiled
with water, flavored with citric or tartaric acid, and colored
with dyes that were too often not fit for human consumption.
The recipes as well as the chemicals were often adapted from

British sources.* To entice this new sweets-eating demographic, confectioners pressed the candy into any shape they thought would appeal to children's imagination. There were guns, jack-knives, wrenches, axes, policemen, soldiers, cigars, and even gin bottles for boys, and babies, purses, shoes, and cupids for girls. Anticipating Cracker Jacks and today's cereals with their Disney-themed toys, the candy companies gave away premiums to both the rich and the poor. The sons and daughters of the plutocracy might buy their sweets in a nifty box shaped like a log cabin, a circus animal, or, in later years, like an honest-to-goodness auto-mobile—with working wheels and all! But even the kids of fac-tory workers could collect premiums in the form of little lead toys and figures.

When Hershey lit the kettles of his steam-powered factory in the late 1800s, the child consumer was an established American reality. He simply had to tap into this market by creating a choco-late-flavored sweet that every youngster could afford. Like Henry Ford, the candy bar tycoon's claim to fame is that he came up with a standardized product at a price affordable to every man, woman, and—most especially—child. As kids grew up with the taste of Hershey's Bars, their eponymous creator transformed the American sweet tooth almost as much as Ford's automobiles altered the once rural landscape. When those young consumers grew up, they made chocolate the taste sensation of the twentieth century, and not just for candy bars but for ice cream, cake, cook-ies, and just about every other dessert.

Pictures of the fortysomething chocolate king depict a man of modest stature and doughy features, just the sort of person

---

* Dr. W. B. O'Shaughnessy reported in an 1830 edition of the *Lancet* that popular English can-dies, many of which were exported to America, contained a wide array of adulterants, includ-ing red oxide of lead, chromate of lead, and red sulphuret of mercury. He also found that the inks used to print candy wrappers contained poisonous dyes, and that "children invariably will suck or eat these papers, from which it is evident the most fatal accidents may occur." American confectioners too often followed British practice.[46]

you'd expect to cook up a batch of candy in the back of his Main Street store. But it had taken many years before Hershey could slow down enough to have his picture snapped. Milton Snavely Hershey grew up dirt poor in rural Lancaster County, the son of a thoroughly dysfunctional family. He was fathered by a flimflam man and raised by a Bible-thumping Mennonite mother who hadn't much use for his father and even less for idleness. There wasn't a lot of fun—or candy—in Milton's childhood. He was set on his road to (much delayed) success when he was apprenticed to a local candy maker at the age of fifteen because the family couldn't pay the bills.

It took years of sequential failures in Philadelphia, New York, Chicago, Denver, and New Orleans before Milton had a genuine hit on his hands, and then it was in no small measure thanks to his mother and loans from her relatives. His first real claim to fame was a milk-rich caramel candy he called "Hershey's Crystal A" that he concocted in 1886 in a rented room in Lancaster, Pennsylvania, just a few miles from his birthplace. The original operation was a small-scale artisanal affair: Milton made the caramels, and his mother and aunt wrapped them in tissue paper. Because of the expensive ingredients and hand labor, the caramels were mostly intended for genteel customers who could pay a premium for candy rich in whole milk and butterfat, all wrapped in a box overgrown with Victorian curlicues.[47] Hershey, however, who remembered his miserable childhood, had his sights on another market, mainly the unwashed children of Lancaster's streets, who could shell out no more than a penny at the corner store. To make the caramels cheap enough, Hershey had to scale up his operation and cut costs. Accordingly, he came out with a line of caramels that used paraffin as a substitute for more expensive butterfat. More important, he turned the artisanal shop into an industrial operation. In 1889, the caramels were being manufactured in a four-story factory.[48] By the late 1890s, Hershey's company was doing a million dollars' worth of business a year and employed fourteen hundred men and women.

In 1900, Hershey took the next step toward efficiency. He sold his caramel company with its massive catalogue of products to concentrate on one item: milk chocolate for the masses. People thought he was nuts to give up on his prosperous business, but it wasn't such a great leap. Milton Hershey had made his fame and fortune with a confection that depended on sugar and milk; he was now just going to add a little cocoa to the mix. Just look at the ingredients on the wrapper of a Hershey's Bar: sugar, milk, cocoa butter, and, only finally, cocoa.

In the late 1890s, imported Swiss chocolate was the flavor du jour, at least among those who could afford it. Candy manufacturers in Germany and England were all trying to duplicate the formula invented by the Swiss chemist Daniel Peter in 1876.[49] Hershey, too, joined the crowd traveling to Switzerland so that he could nose around the local cows and chocolate factories. And, though he did not come home with the secret, the trip apparently wasn't wasted. The caramel tycoon observed that in the Old World, as in America, chocolate candy mostly took the form of fancy bonbons destined for ladies' plump lips. He was also confirmed in his hunch that little folk had little use for all those sophisticated fillings when he attended one tony European get-together and saw youngsters sucking the chocolate coating off the filled confections and leaving their gooey centers behind.

Back home, the cigar fume–belching candy mogul rolled up his sleeves and got to work. Perhaps the result wasn't as smooth as Peter's or Lindt's, and there was a slightly sour tang to the chocolate, but the uncounted thousands (and their kids) who earned little more than a Lancaster toffee puller didn't seem to mind when they could buy the bars for a measly three pennies.* Even-

---

* Europeans have never cottoned much to Hershey's chocolate, using words like barnyard and cheesy to describe it. Hans Scheu, the Swiss president of the Cocoa Merchants' Association, for one, can't stand the stuff. In his view, "Milton Hershey completely ruined the American palate with his sour, gritty chocolate."[50]

tually the price rose to five. But compare that to prices charged by
fancy confectioners in the big cities. In the late 1800s, New York
confectioner Felix Potin of Paris sold his boxed chocolates for up
to seventeen dollars a pound *wholesale.*[51]

What Hershey didn't do, however, was advertise to children.
(He did advertise in trade journals.) Correctly, he understood
that, in an age of print ads that kids couldn't read, there wasn't
any point. Instead, he built an amusement park where tourists
flocked from all over the country. He also sent flashy displays to
retailers to entice both young and old to buy his wares. But, most
important, he kept the price low. Hershey's Bars cost five cents
apiece right through 1968, even if the size of the bar varied quite
a bit from decade to decade.

It's a commonplace in the advertising industry that if you
build brand loyalty early, it can last a lifetime. The same can be
said of flavor preferences. Americans have a soft spot for Hershey's chocolate because they ate it as kids. Many of America's
desserts hearken back to the straightforward tastes of childhood.
Are Oreos the country's bestselling cookie (362 billion sold since
their introduction in 1912) due to the luscious taste sensation
that comes from a union of sugar-flavored Crisco and a chocolate-colored cardboard cookie? No. Like Victorian penny candies, Oreos appeal to kids' liking for uncomplicated flavors and
the urge to play with your food.

Price and attractive displays were important, as Hershey and
others knew all too well, though getting your message across
to preadolescents was a challenge in those early days. It was
really not until the advent of television that food manufacturers would reach that valuable demographic. But once that genie
was unleashed, there was no getting it back in the bottle. By the
1950s, sweets makers of every stripe would surely have agreed
with Howard M. List, then advertising manager of the Kellogg
Company, when he pointed out: "With television, we can almost
sell children our product before they can talk . . . in the old days,
children ate what their mothers bought; now the kids tell their

mothers what to buy." (By this point, American cereal producers were making a product that, from its sugar content alone,
would have been hard to distinguish from cookies and cake.)
Tootsie Rolls (invented in 1896) found a brand-new audience
by sponsoring *The Adventures of Rin Tin Tin* and *The Rocky and
Bullwinkle Show*, and Twinkies (created in 1930) could count on
Howdy Doody and even Superman to hawk their wares.[52] The
coming onslaught of commercials was presaged as early as 1939,
when Mickey Mouse was enlisted by Nabisco to shill their stuff.
In an animated short, "Mickey's Surprise Party," that was shown
in Technicolor at the New York World's Fair, Minnie is seen baking cookies. She wants to make them "just like Mickey's mom
always used to make." Alas, disaster strikes and they are burnt
to a crisp. Then, in the nick of time, our hero arrives with a solution, courtesy of Nabisco. Mickey presents Minnie with a selection of Nabisco products, including Fig Newtons, claiming that
these are his favorite. At the end of the cartoon, motherhood is
dragged in once more to hawk a factory-produced treat when
Mickey reassures his big-eared sweetheart that his mom also
burned her cookies and consequently bought Nabisco as well.[53]

New and Improved

The balance of the scale in favor of factory-produced sweets
began to shift decisively in the years following the Civil War.
Cake recipes, in particular, increasingly came to depend on sugar
rather than eggs to contribute moistness to the finished product,
and bicarbonate of soda instead of eggs or yeast to give them a
lift. "I regard the Royal Baking Powder as the best in the market.
It is an act of simple justice, and also a pleasure, to recommend it
unqualifiedly to American housewives," rang Marion Harland's
endorsement in an 1892 ad in *Scribner's Magazine*.[54] But the

famed culinary authority had long been an enthusiast. Her 1873 opus was one of the first to include recipes for the kind of chemically leavened white cake and yellow cake found at every other birthday party today. She also included instructions for a huckleberry cake made much like the blueberry muffins we are familiar with. The change in technique is startling. In 1847, Eliza Leslie's precocious chocolate cake recipe calls for ten eggs for leavening. Following the standard French technique for making a *biscuit*, she tells you to "beat the whites of ten eggs till they stand alone; then the yolks till they are very thick and smooth." Harland's 1873 chocolate cake calls for proportionately more sugar, less butter, five egg yolks and two whites, plus baking soda to lighten the batter. It would probably take a third of the time to make as Leslie's recipe. It's not that chemical leaveners hadn't been used before. It's just that now they were crowding out every other cake-making technique. Even sponge cake recipes now called for some form of baking soda. An early version of these was called the "Berwick Sponge Cake," undoubtedly a misspelling of Borwick, a British baking powder company. The Royal Baking Powder Company's 1886 *My Receipt* cookbook thoughtfully included this and sixty other sponge cake recipes—all made with Royal baking powder, naturally.

Of course the logical conclusion to this was the cake mix: a factory-produced dessert that you made at home. Though there had been cake mixes before Betty Crocker, it was the product promoted by General Mills' fictional spokesperson that set the standard when it was introduced in 1947. Duncan Hines (named after a real-life restaurant critic) followed the next year. By 1953, *Consumer Reports* would write:

> Not so very long ago, the housewife who went to the bakery store to get her family's dessert, instead of producing it from her own oven, was looked at askance by her more

industrious neighbors. Today there seems to be at least a fair prospect that the situation will be reversed. For the grocery store shelves are replete with ready-mix-cake packages in great variety, and the description of their preparation sounds so simple as to make a trip to the bakery store, by comparison, a major chore.[55]

So now, in a sense, you could have your cake and eat it too. In the late 1800s, women suffered from an inherent contradiction in what was expected from them. On the one hand, the bread-baking homemaker was told over and over that she was society's moral bulwark against the shifting seas of the industrial age; on the other, she was being inculcated in the ideology of progress and consumerism that was washing over America. In the twentieth century, the contradiction was resolved: she learned that she could be a superior mother precisely by becoming a skilled consumer. All it took was filling her home with Royal baking powder ("the keystone in the making of appetizing, wholesome cake, biscuits, muffins, etc."), Jell-O ("Pure, Wholesome, Nutritious. Better than Pies, Cakes or Pastries"), Crisco ("no cooking fat could be daintier or more wholesome"), Baker's chocolate ("pure and healthful"), Campfire marshmallows ("the original food marshmallows"), Kingsford's cornstarch ("the trusted standby of the experienced cook"), and so many more inventions of this wondrous age.[56]

To read some of the advertisements and cookbooks, it's a wonder more of the early American desserts weren't dumped over the sides of the great ship of progress. As early as the 1870s, traditional pies were derogated as heavy and unhealthy. They were still popular, but a trendy cookbook writer like Marion Harland now had to make excuses for including them in her collection. "Not that I recommend pies of any description as healthful daily food—least of all for children," she wrote. "But since they are eaten freely all over our land, let us make them as wholesome and palatable as possible."[57] Yeast was old-fashioned and unreliable, and thus not as healthy or trustworthy as bicarbonate of soda. Molasses was associated with the backward South.

You can see the transformation as you thumb through the Weeks family archives. Mary Weeks's daughter Harriet was born rather unexpectedly in 1864, thirteen years after her sister, even as the armies of North and South ravaged the fields around New Iberia. Little Pattie, as Harriet was known to her family, was what they called a "nervous invalid" in those days. As a consequence, the baby sister was spoiled rotten. She eventually moved to New Orleans, where she terrorized her servants until her death in 1927. She spent much of her time convalescing, which perhaps gave her more time than most to clip and collect recipes. But the carefully pasted scraps of magazines and newspapers are from an altogether different world than her mother's carefully copied instructions for making puddings and syllabubs. Now we see recipes calling for Swans Down cake flour (introduced in 1895), ham cooked in Coca-Cola (first concocted in 1886), and a kind of mousse called a chocolate "marlow" made from Campfire Marshmallows (founded 1917). It's hard to know whether she actually cooked any of these recipes, but even if she didn't, it's safe to say that many others did.

This infatuation with the new wasn't limited to claques of the food industry. It was equally widespread among the cookbook-writing profession. (Admittedly a fine line often divided the two.) The woman who achieved the greatest fame from straddling the intersection of the industrial and the domestic was Fannie Farmer, protégé of the Boston Cooking School, author of the bestselling cookbook, and a great proponent of both science and invention in the home kitchen. For obvious personal reasons, Fannie Merritt Farmer had trouble with the idea of a woman being defined by her role as wife and mother.

Fannie was one of five daughters born to a struggling printer in the Boston area in 1857. She was bright and, despite the family's financial difficulties, looked forward to a rosy future, at least until a debilitating illness (probably polio) crippled her when she was sixteen. As a result, there would be no stream of Victorian beaus offering chocolates to young Fannie. She stayed in bed for months after her illness struck and remained a housebound invalid for years afterward. When she eventually emerged from the household cocoon in her late twenties, she had a noticeable limp and limited prospects at becoming the domestic goddess that was supposedly every young Victorian lady's dream. It was only when she was thirty-one that she found her niche at the Boston Cooking School.

Since the school's founding in 1879, the institution had built its reputation on a scientific approach to cooking. Mrs. Lincoln, the first principal, enjoined her students to "apply the principles of science upon which the health and welfare of her household largely depend." (She also had a short-lived career as the owner of Mrs. Lincoln's Baking Powder Company.) Mrs. Lincoln was especially partial to dessert. The graduates of her "fancy cooking" class concluded their studies with a banquet that began with sweet breads prepared four ways followed by a procession of sweets that included strawberry charlotte, frozen pudding, café parfait, and *gâteau de Princess Louise*. (The last of these was similar to a charlotte.)[58]

Apart from the actual lessons in cooking, what Fannie Farmer absorbed at the Boston Cooking School was that a woman could be a domestic scientist and manager rather than just a "homemaker." In other words, she could become someone who shared the values of a food technologist working in a factory lab. Farmer also learned that the scientific approach is best suited to dessert making, for it is in baking that the domestic scientist most closely resembles the chemist. She continually promoted the use of level measurement, which yields a much more precise quantity than the rounded and heaping teaspoons common in many cookbooks of her time. It is an approach that is invaluable for making a cake but largely superfluous for cooking up a pot roast.

Another quality that Farmer shared with her laboratory brethren was the quest for novelty. She was constantly on the lookout for inspiration, visiting hotels and restaurants to crib culinary ideas and returning to her test kitchen to transform them into recipes her audience could use. Even into her fifties, when her illness had caught up with her and she lectured from a wheelchair, she was ever curious about new, improved recipes. When she died in 1915 she left an estate valued at over $200,000. She would be remembered as the "mother of level measurement" even if more conventional parenthood eluded her.

The inventiveness of cookbook writers like Fannie Farmer as well as the food technologists and recipe developers who worked for corporate America in the twentieth century is way beyond anything professional confectioners on the other side of the Atlantic could ever conceive. In part this was simply a matter of their job description. In America they were paid to innovate, while European confectioners were mostly in the business of keeping their current customers happy. But there was another difference that affected the nature of the sweet inventions on either side of the Atlantic. The *confisseurs* and *Zuckerbäcker* developed recipes for skilled artisans cooking for an elite public, while American domestic economists had to create desserts for relatively unskilled cooks. In the meantime, the chemists devised formulas for industrially produced sweets that could appeal to the lowest common denominator. Despite their limitations, America's test kitchens unleashed an explosion of unbridled creativity. Some of the resulting recipes were inspired, while others were half-baked and some just plain loopy. The architectural wonders of transparent multihued jiggling Jell-O in which gravity-defying bits of canned fruit floated like some drug-induced vision were a little bit of each.*

---

* In Europe, molded jellies had been all the rage a hundred years earlier, but making them was a multiday ordeal requiring the boiling of bones to make gelatin, carefully clarifying and straining and then finally adding the flavor and color. Now, with Jell-O, canned fruit, and an icebox, any homemaker could create an architectural folly worthy of Versailles. Well, almost.

Even putting aside the vast repertoire of factory-made sweets like Hershey's Bars, animal crackers, and Ring Dings, a vast majority of the desserts popularized in the twentieth century were created by food technologists on a deadline. Peanut butter cookies were invented by peanut butter manufacturers to sell their product after it was introduced at the 1904 St. Louis World's Fair, though they didn't really take off until the 1930s, when the Pillsbury Company included a recipe for them in one of its premium cookbooks.[59] Oatmeal cookies were popularized by the Quaker Oats Company when it included a recipe for them on oatmeal packages. The story of chocolate chip cookies most likely begins in the test kitchens of the Boston Cooking School, where melted Baker's brand chocolate bars were originally stirred into a drop cookie dough to make a chocolate drop cookie. The chips came in 1937, introduced by Ruth Wakefield, a graduate of the Framingham Normal School in Massachusetts, which had absorbed the Boston Cooking School. As Wakefield told the story, she was making the earlier chocolate drop cookie recipe when it occurred to her to add the chocolate bar in chunks rather than melting it first. Soon enough, the cookie was popularized when the recipe was broadcast by Betty Crocker (or rather the actor who played her) on her national radio show in 1939.[60] Eventually, Nestlé bought the right to print the recipe on the back of its packages. The brownie recipe also seems to have had its genesis at Framingham, when chocolate was substituted for molasses in a kind of molasses bar cookie. Test kitchens also incubated chiffon cake, cheesecake, devil's food cake, chocolate pudding, and many other American classics.

Does this mean that every American home baker succumbed to back-of-the-package recipes for Nestlé Toll House cookies and Rice Krispies Treats? Of course not. There remained pockets of resistance to this new, improved patisserie, places where regional traditions were especially strong or communities that for one reason or other existed off the grid.

Back in the rural South, the stream of progress tended to flow slower than in New England's bastions of scientific cookery. Recalling his childhood in segregated New Iberia, a writer reminisced about the "sweet potato pies, peach pies, coconut delights, blackberry cobbler, ice cream, pralines [and] fudge"[61] brought to African American church socials in the 1930s and '40s. These are recipes that mostly predate Fannie Farmer and Nabisco, but were they totally immune from the industrial steamroller? I'd bet that what was going into those pie crusts was Crisco, manufactured by the Proctor & Gamble Company, the fudge was made with Carnation evaporated milk, and that by the 1940s the cobbler was topped with Bisquick (introduced by General Mills in 1931).

As Good as Scratch

Today there isn't much difference between North and South when it comes to American home bakers' embrace of factory-made desserts. At least that's the impression I got in New Iberia when I visited the Louisiana Sugar Festival in 2007. Needless to say, there was a bakeoff, or rather a "Sugar Artistry Exhibit and Tasting."

"Oh, I'll bake you cake!" gushed Virginia Latiolais into the phone when I asked her for an interview.

Ms. Latiolais is one of the event's organizers and a locally prominent cake decorator. She is also the pied piper of the Sweet Friends of the Teche Cake Club, a group of ladies who are all alumnae of her cake decorating classes. The group meets each month at a potluck dinner to talk shop and to plan for the big annual event.

Virginia Latiolais and her creations tower above all the others. Though she would probably not make the connection, she is a soul mate to Antonin Carême. She too would certainly consider confectionary a branch of architecture, or perhaps—in her case—of industrial design, as I learned when I finally found her in the hangar-style community center filled with tables of cookies, brownies, and layer cakes. Her latest creation, proudly displayed among lesser sugary still lifes, was a snazzy, two-foot-high John Deere tractor, lovingly detailed in agro green buttercream.

The artist accepted my accolades on her automotive masterwork before steering me to "my" cake, a thing of some magnificence itself. Ms. Latiolais had made me a sky-high doberge (pronounced "doh-besh") cake. This multistoried extravaganza was supposedly invented in New Orleans in the 1930s. The name is likely a corruption of the Hungarian many-layered Dobos torte, though, other than the many layers, the two cakes have nothing in common. My cake was a skyscraper of a half-dozen disks of yellow cake separated by lemon pudding, all stuccoed with white buttercream. The recipe is clearly a descendant of the custard-filled layer cakes that used to inhabit cookbooks in the 1880s, though Ms. Latiolais's approach is a little more modern.[62] This particular cake was made from a cake mix, a pudding mix, and canned frosting.

I ask her whether women still bake at home in rural Louisiana. "Oh, yes. Most people around here, they make their own cakes," the sugar artist assures me. However, she goes on to clarify: "And most of them use a cake mix. You know, most of them don't make a scratch cake, to tell you the truth." This isn't exactly a new phenomenon either. When she was young, the fifty-something baker informs me, "cake mix was in." She sounds like an echo of nineteenth-century home bakers who adopted the reliable chemical leaveners of the industrial age. "Scratch is like a hit or miss, but with a cake mix you just can't miss," she explains. I guess you can't argue with success.

Don't imagine that Louisiana is some sort of regional anomaly in this respect. When *Good Housekeeping* magazine assembled a group of children in 2005 to see if they preferred cakes made from scratch or those that came from a box, the box cakes were the universal favorite.[63] With a little help from Duncan Hines, it would seem that the future of American motherhood is assured.

Red Velvet Cupcakes with Lavender Icing

Cupcakes swept the world in the first decade of the twenty-first century. Why? Because they're fun and easy to make, and they make you feel like a kid again. Admittedly kids may be taken aback at the lavender in the frosting here. Vanilla would be a perfectly adequate substitute, but you would miss out on the outrageous color combination. Though you can use liquid food coloring for the cake (but not for the frosting), paste colors are much more effective. How much you put in is really up to you; just make sure *not* to let good taste get the better of you. The cupcakes themselves are loosely based on a recipe from Magnolia Bakery, the shop made famous on the TV series *Sex in the City*. Given that the show has been broadcast in more than two dozen countries around the world, it isn't entirely surprising that the world is familiar with this all-American treat.

Makes about 2 dozen cupcakes

11 ounces (about 3½ cups) cake flour
6 ounces (¾ cup) unsalted butter, softened
2 cups sugar
3 large eggs, at room temperature

½ teaspoon red paste food coloring
1½ teaspoons pure vanilla extract
3 tablespoons unsweetened cocoa, preferably *not* Dutch process
1 teaspoon salt
1½ cups cultured buttermilk
1½ teaspoons cider vinegar
1½ teaspoons baking soda
1 recipe lavender buttercream (recipe follows)

1. Preheat oven to 350°F. Line two dozen cupcake tins with liners.

2. In a small bowl, sift the cake flour and set aside. In a large bowl, on the medium speed of an electric mixer, cream the butter and sugar until very light and fluffy, about 5 minutes. Add the eggs, one at a time, beating well after each addition. In a small bowl, whisk together the red food coloring and vanilla. Add to the batter along with the cocoa and beat well.

3. Stir the salt into the buttermilk. Add to the batter in three additions alternating with the flour. With each addition, beat until the ingredients are barely incorporated, but do not overbeat.

4. Separately, stir together the cider vinegar and baking soda. Add to the batter and mix well. Using a rubber spatula, scrape down the batter in the bowl, making sure the ingredients are well blended and the batter is smooth.

5. Divide the batter among the prepared tins. Bake for 20–30 minutes, or until a cake tester inserted in the center of the cupcakes comes out clean. Cool on wire racks.

6. When the cupcakes have cooled, spread each with the lavender buttercream.

Lavender Buttercream

You will need lavender extract for this recipe. Making this at home is easy enough if you can get your hands on food-grade (unsprayed) lavender, either fresh or dry. Take ¼ cup of vodka and 1 teaspoon of the dried or 1 tablespoon of the fresh flowers. Purée this in a blender and let sit overnight to let the flowers settle to the bottom. Carefully pour off the flavored vodka. Stick to paste colors here; the liquid may cause the buttercream to separate. This particular buttercream can be a hassle on a really hot day, so turn up the air-conditioner or wait for more temperate weather.

Makes about 4 cups

14 ounces (¾ cup plus 2 tablespoons) unsalted butter, softened
9 egg yolks
1 cup granulated sugar
6 tablespoons water
Paste food coloring
2–4 teaspoons lavender extract (see above)

1. Beat the butter until smooth.

2. In a separate bowl, beat the egg yolks with an electric mixer until thick and foamy.

3. Combine the sugar and water in a small saucepan and boil to the soft ball stage (238°F on a candy thermometer). Very gradually, add the syrup to the egg mixture in a thin stream, beating rapidly after each addition. Beat with an electric mixer until thick and fluffy and room temperature. Beat in the butter, a tablespoon at a time. (It should be a little cooler than room

temperature but not much.) If the mixture looks curdled, keep beating at high speed. If it gets soupy, refrigerate for about 15 minutes and beat again. Finally beat in the food coloring to achieve a nice violet color, and then the flavoring of choice a drop at a time. Refrigerate if necessary until it is of spreading consistency.

FINALE

❊ *Cupcakes and* Macarons ❊

Hisop is a sleek but unpretentious restaurant in one of Barcelona's trendiest shopping districts. The dining room is plain, white, and a little cramped, even though it holds barely a half-dozen tables. The chefs, Oriol Ivern and Guillem Pla, however, are anything but modest in their aspirations. Their cooking is inventive, wacky even, but also tightly disciplined and delicious. Oysters come with a gin and tonic foam, barnacles sit atop cubes of watermelon, seared foie gras is served with cherries and octopus. The young chefs belong to a generation inspired by Ferran Adrià and other proponents of what is generally called molecular gastronomy. Its premise is that chefs should take advantage of the latest advances in food technology to expand their techniques and approaches to cooking.

Dessert gets the same radical makeover as the rest of the menu. At Hisop, my meal of inventive slurps and bites concluded with an arrangement of lab paraphernalia worthy of a science

experiment. One petri dish contained little sugar-covered morsels that turned out to be candied olives. They were chewy and
tasting oddly of licorice. Another displayed an arrangement of
grilled watermelon sprinkled with dehydrated citrus powder
(essentially lemon juice with all the water gone). A glass container
held gin and tonic jellies, which looked like they could be used
for growing microorganisms. But any fear of that was quickly
quenched when the waiter sterilized them with a spray of gin
from an atomizer. The jellies also came with a rack of test tubes
filled with a liquid gin and tonic "essence" that cleverly echoed
their flavors. And if that weren't enough, the fearless artistes also
offered a foie gras crème brûlée on their dessert menu, as well
as pistachio cake served in a puddle of arugula soup with Kaffir
lime ice cream on the side.

Is this the future of dessert? The answer is probably a highly
qualified yes. In Vienna, I asked Karl Schuhmacher, who did so
much to update local pastry in the last thirty years, about this.
He has no doubts that the most creative pastry chefs now work
in restaurants rather than pastry shops, and they keep expanding
the idea of dessert. That restaurant kitchens are where the action
is reflects trends in society as a whole.

In Vienna as in Paris, there is no more need for the ornate
tortes and *gateaux* that used to decorate the tables and sideboards of the bourgeoisie. People hardly entertain at home any
more; they eat out in restaurants. But even then, it's for lunch
or for dinner. How many ladies still meet up with their friends
over coffee and cake on a weekday afternoon? Demel's no longer
makes anywhere near the 150 kinds of *Theegebäck* (tea cookies)
that they used to. Who would buy them? And when would you
serve them? In Paris, the old-fashioned *salons de thé* are patronized by musty matrons—and tourists. Admittedly there is a new
style of *salon de thé*, which has the informality of a Seattle coffee
lounge. Unfortunately, the desserts reflect it. The menus typically

list such things *cake aux carottes* and *muffin à la banane*. The patrons are as likely to be texting their absent friends as engaging in conversation with the person across the table.

The prime reason for these shifts in socializing has to do with women's changing role in society and, more recently, with technology. Certainly in the West, well-to-do women are as likely to be lawyers as housewives. They do not have time for tea or fussing over weekly dinner parties as their Victorian predecessors did. Oh sure, they may still pick up an éclair or apricot tart at the corner patisserie for dessert, but they are just as likely to content themselves with a scoop of ice cream from the freezer. Their status in society no longer depends on their entertaining savoir faire or their aptitude for picking out the trendiest *gâteau*. This is not to say that the sweet makers are an endangered species—on a Saturday afternoon, Vienna's *Zuckerbäcker* are still packed with locals—or that the demand for birthday cakes and wedding cakes has disappeared. On a day-to-day basis, however, there is less pressure on the confectioners to innovate than there was a hundred years back. When people go to the local pastry shop, they expect their favorites to always be there.

Where they are pushing the envelope is in restaurants. Over the last couple of decades, cooking has turned into a worldwide circus with its own acrobats, trapeze artists, trained animals, shills, and pitchmen. Accordingly, the most exciting act garners attention from the media. The chefs on the savory side of the divide were the first to grab the spotlight, but soon enough pastry chefs started attracting their own fan base. It used to be unheard-of for the person in charge of dessert to be mentioned on a menu. Now it is common. As a result, pastry chefs now also feel the pull to explore strange new worlds, to go where no confectioner has gone before. Nowadays it's the only way of advancing their careers, and, let's face it, it's a lot more exciting than rolling out tart crust day in and day out. On the positive side, this has resulted in many talented people being drawn into the field. However, they tend to gravitate to restaurants, where the glamour is, rather than to pastry shops. As you might expect, the continual pressure to chase the latest trend also has its downside. It's much easier to be gimmicky than to be truly innovative.

Restaurants have long served sweets that were different from what you could buy in a pastry shop—such things as soufflés and baked Alaskas—nonetheless, the great majority of the dishes on the dessert menu were no more than gussied-up versions of what you could buy retail. The apple tart might get a scoop of ice cream, the chocolate cake a whirl of custard sauce. Up until the 1970s, French restaurants would often roll around a dessert wagon from which you would choose your final course. It wasn't much different from picking out a pastry from a confectioner's vitrine. This reflected the style of service earlier in the meal. At the fancy places, the main course arrived on a platter, sometimes intended for more than one diner. It was up to the waiter to carve the duck or bone the fish before arranging the dish on the customers' plates. The cook wasn't in the business of making food pretty. In the 1960s, the arrival of nouvelle cuisine in France changed all this. Now chefs began to plate their creations in the kitchen, destining the waiter to be little more than a delivery boy. Desserts too began to be sent out already plated in increasingly complex compositions. Each diner was now served a separate, single-sized dish rather than a slice from something ready-made. Individual soft-centered chocolate cakes were accompanied by ice cream, chocolate truffles, and fruit sauces; *panna cotta* (the much simplified offspring of medieval blancmange) was outfitted with a gaggle of petits fours, fruit, and other gewgaws. Dessert was showy, ostentatious, and, occasionally, hopelessly tacky. In other words, it was what it had always been. But the style was different. A pastry chef no longer had to study architecture but rather abstract painting or perhaps modernist sculpture. The trouble was that, for a *pâtissier* with his or her own shop, these freeform, multi-ingredient compositions were impossible to replicate.

In Paris, Pierre Hermé has sought to tackle this particular conundrum head-on. His solution is to stack his menagerie of flavor and texture in a tall transparent vessel. In his jewel box of a boutique, one counter is now devoted to these layered "verrines" like perfect little towers of cake and cream and a half-dozen other ingredients. The wasabi and grapefruit confection he offered me during our interview is a perfect example. It too plays with convention in the same way as do the chefs at a restaurant like Hisop, and it too is portioned individually so that, even at home, each diner can indulge his or her personal predilections instead of sharing a communal cake or tart. Yet, most important for a retail pastry cook, it is portable. This approach has now spread rapidly all over Paris. I have even spotted Hermé's oversized shot glasses in New York; they will, no doubt, soon be as much of a cliché as his *macarons*. The pastry superstar makes no bones about the fact that he is inspired by what happens in restaurants.

The speed with which information now moves is another factor that is transforming pastry. Hermé, for one, is thrilled by the change. Tapping his iPhone, he grins. "If I hear of a new ingredient, I can find out where to get it in less than five minutes," he boasts. He might add that if he wants to see what a dessert in Sydney looks like, he can see a picture of it on his smart phone just as fast. This accelerated speed of information tends to play to the strengths of restaurant pastry chefs as well. Restaurants generate a great deal of buzz and media attention, at least some of which plays to a global audience.

Some pastry shops have jumped on the globalization bandwagon, turning themselves into worldwide brands. The French, with their long history of exporting and branding luxury goods, have led the way, selling their wares in shops abroad as well as at their Parisian branches. You can buy Hermé's desserts not only in Paris but also at several Japanese locations, including at the gates of the Tokyo Disney Resort. Hermé's former employer, Ladurée, has almost a dozen branches outside of France, with three each in Japan, Switzerland, and the British Isles. Dalloyau, which traces its lineage to the brothers Richard and Charles Dalloyau, who worked at the court of Louis XIV (a descendant opened up a pastry and take-out shop in 1802), now has more shops in both Korea and Japan than it does in France. Dalloyau claims to produce fifty-five metric tons of *macarons* a year. That works out to over five million *macarons*, which, while hardly in the same league as Hershey's, is a long way from the old artisanal confectioners.

In many ways, these operations now resemble other high-end brands like Armani or Rolex that peddle luxury to the bourgeois masses from London to Bangkok. These goods feed the same sort of aspirations that once stimulated demand for Second Empire furniture and *gâteaux Saint-Honoré* in nineteenth-century Paris. In Beijing, Fauchon (another prestigious Paris caterer) was selling *macarons* for about a dollar each in 2008 at a time when the average city wage was about $6,500.[1] The price may be steep, but for locals aiming to impress, it is a luxury they can afford. Other nations have not been as successful exporting their aspirational desserts abroad as the French. (Candy is another matter.) Certainly the Austrians haven't quite figured out how to translate their brand into international success despite the Hotel Sacher's history of shipping its cakes across the oceans. Demel made a brief attempt to open up a shop in New York's Plaza Hotel, but that experiment was short-lived.

Today's globalized networks of business and information mean that dessert fads skip from continent to continent as much as any other trend. Perhaps the most notable dessert craze of the first decade of the third millennium was the *macaron*, especially the exotic kind pioneered by Pierre Hermé. They became as ubiquitous as smart phones. So why the obsession? I have a couple of notions about that. First of all, at their best, *macarons* are genuinely delicious. The intensity and clarity of the flavor translates into pure, immediate pleasure. They are also sufficiently small that they are a practically guilt-free dessert, very important in this day and age when we are told to give up so many pleasures that we may prolong our joyless lives as long as possible. What's more, those flavors are often as exotic as anything dreamed up by the molecular gastronomy chefs; yet, from the consumer, they require only momentary commitment. And, unlike a packaged cookie or candy bar, they are artisanal and thus have the aura of being exclusive. And if that wasn't enough, they're French! Thus, when you eat a masala chai *macaron* (sold at Singapore's Gobi pastry shop), you can pat yourself on the back for your cosmopolitanism and sophistication. Despite the French provenance and name (only a rube would call it a macaroon), there is something informal, dare I say American, about the *macaron*. You eat them with your fingers like cookies or cupcakes.

Which brings us to the other fad that is threatening to turn into a pandemic—cupcakes. These too occasionally come in weird, or at least alien, flavors. In 2010, Singapore's Oni Cupcakes was offering durian cupcakes, flavored with that region's notoriously stinky fruit. In London, the cupcake bakery Violet naturally offers one flavored with the eponymous bloom. Even in Paris, Berko offered a *"Beurre de cacahuète m&m's"* (peanut butter with M&M's) cupcake among its thirty varieties. (OK, peanut butter–flavored desserts may not be weird in America, but they sure are in the fourth Arrondissement.)[2] Though cupcakes may not be as old as *macarons*, they still go back at least 150 years. Also, like the French almond cookie, they used to come in no more than two or three flavors. The one very significant difference between the two confections, however, is that you need virtual no culinary acumen to make a cupcake. In America, at least, most people make it from a cake mix.

The two desserts aren't strictly analogous, but I do think they give you insight into the state of European and American culture today. A comparison of the two underlines the still noticeable differences between our societies but also the way they are converging. Compare the flavors of the two confections. Ladurée, perhaps the best known Parisian *macaron* producer, sells a collection that always includes rose, pistachio, black currant, violet, caramel with salted butter, orange blossom, licorice, lemon, and, of course, chocolate—but no vanilla. At the Los Angeles–based Sprinkles cupcake chain, everyday flavors are limited to variations on vanilla and chocolate (red velvet, marshmallow and chocolate, vanilla and chocolate) and cinnamon sugar. More exotic flavors like coconut and ginger lemon are sold once or twice a week. Crumbs, a New York–based chain bakery, advertises flavors like peanut butter cup, cookie dough, and cookies and cream (topped with an Oreo) among its customers' favorites. It doesn't take a behavioral anthropologist to detect a pattern here.

The Europeans opt for "adult" flavors while Americans go for the uncomplicated tastes of childhood. There is still something of the bourgeois sensibility in the *macaron*. You can show off your savoir vivre and savoir faire by opting for the exotic flavors, since being well traveled and having broad tastes is one of the markers of wealth in contemporary Europe. Exquisitely wrapped boxes of *macarons* are often brought as house gifts, much like chocolates and flowers. And where you bought them matters. In France, connoisseurship in shopping is still highly valued, much as it was a century ago.

The cupcake, on the other hand, is a perfect reflection of the youth culture that has been dominant ever since America's baby boomers hijacked the nation. In the United States, I often get the sense that the ideal age is about sixteen—old enough to drive and have sex (in most states) but still with many of the tastes of childhood. When not at work, the average American man dresses in sneakers, jeans, T-shirt, and a baseball cap, the uniform of a twelve-year-old. To an enormous extent these tastes apply to food as well. Sweet is the favorite flavor in America, in pasta sauce, bread, ketchup, breakfast cereal, and almost all beverages. Another interesting characteristic of the cupcake flavors is how several derive from industrially produced sweets, but this too is characteristic of the American sweet tooth.

As different as the transatlantic cultures are, it's clear that they are gradually turning into one. Walk through a typical European airport and it's hard to tell the Italians from the Americans by dress alone any more. The American cupcake and the French *macaron* may have more in common than what sets them apart. Certainly they are both phenomena of the instant communication age. They share its informal approach and fleeting allegiances. They are a quick promiscuous pleasure to be had between a tweet and an IM. You need no silverware, no ornate café, no physical context. They come in individual servings, not meant to be shared. Given our attention spans today, I wonder how much longer the fad will last. The most recent trend out of France involves marshmallows (*guimauves*), a treat that seems almost as binational and infantile as Jerry Lewis.

When I asked Pierre Hermé what he thought the future would bring, he brought his shoulders up in the classic Gallic gesture. "People always ask me that," the world's most decorated pastry chef observed. "I am not Madame Irma. It is difficult to say." He deliberated a moment. "But I can tell you we have a lot of newcomers in this field. A lot of new talent." I trust that he's right. The pastry cooks will continue to invent new desserts as long as fashion keeps changing and sweet pleasure stays in fashion.

ACKNOWLEDGMENTS

L ike every project of this scale, this one was hardly an individual endeavor. I have been awed and humbled by the generosity people have expressed all over the world to help me out in ways both great and small. In Kolkata, I would have been lost without numerous helping hands including Rajashi Gupta, Ishita Dey, and Sutapa Bhatta and her knowledgeable staff at the Institute of Hotel & Restaurant Management. I also have to thank the confectioners Dhiman Das, Protap Chandra Nag, and Prasanta Nandy for giving me insight into the inner workings of Indian sweetshops, but mainly I need acknowledge a debt of gratitude to Joydeep Chatterjee, who acted as my Virgil in exploring Kolkata's *moira*.

In Istanbul, I am grateful to Faruk and Fatih Güllü at Güllüoğlu. Also in Turkey, I am indebted to historian Mary Işin in more ways than I can count. In Venice, my friend Luca Colferai was always ready with corrections to my Italian and my history. Franco Tonolo and Giuliana Tonolo Piarotto were generous with both doughnuts and information. In Paris, I would like to thank Mary and Phillip Hyman for setting me straight, and Pierre Hermé for taking time out of his busy schedule to analyze dessert, culture, and femininity.

Vienna was a bit of a homecoming for me, and it was no disappointment. Among the people who greeted me with stories and cakes were master confectioners Kurt Nitsche and Karl Schuhmacher, café owner Hans Diglas as well as Astrid Kahl of Demel's, and Christine Koza of the Hotel Sacher. The one person there I can't thank enough is historian Ingrid Haslinger, who helped me immeasurably.

Back in the United States, I experienced the extraordinary Cajun hospitality of Jackie Theriot, Miriam Krepper, and the other organizers of the Louisiana Sugar Cane Festival. Virginia Latiolais, Pat Kahle, Mary Tutwiler, Ben Legendre, and Tommy Thibodeaux all helped me to understand what sugar means to the people who grow and process it. Finally, back home, I'd like to acknowledge the help of the New York Public Library with its awesome collection. Thanks too to my agents Jane Dystel and Miriam Goderich for their faith and hard dealing, and to my editors Cynthia Sherry and Lisa Reardon for all their work on the manuscript. Finally, I would like to thank my wife, Lucia, who was only partly skeptical when I told her I needed to travel round the world to eat cake.

NOTES

Introduction

1 D. Benton, "Role of parents in the determination of the food preferences of children and the development of obesity," *International Journal of Obesity* (2004), 858–69.
2 Admittedly a pacifier works even better. Best is a pacifier and sugar solution combined. See Nora Haouari et al., "The analgesic effect of sucrose in full term infants: a randomised controlled trial," *British Medical Journal* (10 June 1995), 1498–1500; and also R. Carbajal et al., "Randomised trial of analgesic effects of sucrose, glucose, and pacifiers in term neonates," *British Medical Journal* (27 November 1999), 1393–97.
3 For more on the human sweet tooth, see Amanda H. McDaniel and Danielle R. Reed, "The Human Sweet Tooth and Its Relationship to Obesity," in Carolyn D. Berdanier and Naïma Moustaïd-Moussa, *Genomics and Proteomics in Nutrition* (New York: Marcel Dekker, 2004), 54, 60–66.
4 2005 figures; see Faostat website: www.fao.org.

1 Sacred Fudge

1 The study was undertaken by Dr. Sangeeta Patel at the INXS Obesity Medical Centre, admittedly not the most reliable source. First reported on by *The Hindu* and quoted in Matt Preston, "Sugar and Spice," *The Age*, October 14, 2003.
2 Colleen Taylor Sen, *Food Culture in India* (Westport, CT: Greenwood Press, 2004), 149.
3 Stanley A. Wolpert, *A New History of India* (New York: Oxford University Press, 2009), 41– 42.

4   Suchitra Samanta, "The 'Self-Animal' and Divine Digestion: Goat Sacrifice to the God-dess Kālī in Bengal," *Journal of Asian Studies* 53, no. 3 (August 1994), 779–803.
5   According to K. T. Achaya, *A Historical Dictionary of Indian Food* (Delhi and New York: Oxford University Press, 1998), 132, the term *ladduka* (singular *laddu*) first appears in the *Mahābhārata* and the *Sushrutha Samhitā*.
6   Gabriella Eichinger Ferro-Luzzi, "Ritual as Language: The Case of South Indian Food Offerings," *Current Anthropology*, vol. 18, no. 3 (September 1977), 509.
7   K. T. Achaya, *Indian Food: A Historical Companion* (Delhi: Oxford University Press, 1994), 68. *Karai*, also *Korai Kizhangu* (in Tamil), is nut grass (*Cyperus rotundus*), which grows tubers used in traditional Indian medicine.
8   Om Gupta, *Encyclopaedia of India, Pakistan and Bangladesh* (Delhi: Isha Books, 2006), 103.
9   Alexander Hamilton, *A New Account of the East Indies*, vol. 1 (Edinburgh: John Moss-man, 1727), 383.
10 Achaya, *A Historical Dictionary of Indian Food*, 250.
11 Dwijendra Narayan Jha, *The Myth of the Holy Cow* (London: Verso, 2002), 27–29.
12 Achaya, *A Historical Dictionary of Indian Food*, 180.
13 Achaya, *Indian Food*, 35.
14 Indira Chakravarty, *Saga of Indian Food* (New Delhi: Sterling, 1972), 16.
15 The text seems to have accreted sometime between the second century BCE and the fourth CE and occasionally gives more than one version of the same story. Given that the honey story is recounted in several forms, it might be older. See *The Mahāvastu*, trans. John James Jones (London: Luzac, 1952), 291; for sugar and sweetmeat maker references, see 112, 443.
16 There are numerous sources for this. For the pregnancy ritual, see *Village Life in Bengal/Hindu Customs in Bengal* (Philadelphia: Xlibris, 2004), 188.
17 H. A. Rose, "Hindu Birth Observances in the Punjab," *Journal of the Royal Anthropological Institute of Great Britain and Ireland*, vol. 38 (July–December 1908), 226.
18 P. Arundhati, *Royal Life in Mānasôllāsa* (New Delhi: Sundeep Prakashan, 1994), 107.
19 "North India 1600–1938 (Mukerjee)," Global Price and Income History Group website: http://gpih.ucdavis.edu/Datafilelist.htm.
20 See H. A. Rose, "Muhammadan Betrothal Observances in the Punjab," *Man*, vol. 17 (April 1917) and (June 1917), 59–60 and 91–95; and H. A. Rose, "Muhammadan Birth Observances in the Punjab," 249–56. For a description of several forms of *majun*, see Baden Henry Baden-Powell, *Hand-Book of the Manufactures and Arts of the Punjab: With a Combined Glossary and Index of Vernacular Trades and Technical Terms, &C* (Lahore: Punjab Printing Co., 1872), 292.
21 For a relatively recent discussion of the various origin theories, see Glyn James, *Sugarcane* (Oxford: Blackwell Science, 2004), 3–4.
22 Achaya, *A Historical Dictionary of Indian Food*, 110.
23 J. H. Galloway, *The Sugar Cane Industry* (Cambridge, England: Cambridge University Press, 1989), 20.
24 'Allami Abul Fazl, *The Ain I Akbari* (Kolkata: Baptist Mission Press, 1873), 62–63, indicates that rice cost 20 to 40 *dam* per *man* (a Mughal weight measure of about fifty pounds), white sugar 128, and brown, 56 *dam* per *man*. On feeding horses, see 135, on elephants, 130. Contemporary figures come from Faostat, 2005.
25 See Achaya, *A Historical Dictionary of Indian Food*; for *hōlige*, 117, for *murmura*, 97.

26 See P. Arundhati. I have been a little loose with the translation but the details remain much the same. See 163 for the picnic description, 44 and following pages for recipes, 115 and 127 for milk-based desserts. According to the translator, ketaki flowers are now known as kewda (*Pandanus odoratissimus*).

27 On the Mughals, see Wolpert, 108–13, 135, 137.

28 Robert Montgomery Martin, *The History, Antiquities, Topography, and Statistics of Eastern India* (London: W. H. Allen and Co., 1838), 943.

29 Edward Terry, *A Voyage to East-India* (London: J. Wilkie, 1777); see especially section X, 193–99.

30 Noël Deerr, *The History of Sugar* (London: Chapman and Hall, 1949), 51.

31 Abul Fazl, 55.

32 Achaya, *A Historical Dictionary of Indian Food,* 132. There is admittedly a problem with Achaya's assertion, which he traces to a description in the *Ain-i-Akbari*. Having looked at the same translation as he has, I can't find any mention of it.

33 Najmieh Batmanglij, *New Food of Life* (Bloomington, IN: 1stBooks, 2003), 334.

34 These descriptions are quoted in Minakshie Dasgupta, Bunny Gupta, and Jaya Chaliha, *The Calcutta Cookbook* (New Delhi, India: Penguin Books, 1995), where they are credited to K. T. Achaya, "Early Travellers Tales," in *Science Age*, May 1985.

35 See Satya Prakash Sangar, *Food and Drinks in Mughal India* (New Delhi: Reliance, 1999), 16–17. Surdas [also spelled Sûr Dâs] mentions the following sweets and fruits taken at breakfast in the houses of the affluent: milk, butter, and curd; *amrit pakori*; *jalebi khurma*; *ghuja*; *shakarpârâ*; *laddu*; *mâlpûra*; *andarsa*; *khajuri*; *kharik*; *chironji*; raisins; almonds; pistachioes; copra; banana; mango; apricots; cashew nuts; watermelon; dry date; besides *pheni*, etc. Those who could afford it enjoyed a rich dinner including the following vegetables, sweets, and fruits: *Besanpûri, sukhpûri*, and *luchai* [breads]; ghee and *khîr*; *gindori*; *tingari*; *gondpak* and *ilaichipak*; *andarsa, pheni* [sweet] and *lapsi*; *gujha* and *kharik, jalebi*, and *amriti*; raisins and copra, almonds and *chirâri* . . .

36 Sangar, 42.

37 *The East India Military Calendar,* vol. 2 (London: Kingsbury, Parbury, and Allen, 1824), see footnote, 150.

38 Quoted in Krishna Dutta, *Calcutta: A Cultural and Literary History* (Cities of the Imagination) (New York: Interlink Books, 2003), 14.

39 Wolpert, 193.

40 François Bernier, *Voyages de François Bernier* (Paris: imprimé aux frais du. gouvernement pour procurer du travail aux ouvriers typographes, 1830), 310; this is a reprint of the 1699 Amsterdam edition. See also *Le dictionnaire de l'Académie françoise* (Paris: Veuve de Jean Baptiste Coignard, 1694), 230, for a definition.

41 Su-Mei Yu, "Thai Egg-Based Sweets: The Legend of Thao Thong Keap-Ma," *Gastronomica*, Summer 2003, 54. Yu makes some errors in comparing Portuguese and Thai desserts but her description of how *thong yib* is made is fascinating.

42 The information on the family history is mostly taken from a brochure, "Sweetening Lives for 75 Years," put out by the company in around 2006, as well as an interview with Dhiman Das in October 2008.

43 Lál Behári Day, *Govinda Sámanta*, vol. 1 (London: Macmillan and Co., 1874), 155–56.

44 See, for example, Gervase Markham, *The English House-Wife* (London: George Sawbridge, 1675 [the first edition was in 1615]), 153, where he specifically uses buttermilk for clabbering milk.

45 "Bengali sweets out to tempt chocolate lovers," *Times of India* (17 January 2003). A slightly later set of figures comes from Ritwik Mukherjee, "Makeover for mishti," *Business Today* (8 January 2008). He writes that Bengali sweet makers "annually do business worth Rs 6,000 crore [60 billion rupees]." Elsewhere in the piece he notes that the West Bengal Sweetmeat Makers Association has over 100,000 members. Of course the numbers cited by the *Times of India* and *Business Today* aren't strictly comparable, but they do give an impression of the enormous scale of the business.

46 Martin, 943.

47 Herbert Hope Risley, *The Tribes and Castes of Bengal*, vol. 1 (Kolkata: Bengal Secretariat Press, 1892), 312.

48 See Ritendradranath Thakur, "Sandesh," in *Mudir Dokan* (Aruna Prakashan: Kolkata, 2008), 69.

49 On nineteenth-century Kolkata, see Dutta, 23–24 and 104–6.

50 Sweet Talk of Calcutta, Web page: www.angelfire.com/country/bengalifood/food04.html.

51 Jayanta Sengupta, "Nation on a Platter: The Culture and Politics of Food and Cuisine in Colonial Bengal," in *Modern Asian Studies* 44, 1 (2010), 81–98.

52 Dutta, 36.

53 Day, 156.

54 Shib Chunder Bose, *The Hindoos as They Are: A Description of the Manners, Customs, and Inner Life of Hindoo Society in Bengal* (Calcutta: Thacker, Spink and Co., 1883), 51. The book includes a glossary giving the names of a half-dozen contemporary sweetmeats.

55 "Diwali sweets losing their allure," AP wire service (13 October 2008).

2 A Thousand and One Sweet Layers

1 For more on the history of baklava, see Friedrich Unger and Priscilla Mary Işin, *A King's Confectioner in the Orient* (London: Kegan Paul, 2003), 170–76; Priscilla Mary Işın, *Gülbeşeker* (Istanbul: Yapı Kredi Yayınları, 2009), 235–38; and Charles Perry, "The Taste for Layered Bread Among the Nomadic Turks and the Central Asian Origins of Baklava," in *Culinary Cultures of the Middle East* (London: I. B. Tauris, 1994), 89.

2 Nawal Nasrallah, *Delights from the Garden of Eden* (Bloomington, IN: 1stBooks, 2003), 440.

3 Marcus Porcius Cato and Ernest Brehaut, *On Farming* (New York: Columbia University Press, 1933), part LXXVI; see also Jon Solomon, "'Tracta': A Versatile Roman Pastry," *Hermes*, vol. 106, no. 4 (1978), 539–56.

4 For the cooking of medieval Baghdad as well as dishes described in Al-Warrāq's cookbook, see Ibn Sayyār al-Warrāq, *Annals of the Caliphs' Kitchens* (Leiden: Brill, 2007), especially 30, (sugar refining) 388, (*ma'mūniyya*) 405–9, (cannoli) 425, (*lauzīnaj*) 598.

5 Nasrallah, 466.

6 See the descriptions and recipes of *jūdhāba* in Nasrallah, 466; and Maxime Rodison, A. J. Arberry, Charles Perry, and Claudia Roden, *Medieval Arab Cookery* (Blackawton, Devon: Prospect Books, 2001), 412.

7 Odile Redon, Françoise Sabban, and Silvano Serventi, *The Medieval Kitchen: Recipes from France and Italy* (Chicago: University of Chicago Press, 1998), 113.

8 See, for example, the many *torta* recipes in Bartolomeo Scappi, *Opera* (Venice: Michele Tramezzino, 1570).

9 See Charles Perry's translation of *An Anonymous Andalusian Cookbook of the 13th Century*: www.daviddfriedman.com/Medieval/Cookbooks/Andalusian/andalusian9.htm. For footnote, see Scappi, 367.

10 On ancient Mesopotamia, see Henri Limet, "The Cuisine of Ancient Sumer," in *Biblical Archaeologist*, vol. 50, no. 3 (September 1987), 134 and 137. Also Jean Bottero, *The Oldest Cuisine in the World* (Chicago: University of Chicago Press, 2004), 3, 23; and "The Cuisine of Ancient Mesopotamia," in *Biblical Archaeologist*, vol. 48, no. 1 (March 1985), 38.

11 Nasrallah, 525.

12 Herodotus, Andrea Purvis, and Robert B. Strassler, *The Landmark Herodotus: The Histories* (New York: Pantheon Books, 2007), 104.

13 The list is from *La pratica della mercatura*, excerpted in Robert Sabatino Lopez and Irving Woodworth Raymond, *Medieval Trade in the Mediterranean World: Illustrative Documents* (New York: Columbia University Press, 1955), 109–11. The authors speculate that "musciatto" sugar is musk-flavored sugar, which seems implausible given the way Pegolotti speaks of it. He compares its quality to three other grades of sugar, deeming it to be of the lowest quality. My best guess is that *musciatto* comes from Muscat (modern Italian *Mascate*), a major trade entrepôt at the time. Could this be the real origin of the word *muscovado*?

14 Henry Yule, A. C. Burnell, and William Crooke, *Hobson-Jobson: A Glossary of Colloquial Anglo-Indian Words and Phrases, and of Kindred Terms, Etymological, Historical, Geographical and Discursive* (London: J. Murray, 1903), 864.

15 *Asal Katr* in Arabic. The translator notes "that it is 'a fine kind of black honey, treacle' though it is afterwards called cane-honey ('Asal Kasab)." Nasrallah notes that *'asal qaṣab* is "sugarcane honey, which is molasses produced in the process of making cane sugar"; see al-Warrāq, 594.

16 The original name was *kunafa* and meant a very thin bread, which was sometimes sliced into thin strips.

17 Elihu Ashtor, " L'évolution des prix dans le Proche-Orient à la basse époque," *Journal of the Economic and Social History of the Orient* 4 (1961), 32–33.

18 See Deerr, 526–27.

19 See "Prices and wages in Istanbul, 1469–1914," on the International Institute of Social History website: http://iisg.nl/hpw/data.php. An average of seven data points between 1469 and 1528 yields the result of 17.5 grams of silver per kilogram of sugar, while honey runs at 2.8 grams per kilogram.

20 Bernard Lewis, *Wirtschaftsgeschichte des Vorderen Orients in Islamischer Zeit*, Part 1 (Leiden: Brill, 1977), 107–9. Tenth- and eleventh-century Egyptian documents point to the sum of six dinars as the average price of a *kintar* (96.7 kilograms) of sugar in the second half of the eleventh century; one kilogram of sugar in Syria cost .09-.01 dinar; in Egypt during the Mamluk period, a *kintar* of refined sugar cost 7.5 dinars in one mention and 12.5 in another. From 1000 CE to 1400 CE, wheat cost roughly one dinar per 100 kilograms; prices rise after that.

21 Badā' al-Zamān al-Hamadhānī, *Maqāmāt*, translated by W. J. Prendergast, www.sacred-texts.com/isl/mhm/mhm20.htm; but see also Charles Perry, "What to Order in Ninth-Century Baghdad," in *Medieval Arab Cookery*, 217. Theoretically ten silver dirham made up one gold dinar (though it could be as much as twenty, depending on

the period); sources indicate that a soldier's monthly salary was about eighty dirham, but that was in the early ninth century. Ashtor apparently writes that bread cost about one-twentieth of a dirham per ratl, a ratl being about 625 grams in the tenth century. See note 10 in Ṭabarī and Joel L. Kraemer, *Incipient Decline* (Albany: State University of New York Press, 1989), 6.

22 Andrew M. Watson, *Agricultural Innovation in the Early Islamic World* (Cambridge, England: Cambridge University Press, 1983), 96.

23 Lilia Zaouali, *Medieval Cuisine of the Islamic World* (Berkeley: University of California Press, 2007), 9–10. On Ibrāhim's African heritage, see Ibn Khallikān and William Mac-Guckin Slane, *Ibn Khallikan's Biographical Dictionary*, vol. 1 (London: Allen and Co., 1842), 16–19.

24 Al-Warrāq, 125.

25 Muḥammad ibn al-Ḥasan Ibn al-Karīm and Charles Perry, *A Baghdad Cookery Book* (Totnes: Prospect, 2005), 25; on cleaning dishes, see 29.

26 A. J. Arberry, "Studies in Arabic Manuscripts," *Medieval Arab Cookery*, 96–97.

27 See Guillaume Antoine Olivier's *Travels in the Ottoman Empire, Egypt, and Persia* (London: T. N. Longman and O. Rees, 1801), 45.

28 Zaid Sabah, "Instability Makes Holiday Treats a Little Less Sweet," *USA Today* (11 January 2007).

29 See the blog of Laila El-Haddad, www.gazamom .com/2009/08/ramadan-recipes-atayif.

30 See Perry, 103; the recipe repeats in the later expanded version known as *Kitāb Waṣf al-Aṭ'ima al-Mu'tāda*; see also Charles Perry, "The Description of Familiar Foods" in *Medieval Arab Cookery*, 428.

31 Zaouali, 131.

32 For the footnote, see "When everything slows down," *The Economist*, 14–20, August 2010, 36.

33 See Najmieh Batmanglij, *New Food of Life* (Washington, DC: Mage Publishers, 1992), 417; and Poopa Dweck, *Aromas of Aleppo* (New York: Ecco, 2007), 250.

34 *Nuhūd al-'adrā* in Arabic; see Charles Perry, "The Description of Familiar Foods," in *Medieval Arab Cookery*, 416.

35 For more on Unger's experiences in the Ottoman capital, see Unger and Işin, *A King's Confectioner in the Orient* 2–3, 49, 104–5; on *kadayıf*, see 179–82.

36 M. Zeki Oral, "Foods and Breads of the Selçuk (Seljuk) Period," on the Turkish Cuisine website: www.turkish-cuisine.org/english/pages.php?ParentID=1&FirstLevel=8.

37 The Istanbul population figure comes from Albert Habib Hourani and Malise Ruthven, *A History of the Arab Peoples* (Cambridge, MA: Belknap Press of Harvard University Press, 1991), 232; the numbers on the palace from Metin Saip Sürücüoğlu, "Kitchen Organization, Ceremonial and Celebratory Meals in the Ottoman Empire," on the Turkish Cuisine website: www.turkish-cuisine.org/english/pages.php?ParentID =1&FirstLevel=9&SecondLevel=107&LastLevel=112.

38 Jean-Baptiste Tavernier, *Nouvelle relation de l'intérieur du serrail du Grand Seigneur* (Paris: O. de Varennes, 1675), 80.

39 Thomas Dallam, John Covel, and J. Theodore Bent, *Early Voyages and Travels in the Levant*, works issued by the Hakluyt Society, no. 87 (London: Printed for the Hakluyt Society, 1893), 260–62; on the circumcision festivities, 228.

40 Ogier Ghiselin de Busbecq and Edward Seymour Forster, *The Turkish Letters of Ogier Ghiselin de Busbecq* (Baton Rouge: Louisiana State University Press, 2005), 53.

41 On Dernschwam, see Unger and Işın, 7; on contemporary attitudes, see Işın, "A Mirror of Society: Cuisine," on the Turkish Cuisine website: www.turkish-cuisine.org/english /article_details.php?p_id=5&Pages=Articles.

42 Unger and Işın, 176. Also see the Güllüoğlu website quoting Ilber Ortayli writing in the *Istanbul Encyclopaedia*: www .gulluoglu.com.tr/en/kurumsal/dundenbugune .php?id=baklavatarihce.

43 Ayse Alibeyoglu, "Sparring over baklava spills over to Doha," *The Peninsula* (21 May 2006).

3 Sugar and Spice

1 Vincenzo Tanara, *L'Economia Del Cittadino in Villa* (Venice: Bertani, 1661), 39.

2 For Scappi biography, see Terence Scully's translation of Bartolomeo Scappi, *The Opera of Bartolomeo Scappi (1570)* (Toronto: University of Toronto Press, 2008), 12–25.

3 See Bernard Dupaigne, *The History of Bread* (New York: Harry N. Abrams, 1999), 139. He seems to get the Greek name wrong, but otherwise he's right on the mark. On *ciambella*, see Piero Camporesi, *The Magic Harvest* (Cambridge, England: Polity Press, 1993), 16.

4 Athenaeus, *The Deipnosophists*, vol. VI, trans. Charles Burton Gulick (London: W. Heinemann, 1927), 465–501; for the Demeter reference, see 493, for the cheesecake, 487.

5 Patrick Faas, *Around the Roman Table* (New York: Palgrave MacMillan, 2003), 82; for the Pliny quote, see 149.

6 See the Brama Gateway Ukraine website: www.brama.com/art/easter.html.

7 See the Dicionário aberto de calão e expressões idiomáticas website: http://natura .di.uminho.pt/jjbin/dac. On *ganchas*, see the Folclore de Portugal website: http:// folclore-online.com/usos/txt/ganchas_sbras1.html.

8 See Le trésor de la langue française informatisé website: http://atilf.atilf.fr.

9 John Edwards and Apicius, *The Roman Cookery of Apicius* (Seattle, WA: Hartley & Marks, 1984), 174.

10 See the *Spritzgebackenes* recipe in David Friedman's transcription: www .daviddfriedman.com/Medieval/Cookbooks/Sabrina_Welserin.html.

11 Quoted in Waltraud Faissner, *Wie mann die Linzer Dortten macht* (Weitra: Bibliothek der Provinz, 2004), 23.

12 Reinhold C. Mueller and Frederic Chapin Lane, *The Venetian Money Market* (Baltimore: Johns Hopkins University Press, 1997), 648.

13 Philip D. Curtin, *The Rise and Fall of the Plantation Complex: Essays in Atlantic History* (Cambridge, England: Cambridge University Press, 1998), 7–8.

14 See Juergen Schulz, *The New Palaces of Medieval Venice* (University Park: Pennsylvania State University Press, 2004), 199–204; and also the Italian culture and history website: www.boglewood.com/cornaro/xpiscopia.html.

15 Fulcher refers to passing through Laodicea (Latakia) on his way to Valenia (Valeniya); see Edward Peters, *The First Crusade: The Chronicle of Fulcher of Chartres and Other Source Materials* (Philadelphia: University of Pennsylvania Press, 1971), 97.

16 See 1179 Maj. 1, ind XII, Accon—Balduinus IV; quoted in "Sugarcane in Palestine During the Crusaders Reign 492–690 H / 1099–1291 A.D," *An-Najah University Journal for Research—Humanities*, vol. 20, issue 3, 2006, 760. On the weights, see John E. Dotson, "A Problem of Cotton and Lead in Medieval Italian Shipping," *Speculum*, vol. 57, no. 1 (January 1982), 55; see also Elihu Ashtor, "Levantine Weights and Standard Parcels: A Contribution to the Metrology of the Later Middle Ages," *Bulletin of the School of Oriental and African Studies*, vol. 45, no. 3 (1982), 478.

17 Deerr, 76.

18 Benjamin (of Tudela), *The Itinerary of Benjamin of Tudela*, trans. Marcus Nathan Adler (London: Henry Frowde, 1907), 19.

19 Marie-Louise von Wartburg, "Production du sucre de canne à Chypre: Un chapitre de techologie mediévale," in *Coloniser au moyen âge* (Paris: A. Colin, 1995), 130–31.

20 Zaouali, 38.

21 Galloway, 41.

22 For the sugar numbers, see Deerr, 527. Wheat ran about 8 lire per 100 kilograms in the 1400s (there were roughly 6.2 lire to a ducat); see "Prices and wages in northern Italian towns, 1285–1850." For prices in England, see "English prices and wages, 1209–1914"; for Holland, see "The prices of the most important consumer goods, and indices of wages and the cost of living in the western part of the Netherlands, 1450–1800." All three are on the International Institute of Social History website.

23 There is some disagreement about how much slave labor Madeiran sugar plantations employed. According to William D. Phillips, *Slavery from Roman Times to the Early Transatlantic Trade* (Minneapolis: University of Minnesota Press, 1985), 151, in 1500 there were some two thousand slaves in a population of eighteen thousand.

24 Galloway, 51.

25 For an in-depth discussion of Venice's sugar sculptures, see Daniela Ambrosini, "Les honneurs sucrées de Venise," in *Le boire et le manger au XVIe siècle* (Saint-Etienne: Publ. de l'Univ. de Saint-Etienne, 2004), 267–84.

26 For more on the development of the Italian *collazione*, see Claudio Benporat, *Feste e banchetti: convivialità italiana fra Tre e Quattrocento* (Florence: L. S. Olschki, 2001), 93–99.

27 Pompeo Molmenti, *Venice*, vol. 3 (Chicago: A. C. McClurg & Co., 1907), 122–23; for Renée's and Beatrice's feasts, see 295 and 122.

28 I'm translating this from the French edition that came out two years later: Girolamo Ruscelli, *Les Secrets de reverend Signeur Alexis Piemontois. Traduit d'Italien en françois* (Antwerp: Plantin, 1557), 343.

29 Carol Field, *Celebrating Italy* (New York: William Morrow & Co., 1990), 270.

30 According to Deborah Howard, *Jacopo Sansovino Architecture and Patronage in Renaissance Venice* (New Haven, CT: Yale University Press, 1975), 9, his yearly salary was 180 ducats; this would have been 1,116 lire at the time. Palladio made 240 lire per month according to Satya Brata Datta, *Women and Men in Early Modern Venice* (Burlington, VT: Ashgate, 2003), 126.

31 Paolo Paruta, *Della perfettione della vita politica* (Venice: Domenico Nicolini, 1599), 282.

32 Richard Mackenney, *Tradesmen and Traders* (Totowa, NJ: Barnes & Noble Books, 1987), 88–89.

33 For background on the event, see Julia Mary Cartwright Ady, *Isabella d'Este, Marchioness of Mantua, 1474–1539*, vol. 2 (London: J. Murray, 1903), 286–98, for the banquet desription; and Cristoforo di Messisbugo, *Banchetti* (Ferrara: Giovanni de Buglhat and Antonio Hucher Compagni, 1549), 5.

34 Ady, 298.

35 Fernand Braudel, *Civilization and Capitalism, 15th–18th Century*, vol. 1 (New York: Harper & Row, 1982–1984), 221.

36 See Scully's translation of Scappi's *Opera*, 228, 460.

37 Messisbugo, 18.

38 Ken Albala, *Eating Right in the Renaissance* (Berkeley: University of California Press, 2002), 173, 211–12.

39 Molmenti, 291. The bill includes some scant thirty pounds total of three kinds of sugar. I'm assuming these are light pounds (300 grams), typically used for spices, but even if they are the heavier Venetian pounds of around 480 grams, it would still be a relatively paltry amount given how much meat was served.

40 Fabio Parasecoli, *Food Culture in Italy* (Westport, CT: Greenwood Press, 2004), 49.

41 Messisbugo, 43.

42 The figures are for 2005; see the Faostat website.

43 Romoli, Domenico. *La Singolare dottrina di M. Domenico Romoli* (Venice: Gio. Battista Bonfadino, 1593), book 5, ch. 122. June Di Schino and Furio Luccichenti, *Il cuoco segreto dei papi* (Roma: Gangemi, 2007), make the point that he worked for Leo X and Cardinal Rodolfi. In later years, *zuccherini* would refer to candied violets and such; see, for example, Maria Luisa Tibone and Lidia Cardino, *Il confetturiere piemontese* (Sala Bolognese: A. Forni, 1995), 66.

44 Andrew Dalby, *Siren Feasts* (New York: Routledge, 1997), 192.

45 Tanara, 39.

46 *Libro dello scalco di Cesare Evitascandalo* (Rome: Carlo Vullietti, 1609), 137, includes mention of *pan di Spagna* as a specialty of nuns. Scappi's *mostaccioli* are recipe no. 141 (588 in Scully's translation).

47 See Nicolas de Bonnefons, *Les délices de la campagne* (Paris: A. Cellier, 1662), 18; also François Pierre de La Varenne, *Le Cuisinier françois où est enseigné la maniere d'apprêter toute sorte de viandes, de faire toute sorte de pâtisseries & de confitures* (Lyon: Jacques Canier, 1680), 310–18.

48 For *génoise*, see Briand, *Dictionnaire des alimens, vins et liqueurs*, vol. 2 (Paris: Gissey, 1750), 97–98; for *petits pains de sainte Geneviève*, see Charles Philippe d'Albert Luynes, *Mémoires du duc de Luynes sur la cour de Louis XV: 1735–1758* (Paris: Didot, 1860–1865), 251; for an early *paste de Gennes* recipe, see *Traité de confiture* (Paris: T. Guillain, 1689), 53.

49 For the Ferrara origin story, see the Taccuini Storici website: www.taccuinistorici.it /ita/news/moderna/dpani———dolci/ZUPPA-ESTENSE-o-Inglese.html; for Fiesole, see Leo Codacci, in *Civiltà della tavola Contadina*, quoted in the Italian Wikipedia entry; for Naples, see Egano Lambertini, E. Volpe, and Antonio Guizzaro, *Miseria e nobiltà nella storia della cucina napoletana* (Napoli: Tempo lungo, 1999), 221.

50 *Il felsineo: giornaletto settimanale*, no. 1 (June 1840 to May 1841), 301. In Franz Gaudy's *Mein Römerzug* ("My Roman Holiday") (Berlin: Enslin, 1836), 250, the author notes the confusion a visitor might find ordering a zuppa inglese and "expecting to get soup but instead getting a sugar-dusted cake."

51 For one of the earliest examples of what we would recognize as a trifle, see Hannah Glasse, *The Art of Cookery* (London: W. Strahan, etc., 1774), 285.

52 Jane Black, "The Trail of Tiramisu," *Washington Post* (11 July 2007).
53 Vincenzo Cervio, *Il Trinciante di M. Vincenzo Cervio* (Rome: Gabbia, 1593), 131.
54 See the translation in Staphan's Florilegium, Guisados1-art: www.florilegium.org
    /?http%3A//www.florilegium.org/files
    /FOOD-MANUSCRIPTS/Guisados1-art.html.
55 See *Dizionario biografico universale* (Florence: Passigli 1840), 714.
56 *Le mercure galant,* part 2 (October 1682), 101, 159, 176.
57 There are a number of sources for this: see Jeri Quinzio, *Of Sugar and Snow* (Berkeley:
    University of California Press, 2009), 3; and *Ain I 'Akbari*, 55. Elizabeth David and Jill
    Norman make the same point in *Harvest of the Cold Months* (New York: Viking, 1995),
    67.
58 L.S.R., Pierre de Lune, and Audiger, *L'Art de la cuisine française au XVIIe siècle* (Paris:
    Editions Payot & Rivages, 1995), 199-101.
59 The Cavour reference is from John Dickie, *Delizia!* (New York: Free Press, 2008), 178.
    The macaroni was the first course on a menu served to the king for a "*déjeuner*" on
    August 22, 1900; available at the Academia Barilla Gastronomic Library website—His-
    toric Menu Collection. State of Italy—Kingdom of Italy—House of Savoy. COLLOC.
    A.112.24—INV. 1965: www.academiabarilla.com/academia/menu-collection
    /menu-month.aspx.
60 See the baba.it website: www.baba.it/curiosita.htm.
61 Bauli bought two other large brands, Motta and Alemagna, from Nestlé in 2009. See
    "Bauli picks up Motta, Alemagna panettone brands," *Gourmet News*, 25 November
    2009. For Ruggero Bauli's biography, see the Bauli website: www.bauli.it/it/storia.php.
    For the more recent figures, see "Panettone makers want to keep Christmas cake Ital-
    ian," *Reuters*, 12 December 2007.

4 Let Them Eat Cake

1 See Pierre Boyé, *Un roi de Pologne et la couronne ducale de Loraine* (Paris: Berger-
   Levrault et Cie., 1898), 20-24. For Alexandre-Balthazar-Laurent Grimod de La
   Reynière on baba, see *Manuel des amphitryons* (Paris: Capelle et Renand, 1808), 170.
2 Thomas Max Safley, *Charity and Economy in the Orphanages of Early Modern Augsburg,* (Atlantic Highlands, NJ: Humanities Press, 1997), 316; and Eleonora Maria
   Rosalia Herzogin zu Troppau und Jägerndorf, *Freywillig aufgesprungener Granat-Apffel
   des christlichen Samariters* (Nürnberg: Trautner und Schmidt, 1731), 524 (first edition
   was published in 1697 in Grätz).
3 The first reference I've been able to track down, " . . . une douzaine de biscuits de
   Reims, plusieurs tranches de baba au rhum, du gâteau de fleur d'orange, . . . " is in
   George Granville, *Cent proverbes* (Paris: Fournier, 1845), 171. On the newfound popularity of rum, see *Une société de gens de lettres, L'Esprit des journaux, françois et étrang-
   ers*, vol. 4 (Brussels: Weissenbruch, 1805), 113.
4 See the recipe in Louis-Eustache Audot, *La cuisinière de la campagne et de la ville*
   (Paris: Audot, 1853), 440.
5 *L'intermédiaire des chercheurs et curieux*, vol. 40 (Paris: 1899), 733.
6 Pierre Liénard, François Duthu, and Claire Hauguel, *Moi, Nicolas Stohrer, pâtissier du
   Roi, rue Montorgueil, au pied de Saint-Eustache, à Paris* (Paris: Lattès, 1999), 11.
7 For the first French recipe, see *Le pastissier françois* (Paris: Jean Gaillard, 1653), 1-7.
   The claim about the early *gâteau feuillé* appears in Maguelonne Toussaint-Samat, *La*

très belle et très exquise histoire des gateaux et des friandises (Paris: Flammarion, 2004), 168–70, and other secondary sources. The Medici coronation menu is in "Festin donné à al royne Catherine au logis episcopal de l'évesché de Paris, le dix-neuvieme jour de jouing 1549," in Félix Danjou and L. Cimber, eds., *Archives curieuses de l'histoire de France*, series I, vol. 3, 419.

8   These were intended "pour le service de la pucelle," which Jane Hinson, in her translation, renders as for "for young women," but "maidens" is probably closer to the original sense.

9   Sugar cost sixteen *sols* for two *livres* and presumably these were the light pounds (367 grams in Paris) typically used for spices. A *livre* of columbine ginger cost eleven *sols* and a half-*livre* of ground cinnamon was five *sols*. See Jean Bruyant et al., *Le ménagier de Paris*, vol. 2 (Paris: Impr. de Crapelet, 1846), 109–11.

10 On the emperor's visit, see "Cest la maniere comment lempereur entra a paris et fu le lundi IIII iour de Janvier lan LXXVII," Archives Départamentales du Nord v Lille, signature B 654, no. 10, 688. For the *lait lardé* recipe, see the Vatican *Viandier*: www.uni-giessen.de/gloning/tx/vi-vat.htm.

11 *Le Ménagier de Paris*, 107, 108.

12 For the Sion manuscript, see www.uni-giessen.de/gloning/tx/viandier-sion.htm; for the 1392, www.uni-giessen.de/gloning/tx/vi-vat.htm; 15th C. Viandier see www.uni-giessen.de/gloning/tx/viand15.htm.

13 Leonie Frieda, *Catherine de Medici: Renaissance Queen of France* (New York: Fourth Estate, 2003), 13; on her prodigious appetite, 145 and 382.

14 On both the Italian influence and anti-Italianism, see Henry Heller, *Anti-Italianism in Sixteenth-Century France* (Toronto: University of Toronto Press, 2003), especially 8, 10, 39, and 189.

15 Danjou and Cimber, 418.

16 *Estris* are presumably the same as the *éstrié* defined as "a kind of bread, or paste, of fine flower [sic] kneaded with water, white wine, the yolk of eggs, salt and sugar" by Randle Cotgrave, *A French and English dictionary* (London: Anthony Dolle, 1673), n.p.

17 A *livre* of ginger cost thirty-two *sols*, cinnamon forty-eight *sols*, and the sugar now cost nine *sols*; the order was for nineteen *livres*, which I am again assuming were the light pounds of 367 grams.

18 Barbara Ketcham Wheaton, *Savoring the Past* (Philadelphia: University of Pennsylvania Press, 1983), 52.

19 See the dictionary of the Académie Française and also Léopold Favre et al., *Dictionnaire historique de l'ancien langage François*, vol. 3 (Paris: Favre, 1877), 16.

20 Bonnefons, 17. Latini also has a recipe for *biscottini di Savoia* "detti quì in Napoli Mostaccere," which are basically ladyfingers, 166.

21 Domenico Romoli, *La Singolare dottrina di M. Domenico Romoli* (Venice: Gio. Battista Bonfadino, 1593), 374.

22 La Varenne, 322.

23 Pierre Richelet, *Dictionnaire françois de P. Richelet* (Geneva: Jean Jacques Dentand, 1694), see "Augmentation," 1.

24 Antonio Colmenero de Ledesma and Renée Moreau, *Du Chocolate discours curieux* (Paris: Sebastien Cramoisy, 1643), 54 (the book is a translation of the Spanish original from 1631).

25 On Marie, see J. H. Shennan, *The Bourbons* (London: Hambledon Continuum, 2007), 64–70.

26 For a statistical breakdown of sweetened foods, see Jean-Louis Flandrin, *Arranging the Meal* (Berkeley: University of California Press, 2007), 80–84. For the *Léscole* example, see the 1713 ed. published as *L'école* [sic] *parfaite des officiers de bouche* (Paris: Pierre Ribou), 393 and 464.

27 Both d'Aulnoy's and Bouchard's reaction are described in Jean-Louis Flandrin, "Dietary Choices and Culinary Technique, 1500–1800," in *Food: A Culinary History from Antiquity to the Present*, eds. Jean-Louis Flandrin, Massimo Montanari, and Albert Sonnenfeld (New York: Penguin, 2000), 410.

28 Joan E. DeJean, *The Essence of Style* (New York: Free Press, 2005), 268–70.

29 Martin Lister, *A Journey to Paris* (London: Jacob Tonson, 1699), 181.

30 Jeroen Duindam, *Vienna and Versailles* (Cambridge, England: Cambridge University Press, 2007), 172.

31 Massialot notes the date but not the year, but 1690 is the most probable choice; see *Le cuisinier roïal et bourgeois* (Paris: Prudhomme, 1705), 36–38. For a diagram of the layout of dishes, see plate 8, between pages 80 and 81.

32 *Nouvelle instructions pour les confitures, les liqueurs et les fruits* (Paris: C. de Sercy, 1698), plate after page 458.

33 L.S.R., 168.

34 Antoine Furetière, *Dictionnaire universel* (The Hague and Rotterdam: A. et R. Leers, 1690), n.p.

35 Page 501 in the 1713 edition.

36 For prices in Holland and Paris, see "The prices of the most important consumer goods, and indices of wages and the cost of living in the western part of the Netherlands, 1450–1800" and "Prices, wages and rents in Paris, 1450–1789" on the International Institute of Social History website.

37 See Bertram M. Gordon, "Chocolate in France," in *Chocolate: History, Culture and Heritage*, eds. Louis Grivetti and Howard-Yana Shapiro (Hoboken, NJ: Wiley, 2009), 570–71.

38 DeJean, 136.

39 Philippe Sylvestre Dufour, *Traitez nouveaux & curieux du café, du thé et du chocolate* (The Hague: Adrian Moetjens, 1693), 28.

40 Marie de Rabutin-Chantal Sévigné, *Lettres de Madame de Sévigné: de sa famille et de ses amis*, vol. 9 (Paris: J. J. Blaise, 1820), 328.

41 Quinzio, 60.

42 DeJean, 140.

43 Nicolas de Blégny, *Les Adresses de la ville de Paris avec le trésor des almanachs, livre commode*, vol. 1 (Paris: D. Nion, 1691), 300.

44 Thomas Corneille, *Le grand dictionnaire des arts et des sciences, M–Z* (Paris: Coignard & Coignard, 1696), 244; the 1727, 1758, 1781 editions give a similar definition, as does the 1851 edition, though there is now a reference to a "*sorbet glacée*" and a "*sarbotière*," or ice cream freezer.

45 For the original wording, see Pierre Jean Baptiste Le Grand d'Aussy, *Histoire de la vie privée des François*, vol. 3 (Paris: Simonet, 1815), 106. How you translate the phrase depends on how you interpret the punctuation and grammar. Scholars have differed on this seemingly trivial detail. *Eaux de gelées* seems straightforward enough. A contemporary French–Italian dictionary tells us that *eaux gelées* were called *acque gelate*, or "frozen waters," in Italy. It also gives as an example of usage: "to drink frozen water." So presumably these were either iced in the sense of "iced tea" or possibly the consis-

tency of a slushie, but in neither case could they be confused with ice cream. The *glaces de fruit* is where the trouble comes in. Though this could conceivably be interpreted as glazed (i.e., candied) fruit, I think that unlikely given the way the sentence is written. It is more probable that the statute is intended to mean *eaux gelées* and *eaux glacées* (or *"eaux glaces,"* as it was occasionally written), which had the clear meaning of a frozen dessert at the time.

46 *Nuovo dizzionario italiano francese e francese italiano* (Geneva: Widerhold, 1677), 389.

47 Charles Kunstler, *La vie quotidienne sous Louis XVI* (Paris: Hachette, 1950), 263-64.

48 On the newfound popularity of hard liquor, see Lister, 168.

49 Dufour, 34, 311.

50 J. J. Machet, *Le Confiseur moderne* (Paris: Chez Maradan, 1803), 89.

51 Grivetti and Shapiro, 613.

52 Dufour, 315.

53 François Massialot, *Nouvelle instruction pour les confitures, les liqueurs, et les fruits* (Paris: Charles de Sercy, 1692), 171.

54 Gillier, *Le cannameliste français* (Nancy: J. B. H. Leclerc, 1768), 105, 183.

55 L.S.R., 180.

56 The 1689 *Traité de confiture* includes a recipe for something called *"massepin soufflé,"* but this is more like today's recipe for a macaron; *Le Nouveau Confiturier* (1698, attributed—somewhat improbably—to La Varenne) calls a similar sweetmeat a *"maspin leger."*

57 The date of Carême's birth is not known with certainty; see Ian Kelly, *Cooking for Kings* (New York: Walker & Co., 2004), 32.

58 See Antonia Fraser, *Marie Antoinette* (New York: N. A. Talese/Doubleday, 2001), 135 and 418; also Edward Latham, *Famous sayings and their authors* (London: Swan Sonnenschein, 1906), 175. Oddly, the compiler misquotes Louis XVIII in the anecdote about the meat pie, substituting Marie Antoinette for the Marie Thérèse of the original text.

59 See, for example, Grimod de La Reynière, *Manuel des amphitryons* (1804 edition), 217.

60 Frances Shelley and Richard Edgcumbe, *The Diary of Frances Lady Shelley*, vol. 1 (New York: C. Scribner's, 1912), 137.

61 For this Carême quotation and the next, see Kelly, 61-62 and 100; for more on his relationship with Rothschild, see 203 and 209.

62 Wheaton, 161.

63 DeJean, 113.

64 *"Krem ze smetany"* is in *Hospodařská Pražská Kuchařka* (Prague: Cýs. král. dwořská knihtiskárna, 1820), 466; *Zitronem Gelee* are in François Le Goullon, *Der elegante Theetisch* (Vienna: Haas, 1816), 21; "Meringhe" in Vincenzo Corrado, *Il credenziere di buon gusto* (Naples: S. Giordano, 1820), 53, *compotas* in Juan de la Mata, *Arte de reposteria* (Madrid: Josef Herrera, 1786), 58-67.

65 See Bonnie G. Smith, *Ladies of the Leisure Class: The Bourgeoises of Northern France in the Nineteenth Century* (Princeton, NJ: Princeton University Press, 1981).

66 On French consumer taste at midcentury, see Whitney Walton, *France at the Crystal Palace* (Berkeley: University of California Press, 1992).

67 A. Husson and L. Foubert, "Produits de la boulangerie et de la pâtisserie," in *Exposition universelle de 1867 à Paris. Rapports du Jury international.* Tome onzième: Groupe VII. Aliments (frais ou conservés) a divers degrés de préparation—Classes 67 à 73 (Paris: Imprimerie administrative de Paul Dupont, 1868).

68 Alexandre-Balthazar-Laurent Grimod de La Reynière and Jean-François Coste, *Almanach des gourmands: servant de guide dans les moyens de faire excellente* (Paris: Maradan, 1810), 152, 227, 271.

69 The quotation is from the English translation, Jules Gouffé, *The Royal Book of Pastry and Confectionery*, trans. Alphonse Gouffé (London: Sampson Low, Marston, Low, & Searle, 1874), 2–3.

70 Ken Albala, *Eating Right in the Renaissance* (Berkeley: University of California Press, 2002), 212.

71 The translation is from Jean-Jacques Rousseau, *Émile: or, Treatise on Education*, trans. William Payne (New York and London: D. Appleton and Co., 1911), 291. The translator renders *laitage* as "milk, butter, cream," *sucreries* as "sweetmeats," *pâtisserie* as "pastry," and *entremets* as "dessert."

72 Jean Anthelme Brillat-Savarin, *Physiologie du goût*, vol. 1 (Paris: Bibliothèque Nationale, 1866), 143.

73 Victor Hugo, *Les misérables*, Lee Fahnestock, trans. (New York: New American Library, 1987), 137.

74 See "Craftsmen" on the International Institute of Social History website.

75 Grimod de la Reynière, *Almanach des gourmands* (1810), 215–16, gives two restaurant prices, one for a dinner costing two louis (twenty-four francs to a louis) and another for forty sous (two francs), which must have been a cheap place indeed; for vanilla price, see 56. For the Pierre Lacam mention, see *Le mémorial historique et géographique de la pâtisserie*, 4th ed. (Paris: chez l'auteur, 1898), 161–62. For more detail on the introduction into the Indian Ocean, see A. Delteil, *La vanille* (Paris: Augustin Challamel, 1884), 7–8.

76 *Almanach des gourmands* (1810), 273; for the pastry shop numbers, see M. Bucan, "Rapport sur les produits de la boulangerie et de la pâtisserie," in *Exposition universelle internationale de 1878 à Paris. Rapports du jury international*. GROUPE VII.—Classe 70. (Paris: Imprimerie nationale, 1880), 12.

77 Lacam, 132, 133, and 214.

78 It definitely appears in the third edition of Urbain Dubois, *Cuisine de tous les pays* (Paris: E. Dentu, 1872), 532; it may well appear as early as the 1868 edition, which I have not seen; for a custard-based variation, see Urbain Dubois, *Grand livre des pâtissiers et des confiseurs* (Paris: E. Dentu, 1883), 266.

79 Frances Sheafer Waxman, *A Shopping Guide to Paris and London* (McBride, Nast & Company, 1912), 88–89; Helen de Coulevain (writing under the pseudonym of Pierre) said much the same thing in *On the Branch* (New York: E. P. Dutton, 1910), 216 (the book was first published in French in 1903).

80 Armand Husson, *Les consommations de Paris* (Paris: Hachette et cie, 1875), 372; for tea statistics, see 419. For more on tea-drinking etiquette, see Louise Alquié de Rieusseyroux d'Alq, *Le nouveau savoir-vivre universel*, vol. 2 (Paris: Bureaux des causeries familières, 1884), 192–95; see also the introduction to Alfred Suzanne, *La cuisine anglaise et la pâtisserie: traité de l'alimentation en Angleterre* (Paris: L'Art culinaire, 1894).

81 See, for example, Alexandre Dumas, *Grand dictionnaire de cuisine* (Paris: A. Lemerre, 1873), 77; or Antoine Gogué, *La cuisine française* (Paris: L. Hachette, 1876), 44.

82 D'Alq, 82. For a more "modern" approach, see Comtesse de Tramar, *Usages mondains* (Paris: Victor-Havard, 1901), 175–76. Yet even as late as 1922, an admittedly somewhat dated edition of F. G.-M., *Manuel de politesse à l'usage de la jeunesse* (Paris: J. de Gigord, 1922), 58, had you putting dessert on the table from the beginning.

83 On Marie Antoinette, see Fraser, 393; for filled macarons, see, for example, Joseph Favre, *Dictionnaire universel de cuisine pratique* (Paris: l'auteur, 1905), 1280.

5 Schlag and Strauss

1 For Wohlfahrth's handbill and description of his premises, see Federico von Berzeviczy-Pallavicini, Gotthard Böhm, and Christian Brandstätter, *Die k.k. Hofzuckerbäckerei Demel* (Vienna: Verlag Christian Brandstätter, 1976), 10.

2 On the congress, see Duff Cooper, *Talleyrand* (Palo Alto, CA: Stanford University Press, 1932), 245; and Auguste Louis Charles La Garde-Chambonas (comte de), Albert Dresden Vandam, and Maurice Fleury, *Anecdotal recollections of the Congress of Vienna* (London: Chapman & Hall, 1902), 1–2 (the original French version was first published around 1820).

3 David King, *Vienna 1814* (New York: Harmony Books, 2008), 79.

4 *Spanische Winde* shows up in Gottlieb Rammelt, *Vermischte oekonomische Abhandlungen*, vol. 2 (Halle: Johann Gottfried Trampe, 1771), 100, as a name for a morning glory (*Convolvulus hederaceus*); for recipes, see F. G. Zenker, *Der Zuckerbäcker für Frauen mittlerer Stände* (Vienna: C. Haas, 1834), 54–58, and other contemporary books. An early mention in Christian Friedrich Germershausen, *Die Hausmutter in allen ihren Geschäfften*, vol. 5 (Leipzig: Johann Friedrich Junius, 1785), implies that they were small since they were sold by the dozen, much like meringues. For a *Russische-Torte* recipe, see Otto Julius Bierbaum, *Conditorei-Lexikon* (Strasbourg: Strassburger Druckerei und Verlagsanstalt, 1898), 467.

5 The Franz Josef quotation appears in Ann Tizia Leitich and Maria Franchy, *Wiener Zuckerbäcker: eine süsse Kulturgeschichte* (Vienna: Amalthea, 1980), 61. For a list of confectioners and the dates they acquired *Hoflieferant*, the seal of imperial patronage, see Kulturkreis Looshaus, *Der Süsse Luxus* (Vienna: Kulturkreis Looshaus, 1996), 32.

6 Duindam, 77.

7 Ingrid Haslinger, "Von Confecturn, Chocolade und Gefrornem die ehemaligen k. u. k. Hofzuckerbäcker: Die Geschichte der Zuckerbäckerei in Österreich und Ungarn," in *Der Süsse Luxus*, 12.

8 For more on the *mandoletti* sellers, see Leitich and Franchy, 41 and 44. For the later recipe, see Bierbaum, 411.

9 Ingrid Haslinger, "The Table of the Habsburgs from 1740 to 1918," unpublished lecture (2006).

10 Michael Kelly, *Reminiscences of Michael Kelly, of the King's Theatre, and Theatre Royal Drury Lane, Including a Period of Nearly Half a Century* (London: Colburn, 1826), 208.

11 Marcel Brion, *Daily Life in the Vienna of Mozart and Schubert* (New York: Macmillan, 1962), 28, 187.

12 Gallaway, 5.

13 See Olivier de Serres, *Le théâtre d'agriculture et mesnage des champs* (Paris: I. Metayer, 1600), 639. On Achard, see the Deutsches Museum website: www.deutsches-museum .de/en/exhibitions/materials-production/agriculture/sugar-refining. On Baron de Koppy, see Harvey Washington Wiley, *The Sugar-Beet Industry* (Washington, DC: Government Printing Office, 1890), 15. On production numbers, see United States, *The World's Sugar Production and Consumption, Showing the Statistical Position of Sugar at the Close of the Nineteenth Century* (Washington, DC: Government Printing Office, 1902), 2760.

14 Johann Georg Kohl, *Austria, Vienna, Hungary, Bohemia and the Danube, Galicia, Styria, Moravia, Buckovina, and the Military Frontier* (London: Chapman and Hall, 1843), 126, 205.

15 Menon still makes the distinction in 1742, but very few (if any?) French nineteenth-century sources divide up the chapters this way even if specifically *gras* (meat day) versus *maigre* (fast day) dishes are mentioned throughout the texts.

16 Karolína Vávrová, *Pražská Kuchařka* (Prague: Ant. Felkla, 1881), 408–10. I am translating *jídla moučná* as *Mehlspeisen*.

17 *Von Speisen, natuerlichen und kreuter Wein, aller verstand* (Frankfurt: 1531); see http://cs-people.bu.edu/akatlas/Speisen/recipes.html for a translation.

18 *Gazzetta universale: o sieno notizie istorice, politiche, di scienze, arti agricoltura, ec*, vol. 17 (1790), 254.

19 Prices are from Germershausen, 289 and 292. A thaler was worth some 23.4 grams of silver in the second half of the eighteenth century, while in 1781 the nominal wage for a craftsman would have been about 4.73 grams in Leipzig; see "Prices and Wages in Leipzig, 1547–1914" on the International Institute of Social History website.

20 See, respectively, G. Fr. Zenker, *Der Zuckerbäcker für Frauen mittlerer Stände* (Vienna: Haas, 1827), 190, and Zenker, *Comus-Geheimnisse über Anordnung häuslicher und öffentlicher, kleinerer und größerer Gastmahle, Pickeniks, Theezirkel [et]c*, (Vienna: Haas, 1827), 151–52; I am translating *Tunkgebäcke* as iced cookies on the suggestion of Ingrid Haslinger.

21 Magdalena Dobromila Rettigová, *Kafíčko a wsse co ge sladkého* (Prague: Jar. Pospjssil, 1845), 20–21.

22 Ulla Heise, *Coffee and Coffee-Houses* (West Chester, PA: Schiffer, 1987), 50.

23 Katharina Prato-Scheiger and Viktorine Leitmaier, *Die süddeutsche küche*, 34th ed. (Graz: Verlagsbuchhandlung "Styria," 1903), 763.

24 See Kohl, 524 and 145.

25 Gerhard Robert Walther von Coeckelberghe-Dützele, *Die K.K. Burg in Wien: ein Wegweiser für Fremde und Einheimische*, 63–64; for the dates on Milani, see Heise, 100.

26 Heise, 16 and 104.

27 Franz Maier-Bruck, *Das grosse Sacher-Kochbuch* (Munich: Schuler, 1975), 526.

28 This was certainly true in Prague at least; see O. Klauber, *Prag und Umgebungen: Praktischer führer*, vol. 26 (Berlin: W. A. Goldschmidt, 1902), 30–31.

29 The guidebook quotation is in Fr. Förster, *The Illustrated English Guide Through Vienna and Its Environs* (Vienna: A. Hölder, 1873), xii; the regulation is quoted in *Susse Luxus*, 13.

30 Bernard Dupaigne, *The History of Bread* (New York: Harry N. Abrams, 1999), 210; see also "European Delicacies," www.euroconsulting-geie.net/site/images/stories/doc/turismo/European%20delicacies.pdf.

31 For English gingerbread prices, see Arthur George Liddon Rogers, *A History of Agriculture and Prices in England*, vol. 1, 630. On Deventer gingerbread, see Gaitri Pagrach-Chandra, *Windmills in My Oven: A Book of Dutch Baking* (Totnes: Prospect, 2002), 67.

32 See Anneliese Harding, "The Edible Mass Medium—Traditional Cookie Molds of the 17th, 18th and 19th Centuries," www.cookiemold.com/CookieMolds-History.html.

33 "Linzer Torte selbst gemacht," *Oberösterreichische Nachrichten* (10 November 2007).

34 See Faißner.

35 For an online version, see www.uni-giessen.de/gloning/tx/rumpturt.htm; for a
    translation: http://clem.mscd.edu/~grasse/GK_turten1.htm.

36 See Balthasar Staindl, *Ein sehr Künstlichs vnd nutzlichs Kochbuoch* (1569), online
    access at www.uni-giessen.de/gloning/tx/staind69.htm; *Ein New Kochbuch*, c.
    1581, where they are called "turten": http://clem.mscd.edu/~grasse/GK_Rumpolt1.htm; but
    especially see the recipes in *Das Kochbuch der Sabina Welserin* (Augsburg ?, c.
    1553) with its dozens of *Torten* recipes.

37 *Ein Koch—Und Artzney-Buch*, Gedruckt zu Grätz / Bey denen Widmanstetterischen
    Erben 1686, 8–9 and 51; see the transcription at www.uni-giessen.de/gloning/tx
    /graz2.htm.

38 Massialot, 174.

39 Thirteen gulden was equivalent to 780 Kreuzer. In 1760, bread cost 3.2 kreuzen per
    kilogram, wine 2.33 pfenning per liter (4 pfenning equaled 1 Kreuzer); see A. F. Pri-
    bram, *Materialien zur Geschichte der Preise und Loehne in Oesterreich*, Band I (Carl
    Ueberreuters: Vienna, 1938); see also W. G. Clarence-Smith, *Cocoa and Chocolate,
    1765–1914* (London: Routledge, 2000), 164. Ingrid Haslinger noted to me in an e-mail
    that there were complaints about the costs.

40 *Susse Luxus*, 10–11. N.B. there is an error in the text regarding the proper weight of a
    "loth"; it is 17.5 grams, not 75 grams.

41 Neudecker; see unpaginated recipe list at the end.

42 *Susses Gold*, 58.

43 For the legal definition, see Kunz, 6. The text of the letter appears in Maier-Bruck,
    564–65. For the Sacher article, see "Der Alte Sacher," *Neues Wiener Tagblat* (20 Decem-
    ber 1906), 8–9.

44 See especially Maier-Bruck's Sacher-sanctioned *Grosse Sacher Kochbuch*, 564.

45 The American mention is in *Current Literature*, vol. 6, January–April 1891, 405. For
    the Viennese guidebook, see *Wienerstadt: Lebensbilder aus der Gegenwart* (Vienna: F.
    Temsky, 1895), 235.

46 For the earlier versions, see Scheibenbogen, 94, and Louise Seleskowitz, *Wiener Koch-
    buch* (Wien: W. Braumüller, 1908), 395. For later variations, see *Gute Küche Wiener
    Kochbuch* (Vienna: Bibliothek der *Illustrierten Kronenzeitung*, n.d. but likely between
    1918 and 1938); for online access: www.literature.at/viewer.alo?objid=12443&page=2
    &viewmode=overview; also Marie Dorninger, *Burgerliches Wiener Kochbuch* (Vienna:
    Dorninger, 1906) 418–19.

47 See the Supreme court decision of 11 November 1958, no. 4Ob321/58, accessible
    online at: www.ris.bka.gv.at/Dokument.wxe?Abfrage=Justiz&Dokumentnummer
    =JJT_19581111_OGH0002_0040OB00321_5800000_000.

48 See Peter Pöch, "Austria," in Dennis Campbell and Susan Cotter, *Unfair Trading
    Practices* (London: Kluwer Law International, 1997), 33; and ÖBl [Austrian Supreme
    Court] 1963, 6.

49 The numbers are from the hotel's promotional material; the information about the
    secretiveness of the recipe is from an interview with Christine Koza, the hotel's PR
    representative, on December 11, 2008.

50 For a nuanced analysis of the relationship of the Viennese middle class to the arts, see
    Carl E. Schorske, *Fin-de-Siècle Vienna* (New York: Knopf, 1979), 5–10.

51 See recipe for "Panama Torta" in *Živena: časopis pre kultúrne a ženské záujmy* (March
    1911), 71.

52 See the many recipes in Sophie Meissner, *Modernes Kochbuch* (Wien: A. Hartleben, 1901).

53 George Lang, *The Cuisine of Hungary* (Atheneum: New York, 1982), 61–63.

6 A Democracy of Sweetness

1 Hershey's net sales in 2006: $4,944.2 million according to the 2006 "Annual Report to Stockholders"; kiss numbers are from the Hershey's website: www.hersheys.com/kisses /about/making.asp.

2 USDA; the statistics are for 2010. See "Table 20a—U.S. sugar deliveries for human consumption by type of user, calendar year" on the USDA Economic Research Service website: www.ers.usda.gov/Briefing/sugar/Data.htm.

3 Wendy A. Woloson, *Refined Tastes* (Baltimore: Johns Hopkins University Press, 2002), 74.

4 Michael Krondl, *Around the American Table* (Holbrook, MA: Adams, 1995), 85.

5 Karo website: www.karosyrup.com/history.asp; for more background on corn syrup, see Betty Fussell, *The Story of Corn* (New York: Knopf, 1992), 269.

6 Laura Ingalls Wilder, *Little House on the Prairie* (New York: HarperCollins, 2006 [first edition was 1935]), 204.

7 William Weeks Hall and Morris Raphael, *The Weeks Hall Tapes* (New Iberia, LA: M. Raphael Books, 1983), 38–39.

8 Michael G. Wade, *Sugar Dynasty: M. A. Patout & Son, Ltd., 1791–1993* (Lafayette, LA: Center for Louisiana Studies, University of Southwestern Louisiana, 1995), 77.

9 Stephen Schmidt, "Cakes," in *Encyclopedia of Food and Drink in America* (Oxford, England: Oxford University Press, 2004), 60.

10 See, for example, the transparent pudding recipe in John Farley, *The London Art of Cookery* (London: J. Scatcherd and J. Whitaker, 1787), 189. An early mention of chess pie appears in *American Agriculturist*, vol. 25 (October 1866), 342.

11 See the much enlarged 1888 edition: Mrs. Beeton (Isabella Mary), *The Book of Household Management* (London, New York: Ward, Lock & Co., 1888), 849 and 1260.

12 Thomas Mawe and John Abercrombie, *The Universal Gardener and Botanist* (London: G. Robinson, 1778), entry under pompion n.p.

13 Hannah Woolley, *The Queen-Like Closet* (London: R. Lowndes, 1672), 227.

14 See, for example, Richard Briggs, *The English Art of Cookery* (London: G.G.J. and J. Robinson, 1788).

15 Richard Bradley, *The country housewife and lady's director* (London: R. Bradley, 1732), 108.

16 Louis Antoine Godey and Sarah Josepha Buell Hale, eds., *Godey's Lady's Book and Magazine*, vols. 62–63 (1861), 555.

17 Amelia Simmons, *American Cookery* (Hartford: Hudson & Goodwin, 1796), 43.

18 See Noah Webster, *An American Dictionary of the English Language* (Springfield, MA: G. and C. Merriam, 1848), 106.

19 In Alphonse's translations of his brother Jules Gouffé's books, the former was listed as Victoria's head pastry cook.

20 For the weight, see "Scraps of News," *Latter-Day Saints' Millennial Star,* vol. 33 (28 March 1871), 207. "The Royal Marriage," *New York Times* (March 22, 1871), mentions the fact that there were "two immense wedding cakes" but offers no other details.

21 Estelle Woods Wilcox, *Practical Housekeeping* (Minneapolis: Buckeye Publishing Co., 1883), 360.

22 Christian Isobel Johnstone, *The Cook and Housewife's Manual* (London: Simpkin, Marshall, 1847), 534.

23 Both this quote and the next are in Woloson, 176 and 169.

24 *The Gentleman's Magazine,* vol. 102, part 2 (December 1832), 492.

25 "Victorian Royal Wedding Cake Sale," BBC website (16 April 2009): http://news.bbc.co.uk/2/hi/uk_news/england/west_midlands/8003074.stm.

26 Eggs were twelve cents per dozen in Vermont in 1850, wages sixty-seven cents per day including board; see "Vermont 1780–1943" on the Global Price and Income History Group website.

27 Footnote: Gouffé, 75.

28 Washington Irving, *A history of New-York*, vol. 1 (Philadelphia: Inskeep and Bradford, 1812), 157; for the English doughnut reference, see William Hone, *The Year Book of Daily Recreation and Information* (London: T. Tegg, 1832), 1592.

29 "'Old Salt' Doughnut Hole Inventor Tells Just How Discovery Was Made and Stomach of Earths Saved," *Washington Post* (6 March 1916), ES9.

30 Frank Moore, *The Rebellion Record*, vol. 2 (New York: Putnam, 1862), 78.

31 Marion Harland, *Common Sense in the Household* (New York: Scribner, Armstrong & Co., 1873), 312.

32 For early American sugar statistics, see Alfred S. Eichner, *The Emergence of Oligopoly* (Baltimore: Johns Hopkins University Press, 1969), 28.

33 Harland, 20.

34 Weeks Hall, 42.

35 Laura Ingalls Wilder, *First Four Years* (New York: Harper & Row, 1971), 13.

36 Literacy rates among white women were about 50 percent at the start of the nineteenth century, 90 percent in 1870. See Catherine Hobbs, *Nineteenth-Century Women Learn to Write* (Charlottesville: University of Virginia Press, 1995), 2. In France, comparable figures were 28 percent in 1801 and 52 percent in the early 1850s; see endnote, Alison Finch, *Women's Writing in Nineteenth-Century France* (Cambridge, England: Cambridge University Press, 2000), 265.

37 Susan Marks, *Finding Betty Crocker* (New York: Simon & Schuster, 2005), 168, 170; for the ad, see "BettyCrocker2.mpg" on the Internet Archive website: www.archive.org/details/ ThreeClassic1950sBettyCrockerCakeMixCommercials.

38 Woloson, 120.

39 On sex and chocolate candy in America, see Woloson, 13, 128, and 130.

40 For more on the Bakers, see the Bostonian Society, *Sweet History: Dorchester and the Chocolate Factory* (2005), online access at www.bostonhistory.org/bakerschocolate. On the slave owners, see 24, on the advertising blitz, 10–12.

41 See Eliza Leslie, *The Lady's Receipt-Book* (Philadelphia: Carey and Hart, 1847).

42 On Hershey, see Katherine Binney Shippen and Paul A. W. Wallace, *Milton S. Hershey* (Hershey, PA: Milton Hershey School, 1973), 9; the *Once a Week* quotation and the Henrion numbers are, respectively, in Woloson, 36 and 33.

43 On the product line, see Frank A. Kennedy, "The Biscuit Industry," in *One Hundred Years of American Commerce*, vol. 2 (New York: Haynes, 1895), 625; on marshmallows, see Tim Richardson, *Sweets* (Bloomsbury, NY: Bloomsbury, 2002), 213.

44 Woloson, 7.

45 Stanley L. Engerman and Robert E. Gallman, *The Cambridge Economic History of the United States: The Long Nineteenth Century* (New York: Cambridge University Press, 2000), 211.

46 Woloson, 55.

47 Michael D'Antonio, *Hershey: The Extraordinary Life of Wealth, Empire, and Utopian Dreams* (Simon and Schuster, 2006), 54. On the ingredients in the caramels, see Paul Wallace, *Milton S. Hershey* (Hershey's archives, manuscript), 97.

48 Shippen and Wallace, 16.

49 There is some confusion about whether this happened in 1875 or 1876. I'm going with the later date based on, among others, Robin Dand, *The International Cocoa Trade* (Cambridge, England: Woodhead, 1995), 13.

50 Joël Glenn Brenner, *The Emperors of Chocolate* (New York: Random House, 1999), 111.

51 Woloson, 120.

52 Superman shilled in a comic book rather than on TV.

53 See "Mickey's Surprise Party" (1939) on YouTube: www.youtube.com/watch?v =aXqq7HKvm38.

54 See *Scribner's Magazine* (June 1892), 27.

55 "Cake Mixes: CU's consultants tasted and examined ready-mix cakes to find which brands were best," *Consumer Reports* (September 1953), 385–87; quoted on the Food Timeline website: www.foodtimeline.org/foodcakes.html#aboutcakemixes.

56 For Royal baking powder and Baker's cocoa, see *Journal of Home Economics* (December 1920), 4, 13; for Crisco, see Truman Armstrong De Weese, *The Principles of Practical Publicity* (Philadelphia: George W. Jacobs, 1908), 163; for Campfire marshmallows, see *Boys' Life* (June 1925), 57; for Kingsford cornstarch, see *American Magazine* (October 1910), 116.

57 Harland, 350.

58 For the quotation, see Mary J. Lincoln, *Mrs. Lincoln's Boston Cook Book* (Boston: Roberts Brothers, 1895), vii; for the menu, Laura Shapiro, *Perfection Salad* (New York: Random House, 2001), 63.

59 Becky Mercuri, "Cookies," in *Encyclopedia of Food and Drink in America* (Oxford, England: Oxford University Press, 2004), 318. The first peanut butter cookie mention I have been able to find shows up in Frances Elizabeth Stewart, *Lessons in Cookery* (Chicago, New York: Rand McNally & Co., 1918), 131. Pillsbury's *Balanced Recipes* contains a recipe for Peanut Butter Balls made much like they are today; see What's Cooking America website: http://whatscookingamerica.net/History/CookieHistory.htm.

60 Nancy K. Young, *The Great Depression in America: A Cultural Encyclopedia* (Westport, CT: Greenwood, 2007), 126.

61 Glenn R. Conrad, *New Iberia: Essays on the Town and Its People* (Lafayette: Center for Louisiana Studies, University of Southwestern Louisiana, 1979), 438.

62 See, for example, Estelle Woods Wilcox, *The New Practical Housekeeping* (Minneapolis: Home Publishing Co., 1890), 73.

63 Interview with *Good Housekeeping* food editor Susan Westmoreland, October 2007.

Finale

1 The source on the price of *macarons* is "Fauchon Beijing" on Off & On blog: http://mooyong.blogspot.com/2008/07/fauchon-beijing.html; wage data is from "Beijing workers' average annual wage income," *China Financial Daily*, 25 March 2009.

2 See Alexandra Marshall, "Paris Sweets: Ceci N'est Pas un Macaron," *New York Times*, 20 April 2010.

SELECTED BIBLIOGRAPHY

———⊗⊗⊗———

The following texts do not by any means include all the sources I consulted; they are, however, crucial to understanding the subject. For a more comprehensive list, see the endnotes. Many of the books, especially those published before 1910 or so, are now available online. Google Books is invaluable, and so are the digitized collections of the French Bibliothèque Nationale (http://gallica.bnf.fr). Another resource worth looking at is the online collection of the University of Barcelona library (www.bib.ub.edu /fileadmin/imatges/llibres/grewe.htm). The Czech National Library is also gradually digitizing its nineteenth-century collection (http://kramerius.nkp.cz). For predominantly German texts, see Thomas Gloning's remarkable website: www.uni-giessen.de /gloning/kobu.htm. Finally, both Global Price and Income History Group (http://gpih .ucdavis.edu/index.htm) and the International Institute of Social History (http://iisg.nl/hpw /data.php) have terrific collections of databases on food prices and wages around the world.

Abul-Fazl, 'Allami, H. Blochmann, and H. S. Jarrett. *The Ain I Akbari.* Calcutta: Baptist Mission Press, 1873.

Achaya, K. T. *A Historical Dictionary of Indian Food.* Delhi and New York: Oxford University Press, 1998.

———. *Indian Food: A Historical Companion.* Delhi: Oxford University Press, 1994.

Albertano, Jean, Jean Bruyant, Jean Renault, and Julia P. Wightman. *Le ménagier de Paris: traité de morale et d'économie domestique.* Paris: Impr. de Crapelet, 1846.

Ambrosini, Daniela. "Les honneurs sucrés de Venise." In *Le boire et le manger au XVIe siècle: actes du XIe colloque du Puy-en-Velay,* ed. Marie Viallon-Schoneveld, 267–84. Saint-Etienne: Publ. de l'Univ. de Saint-Etienne, 2004.

Arundhati, P. *Royal Life in Mānasôllāsa.* New Delhi: Sundeep Prakashan, 1994.

Athenaeus, and Charles Burton Gulick. *The Deipnosophists.* Volume VI. London: W. Heinemann, 1927.

Audiger. *La Maison réglée et l'art de diriger la maison d'un grand seigneur et autres . . . avec la véritable méthode de faire toutes sortes d'essences, d'eaux et de liqueurs . . .* Amsterdam: P. Marret, 1700.

Banerjee, Sumanta. *The Parlour and the Streets: Elite and Popular Culture in Nineteenth Century Calcutta.* Calcutta: Seagull Books, 1989.

Banerji, Chitrita. *Eating India: An Odyssey into the Food and Culture of the Land of Spices.* New York: Bloomsbury, 2007.

———. *Land of Milk and Honey: Travels in the History of Indian Food.* Oxford, England: Seagull Books, 2007.

Basu, Tara Krishna, Richard Stevenson, Tara Krishna Basu, and Basanta Coomar Bose. *Village Life in Bengal.* Philadelphia: Xlibris, 2004.

Batmanglij, Najmieh. *New Food of Life.* Bloomington, IN: 1stBooks, 2003.

Beecher, Catharine Esther. *Miss Beecher's Domestic Receipt-Book Designed as a Supplement to Her Treatise on Domestic Economy.* New York: Harper, 1850.

Bernier, François. *Voyages de François Bernier.* Paris: imprimé aux frais du gouvernement four procurer du travail aux ouvriers typographes, 1830. Reprint of 1699 Amsterdam edition.

Berzeviczy-Pallavicini, Federico von, Gotthard Böhm, and Christian Brandstätter. *Die k.k. Hofzuckerbäckerei Demel: Ein Wiener Märchen.* Vienna: Verlag Christian Brandstätter, 1976.

Bhattacharya, Tania, Anindita Mitra, and Suktara Ghosh. "Sweet talk," *The (Kolkata) Telegraph.* 4 October 2008.

Bierbaum, Otto Julius. *Conditorei-Lexikon: Alphabetisches Hand- und Nachschlagebuch über alle Erzeugnisse der Conditorei und verwandter Branchen für Conditoren, Fein-, und Pastetenbäcker, Lebküchler und Hausfrauen.* Strasbourg: Strassburger Druckerei und Verlagsanstalt, 1898.

Black, Jane. "The Trail of Tiramisu." *Washington Post.* 11 July 2007.

Bose, Chunder Shib. *The Hindoos as They Are: A Description of the Manners, Customs, and Inner Life of Hindoo Society in Bengal.* Calcutta: Thacker, Spink and Co., 1883.

Bose, Pramatha Nath. *A History of Hindu Civilisation During British Rule.* Vol II. Calcutta: W. Newman & Co., 1894.

Bose, Shib Chunder. *The Hindoos as They Are: A Description of the Manners, Customs, and Inner Life of Hindoo Society in Bengal.* Calcutta: Thacker, Spink and Co., 1883.

The Bostonian Society. *Sweet History: Dorchester and the Chocolate Factory.* 2005. www.bostonhistory.org/bakerschocolate.

Bottéro, Jean. "The Cuisine of Ancient Mesopotamia." *The Biblical Archaeologist,* vol. 48, no. 1 (March 1985), 36–47.

Brion, Marcel. *Daily Life in the Vienna of Mozart and Schubert.* New York: Macmillan, 1962.

Camporesi, Piero. *The Magic Harvest: Food, Folklore, and Society.* Cambridge, England: Polity Press, 1993.

Carême, Marie Antonin. *Le Pâtissier Royal Parisien, Ou Traité Élémentaire Et Pratique De La Pâtisserie Ancienne Et Moderne.* Second edition. Paris: chez l'Auteur, 1828.

Chakravarti, Taponath. *Food and Drink in Ancient Bengal.* Calcutta: K. L. Mukhopadhyay, 1959.

Chakravarty, Indira. *Saga of Indian Food: A Historical and Cultural Survey.* New Delhi: Sterling Publishers, 1972.

Conrad, Glenn R. *New Iberia: Essays on the Town and Its People.* Lafayette: Center for Louisiana Studies, University of Southwestern Louisiana, 1979.

Conrad, Glenn R., and Ray F. Lucas. *White Gold: A Brief History of the Louisiana Sugar Industry, 1795–1995.* Louisiana life series, no. 8. Lafayette, LA: Center for Louisiana Studies, University of Southwestern Louisiana, 1995.

D'Alq, Louise Alquié de Rieusseyroux. *Le nouveau savoir-vivre universel.* Volume 2. Paris: Bureaux des causeries familières, 1884.

D'Antonio, Michael. *Hershey: Milton S. Hershey's Extraordinary Life of Wealth, Empire, and Utopian Dreams.* New York: Simon & Schuster, 2006.

Dasgupta, Minakshie, Bunny Gupta, and Jaya Chaliha. *The Calcutta Cookbook: A Treasury of over 200 Recipes from Pavement to Palace.* New Delhi, India: Penguin Books, 1995.

David, Elizabeth, and Jill Norman. *Harvest of the Cold Months: The Social History of Ice and Ices.* New York: Viking, 1995.

Deerr, Noël. *The History of Sugar.* London: Chapman and Hall, 1949.

DeJean, Joan E. *The Essence of Style: How the French Invented High Fashion, Fine Food, Chic Cafés, Style, Sophistication, and Glamour.* New York: Free Press, 2005.

"Der Alte Sacher," *Neues Wiener Tagblat.* 20 December 1906: 8–9.

Dickie, John. *Delizia!: The Epic History of the Italians and Their Food.* New York: Free Press, 2008.

Duindam, Jeroen. *Vienna and Versailles.* New studies in European history. Cambridge: Cambridge University Press, 2007.

Dupaigne, Bernard. *The History of Bread.* New York: Harry N. Abrams, 1999.

Dutta, Krishna. *Calcutta: A Cultural and Literary History.* Cities of the Imagination. New York: Interlink Books, 2003.

Faißner, Waltraud. *Wie mann die Linzer Dortten macht: historische Rezepte zur "Linzer Torte" aus der Kochbuchsammlung der Bibliothek des Oberösterreichischen Landesmuseums.* Studien zur Kulturgeschichte von Oberösterreich, Bd. 13. Weitra: Bibliothek der Provinz, 2004.

Ferguson, Priscilla Parkhurst. *Accounting for Taste: The Triumph of French Cuisine.* Chicago: University of Chicago Press, 2004.

Ferro-Luzzi, Gabriella Eichinger. "Ritual as Language: The Case of South Indian Food Offerings." *Current Anthropology,* vol. 18, no. 3 (September 1977), 507–14.

"Festin donné à la royne Catherine au logis episcopal de l'évesché de Paris, le dix-neuvieme jour de jouing 1549," in Félix Danjou and L. Cimber, eds., *Archives curieuses de l'histoire de France,* series I, volume 3.

Flandrin, Jean Louis. *Arranging the Meal: A History of Table Service in France.* California Studies in Food and Culture, 19. Berkeley: University of California Press, 2007.

Galloway, J. H. *The Sugar Cane Industry: An Historical Geography from Its Origins to 1914.* Cambridge studies in historical geography, 12. Cambridge [England]: Cambridge University Press, 1989.

Germershausen, Christian Friedrich. *Die Hausmutter in allen ihren Geschäfften.* Volume 5. Leipzig: Johann Friedrich Junius, 1785.

Ghose, Nand Lal. *A Guide for Indian Females from Infancy to Old Age, Comprising Manners, Customs Rules, & C.* Lahore: Sant Singh Luther Oriental Press, 1896.

Gilliers. *Le cannameliste français, ou nouvelle instruction pour ceux qui desirent d'apprendre l'office: rédigé en forme de dictionnaire.* Nancy: J. B. H. Leclerc, 1768.

Gouffé, Jules. *The Royal Book of Pastry and Confectionery.* London: Sampson Low, Marston, Low & Searle, 1874.

Grimod de La Reynière, Alexandre-Balthazar-Laurent, and Jean-François Coste. *Alman-ach des gourmands, servant de guide dans les moyens de faire excellente chère*. Paris: Maradan, 1804.

Grimod de La Reynière, Alexandre-Balthazar-Laurent. *Manuel des amphitryons*. Paris : Capelle et Renand, 1808.

Grivetti, Louis, and Howard-Yana Shapiro. *Chocolate: History, Culture, and Heritage*. Hobo-ken, NJ: Wiley, 2009.

Hackert, Fritz. "Cafes, Feuilletons, and Cabarets in Vienna 1900." In *Vienna: The World of Yesterday, 1889–1914*, ed. Stephen Eric Bronner and F. Peter Wagner, 20–32. Amherst, NY: Humanity Books, 1999.

Hagger, Conrad. *Neues saltzburgisches Koch-Buch, für hochfürstliche und andere vornehme Höfe, Clöster . . . wie auch für einschichtige, gesund und krancke Persoënen . . . mit mehr dann 2500. Speisen, und 318. in schönen Kupffergestochenen Formen . . . Bestehend aus 4. Theilen, in 8. Büchern eingetheilt*. Augsburg: J. J. Lotter, 1718.

Hall, William Weeks, and Morris Raphael. *The Weeks Hall Tapes*. New Iberia, LA: M. Raphael Books, 1983.

Hamilton, Alexander. *A New Account of the East Indies*. Edinburgh: John Mossman, 1727.

Hansgirgová, Františka. *Nová česká kuchařka, aneb, Navedení ku připravování všelikých pokrmů, hodících se pro skrovnou i skvostnější domácnost*. Prague: I. L. Kober, 1864.

Harland, Marion. *Common Sense in the Household: A Manual of Practical Housewifery*. New York: Scribner, Armstrong & Co., 1873.

Hellerstein, Erna Olafson. *Women, Social Order, and the City Rules for French Women, 1830–1870*. Dissertation, University of California at Berkeley, 1980.

Heise, Ulla. *Coffee and Coffee-Houses*. West Chester, PA: Schiffer, 1987.

Hess, Karen. *Martha Washington's Booke of Cookery: And Booke of Sweetmeats: Being a Fam-ily Manuscript, Curiously Copied by an Unknown Hand Sometime in the Seventeenth Century, Which Was in Her Keeping from 1749, the Time of Her Marriage to Daniel Curtis, to 1799, at Which Time She Gave It to Eleanor Parke Curtis, Her Granddaughter, on the Occasion of Her Marriage to Lawrence Lewis*. New York: Columbia University Press, 1995.

Hyman, Mary. "The Apothecary's Table." *Slow: The International Herald of Taste*. Issue no. 16, January–March 2000.

Ibn Sayyār al-Warrāq, al-Muzaffar ibn Nasr, Nawal Nasrallah, Kaj Öhrnberg, and Sahbān Murūwah. *Annals of the Caliphs' Kitchens: Ibn Sayyār Al-Warrāq's Tenth-Century Baghdadi Cookbook*. Leiden: Brill, 2007.

Ibn al-Karīm, Muḥammad ibn al-Ḥasan, and Charles Perry. *A Baghdad Cookery Book: The Book of Dishes (Kitāb Al-Ṭabīkh)*. Petits Propos Culinaires, 79. Totnes: Prospect, 2005.

Işın, Priscilla Mary. *Gülbeşeker: Türk Tatlıları Tarihi*. Second edition. Istanbul: Yapı Kredi Yayınları, 2009.

James, Glyn. *Sugarcane*. Oxford: Blackwell Science, 2004.

Kale, Steven D. *French Salons: High Society and Political Sociability from the Old Regime to the Revolution of 1848*. Baltimore: Johns Hopkins University Press, 2004.

Kelly, Ian. *Cooking for Kings: The Life of Antonin Carême, the First Celebrity Chef*. New York: Walker & Co., 2004.

Kohl, Johann Georg. *Austria, Vienna, Hungary, Bohemia and the Danube, Galicia, Styria, Moravia, Buckovina, and the Military Frontier*. London: Chapman and Hall, 1843.

Kulturkreis Looshaus. *Der süsse Luxus: die Hofzuckerbäckerei und die ehemaligen K.U.K. Hofzuckerbäcker: eine Ausstellung des Kulturkreises Looshaus*. Vienna: Kulturkreis Looshaus, 1996.

Kunz, Friedrich. "Die Sachertorte—ein süßer Mythos aus Wien." In *BMI Aktuell*, September 2005, 4–7. www.backmittelinstitut.de/255-0-die-sachertorte.html.

L.S.R., Pierre de Lune, and Audiger. *L'Art de la cuisine française au XVIIe siècle: L.S.R., l'art de bien traiter. Pierre de Lune, le cuisinier. Audiger, la maison réglée.* Les grands classiques de la gastronomie. Paris: Editions Payot & Rivages, 1995.

Lacam, Pierre. *Le mémorial historique et géographique de la pâtisserie, contenant 2,200 recettes de pâtisserie, glaces & liqueurs, orné de gravures dans le texte.* 4th edition. Paris: En vente chez l'auteur, 1898.

Latini, Antonio. *Lo scalco alla moderna.* Lodi: Bibliotheca culinaria, 1993.

Lancelot de Casteau. *Ouverture de Cuisine.* Liège: Leonard Streel, 1604. www.uni-giessen.de /gloning/tx/ouv3.htm.

Lansdale, Maria Hornor. *Vienna and the Viennese.* Philadelphia: H. T. Coates & Co., 1902.

La Varenne, François Pierre de, and Terence Scully. *La Varenne's Cookery: The French Cook; the French Pastry Chef; the French Confectioner.* Blackawton, Totnes, UK: Prospect Books, 2006.

Le Goullon, François. *Der elegante Theetisch oder die Kunst, einen glänzenden Zirkel auf eine geschmackvolle und anständige Art ohne grossen Aufwand zu bewirthen.* Vienna: Haas, 1816.

Leitich, Ann Tizia, and Maria Franchy. *Wiener Zuckerbäcker: eine süsse Kulturgeschichte.* Vienna: Amalthea, 1980.

Le pastissier françois. Paris: Jean Gaillard, 1653.

Leslie, Eliza. *New Receipts for Cooking.* Philadelphia: T. B. Peterson, 1854.

Leslie, Eliza. *The Lady's Receipt-Book: A Useful Companion for Large or Small Families.* Philadelphia: Carey and Hart, 1847.

Leslie, Eliza. *Seventy-Five Receipts for Pastry, Cakes, and Sweetmeats.* Boston: Munroe and Francis, 1832.

Liénard, Pierre, François Duthu, and Claire Hauguel. *Moi, Nicolas Stohrer, pâtissier du Roi, rue Montorgueil, au pied de Saint-Eustache, à Paris.* Paris: Lattès, 1999.

Limet, Henri. "The Cuisine of Ancient Sumer." *Biblical Archaeologist*, vol. 50, no. 3 (September 1987), 132–47.

Lister, Martin. *A Journey to Paris in the Year 1698.* London: Jacon Tonson, 1699.

Magne, Émile. *La vie quotidienne au temps de Louis XIII.* Paris: Hachette, 1942.

Maier-Bruck, Franz. *Das grosse Sacher-Kochbuch: die österreichische. Küche.* Munich: Schuler, 1975.

Martin, Robert Montgomery. *The History, Antiquities, Topography, and Statistics of Eastern India Comprising the Districts of Behar, Shahabad, Bhagulpoor, Goruckpoor, Dinajepoor, Puraniya, Rungpoor, & Assam, in Relation to Their Geology, Mineralogy, Botany, Agriculture, Commerce, Manufactures, Fine Arts, Population, Religion, Education, Statistics, Etc.* London: W. H. Allen and Co., 1838.

Martin, Robert Montgomery. *History of the British Colonies.* London: J. Cochrane and Co., 1834.

———. *Statistics of the Colonies of the British Empire in the West Indies, South America, North America, Asia, Austral-Asia, Africa, and Europe.* London: W. H. Allen and Co., 1839.

Martino. "Libro de arte coquinaria." In *Arte della cucina. Libri di ricette, testi sopra lo scalco, i trincianti e i vini. Dal XIV al XIX secolo.* A cura di Emilio Faccioli. Vol. 1. Milano, 1966, 115–204.

Massialot, François. *Nouvelle instruction pour les confitures, les liqueurs, et les fruits: avec la maniere de bien ordonner un dessert, & tout le reste qui est du devoir des maîtres d'hôtels, sommeliers, confiseurs, & autres officiers de bouche : suite du Cuisinier roïal & bourgeois: egalement utile dans les familles, pour sçavoir ce qu'on sert de plus à la mode dans les repas, & en d'autres occasions.* Second edition. Paris: Charles de Sercy, 1698.

————. *Nouvelle instruction pour les confitures, les liqueurs, et les fruits: où l'on apprend à confire toute sorte de fruits, tant secs que liquides & divers ouvrages de sucre qui sont du fait des officiers & confiseurs, avec la maniere de bien ordoner un fruit: suite du Nouveau cuisinier royal & bourgeois, également utile aux maître-d'hôtels & dans les familles pour sçavoir ce qu'on sere de plus à la mode dans les repas.* Paris: Claude Prudhomme, 1716.

Mendosa, Gilda. *The Best of Goan Cooking.* New Delhi, India: UBS Publishers' Distributors, 2004.

Menon. *La science du maître d'hôtel confiseur: à l'usage des officiers, avec des observations sur la connaissance et les propriétés des fruits . . . suite du Maître d'hôtel cuisinier.* Paris: Paulus-Du-Mesnil, 1750.

————. *La science du maître d'hôtel cuisinier, avec des observations sur la connaissance et propriété des alimens.* Paris: Chez Paulus-Du-Mesnil, 1749.

Messisbugo, Cristoforo di. *Banchetti compositioni di vivande, et apparecchio generale.* Ferrara: Giovanni de Buglhat and Antonio Hucher Compagni, 1549.

Molmenti, Pompeo, and Horatio F. Brown. *Venice, Its Individual Growth from the Earliest Beginnings to the Fall of the Republic.* Chicago: A. C. McClurg & Co., 1907.

Nasrallah, Nawal. *Delights from the Garden of Eden: A Cookbook and a History of the Iraqi Cuisine.* Bloomington, IN: 1stBooks, 2003.

Neubauer, Leopold. *Widenská Kuchařská Knjha, aneb Ponáwrženj, gak se Massyté a Postnj Gjdla bez welkého Nákladu, a wssak předce od dobré Chutj připrawitj mohau.* Brno: Jan Jiří Gastl, 1792.

Neudecker, Maria A. *Die Baierische Köchinn in Böhmen: Ein Buch, das sowohl für Herrschafts-, als auch für gemeine Küchen eingerichtet ist, und mit besonderem Nutzen gebraucht werden kann.* Salzburg: Mayer, 1819.

Parmar, Pramila. *Mithai: A Collection of Traditional Indian Sweets.* New Delhi, India: UBSPD, 1994.

Prato, Katharina. *Die süddeutsche Küche auf ihrem gegenwärtigen Standpunkte.* Graz: Verlags-Buchhandlung "Styria," 1890.

Preston, Matt. "Sugar and Spice," *The Age,* 14 October 2003.

Quinzio, Jeri. *Of Sugar and Snow: A History of Ice Cream Making.* Berkeley: University of California Press, 2009.

Redon, Odile, Françoise Sabban, and Silvano Serventi. *The Medieval Kitchen: Recipes from France and Italy.* Chicago: University of Chicago Press, 1998.

Rettigová, Magdalena Dobromila. *Kafíčko a wsse co ge sladkého.* Prague: Jar. Pospjssil, 1845.

Richardson, Tim. *Sweets.* Bloomsbury, NY: Bloomsbury, 2002.

Rodison, Maxime, A. J. Arberry, Charles Perry, and Claudia Roden. *Medieval Arab Cookery.* Blackawton, Devon: Prospect Books, 2001.

Romoli, Domenico. *La Singolare dottrina di M. Domenico Romoli.* Venice: Gio. Battista Bonfadino, 1593.

Rose, H. A. "Hindu Betrothal Observances in the Punjab," *Journal of the Royal Anthropological Institute of Great Britain and Ireland,* vol. 38 (July–December 1908), 409–18.

Rose, H. A. "Hindu Birth Observances in the Punjab," *Journal of the Royal Anthropological Institute of Great Britain and Ireland,* vol. 37 (July–December 1907), 220–36, and vol. 38 (July–December 1908), 409–18.

Rose, H. A. "Muhammadan Betrothal Observances in the Punjab," *Man,* vol. 17 (April 1917), 58–62, and (June 1917), 91–97.

————. "Muhammadan Birth Observances in the Punjab," *Journal of the Royal Anthropological Institute of Great Britain and Ireland*, vol. 37 (July–December 1907), 237–60.

Rumpolt, Marx. *Ein new Kochbuch*. Frankfurt: J. Feyerabendt, 1581.

Ruscelli, Girolamo. *Les Secrets de reverend Signeur Alexis Piemontois. Traduit d'Italien en françois*. Antwerp: Plantin, 1557.

Sabban, Françoise, and Silvano Serventi. *La gastronomie au Grand siècle: 100 recettes de France et d'Italie*. Paris: Stock, 1998.

Sangar, Satya Prakash. *Food and Drinks in Mughal India*. New Delhi: Reliance, 1999.

Scappi, Bartomoleo. *Opera di M. Bartolomeo Scappi, cuoco secreto di Papa Pio V diuisa in sei libri*. Venice: Michele Tramezzino, 1570.

Scappi, Bartolomeo, and Terence Scully. *The Opera of Bartolomeo Scappi (1570): l'arte et prudenza d'un maestro cuoco*. Toronto: University of Toronto Press, 2008.

Scheibenbogen, Antoine. *Cuisine et pâtisserie austro-hongroises*. Paris: L'auteur, 1896. Reprint, Nîmes: C. Lacour, 1993.

Sen, Colleen Taylor. *Food Culture in India*. Food Culture Around the World. Westport, CT: Greenwood Press, 2004.

Shapiro, Laura. *Perfection Salad*. New York: Random House, 2001.

Sherring, M. A. *Hindu Tribes and Castes*. Calcutta: Thacker, Spink & Co., 1872.

Shippen, Katherine Binney, and Paul A. W. Wallace. *Milton S. Hershey*. Hershey, PA: Milton Hershey School, 1973.

Silva, António. *Doçaria conventual portuguesa*. Lisbon: Texto Editores, 2005.

Simmons, Amelia. *American Cookery, or, The Art of Dressing Viands, Fish, Poultry, and Vegetables: And the Best Modes of Making Pastes, Puffs, Pies, Tarts, Puddings, Custards, and Preserves: and All Kinds of Cakes, from the Imperial Plumb to Plain Cake, Adapted to This Country, and All Grades of Life*. Hartford, CT: Printed by Hudson & Goodwin for the author, 1796.

Smith, Andrew F. *Encyclopedia of Food and Drink in America*. Oxford, England: Oxford University Press, 2004.

Tanara, Vincenzo. *L'Economia Del Cittadino in Villa*. Venice: Bertani, 1661.

Terry, Edward. *A Voyage to East-India; Wherein Some Things Are Taken Notice of, in Our Passage Thither, but Many More in Our Abode There, Within That Rich and Most Spacious Empire of the Great Mogul: Mixt with Some Parallel Observations and Inferences Upon the Story, to Profit As Well As Delight the Reader*. London: J. Wilkie, 1777.

Tibone, Maria Luisa, and Lidia Cardino. *Il confetturiere piemontese*. Sala Bolognese: A. Forni, 1995.

Toussaint-Samat, Maguelonne. *A History of Food*. Cambridge, MA: Blackwell Reference, 1993.

————. *La très belle et très exquise histoire des gâteaux et des friandises*. Paris: Flammarion, 2004.

Unger, Friedrich, and Priscilla Mary Işin. *A King's Confectioner in the Orient: Friedrich Unger, Court Confectioner to King Otto I of Greece*. Kegan Paul Library of Culinary Arts. London: Kegan Paul, 2003.

Vávrová, Karolína. *Pražská Kuchařka*. Prague: Ant. Felkla, 1881.

Veblen, Thorstein. *The Theory of the Leisure Class*. Modern Library Classics. New York: Modern Library, 2001.

Wagner, Christoph. *Süsses Gold: Kultur- und Sozialgeschichte des Wiener Zuckers*. Vienna: Brandstätter, 1996.

Walton, Whitney. *France at the Crystal Palace: Bourgeois Taste and Artisan Manufacture in the Nineteenth Century*. Berkeley: University of California Press, 1992.

Watson, Andrew M. *Agricultural Innovation in the Early Islamic World: The Diffusion of Crops and Farming Techniques, 700–1100.* Cambridge Studies in Islamic Civilization. Cambridge, England: Cambridge University Press, 1983.

Wechsberg, Joseph. *The Cooking of Vienna's Empire.* New York: Time-Life Books, 1968.

Weeks, Mary Palfrey. Manuscript recipe book of Mary Palfrey Weeks from the Shadows-on-the-Teche Archives, a National Trust Historic Site, New Iberia, LA.

Wheaton, Barbara Ketcham. *Savoring the Past: The French Kitchen and Table from 1300 to 1789.* Philadelphia: University of Pennsylvania Press, 1983.

Woloson, Wendy A. *Refined Tastes: Sugar, Confectionery, and Consumers in Nineteenth-Century America.* Baltimore: Johns Hopkins University Press, 2002.

Wolpert, Stanley A. *A New History of India.* New York: Oxford University Press, 2009.

Yu, Su-Mei. "Thai Egg-Based Sweets: The Legend of Thao Thong Keap-Ma." *Gastronomica,* Summer 2003.

Zaouali, Lilia. *Medieval Cuisine of the Islamic World: A Concise History with 174 Recipes.* Berkeley: University of California Press, 2007.

Zenker, G. Fr. *Comus-Geheimnisse über Anordnung häuslicher und öffentlicher, kleinerer und größerer Gastmahle, Pickeniks, Theezirkel [et]c.: über das Credenzen des Nachtisches, der Weine u.s.w. und wie Tafeln nach den Regeln der Kunst und des Geschmacks zu decken und zu serviren sind; Nebst einer vollständigen Anleitung zur Transchirkunst; Für Herrschaften und bürgerl. Familien, Gastgeber [et]c.; Als Fortsetzung der . . . Kochbücher desselben Verfassers, und als Anhang zu jedem Kochbuche brauchbar; Mit erläuternden Kupfertafeln.* Vienna: Haas, 1827.

———. *Der Zuckerbäcker für Frauen mittlerer Stände. Anweisung zur leichten und wenig kostspieligen Bereitung der auserlesensten Confitüren, Kunstgebäcke, Getränke, Gefrornen &c. &c.* Vienna: Haas, 1834.

Zubaida, Sami, and Richard Tapper. *Culinary Cultures of the Middle East.* London: I. B. Tauris, 1994.

INDEX

403